Chalk Work.

The blackboard has been well called the great weapon of the modern educator; this is especially true in reference to instruction in an art dealing with lines, curves and figures.

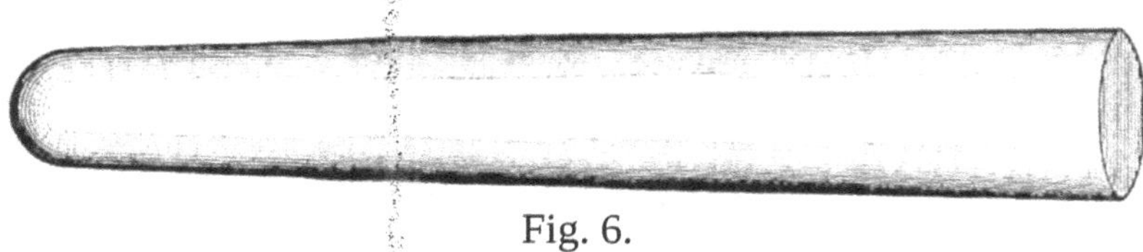

Fig. 6.

Many a man can chalk out on a blackboard, or on a piece of sheet-iron, or on the floor, just what he wants to show, and make his meaning very plain; hence, in every workshop, and many other places, a blackboard is more than useful, and it has been said that no draughting office is complete without one.

Fig. 6 represents a chalk-crayon.

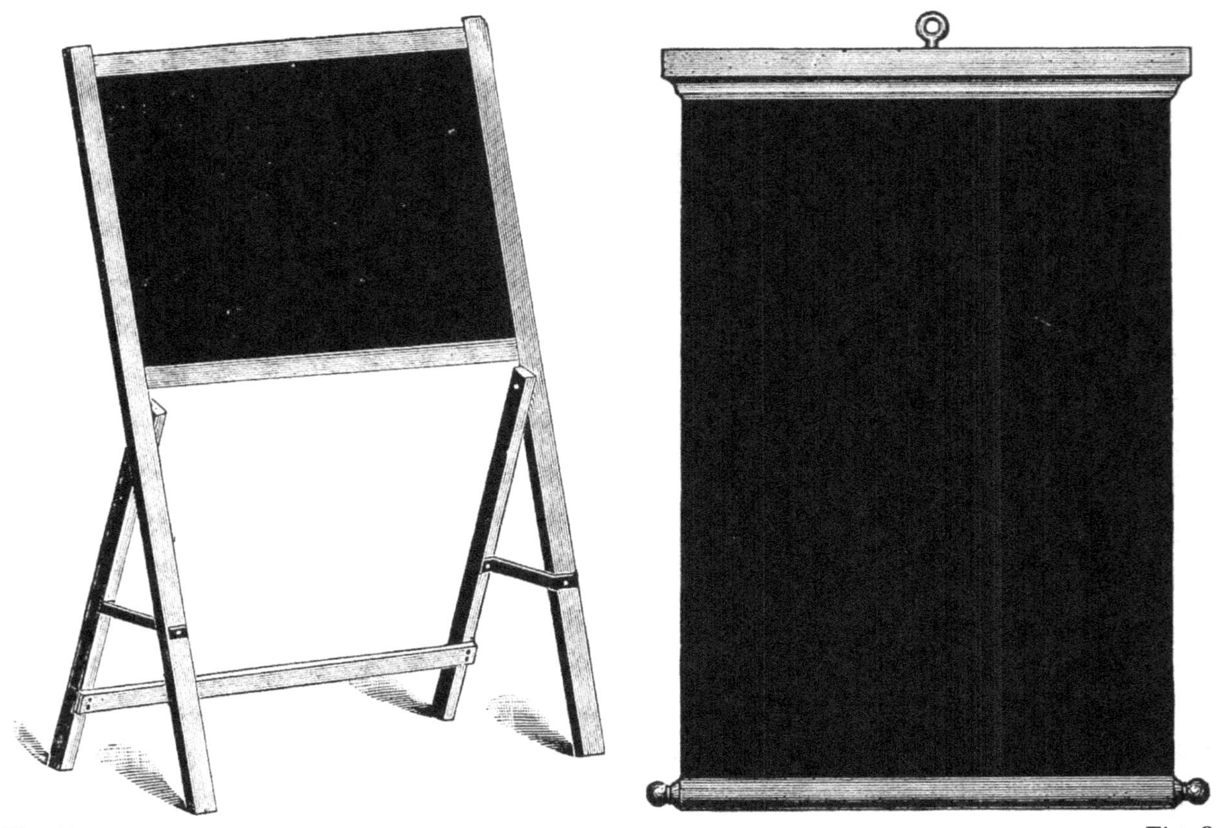

Fig. 7.   Fig. 8.

Figs. 7 and 8 need no explanation, as they represent two forms of the well-known blackboard.

Chalk lines have this advantage—they are easily altered or rubbed out when not needed any longer. The work executed upon a blackboard is mostly done by hand, without aid from instruments; a few tools, however, are useful—such as, 1, large wooden blackboard compasses holding a crayon, which are made and sold by the trade in size twelve inches to thirty inches in length; 2, a straight-edge; and 3, some crayons. With the compasses circles and part of the circle can be made, and with the straight-edge the larger lines can be drawn.

These instruments are shown on page 29, and are, 1, compasses, for holding chalk for making circles; 2, a tee-square; 3, a straight-edge; 4, a protractor for measuring angles; 5, a triangle 60° and 30°; 6, a brass holder for crayons.

Blackboard Drawing.—The use of a blackboard comes principally and properly under the head of free-hand drawing, but its importance is such that a separate division of the volume is assigned to it.

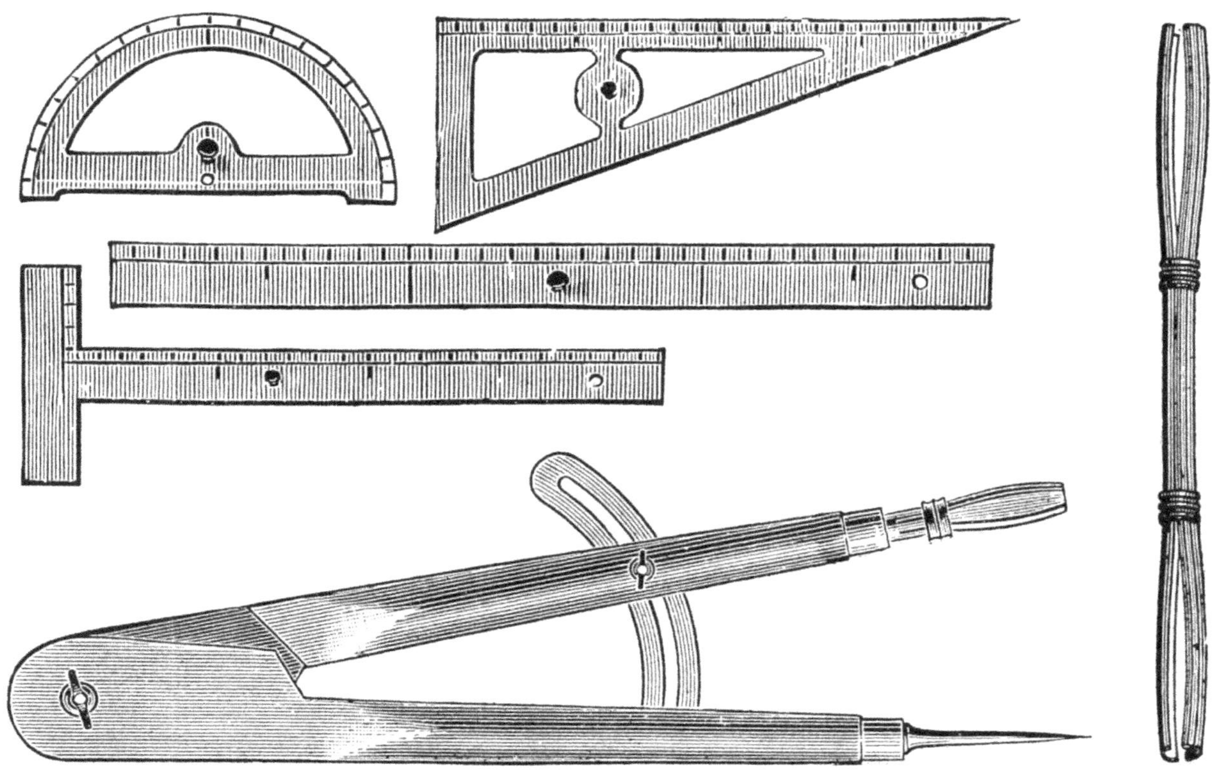

Thus, chalk-work may be considered the first lesson in "free-hand," as all the examples can also be most profitably practiced with pencil and paper.

Very rapid drawing upon the board should not be encouraged, as it is likely not to be accurate enough; again, the board should be entirely free from grease. Cloths, sponges or chamois skin rubbers may be used to erase or change the chalk marks. Vertical lines should be drawn from above downward; short lines should be drawn with the fingers alone, those somewhat longer with the hand, using the wrist-joint; the still longer lines with the forearm, using the elbow-joint; those longer yet with the whole arm, using the shoulder-joint; lines should always be drawn with a uniform motion, slow enough for the eye to follow.

Practice in chalk-work should alternate with sketching in a sketchbook and with geometrical drawing—to be hereafter described. The student should practice a short time on the board, at least once a week; large sizes are the most profitable for the representations to be made; when drawing in different directions the hand should be turned, not the paper or board; the hand should never be allowed to obstruct the sight, hence the hand and fingers should be held in a position of freedom—with fingers not nearer than $1\frac{1}{2}$ or 2 inches from the board.

NOTE.—The first lesson of any kind the author received in drawing was to make a straight line; this was effected by holding the pencil nearly erect and guiding it along by the aid of the little finger held pressed against the edge of a board; this was a useful item of knowledge, as proved by passing years.

A well-known artist, in telling his early experience, said: "The first thing I was taught was to draw a line, divide it, erect a perpendicular from its center, and afterwards to divide the angle made by the perpendicular." In answer to a question asking how long he was kept at the lines, he replied, "about two months—or a month or two," indicating that even the longer time would have been well spent in learning to draw a straight line.

PREPARATORYPRACTICEINDRA WING.

Every visible object is bounded by lines which enable the observer to determine its shape. If these lines are straight or curved, the shape of the object is regular; if broken, the shape of the object is irregular.

The elements, then, of form are lines, straight, curved, or broken, and these, therefore, furnish the beginning of all instruction in free-hand or mechanical drawing.

PERPENDICULARLINES.

Fig. 15 shows six lines—upright and perpendicular, with points or "dots" indicated at the top and bottom of each line; to draw these, proceed thus:

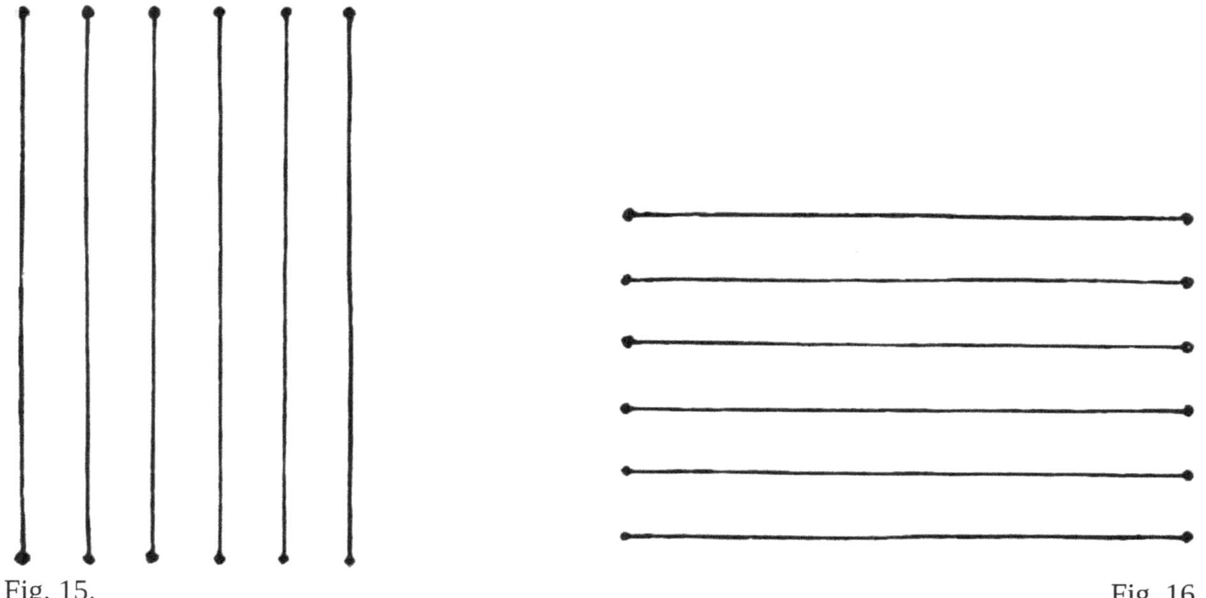

Fig. 15.   Fig. 16.

The learner should stand with his right shoulder opposite the board, and the weight of the hand and the arm should be allowed to fall naturally; now, make on the board two points, one being six inches above the other, these being merely "dots," shown at the ends of the lines, figs. 15, etc., and made with two motions; the line between the points should now be drawn not too quickly from the upper to the lower point; three movements of the hand and arm complete the line; to draw the other five lines the movements have simply to be repeated.

If the student pronounces to himself "one," "two," "three," at each motion, it will be helpful; in this exercise, fig. 15, the aim is to make six lines, each line being parallel to the first. Again, in the example, it is intended that the lower point should be made first, next the upper, and lastly the line drawn from the upper to the lower point, but the order may be reversed; at *one* the upper point, at *two* the lower, at *three* the stroke upwards to complete the line.

HORIZONTALLINES.

To make these as shown in fig. 16, proceed as follows: With the word *one* make a point, with *two* another point six inches at the left, with *three* draw a straight line from the left point to the right. All added lines should be parallel: for practice, reverse the process thus, *one*, make a "point," at *two* another point at the right, at *three* draw line to the left.

The student will note that the two motions—at the words *one* and *two*—are to fix the positions of the ends of the lines; this practice will be found useful in the most advanced examples and an item of elementary practice never to be forgotten—like the help to be derived by the first round of a ladder.

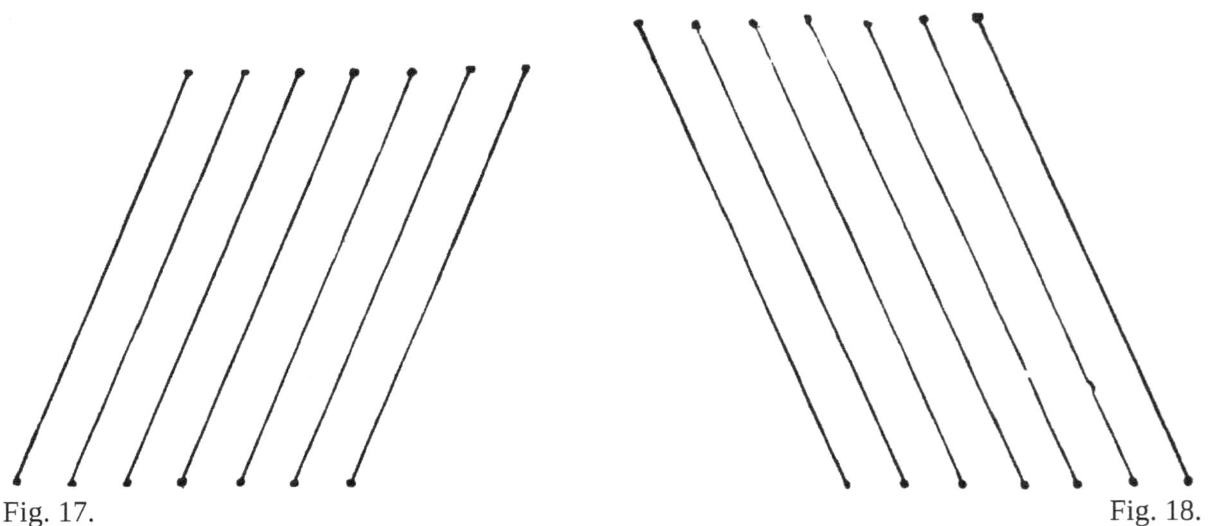

Fig. 17.   Fig. 18.

OBLIQUELINES.

In drawing oblique straight lines as shown in fig. 17, at the word *one* let the student make the lower point; at the word *two* the upper, a little to the right of the lower; at the word *three* draw a line quickly from the upper to the lower point. In pronouncing the words *one, two, three,* let the student make the additional parallel lines.

As shown in fig. 18, at the word *one* make the lower point; at the word *two* the upper point, a little *to the left*; at the word *three* draw a line rapidly from the upper to the lower point, and "timing" the process by repeating *one, two, three,* make the additional parallel lines.

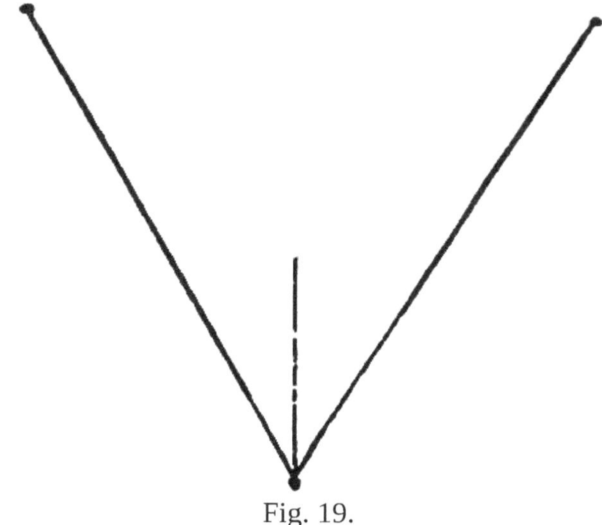

Fig. 19.

BROKENLINES.

A broken line is composed of two or more straight lines at angles to each other (see fig. 19). To draw them begin (saying) *one*, make a point; *two* a point below at the left; *three*, a point above at the left; *four*, draw a line from the left hand point to the lower point; at the word *five*, from the lower point to the upper right hand point. For practice draw numerous lines in the same way, keeping them parallel to each other, as shown in fig. 20.

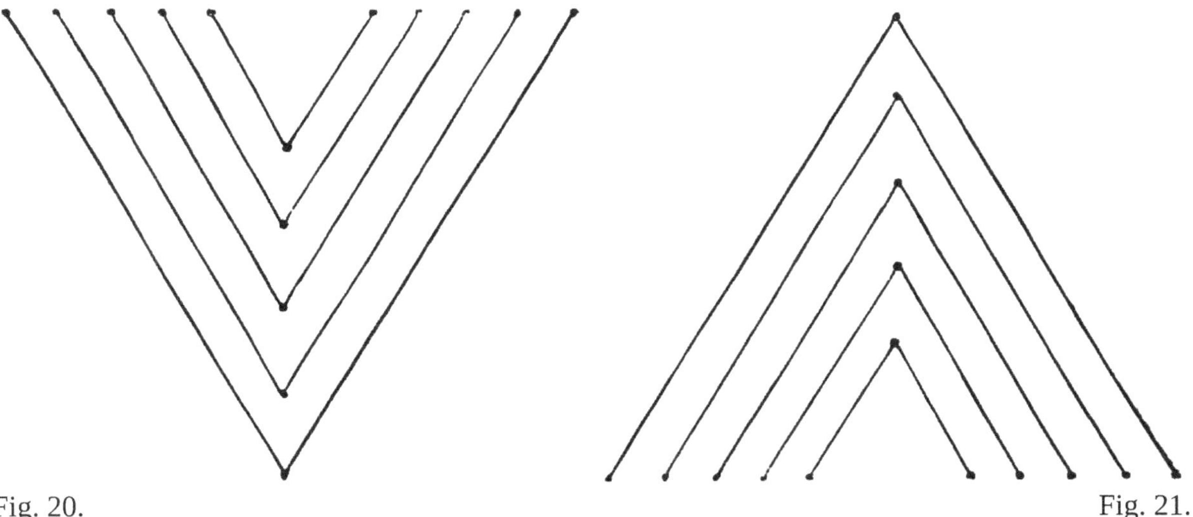

Fig. 20.

Fig. 21.

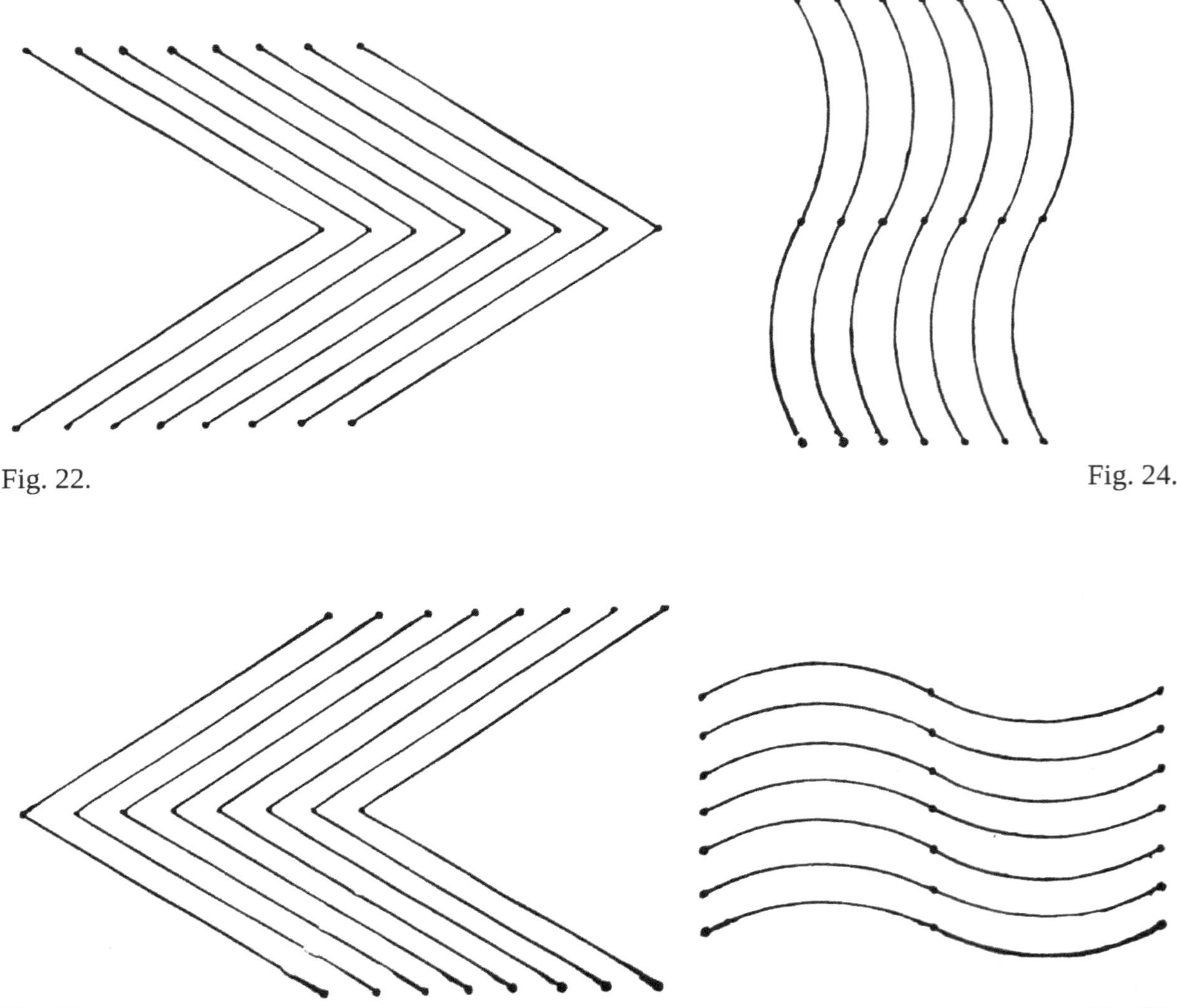

Fig. 22.

Fig. 24.

Fig. 23.

Fig. 25.

In example, fig. 21, the arrangement of the points is changed—let the student draw at the words, as follows: *One,* a point; *two,* a point above at the left; *three,* a point below at the left; *four,* draw from the point at the left to the upper point; *five,* from the upper point to the lower right hand point; continue to add parallel lines to complete the figure as shown.

Figs. 22 and 23 are given as examples to practice, making first the points and then the connecting lines and afterward the parallel lines to complete the figures.

CURVEDLINES.

To draw curved lines, as shown in fig. 24. At the word *one*, point; at the word *two*, point three inches directly above; *three*, at the same distance above again make a point; now draw a curve as shown, joining the middle point and the upper point; now draw the curve as shown below it; finally complete figure as shown.

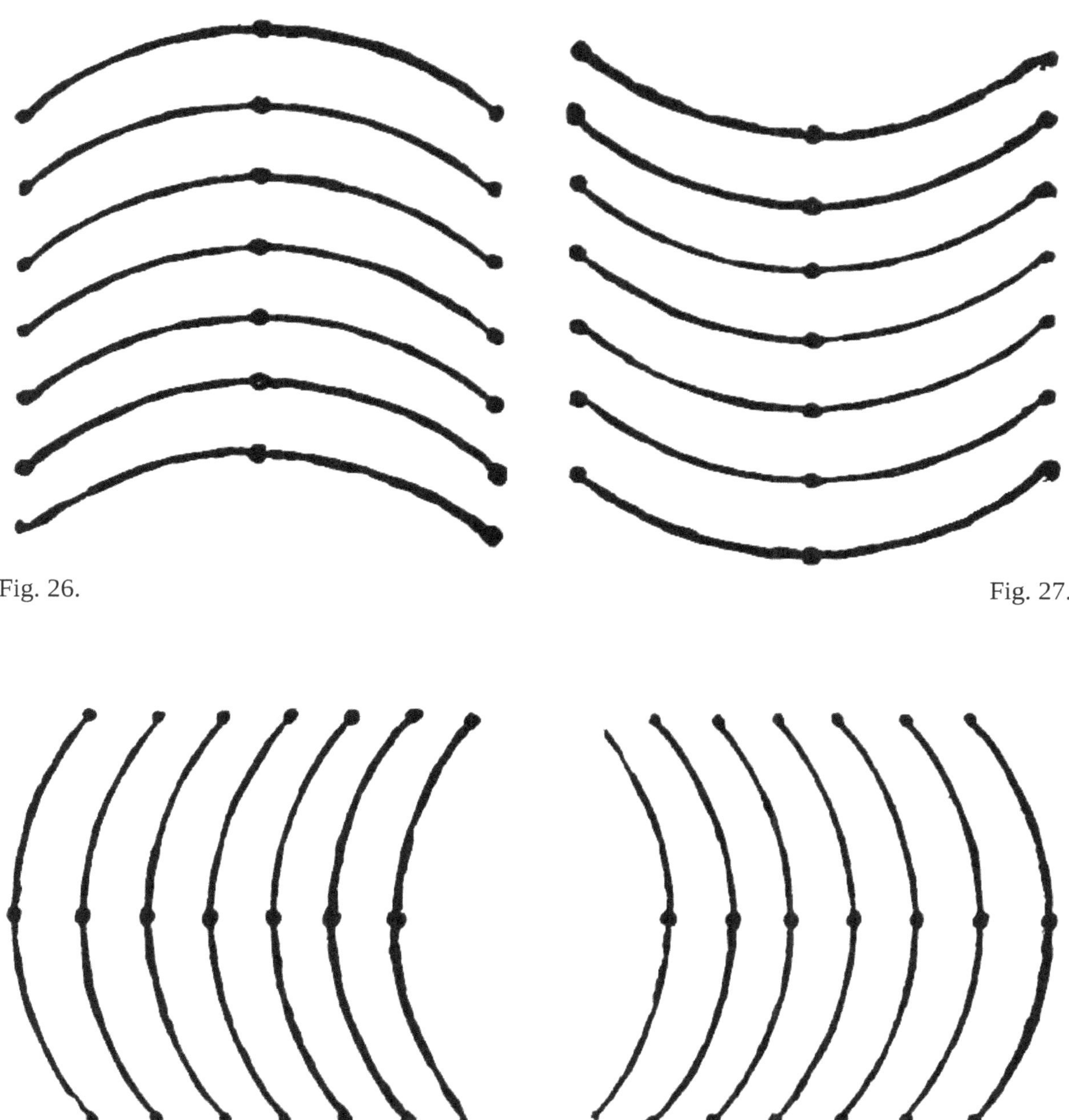

Fig. 26.

Fig. 27.

Fig. 28.

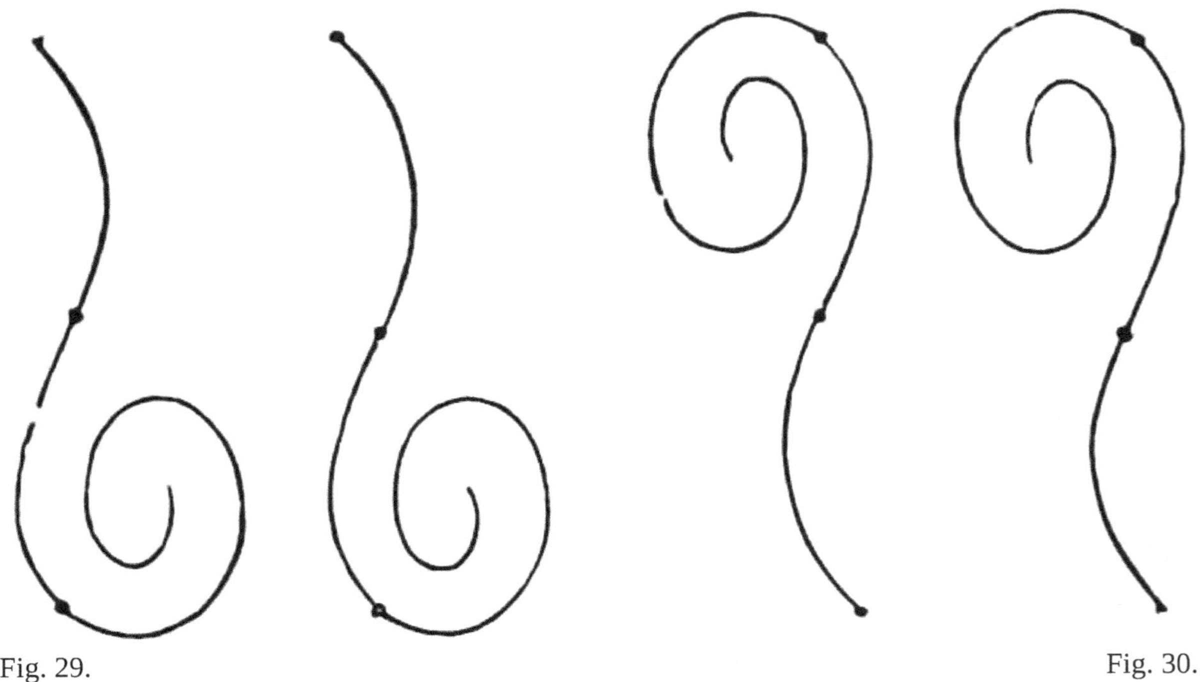

Fig. 29.   Fig. 30.

Figs. 25 to 30 are to be practiced, making first the points and then connecting them by the curves to complete the figures.

When two or more students are working together, with each having a blackboard, the counting may be in concert—or a teacher could count for a class. In these line examples care should be used in making them of uniform length. There is a difference to be noted between a crooked line and a broken line, the latter being a straight line and the former deviating from it.

Square chalk crayons are the best for hand work, as lines of an even or uniform width can be drawn with them.

A very fine effect is produced by using two thicknesses of chalk, one being double the thickness of the other; the heavy lines being used on the shade side of objects will produce a good effect, giving thickness and body to the object.

Round chalk crayons are used in the compasses to draw circles, but hand lines drawn with them are not so neat as those produced with the square-shaped chalk.

To obliterate or remove the construction, or false lines made on the blackboard, a wooden handle two inches in diameter with a cone end 3 or 4 inches long, covered with chamois skin or soft cloth tightly wrapped round the cone and fastened with a tack or drawing pin, makes the best implement to erase lines not required, the point of the cone will remove these without destroying the lines or curves which meet them.

Sponges, chamois skin or cloth rubbers are used to rub out the chalk drawings and clean the blackboard.

The best height for a diagram on the blackboard is not higher than the head, nor lower than the elbow.

Horizontal lines should be made from the left to the right; the body and arm being moved with the hand, and kept in the same relative position with it, will steady the hand.

Curved lines to the left should be drawn first, enabling the eye to take in not only the curve in process of formation but that already made.

Passing the crayon in the hand, over the intended curve previous to marking it, will guide the eye and give confidence to the hand in chalking the curve.

A proper distance from the blackboard is essential, the face being about two feet away from it.

Draw with the whole arm extended from the shoulder-joint, not from the elbow or wrist.

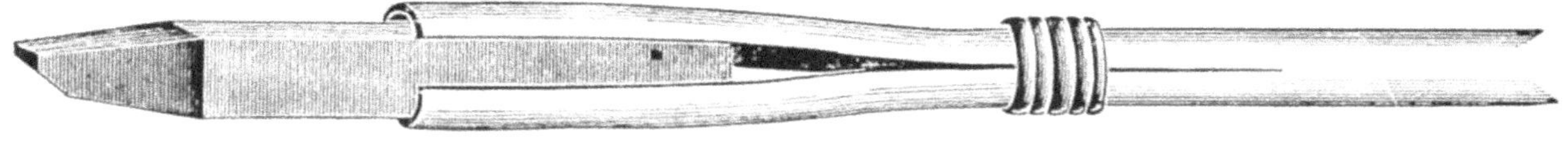

Fig. 31.

"There are more ways than one of telling things: by speech, by writing, by printing, also by pictures and drawings." Knowles

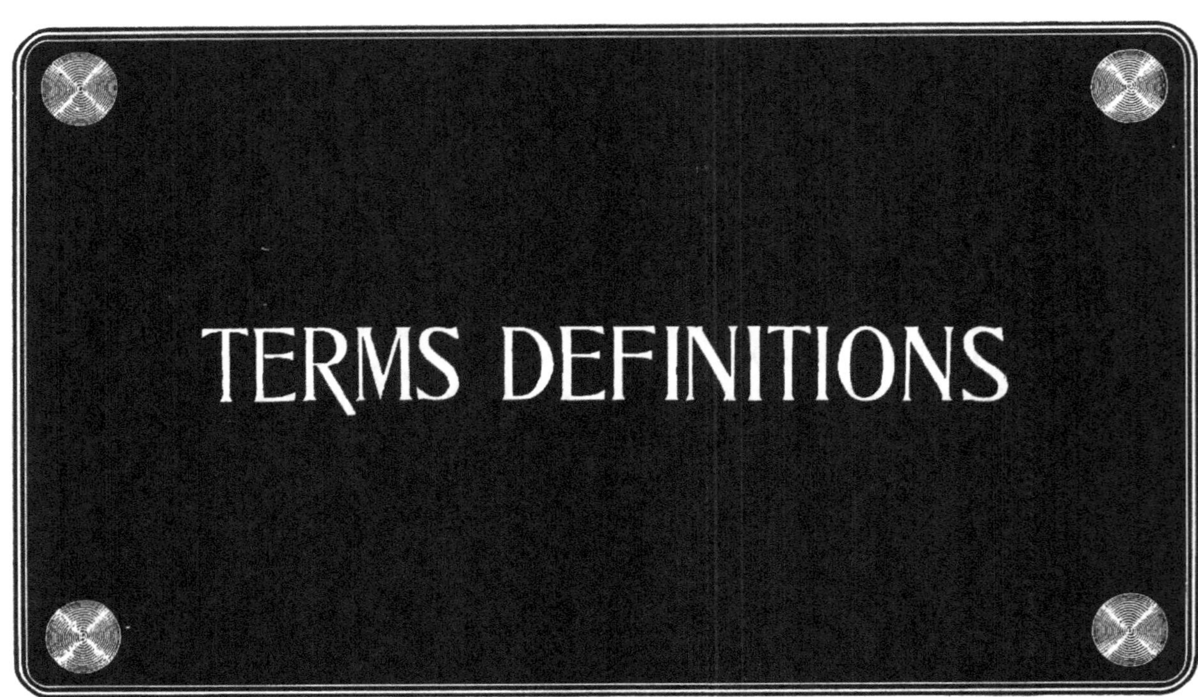

TERMS DEFINITIONS

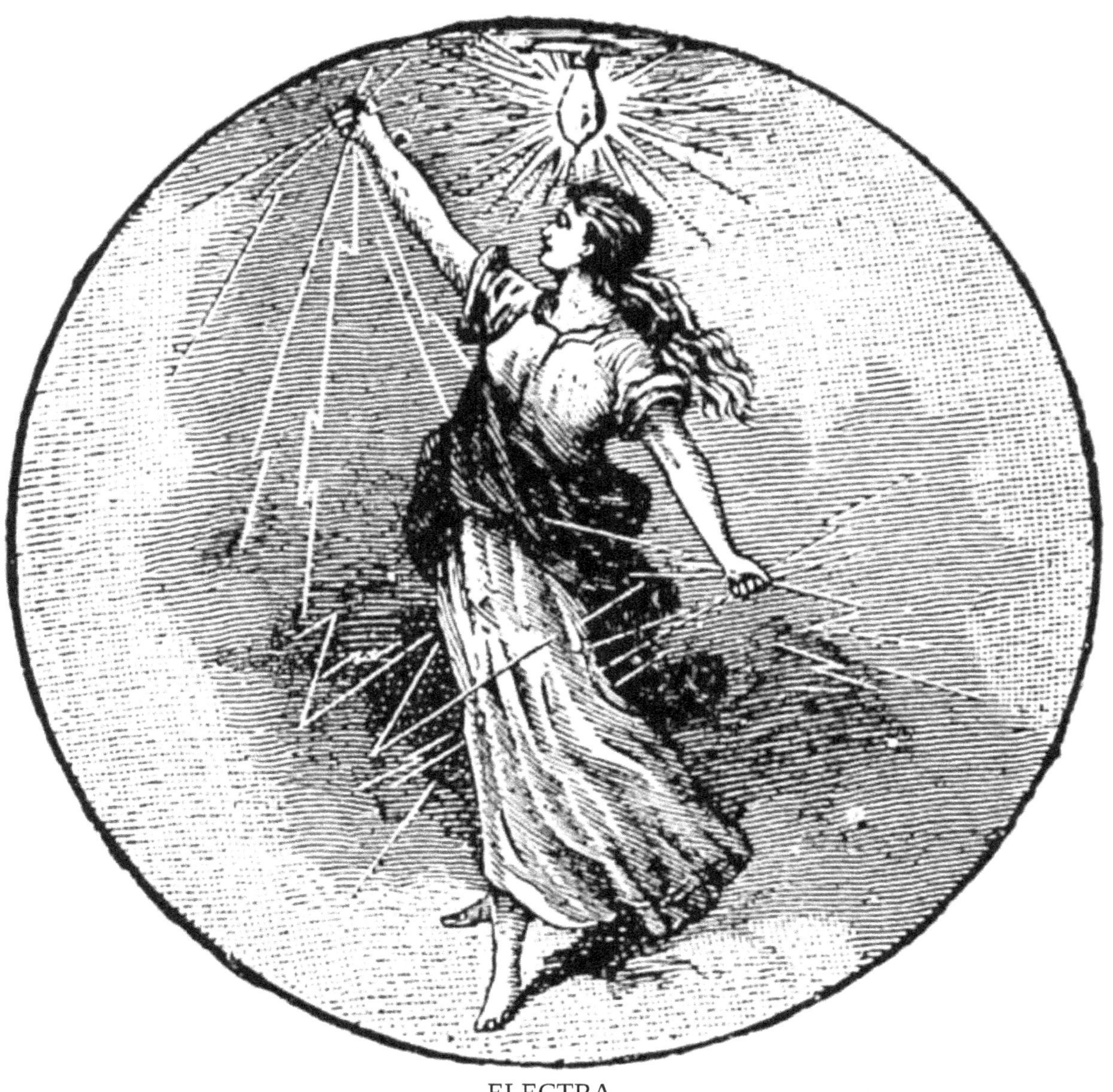

ELECTRA.

Preliminary Terms and Definitions.

Like all the arts, drawing has a nomenclature of its own, and nothing can be more helpful to the beginner than to know the name of things relating to the art of drawing. This is a language almost peculiar to itself, and used daily and hourly by many thousands of superintendents, foremen and master mechanics, as well as by owners, designers and draughtsmen, hence its introduction at this early stage.

ALTITUDE.—This is the elevation of an object above its base, or the perpendicular distance between the top and bottom of a figure.

ANGLE is the difference in the direction of two lines which meet or tend to meet. The lines are called *the sides* and the point of meeting, the *vertex* of the lines.

To make an angle apparent, the two lines must meet in a point, as *A B* and *A C*, which meet in the point *A*, as shown in fig. 33.

Angles are measured by degrees.

A *Degree* is one of the three hundred and sixty equal parts of the space about a point in a plane.

Angles are distinguished in respect to magnitude by the terms Right, Acute and Obtuse Angles.

A *Right Angle* is that formed by one line meeting another, so as to make equal angles with that other.

The lines forming a right angle are *perpendicular to each other*.

An *Acute Angle* is less than a right angle. See Fig. 35.

An *Obtuse Angle* is greater than a right angle. See Fig. 36.

Obtuse and acute angles are also called *oblique angles*; and lines which are neither parallel nor perpendicular to each other are called *oblique lines*.

The *Vertex* or *Apex* of an angle is the point in which the including lines meet.

An angle is commonly designated by a letter at its vertex; but when two or more angles have their vertices at the same point, they cannot be thus distinguished.

For example, when the three lines *A B*, *A C*, and *A D* in fig. 37 meet in the common point *A*, we designate either of the angles formed, by three letters, placing that at the vertex between those at the opposite extremities of the including lines. Thus, we say, the angle *B A C*, etc.

APEX.—The summit or highest point of an object.

ARC.—See circle.

AXIS OF A SOLID.—An imaginary straight line passing through its center.

AXIS OF A FIGURE.—A straight line passing through the center of a figure, and dividing it into two equal parts.

BASE.—The base of a solid figure is that on which it stands—the lowest part.

BISECT.—To divide into two equal parts.

BISECTOR.—A line which bisects.

CIRCLE.—A *Circle* is a plane figure bounded by one uniformly curved line, all of the points in which are at the same distance from a certain point within, called the *Center*.

The *Circumference* of a circle is the curved line that bounds it.

The *Diameter* of a circle is a line passing through its center, and terminating at both ends in the circumference, as *A C B*.

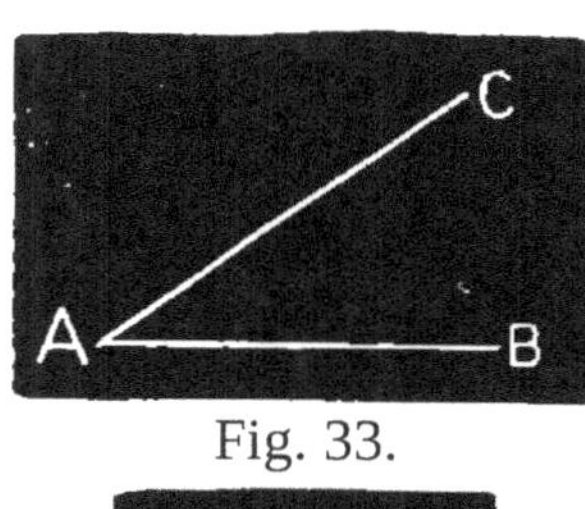

Fig. 33.

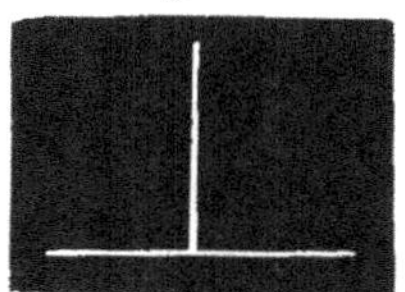

Fig. 34.

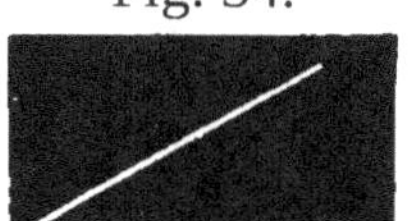

Fig. 35.

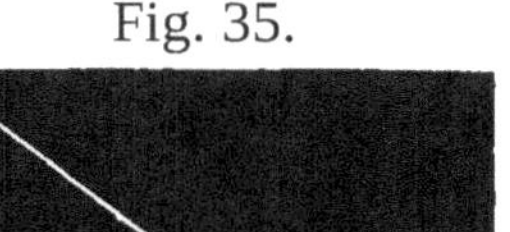

Fig. 36.

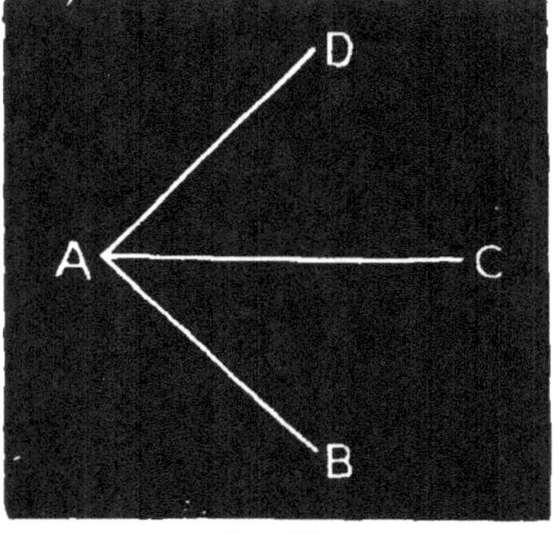

Fig. 37.

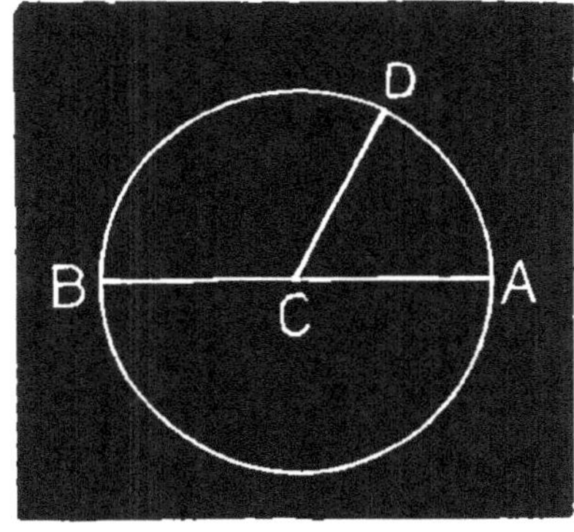

Fig. 38.

The *Radius* of a circle is a line extending from its center to any point in the circumference. It is one-half of the diameter. All the diameters of a circle are equal, as are also all the radii *C D*, *C B* and *C A.*

An *Arc* of a circle is any portion of the circumference, as *B D* and *A D.*

Semi-Circle.—Half a circle formed by bisecting it with a diameter, as *A C B.* Fig. 38.

An angle having its vertex at the center of a circle is measured by the arc intercepted by its sides. Thus, the arc *A D* measures the angle *A C D*, and in general, to compare different angles, we have but to compare the arcs, included by their sides, of the equal circles having their centers at the vertices of the angles.

CIRCUMSCRIBE.—To draw a line of figures about or outside, such as a circle drawn around a square touching its corners or angles.

Inscribe.—To draw a line or figure inside or on the interior, such as a circle drawn within a square touching its sides.

CONCAVE.—Curving inwardly.

CONE.—A solid body or figure having a circle for its base, and its top terminated in a point or vertex.

CONSTRUCTION.—The making of any object.

CONTOUR.—The outline of the general appearance of an object.

CONVERGENCE.—Lines extending towards a common point.

CONVEX.—Rising or swelling into a round form—the opposite to concave.

CORNER.—The point of meeting of the edges of a solid, or the two sides of a plane figure.

CROSS-HATCHES.—In free-hand drawing the use of lines crossing each other to produce light and shade effects.

CURVE.—A line of which no part is straight.

Reversed Curve.—One whose curvature is first in one direction and then in the opposite direction.

Spiral Curve.—A plain curve which winds about and recedes, according to some law, from its point of beginning, which is called its center.

CYLINDER.—A solid bounded by a curved surface and by two opposite faces called bases; the bases may be any curved figures and give the name to the cylinder; thus a circular cylinder is one whose bases are circles.

CYLINDRICAL.—Having the general form of a cylinder.

DEGREE.—The 360th part of a circle.

DESCRIBE.—To make or draw a curved line; to draw a plan.

DESIGN.—Any arrangement or combination to produce desired results in industry or art. To delineate a form or figure by drawing the outline—a sketch.

DEVELOP.—To unroll or lay out.

DIAGONAL.—A right line drawn from angle to angle of a quadrilateral or many angled figure and dividing it into two parts.

DIAMETER.—A right line passing through the center of a circle or other round figure terminated by the curve and dividing the figure symmetrically into two equal parts.

EDGE.—The intersection of any two surfaces.

ELEVATION.—The term elevation, vertical projection and *front view*—applied to drawings—all have the same meaning.

FACE.—One of the plane surfaces of a solid; it may be bounded by straight or curved edges.

FINISHING.—Completing a drawing whose lines have been determined by erasing unnecessary lines and strengthening and accentuating where this is needed.

FORESHORTENING.—Apparent decrease in length, owing to objects being viewed obliquely; thus a wheel, when seen obliquely, instead of appearing round, presents the appearance of an ellipse.

FREE-HAND.—Executed by the hand unaided by instruments.

GENERATED.—Produced by.

GEOMETRIC.—According to geometry.

HALF-TINT.—The shading produced by means of parallel equidistant lines.

HEMISPHERE.—Half a sphere obtained by bisecting a sphere by a plane.

HORIZONTAL.—Parallel to the surface of smooth water. In drawing, a line drawn parallel to the top and bottom of the sheet is called horizontal.

INSCRIBE.—See circumscribe—its opposite.

INSTRUMENTAL.—By the use of instruments.

LINE.—A line has length, only, as A C; a right line is a straight line, the shortest line that can be drawn between two points, A———C.

Straight. One which has the same direction throughout its entire length.

Curved. One no part of which is straight.

Broken. One composed of different successive straight lines.

Mixed. One of straight and curved lines.

Center. A line used to indicate the center of an object.

Construction. A working line used to obtain required lines.

Dotted. A line composed of short dashes. - - - - - -

Dash. A line composed of long dashes. — — —

Dot and *Dash.* A line composed of dots and dashes alternating. — · — · —

Dimension. A line upon which a dimension is placed.

Full. An unbroken line, usually representing a visible edge. ———

Shadow. A line about twice as wide as the ordinary full line.

A straight line is often called simply a line, and a curved line a curve.

LONGITUDINAL.—In the direction of the length of an object.

MODEL.—A form used for study.

OBLIQUE.—Neither horizontal nor vertical.

OBLONG.—A rectangle with unequal sides.

OVAL.—A plane figure resembling the longitudinal section of an egg; or elliptical in shape.

OVERALL.—The entire length.

PARALLEL.—Having the same direction and everywhere equally distant.

PATTERN.—That which is used as a guide or copy in making things.
> *Flat.* One made of paper or other thin material.
> *Solid.* One which reproduces the form and size of the object to be made.

PERIMETER.—The boundary of a closed plane figure.

PERPENDICULAR.—At an angle of 90°.

PERSPECTIVE.—View; drawing objects as they appear to the eye from any given distance and situation, real or imaginary.

PLAN.—Plan, horizontal projection and *top view* have the same meaning.

PLANE FIGURE.—A part of a plane surface bounded by straight or curved lines, or by both combined.

POLYGON.—A plane figure bounded by straight lines called the sides of the polygon. The least number of sides that can bound a polygon is three. Polygons bounded by a greater number of sides than four are denominated only by the number of sides.

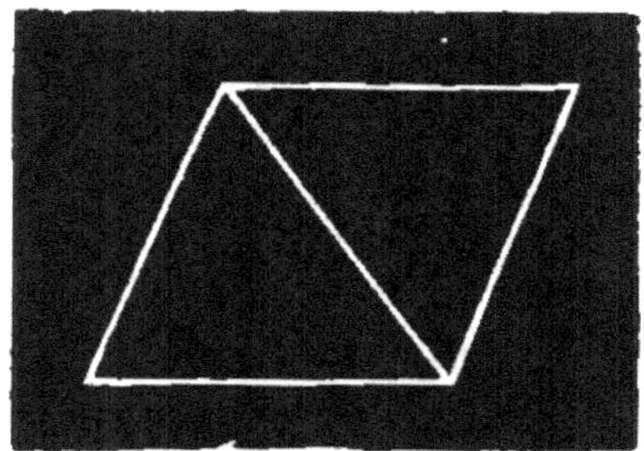

Fig. 39.

A polygon of five sides is called a *Pentagon*; of six, a *Hexagon*; of seven, a *Heptagon*; of eight, an *Octagon*; of nine, a *Nonagon*, etc.

Diagonals of a polygon are lines joining the vertices of angles not adjacent.

The *Perimeter* of a polygon is its boundary considered as a whole.

The *Base* of a polygon is the side upon which the polygon is supposed to stand.

The *Altitude* of a polygon is the perpendicular distance between the base and a side or angle opposite the base.

A *Quadrilateral* is a polygon having four sides and four angles.

A *Parallelogram* is a quadrilateral which has its opposite sides parallel.

The side upon which a parallelogram stands and the opposite side are called respectively its lower and upper bases.

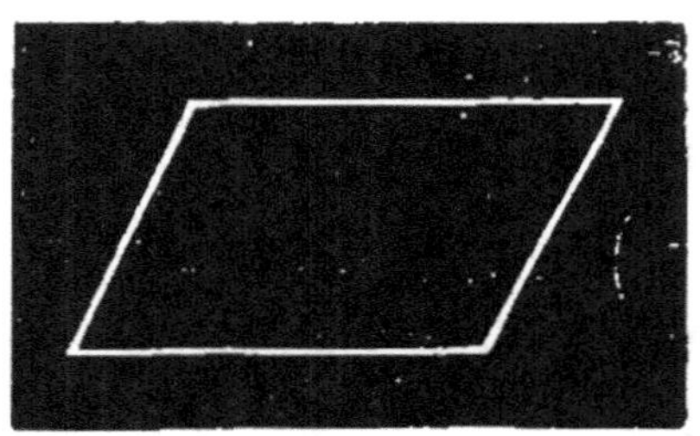

Fig. 40.

A *Rectangle* is a parallelogram having its angles right angles.

A *Square* is an equilateral rectangle, fig. 41.

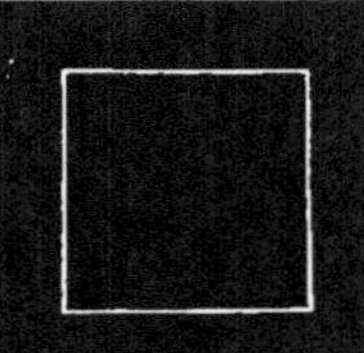

Fig. 41.

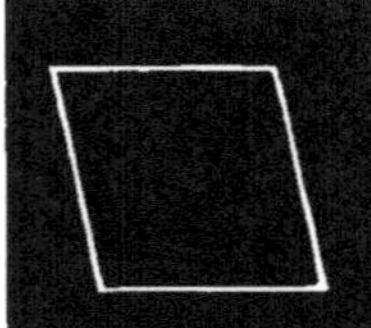

Fig. 42.

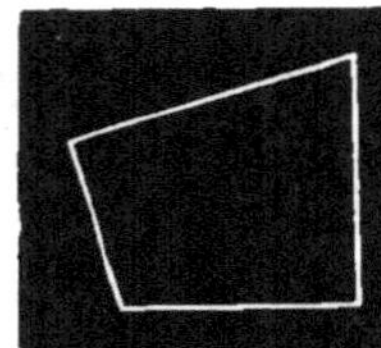

Fig. 43.

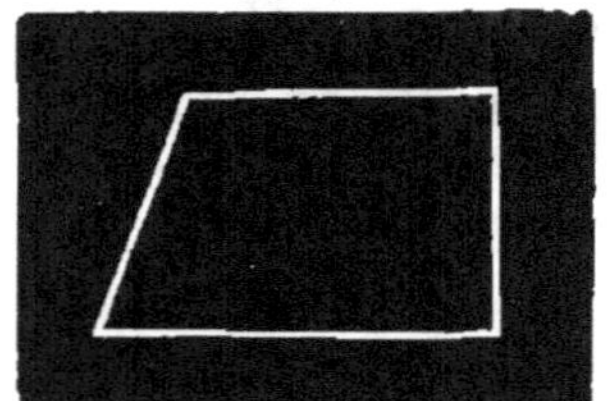

Fig. 44.

A *Rhomboid* is an oblique-angled parallelogram.

A *Rhombus* is an equilateral rhomboid, fig. 42.

A *Trapezium* is a quadrilateral having no two sides parallel, fig. 43.

A *Trapezoid* is a quadrilateral in which two opposite sides are parallel, and the other two oblique, fig. 44.

A **POLYHEDRON** is a solid bounded by planes. There are five regular solids which are shown in figs. 45, 46, 47, 48 and 49. A regular solid is bounded by similar and regular plane figures.

Fig. 45.—The *tetrahedron,* bounded by four equilateral triangles.

Fig. 46.—The *hexahedron,* or cube, bounded by six squares.

Fig. 47.—The *octahedron,* bounded by eight equilateral triangles.

Fig. 48.—The *dodecahedron,* bounded by twelve pentagons.

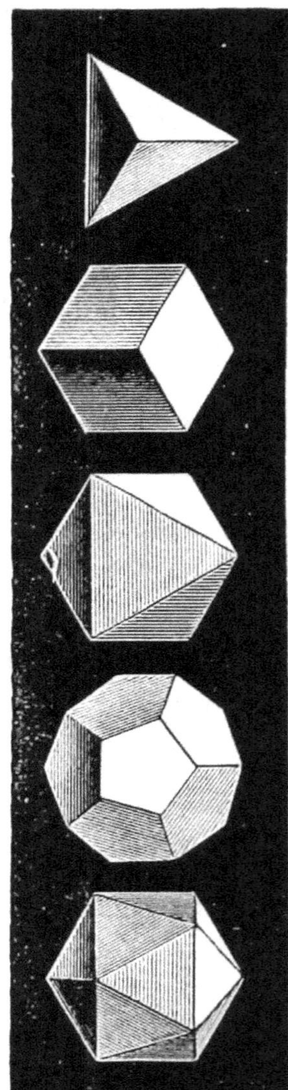

Figs. 45-49.

Fig. 49.—The *icosahedron*, bounded by twenty equilateral triangles.

PRISM.—A solid whose bases or ends are very similar plane figures, and whose sides are parallelograms; prisms are called triangular, square, etc., according as the bases are triangles, squares, etc.

PRODUCE.—To continue or extend.

PROFILE.—An outline or contour.

PROJECTION.—The view of an object obtained upon a plane by projecting lines perpendicular to the plane.

QUADRANT.—The fourth part; a quarter; the quarter of a circle.

QUADRISECT.—To divide into four equal parts.

SECTION.—A projection upon a plane parallel to a cutting plane which intersects any object. The section generally represents the part behind the cutting plane, and represents the cut surfaces by diagonal lines.

SECTIONAL.—Showing the section made by a plane.

SHADOW.—Shade and shadow have about the same meaning.

SOLID.—A solid has three dimensions—length, breadth and thickness.

SPHERE.—A solid bounded by a curved surface every point of which is equally distant from a point within called the center.

SURFACE.—The boundary of a solid. It has but two dimensions—length and breadth. Surfaces are plane or curved.

A *Plane Surface* is one upon which a straight line can be drawn in any direction.

A *Curved Surface* is one no part of which is plane.

The surface of the sphere is curved in every direction, while the curved surfaces of the cylinder and cone are straight in one direction.

The surface of a solid is no part of the solid, but is simply the boundary of the solid. It has two dimensions only, and any number of surfaces put together will give no thickness.

SYMMETRY.—*Design.* A proper adjustment or adaptation of parts to one another and to the whole.

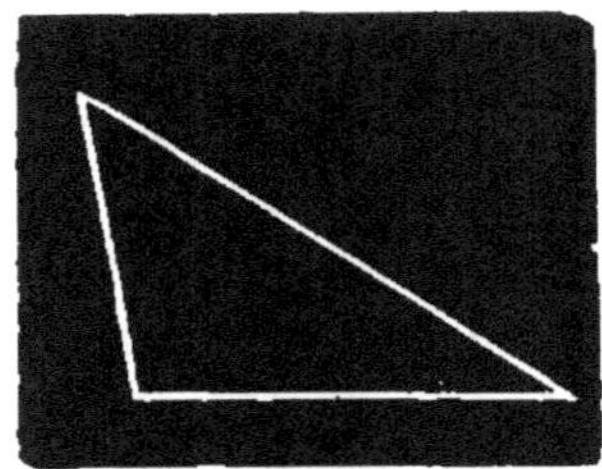

Fig. 50.

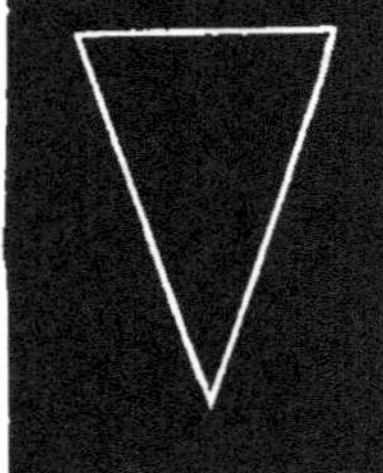

Fig. 51.

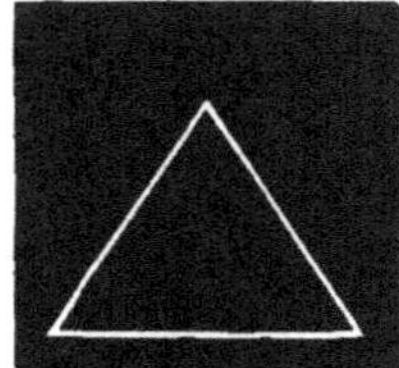

Fig. 52.

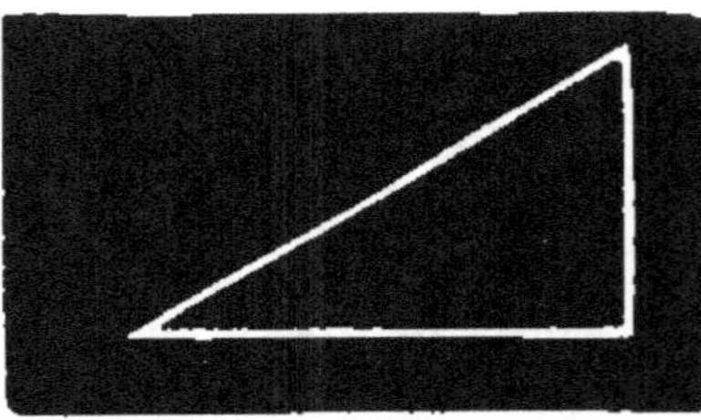

Fig. 53.

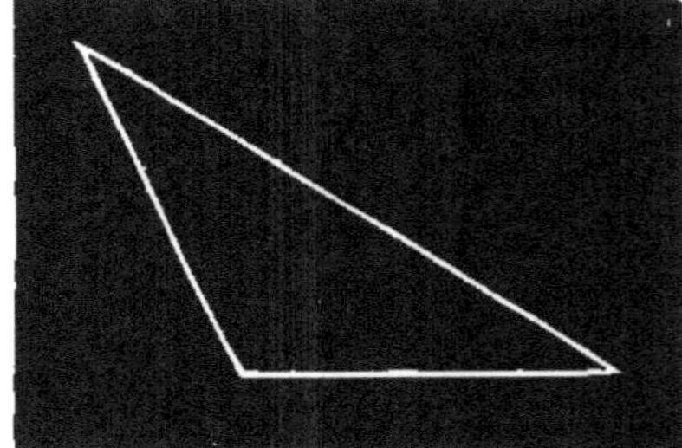

Fig. 54.

TRISECT.—To divide into three equal parts.

TRIANGLE.—A triangle is a polygon having three sides and three angles. *Tri* is a Latin prefix signifying three; hence a Triangle is literally a figure containing three angles.

A *Scalene Triangle* is one in which no two sides are equal. See fig. 50.

An *Isosceles Triangle* is one in which two of the sides are equal. See fig. 51.

An *Equilateral Triangle* is one in which the three sides are equal. An *Equiangular Triangle* is one having its three angles equal. An *Acute-Angled Triangle* is one in which each angle is acute.

A *Right-Angled Triangle* is one which has one of the angles a right angle. See fig. 53.

An *Obtuse-Angled Triangle* is one having an obtuse angle. Fig. 54.

Equiangular triangles are also equal sided, and vice versa.

VERTICAL.—Upright or perpendicular. Vertical and perpendicular are not synonymous terms.

VERTEX.—See Angle, Quadrilateral, Triangle. The vertex of a solid is the point in which its axis intersects the lateral surface.

VIEW.—See Elevation. Views are called front, top, right or left side, back, or bottom, according as they are made on the different planes of projection. They are also sometimes named according to the part of the object shown, as edge view, end view, or face view.

WORKING DRAWING.—One which gives all the information necessary to enable the workman to construct the object.

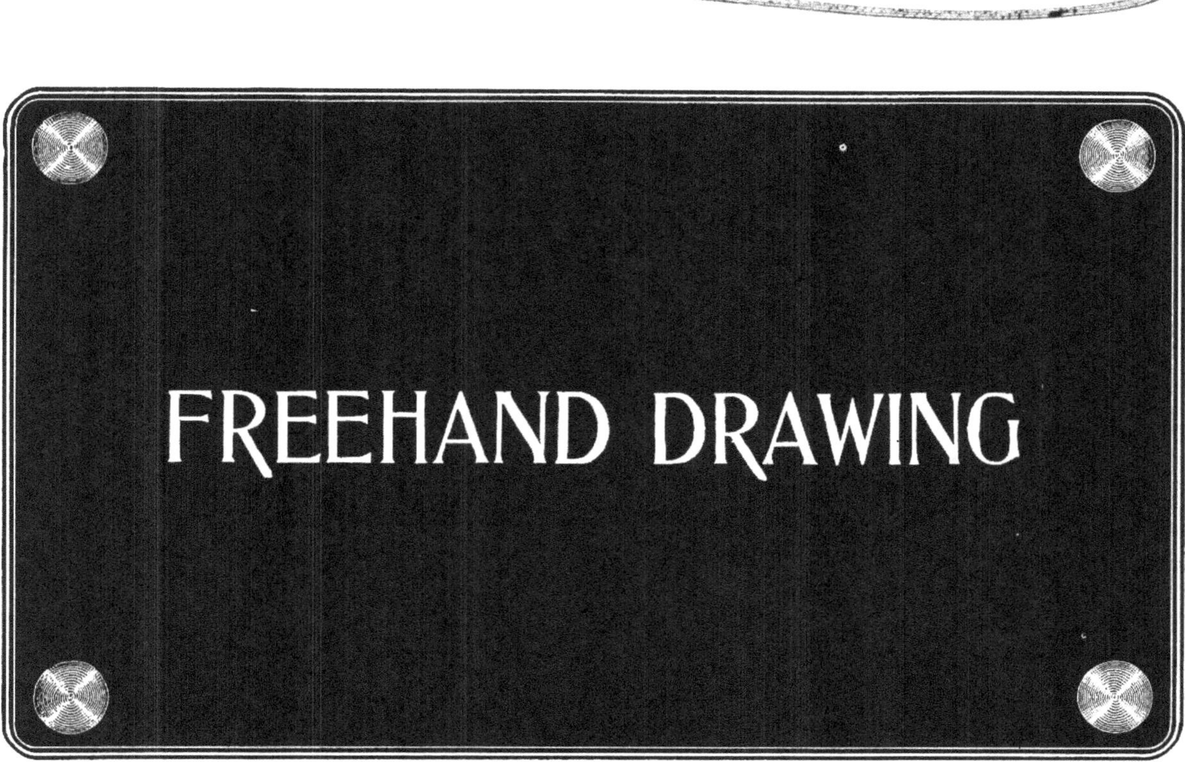

FREEHAND DRAWING

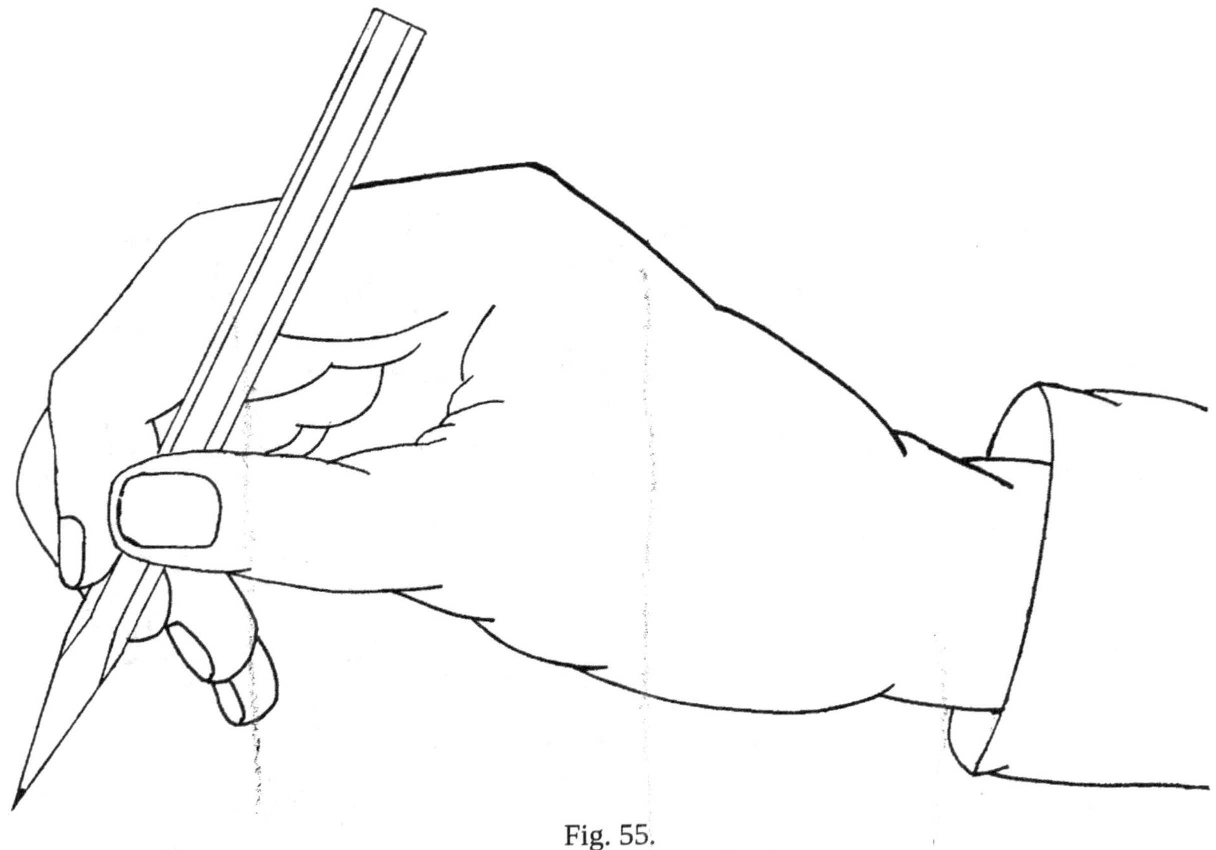

Fig. 55.

Free-Hand Drawing.

A free-hand drawing is executed with the unaided hand and eye, without guiding instruments or other artificial help. It is necessary to be known that all drawing required cannot possibly be done by rule and compass, but that some portions must be drawn "free-hand," trusting to the eye alone.

Hence, it is important that the student should be able to sketch at sight from objects he may see, or to draw roughly, with a piece of chalk or a pencil, pieces of mechanism required to be represented.

Practice in free-hand should go along with mechanical drawing as progress is made, and thus cultivating both branches equally.

"A simple sketch will often," as has been rather roughly said, "express more than yards of talk."

Even a slight sketch refreshes the memory, and in the case of the preparation of a complete set of drawings, with a view to the making of a thoroughly finished mechanical drawing, the proper course to pursue is, to make a general sketch, letter the various parts for reference, and then prepare a series of detailed sketches, similarly lettered, and diffuse with dimensions.

Everyone, whatever his specialty, feels to-day that the ability to sketch rapidly and clearly is among the absolute necessities for correct and prompt transactions of business, in giving and executing orders and doing business with persons outside his profession.

Mistakes and misunderstandings may be averted by means of rough sketches taken at the time and shown for confirmation; this also saves assistants from getting into trouble, especially if they pin the sketch to the order, for reference, in case of the arising of any dispute. These are a few of the advantages of knowing how to sketch quickly and correctly.

In "free-hand" any sort of pencil is better than none, but there is a considerable advantage in having a good serviceable article—a pencil not too soft nor too hard, and one which will retain its point for some little time.

Fig. 55 shows the approved position in which the pencil should be held while sketching. The pencil should be held firmly between the thumb and first finger of the right hand; press the second finger against the pencil at the opposite side to the thumb pressure, so that the pencil is firmly held by the contact of the thumb and two fingers—the third and fourth fingers just coming into easy reach of the paper surface—the wrist or ball of the hand resting lightly on the surface of the work—the arm resting on the desk or drawing-board for steadiness.

The motion of the pencil is produced from the movement of the fingers and thumb, principally in the vertical strokes, and the horizontal strokes are produced by fingers and thumb, combined with a wrist or elbow motion; the oblique lines and curves are produced with a free movement, with nothing cramped or confined about the finger joints.

POSITION.

It should be observed that nothing is more prejudicial to good execution than the habit of leaning over the paper, which ought to be placed on a surface sufficiently inclined to bring every portion equally under the eye, thus obviating the necessity of leaning forward. All support to the figure should be obtained by resting on the left arm, the right being left free for work. By attention to these rules that awkwardness of position, so detrimental to a good figure, will be avoided. It is better to have the light on the left hand, as in this direction the shadow of the pencil does not interfere with the view of the drawing.

HOW TO CUT A PENCIL.

Hold the pencil firmly in the left hand, as in the drawing, allowing about an inch to project beyond the fingers, and turn it gradually as the knife removes the wood. The knife should be held so that the blade alone projects beyond the fingers, and the part of it nearest the handle used for cutting. The pencil should be placed against the inside of the thumb of the right hand, as in the drawing (fig. 56), and the wood removed by slight shaving. The lead should not be cut at the same time as the wood, but rested on the thumb and pared gently afterwards; by attention to these directions the pencil will be economized.

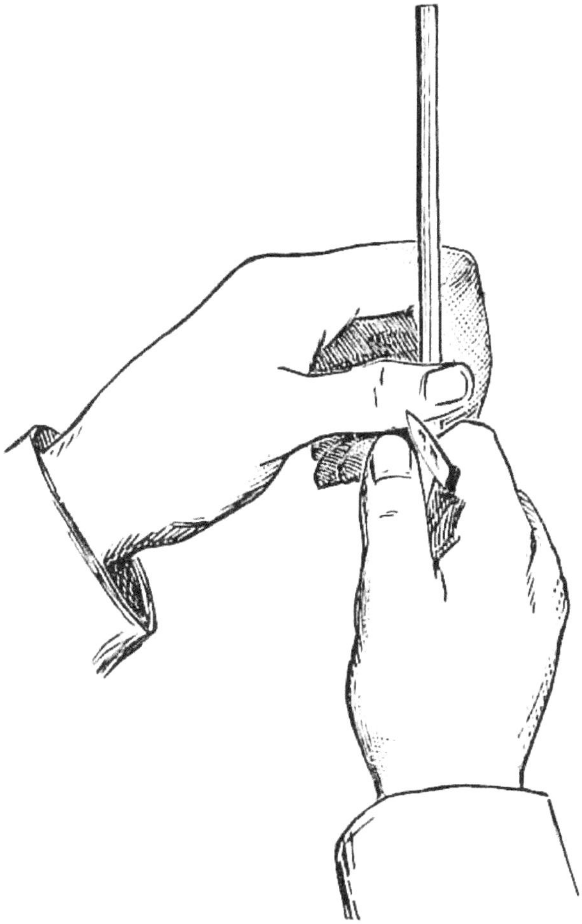

Fig. 56.

HOW TO DRAW STRAIGHT LINES.

Before a line is drawn, the point at which it is to commence and the point where it is to end, should be known; and let it be distinctly understood that *this judgment of the eye*, and placing of points, should invariably precede the drawing of every line.

The first effort should, therefore, be to produce a line of points exactly parallel with the upper edge of the paper, and at equal distances from each other. Commence with point *A* and place the point *B* carefully level with it, now place a slip of paper against these points in the original, mark their distance apart, and see if the same proportion has been given in your copy; if not, make the necessary correction. Proceed with the next point, examine it, and so on to the end of the line. When this is complete, examine each point in succession, to try if it is at the same distance from the top of the paper; when this is correct, proceed to draw the first level line. Hold the pencil as in the drawing, fig. 57, keeping the elbow near the side; join *A* to *B* by one light, steady stroke, produced by a movement of the wrist, and add stroke upon stroke until the line is of the required depth. Continue this process to the end of the line of points. Now place the point *D* at the right distance below the *A*, proceed with the points for another line as before, and continue the lines until the paper is covered. In producing the stroke the pencil should not be jerked, or any stop be made between the points, but the movement should be even throughout, and it is much better to produce each line by several soft strokes, as *the repetition of delicate lines induces lightness of touch and freedom of hand*; and it is also no small advantage that lines thus produced are more easily removed by the India rubber, should they require correction.

TO DRAW THE FIRST OBLIQUE LINE.

Prepare three rows of points down the side of the paper, on the left hand; examine them to see that they are at equal distances from the side and from each other; hold the pencil as in the drawing, fig. 58, move the elbow a little from the side, and join the points *A* and *B* with one light line, produced by a movement of the fingers and thumb, repeating the strokes until the line is of the requisite depth; proceed to join *B* to *C*, taking care previously to bring the hand a little down the paper, as the line from *A* to *C* is too long to be produced from one position. When the three rows of points are filled, make another set, examine them and proceed as before. By these means the paper will be covered with oblique lines, and if the points have been placed exactly, the sheet will have a neat and regular appearance.

NOTE.—The drawings of hands are introduced to show the positions for holding the pencil, and are not intended for copying.

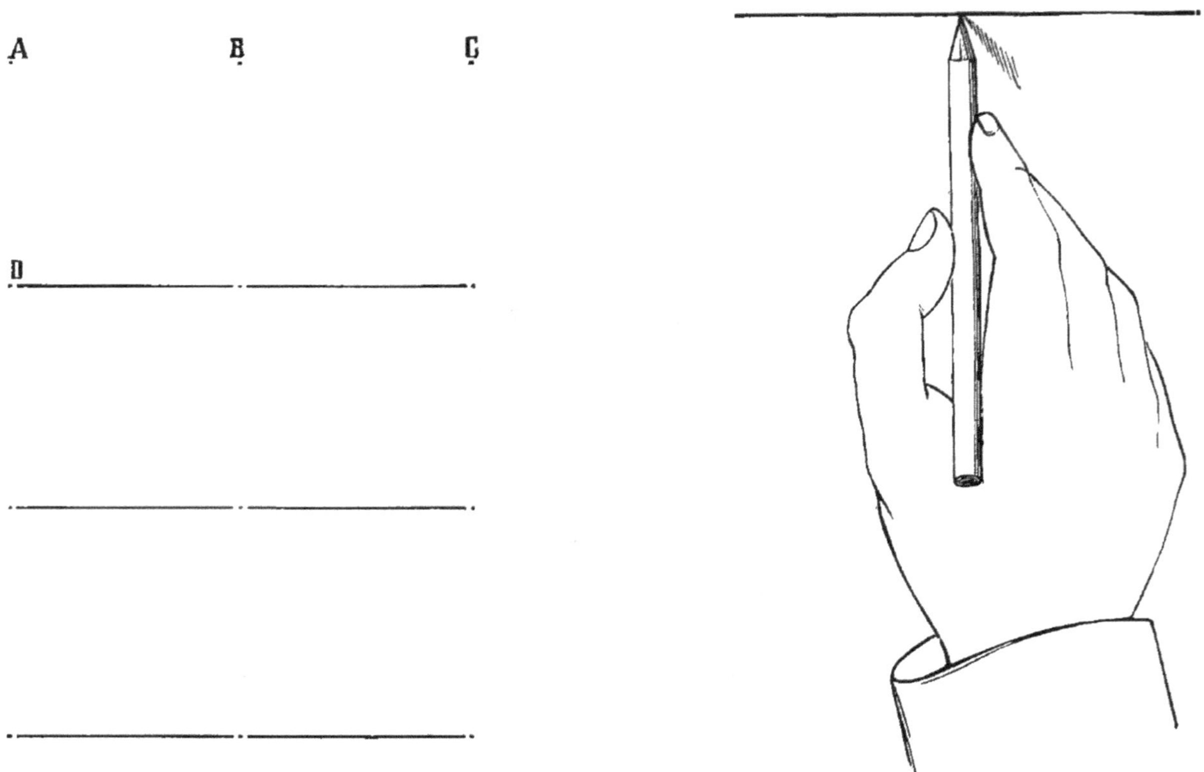

Fig. 57.

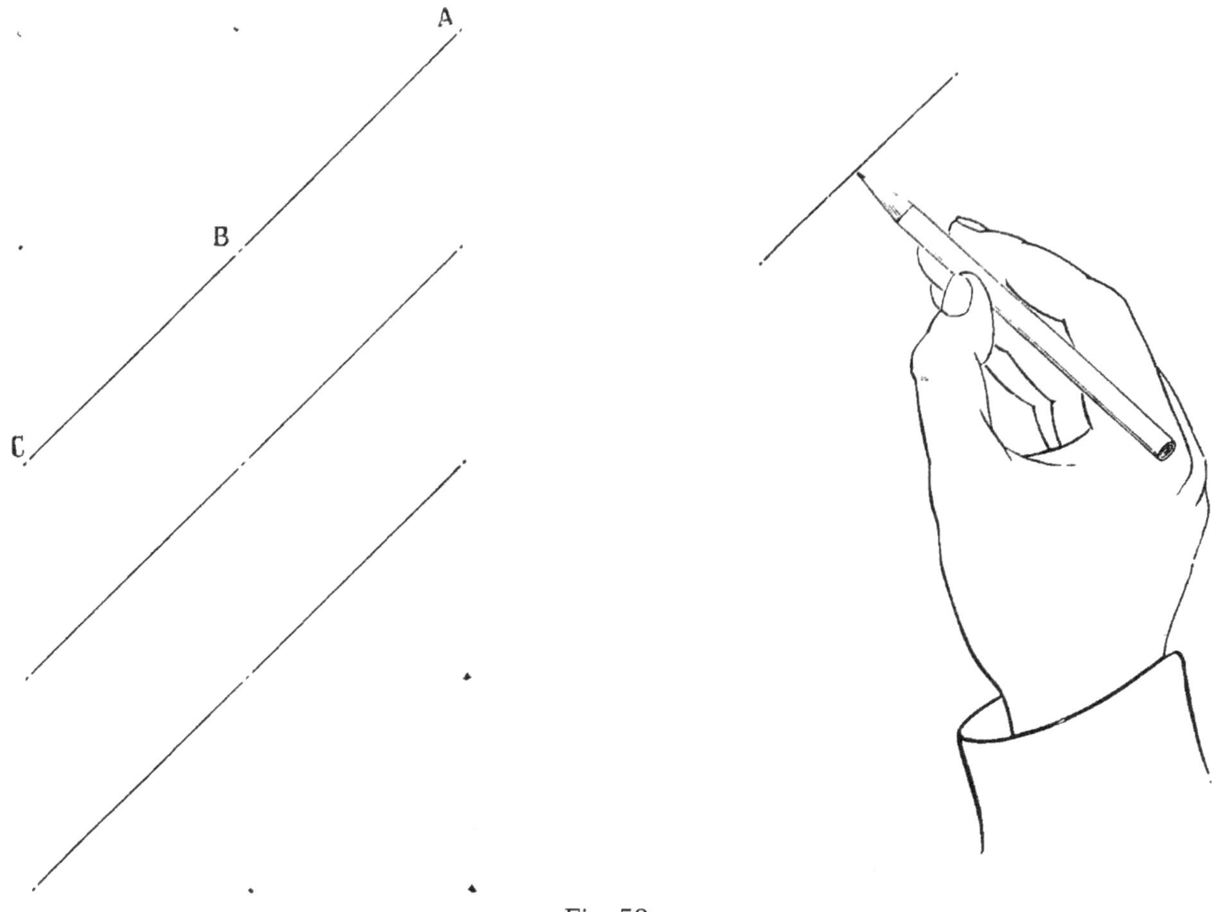

Fig. 58.

It is a common, and at the same time highly injurious habit, to draw this line by a movement of the wrist, the fingers remaining rigid. This may be detected by watching the action of the thumb; if it bends as the line is produced, all is right; but if it does not the wrist is at work.

TO DRAW THE UPRIGHT OR PERPENDICULAR LINE.

This line demands the greatest attention, and any care bestowed upon it will be amply repaid in the after studies.

Commence by placing a line of points down the side of the paper, examine them very carefully to see that they are all the same distance from its edge, hold the pencil as in the drawing, fig. 59, move the elbow well out from the side, and join the points by a movement of the fingers and thumb. When one line is complete, place the points for the next, and examine them from the edge of the paper, not from the line just drawn. Proceed in this manner until the paper is covered.

There is in most cases a tendency to place the points for this line in a slightly inclined direction, as in writing, though in some instances the tendency is the opposite, a thoroughly correct eye in this respect being a rare gift: and it may be useful to suggest that the paper be so placed that the line of points to be produced may be exactly in front of the eye.

TO DRAW THE SECOND OBLIQUE LINE.

Prepare three rows of points down the side of the paper, examine them for correctness of position, hold the pencil as in the drawing, fig. 60, remove the elbow as far as possible from the side, and join the points by a movement of the fingers and thumb, and continue the exercise until the paper is covered.

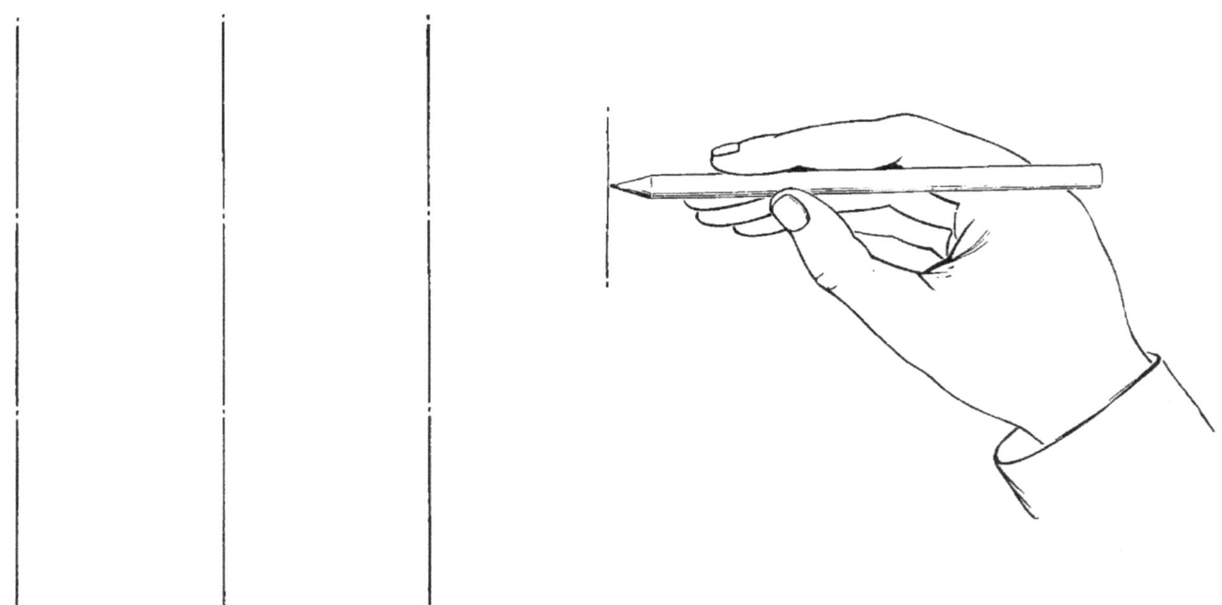

Fig. 59.

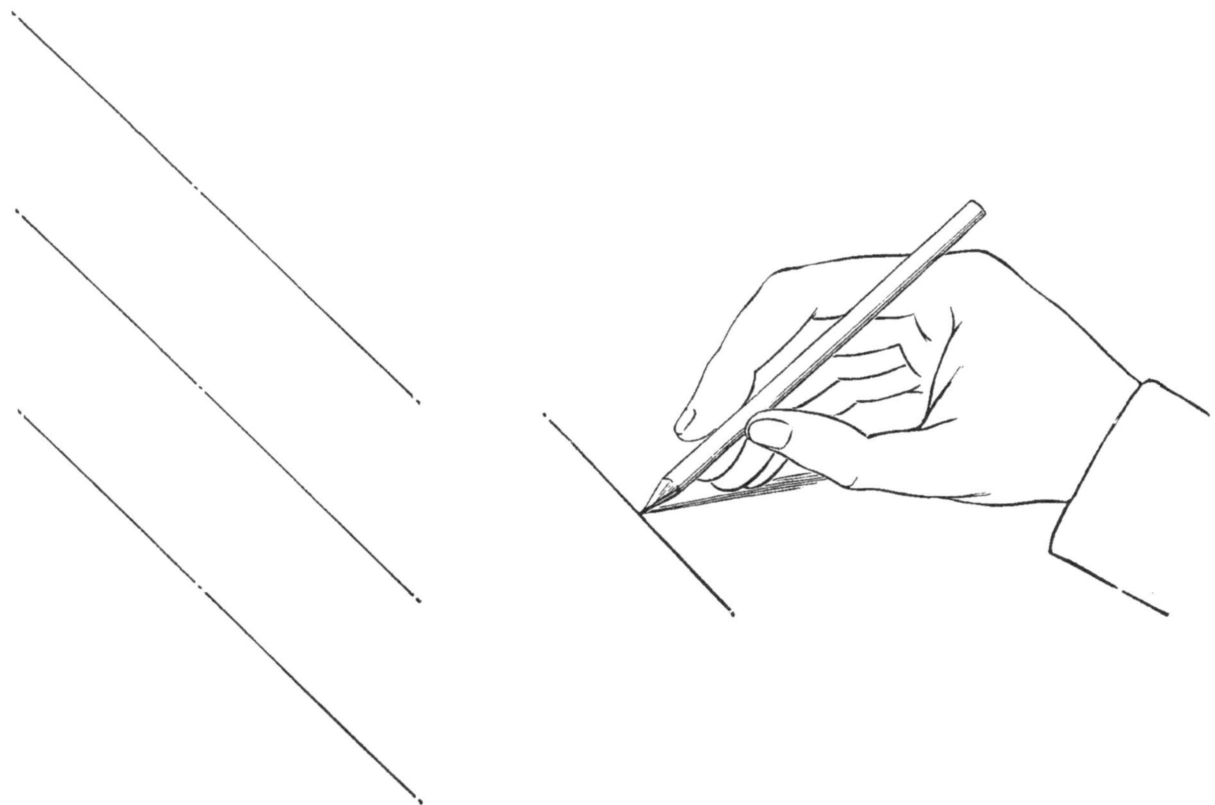

Fig. 60.

It will be noticed that each change in direction of the line to be drawn, has been accompanied with a corresponding change in the position of the elbow and wrist. The following simple rule will assist the memory when placing the hand for any given line; the pencil should be held so that it may form a T with the line to be drawn:

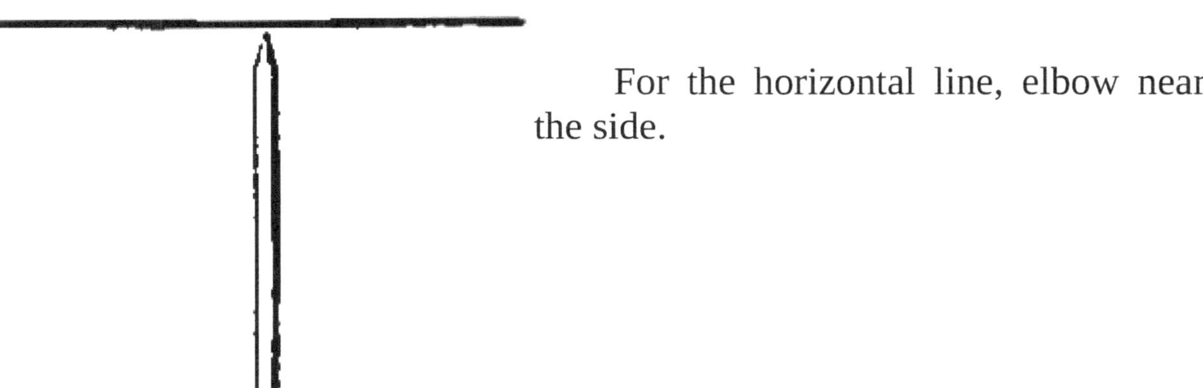

For the horizontal line, elbow near the side.

For the first oblique, elbow a little removed.

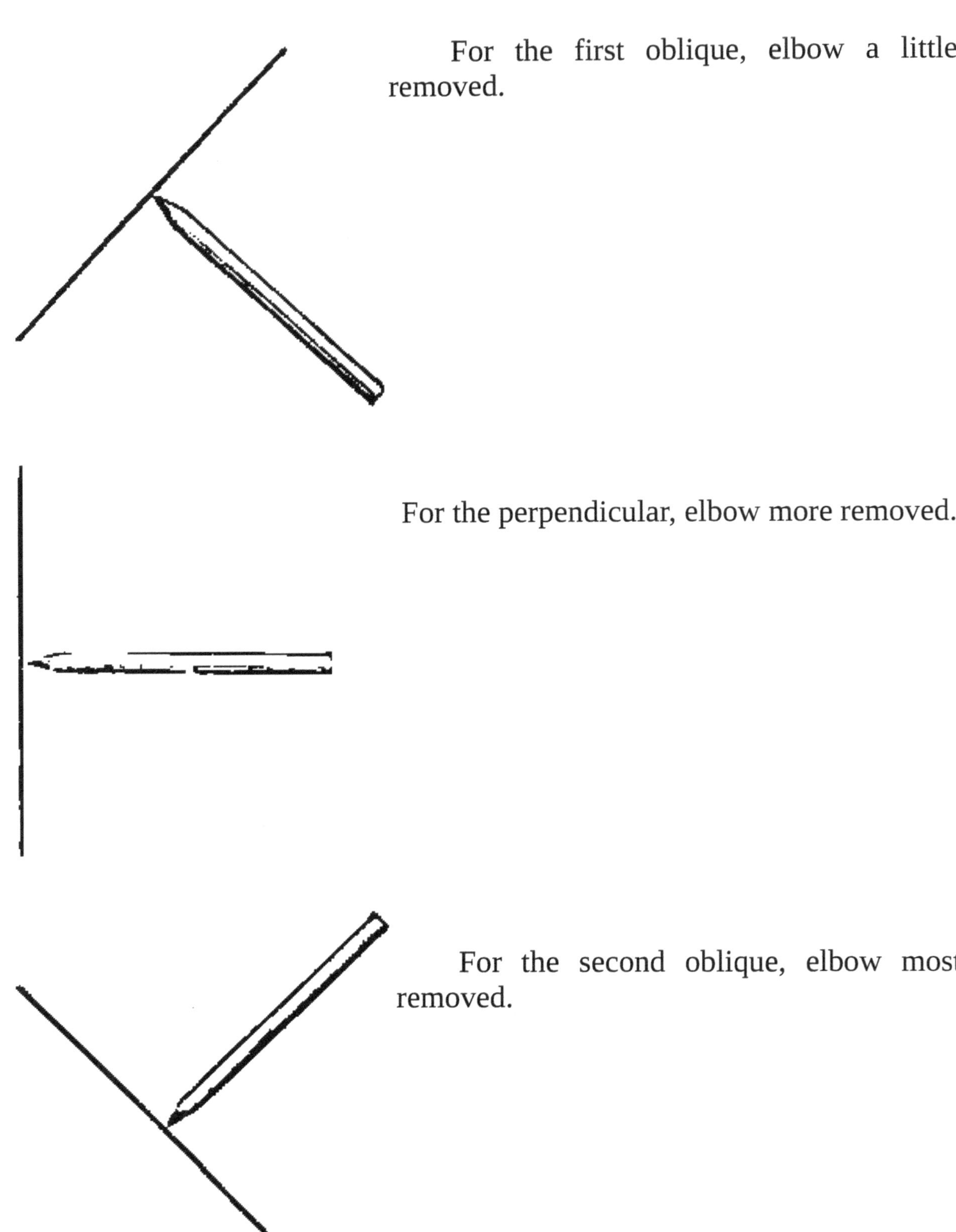

For the perpendicular, elbow more removed.

For the second oblique, elbow most removed.

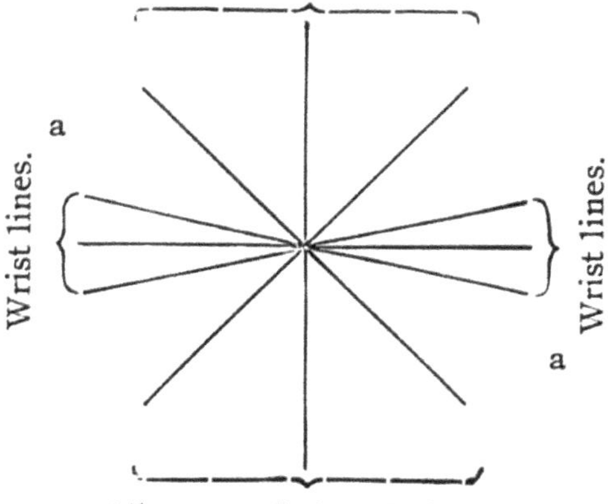

It may also be interesting to notice, with regard to the movements by which lines are produced, that they are divided into two systems; the first is that of the wrist, which includes the horizontal, and lines in nearly the same direction; the second is that of the fingers and thumb, by which all other lines are formed. The following diagram exhibits the two systems and their various lines grouped, and it will be observed that there is a space marked (a) between the two sets, which may be considered neutral ground. Lines in this direction may be produced by either movement, as may be most convenient, but it will always be found that these lines are the most trying to the hand.

ON FIGURES FORMED OF STRAIGHT LINES.

Before commencing this subject, let it be clearly understood that future success will, in a great measure, depend upon the amount of care bestowed upon it. The aim should be to obtain absolute accuracy, and for this end the copies should be tested by the most careful measurements, and corrected until they are true with the originals, but it should be distinctly understood that these measurements are only to be made after the eye and hand have done their best.

NOTE.—To some it may appear that too much time and care has been bestowed on mere lines, but let it be understood that a good system of line drawing is the basis of all education—the slightest outline by a hand thus trained has a bold, free and masterly character; and with regard to shading, which is simply an aggregation of good lines, it is only by such a practiced hand its most charming effects can be produced.

Fig. 66: Place the points *A*, *B*. Examine them to see that they are the same distance apart as in the original, and that they are level; place the point *C* exactly under *A*, and make *A C* equal in distance to *A B*; now place the point *D* opposite *C* and under *B*; try the distances between each point to see that they are the same; divide each side by a point half way, and then draw the lines.

Fig. 67: Repeat the last figure and add the lines *A* and *B*, taking great care that the points for them are correctly placed.

Fig. 68: Commence with the square as before; then join the half-way points.

Fig. 69: After the square is drawn, place the points *A* and *B* at the right height above the half-way points, and *C*, *D* at the proper distance from the corners, then draw the figure.

Fig. 70: The greatest care should be taken with the squares for this and the following figure, as the slightest error in them will destroy the symmetry of the drawing within; when the square is completed, join the opposite corners, and place on the crossed lines the points *B*, *C*, *D*, *E*; examine these to see that they are each at the same distance from the centre *A*, and that this distance is equal to the space from *A* to the sides of the square; when all are proved to be correct, complete the figure.

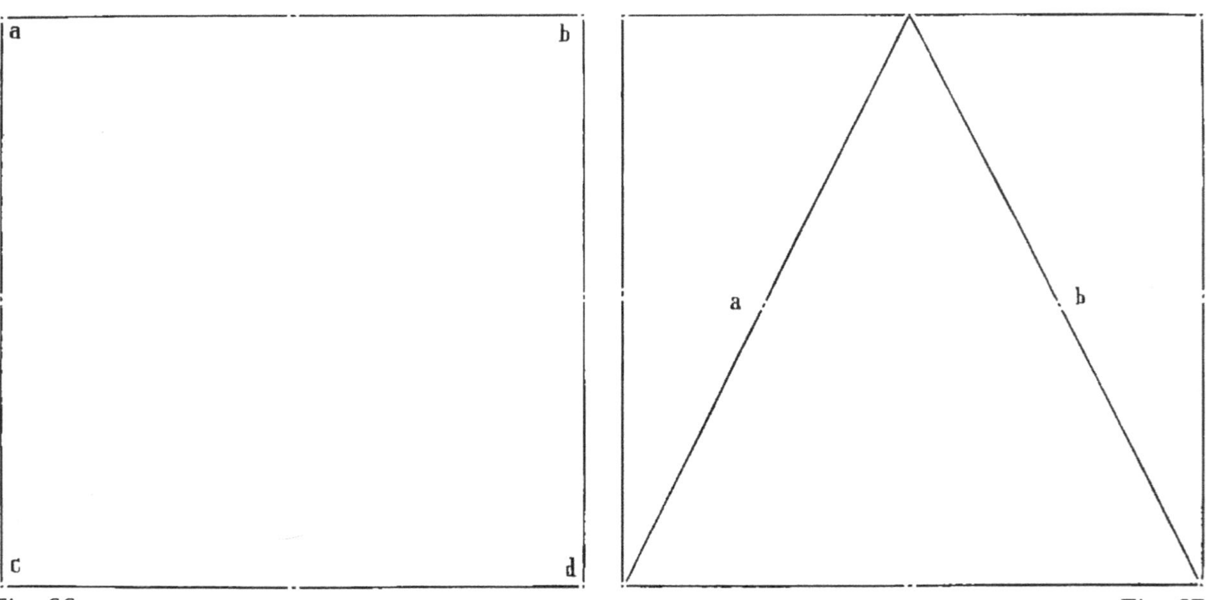

Fig. 66.　　　　Fig. 67.

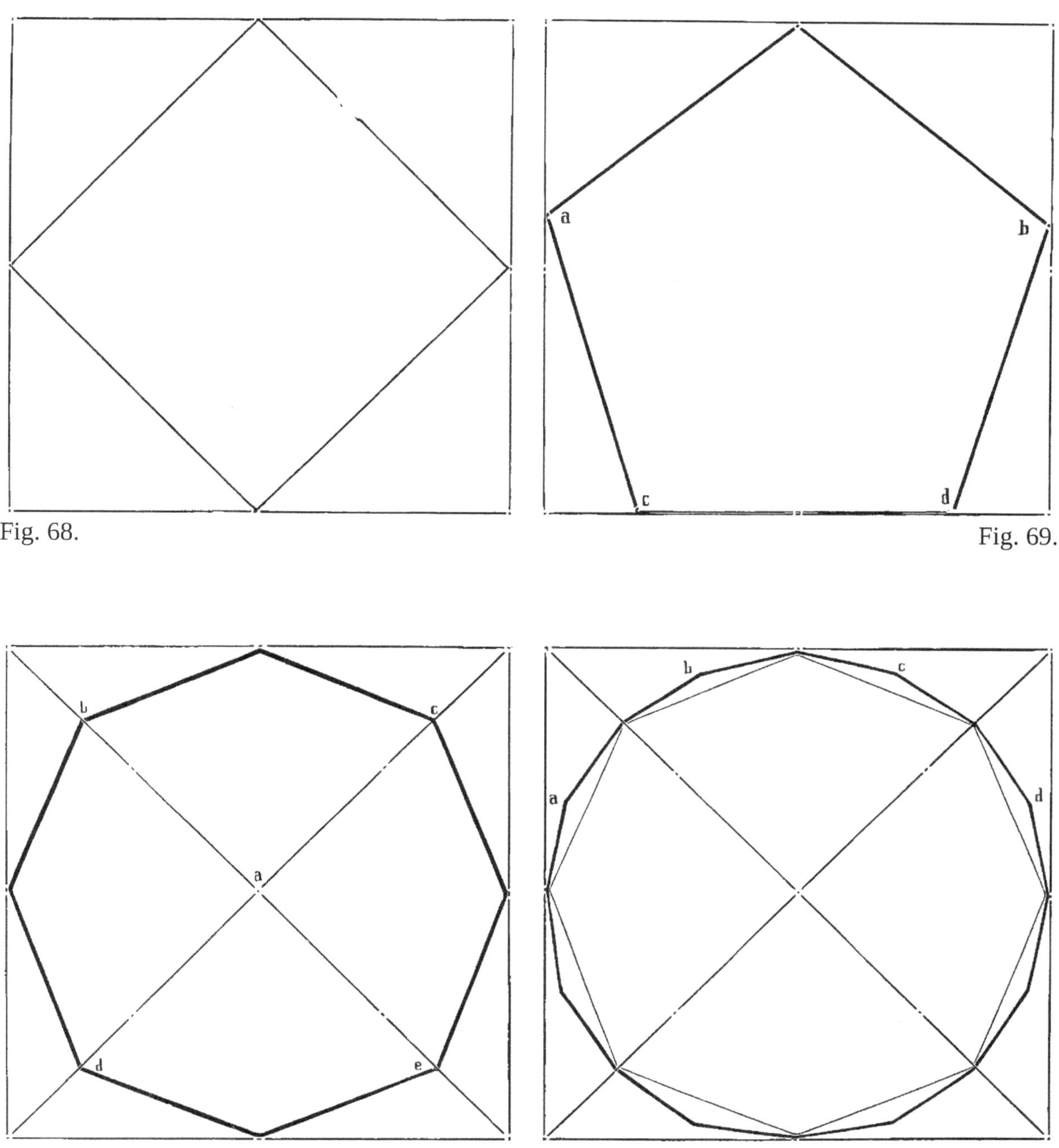

Fig. 68.

Fig. 69.

Fig. 70.

Fig. 71.

Fig. 71: Repeat the last drawing with, if possible, greater exactness, and outside the octagon place the points *A*, *B*, *C*, *D*, etc.; examine each of these points to see that they are all at the same distance from the centre, and then complete the figure.

ON CURVED LINES.

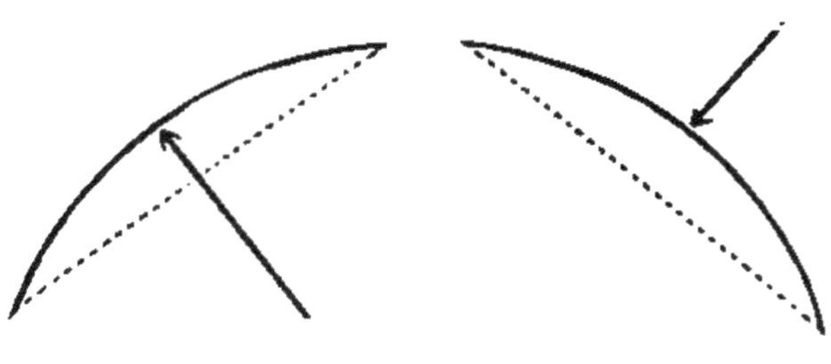

The right position of the hand for drawing any curved line is that required for a straight line which would touch the extremities of the curve. The straight lines given in the exercises are valuable, not only as a guide to the position of the hand, but as an assistance to the eye when forming the curves or examining them after they are produced.

The direction given for drawing a straight line was to form it by one steady movement from point to point, without any jerk or stop by the way. This instruction requires to be changed for the curve, *which is better produced by several short strokes*, thus:

or by overlapping lines, any outside bits being cleared away with India rubber.

These exercises will test the drawing power and try the patience of the pupil, but they are worthy of all the care which can be bestowed, which in future efforts will meet with its full reward.

Fig. 76: Draw first the square as directed in the previous lesson, join the points *A, B, C* and add the short lines at *E* and *F*, proceed with the curve *A B*, drawing it with faint lines at first, and adding stroke upon stroke until the required depth is obtained; the curve *A C* is more difficult to produce, in consequence of the formation of the hand; it should, therefore, be drawn in shorter pieces, joining them together afterwards by over strokes.

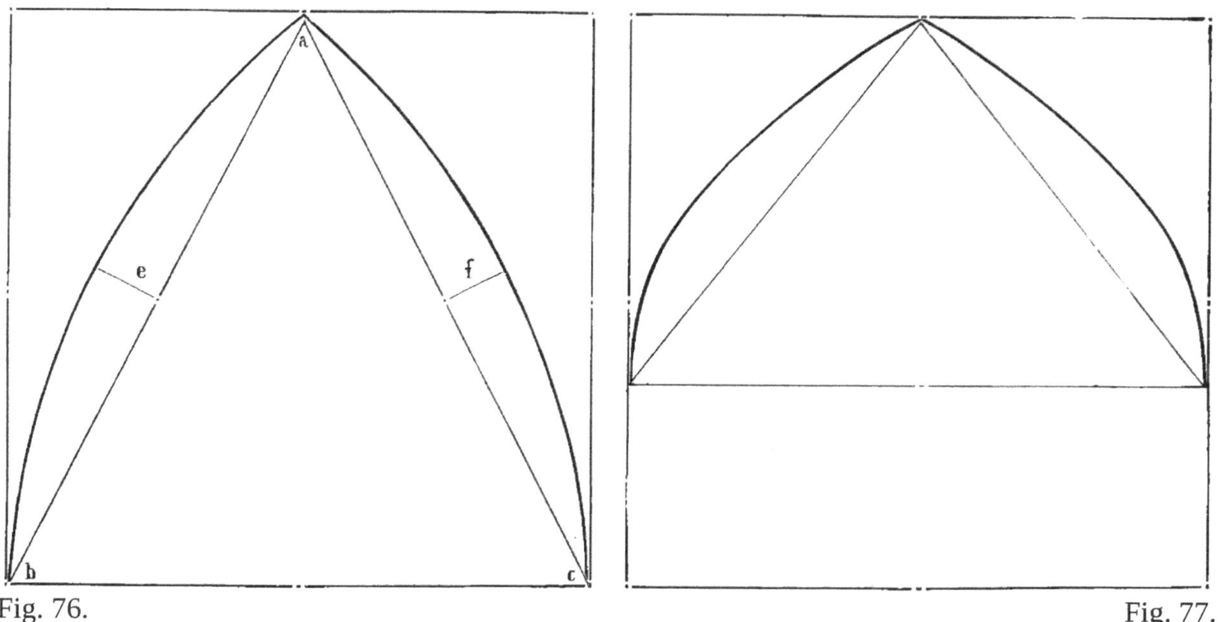

Fig. 76.   Fig. 77.

Fig. 77: Draw the square and straight lines first, then add the curves, taking care to give the greatest fullness at the right place.

Fig. 78: Draw the square and straight lines, proceed with the curves, taking care to make each of the same proportion.

Figs. 79 and 80: The ovals contained in these figures are simply foreshortened circles, and as such forms are of frequent occurrence in sketching from objects, in bridges, wheels, ends of timber, etc., they should be carefully studied; the greatest difficulty is to turn the narrow ends, and prevent their looking like corners. For this purpose it is better to draw the short curves first, thus:
and then join the longer sides to them.

Fig. 81: If this figure can be drawn correctly, a great success has been achieved; the circle is a most difficult form to delineate, and without system could not be accomplished. Draw the square and straight lines within it with great care, examine each point of the octagon to see that it is at the same distance from the centre, and then draw the circle.

EXAMPLES FOR PRACTICE.

Several figures, 83 to 96, representing more or less familiar parts of machines, utilities, etc., are introduced for practice in free-hand, but—

It must be noted that even in free-hand the wise student will occasionally use the straight edge and compasses, so as to make his first attempts fairly creditable. Many good draughtsmen have begun by simply copying such figures and illustrations as are used throughout this volume and other similar sources; perhaps there is nothing better for practice or training than the copying and reproducing of samples of good mechanical drawings, yet it must always be remembered that advancement in free-hand must be made in the line of less to greater efforts, and that the why and wherefore will be constantly asked by the aspiring student; that good and correct drawings are to be aimed for at all times in every line and dimension —never forgetting the law of proportion in the smallest outlines of objects to be represented.

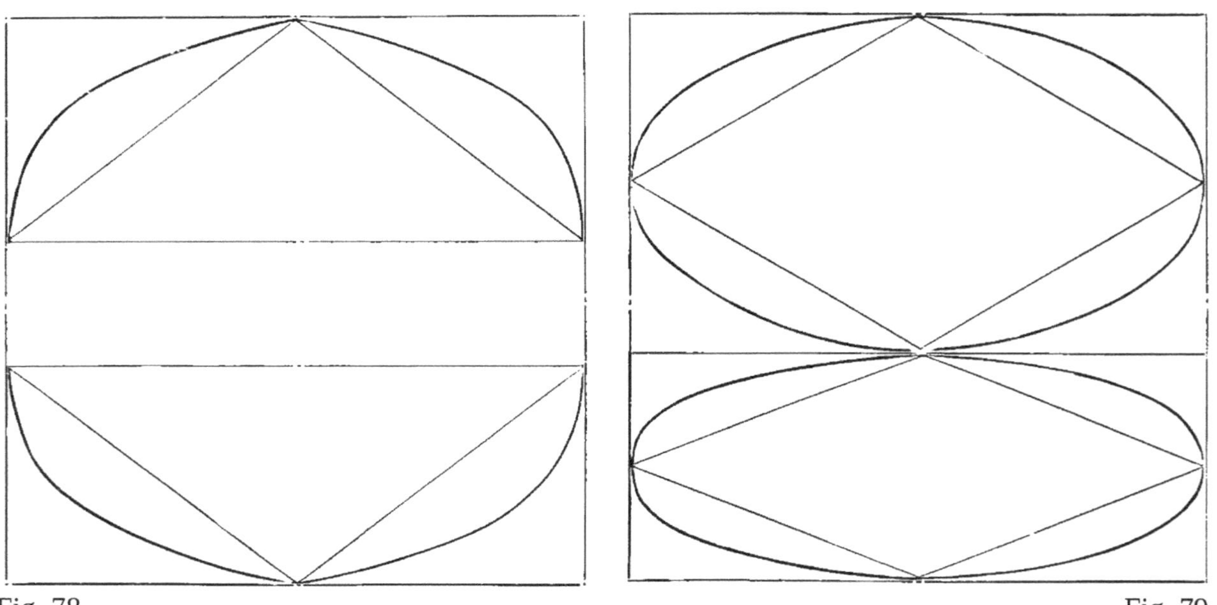

Fig. 78. Fig. 79.

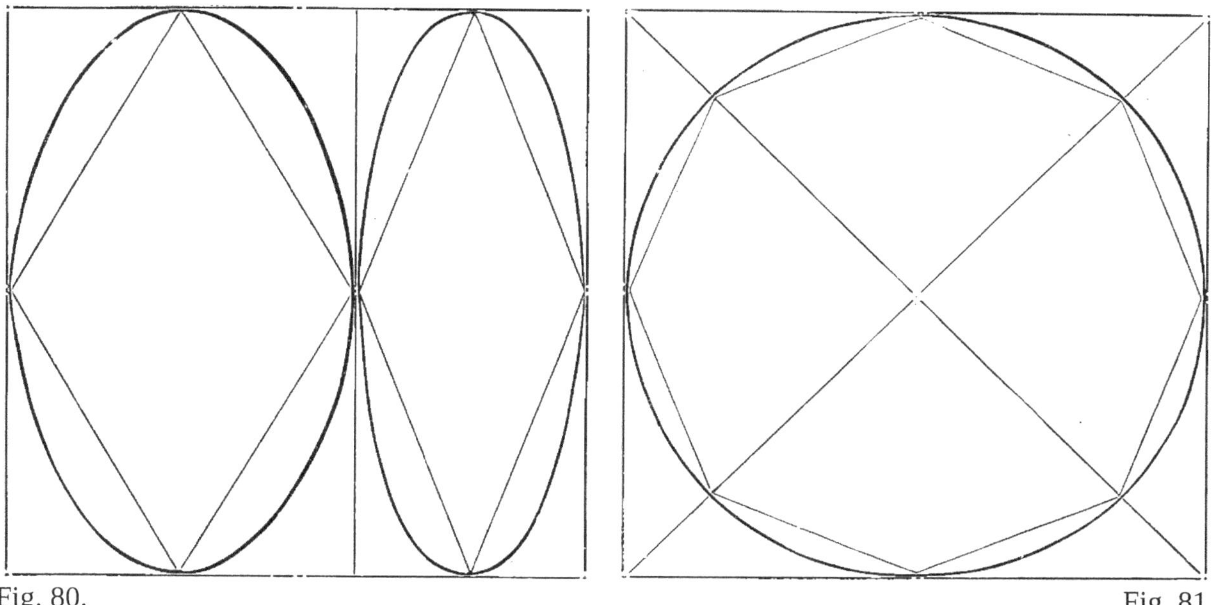

Fig. 80.   Fig. 81.

Fig. 83 is a section, or end view of a bar of angle iron; the student will find helpful practice in attempting this figure; he may be allowed to use a straight-edge in drawing the lines, but no measurements; the work should be tested on completion by a rule, or better by penciling from the original on tracing paper, and comparing the free-hand with the copy, when the defective proportions, if any, will be clearly exhibited.

Fig. 84 is a section of tee iron, and fig. 85 is a section of channel iron. These three figures on page 75 should be practiced alternately, although seeming similar in shape.

Fig. 86 is a side and end view of an angle plate shaded. Fig. 87 is a wrench shaded.

Examples of bolt ends are shown in the two next numbers; fig. 88 exhibits the common square-head bolt, and fig. 89 the hexagon or six-sided bolt-head; these are also examples of *straight-line shading*. Fig. 90 is a lathe-dog, and shows an example of *curved shading*; fig. 92 is an engine crank, and an example of *straight and curved shading*; fig. 91 is a screw clamp.

Fig. 93 is a section of boiler plates riveted together; a caulking tool is also shown.

In the example, fig. 94—a hand-wheel—the principal difficulty, even for the most advanced student in free-hand, will be in drawing the circles; a coin, if convenient, can be used to scribe about, in drawing these; the other parts can afterwards be filled in around the circle. Fig. 96 is introduced for practice in penciling and shading; the figure represents a water-wheel on a stone pier.

The familiar oil can is shown in fig. 95. These all are excellent objects for practice.

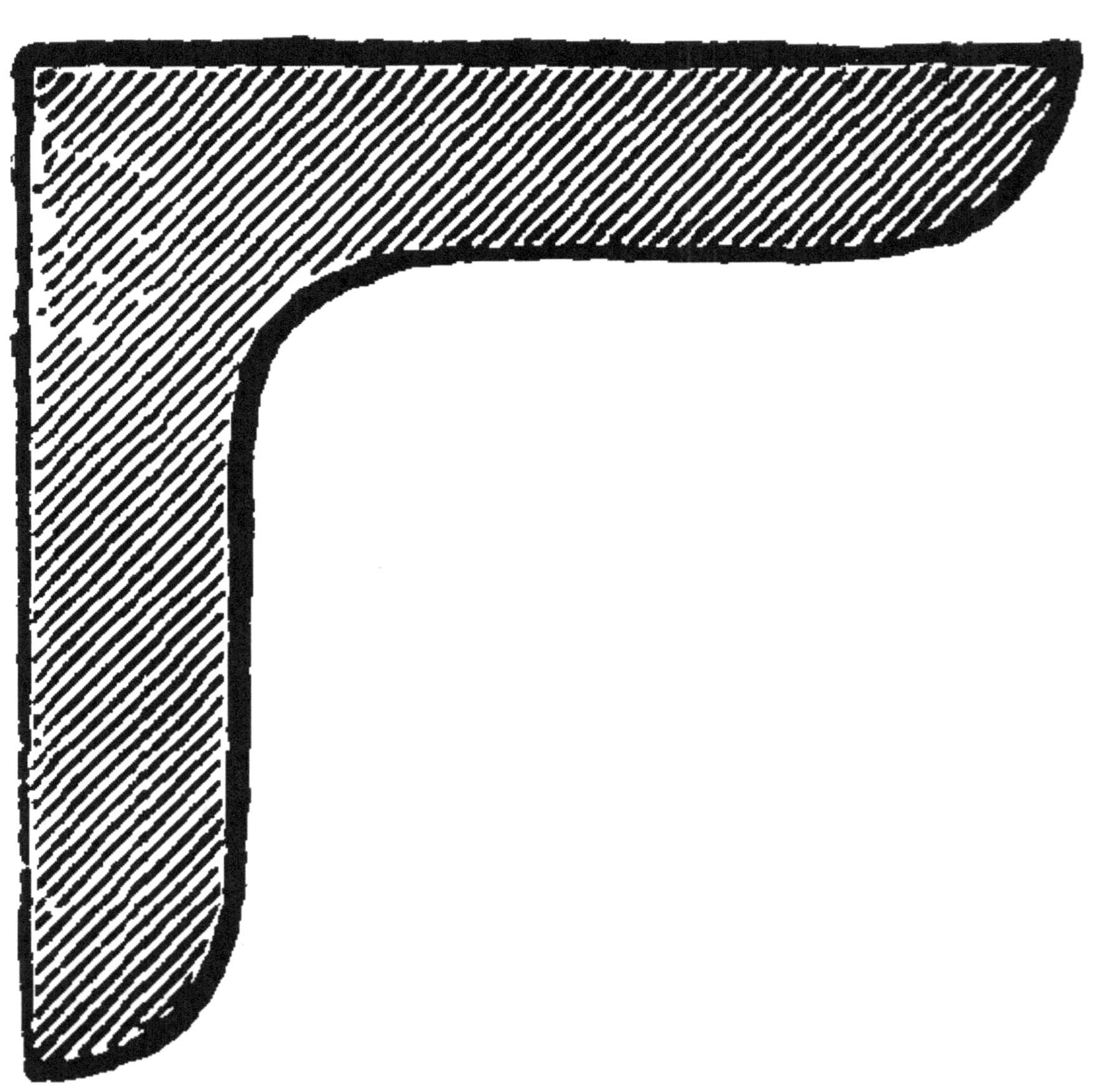

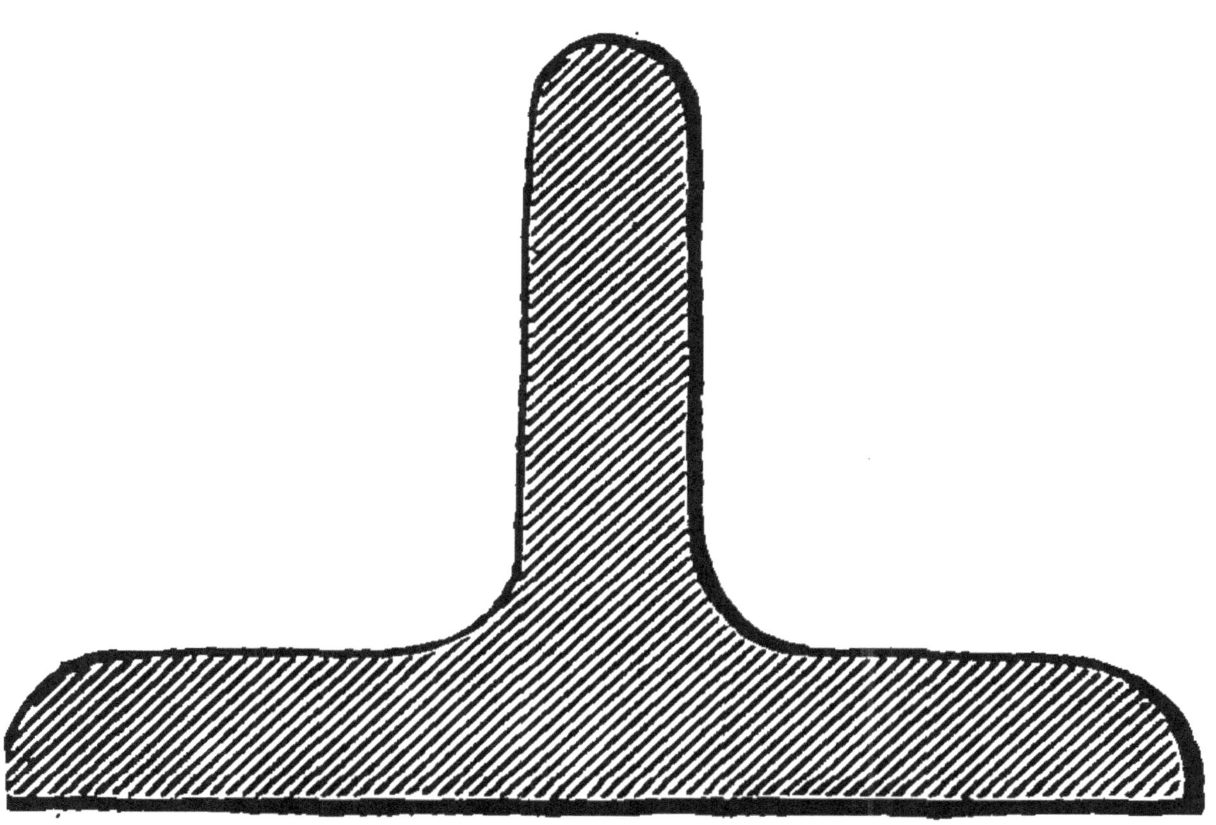

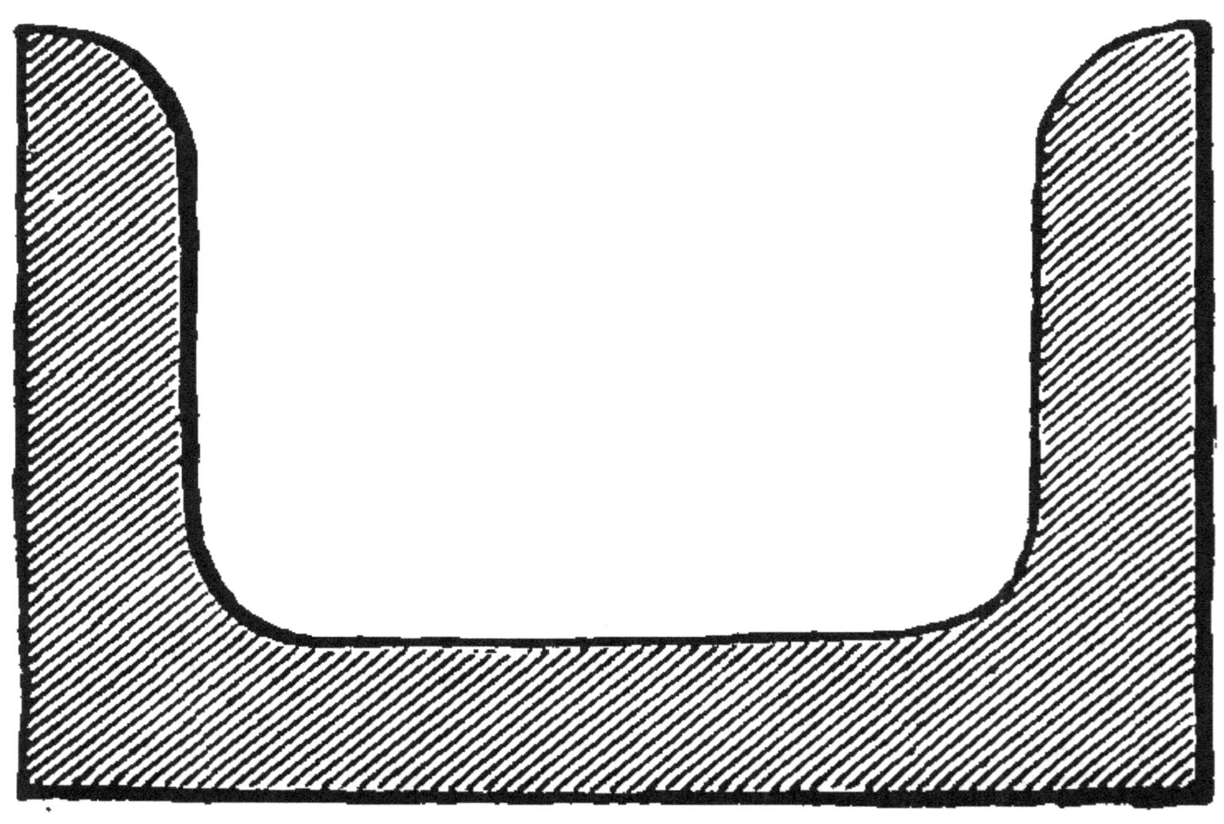

Fig. 83.—Fig. 84.—Fig. 85.

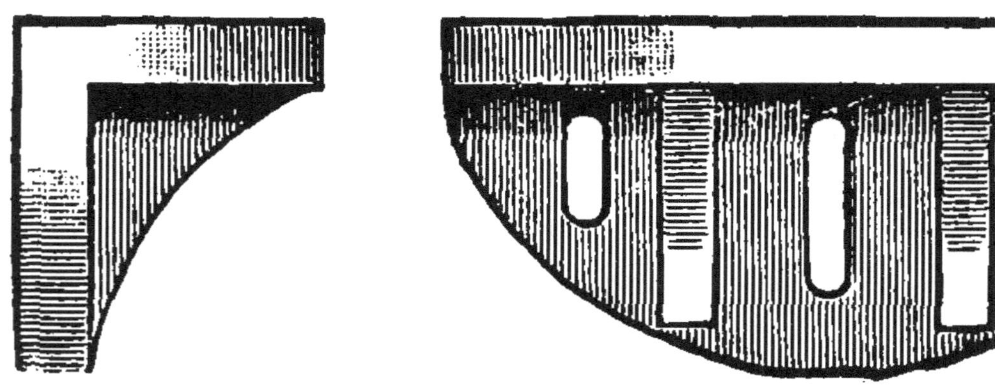

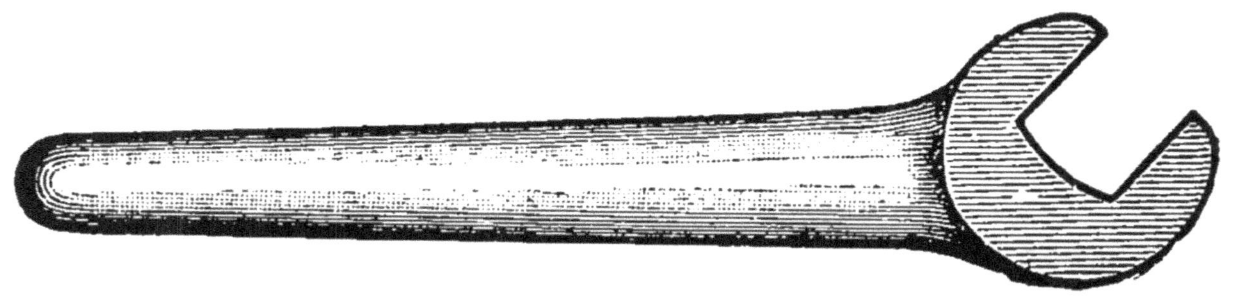

Fig. 86.   Fig. 87.

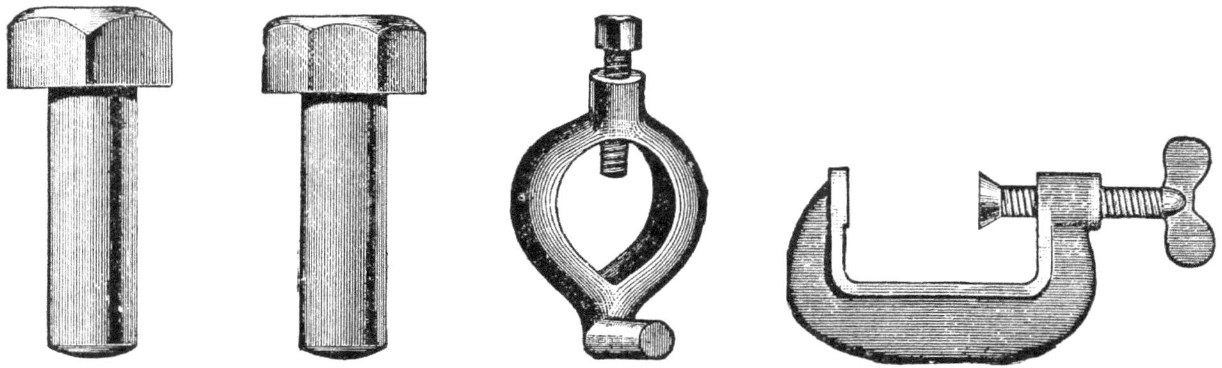

Fig. 88.—Fig. 89.—Fig. 90.—Fig. 91.

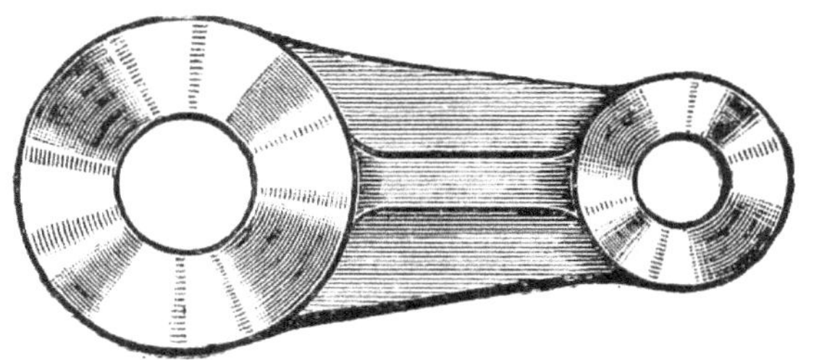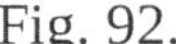

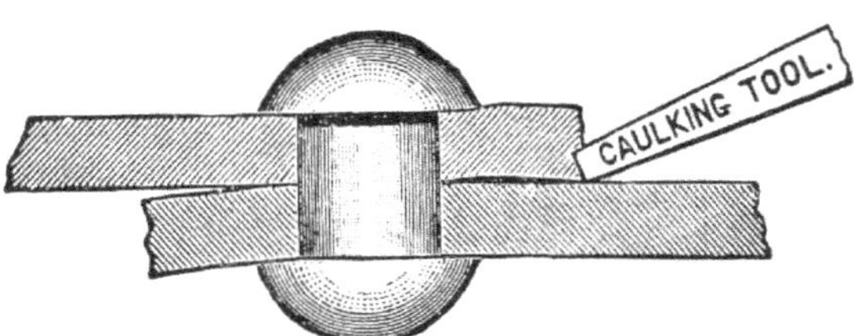

Fig. 92.   Fig. 93.

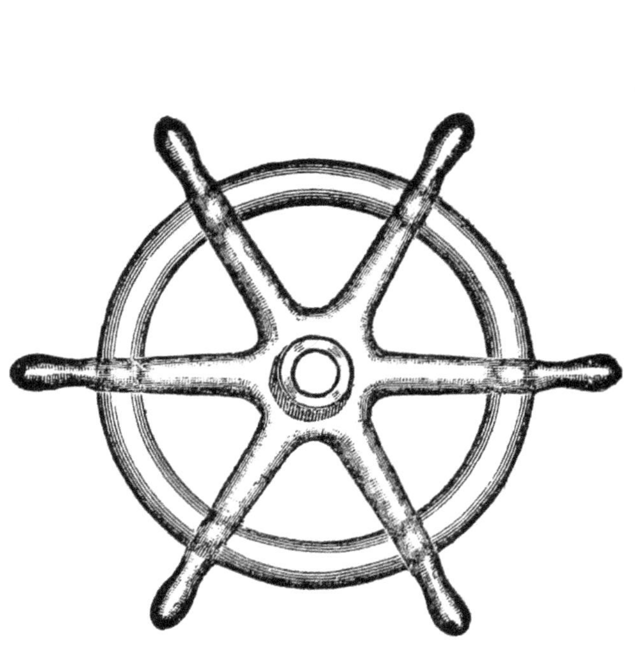

Fig. 94.

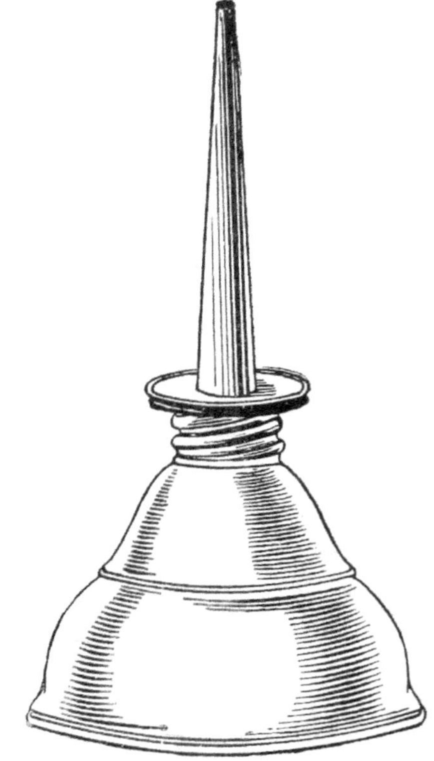

Fig. 95.

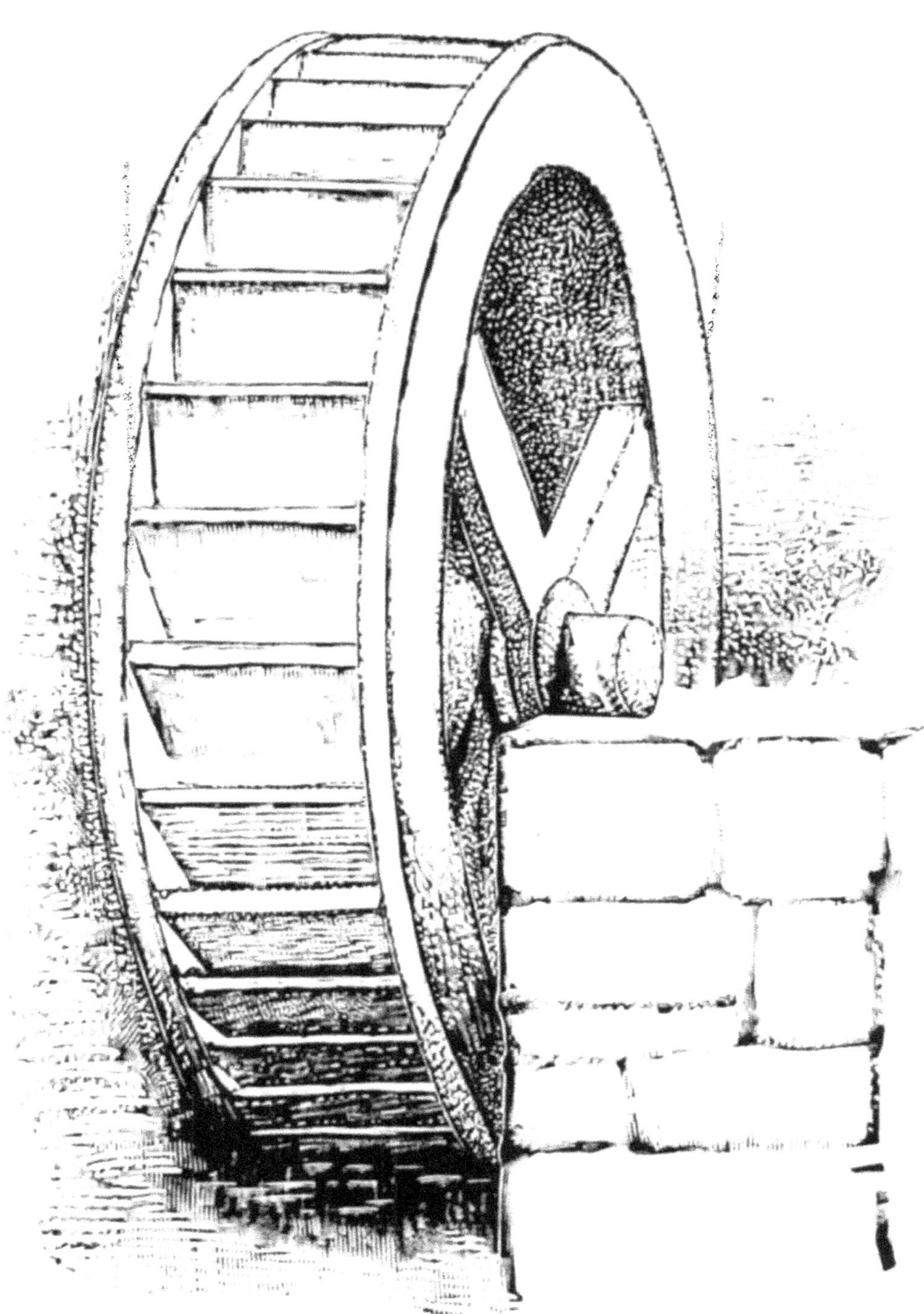

Fig. 96.

GEOMETRICAL DRAWING

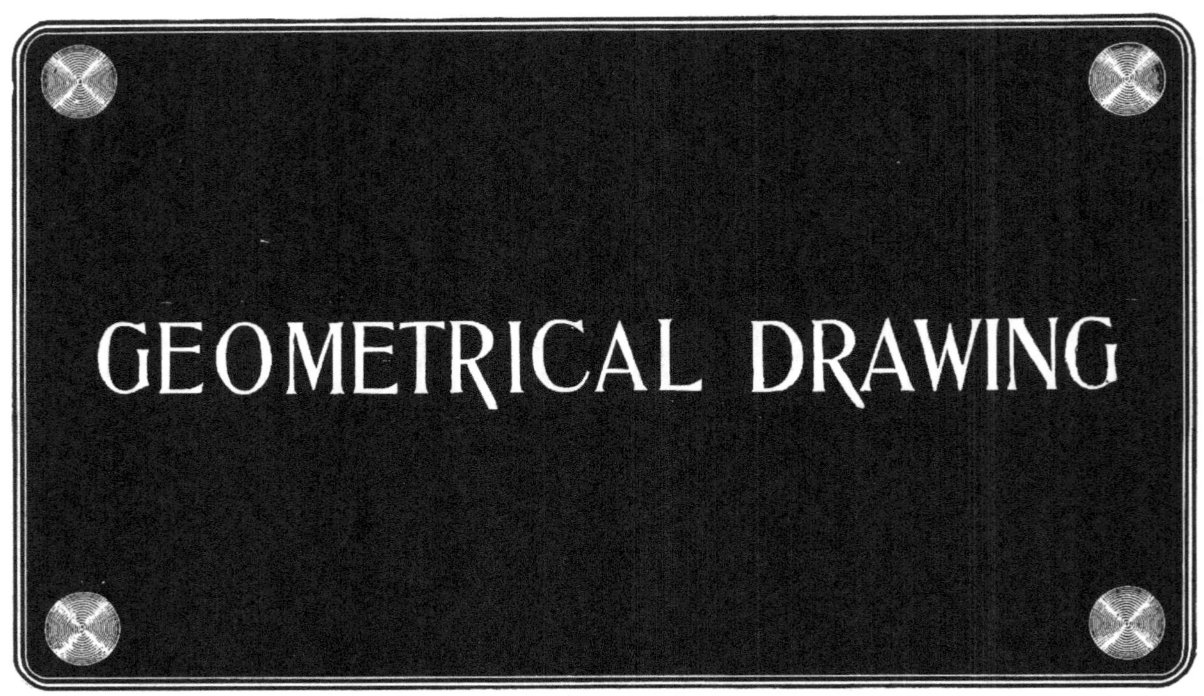

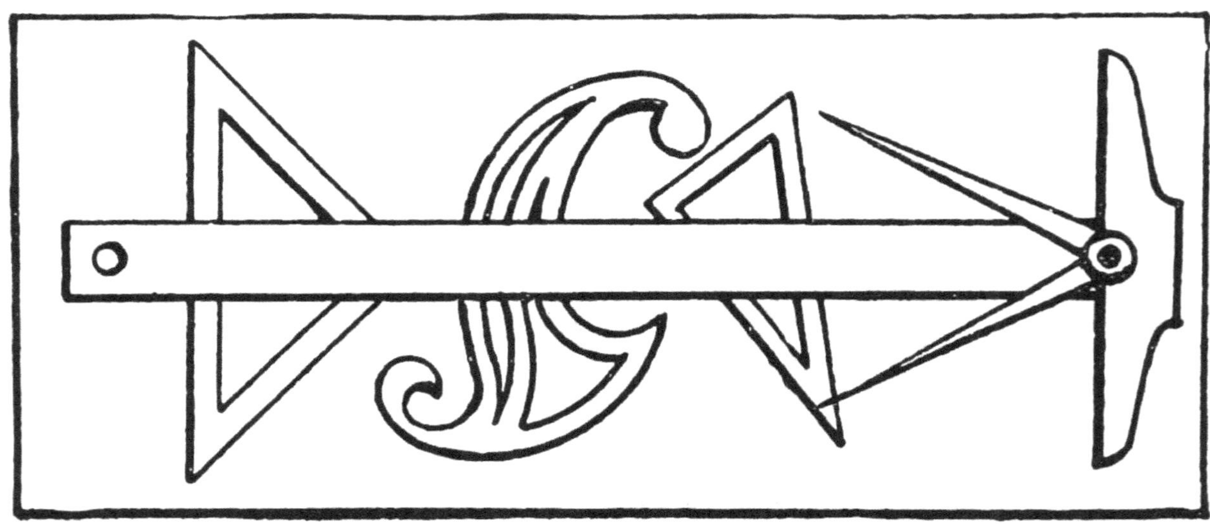

Geometrical Drawing.

Geometry is the science of measurement; it has been known for more than three thousand years; many lives have been devoted to its development, and it exists to-day as the foundation of all mathematics.

Geometrical drawing is the art of representing, to the eye, the problems "worked out" by geometricians, and the importance of a knowledge of geometrical drawing is paramount. The student will find that the figures delineated and explained in the next few pages constantly occur in mechanical drawing. Says Walter Smith, State Director of Art Education in Massachusetts, "I have never known a case where a student did not progress more satisfactorily in his studies after a course of practical geometry."

The elementary conceptions of geometry are few:

1.—A point.

2.—A line.

3.—A surface.

4.—A solid, and

5.—An angle.

All of which elements are used in mechanical drawings.

From these, as data, a vast number of mathematical problems have been deduced; of which a few of the most elementary will be illustrated in this work; but these few will repay the attention of the student.

In "freehand" drawing the crayon and pencil are used; in geometrical drawings the dividers, as shown in illustration, fig. 97, together with a rule, are all that is necessary to accomplish the work.

A problem is something to be done, and geometry has been defined as the science of measurement; the relation between geometry and mechanical drawing is very close, hence the term "geometrical problem."

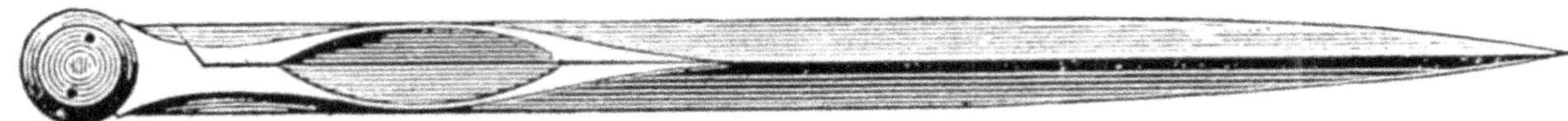

Fig. 97.

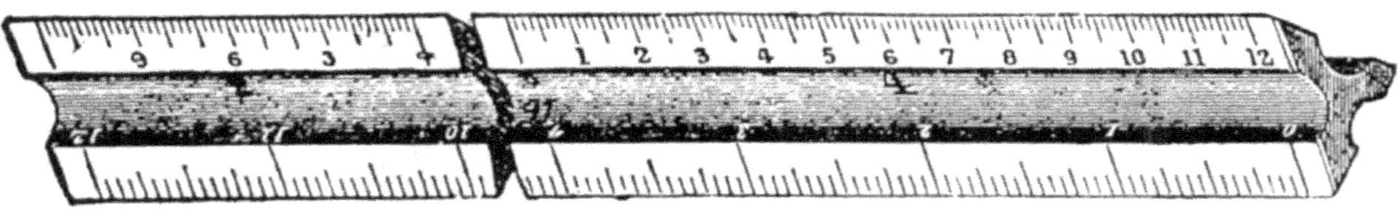

Fig. 98.

Before proceeding with the examples, a few elementary statements belonging to the science of geometry are presented; these will be useful to the student, not only while "doing" the problems, but in many cases of every-day—future—experience.

Geometry is one of the oldest and simplest of sciences; it may be defined as *the science of measurement*; geometry is *the root* from which all regular mathematical calculations issue. It has claimed the best thought of practical men from the times of the Greeks and Romans two thousand years ago; they derived their knowledge of the science from the Egyptians, who in turn were indebted to the Chaldeans and Hindoos in times beyond any authentic history; hence it was under the operations of the laws explained in geometry, that the pyramids of Egypt and the temples of Greece were constructed, as well as the engines of war and appliances of peace of ancient times.

A point is mere position, and has no magnitude.

A line is that which has extension in length only. The extremities of lines are points.

A surface is that which has extension in length and breadth only.

A solid is that which has extension in length, breadth and thickness.

An angle is the difference in the direction of two lines proceeding from the same point.

Lines, Surfaces, Angles and Solids constitute the different kinds of quantity called *geometrical* magnitudes.

Parallel lines are lines which have the same direction; hence parallel lines can never meet, however far they may be produced;

for two lines taking the same direction cannot approach or recede from each other.

An *Axiom* is a self-evident truth, not only too simple to require, *but too simple to admit of demonstration.*

A *Proposition* is something which is either proposed to be done, or to be demonstrated, and is either a problem or a theorem.

A *Problem* is something proposed to be done.

A *Theorem* is something proposed to be demonstrated.

A *Hypothesis* is a supposition made with a view to draw from it some consequence which establishes the truth or falsehood of a proposition, or solves a problem.

A *Lemma* is something which is premised, or demonstrated, in order to render what follows more easy.

A *Corollary* is a consequent truth derived immediately from some preceding truth or demonstration.

A *Scholium* is a remark or observation made upon something going before it.

A *Postulate* is a problem, the solution of which is self-evident.

Let it be granted—

I. That a straight line can be drawn from any one point to any other point;

II. That a straight line can be produced to any distance, or terminated at any point;

III. That the circumference of a circle can be described about any center, at any distance from that center.

The common algebraic signs are used in Geometry, and it is necessary that the student in geometry should understand some of the more simple operations of algebra. As the terms circle, angle, triangle, hypothesis, axiom, theorem, corollary and definition are constantly occurring in a course of geometry, they are abbreviated as shown in the following list:

Addition is expressed by	+
Subtraction is expressed by	-
Multiplication is expressed by	×
Equality and Equivalency are expressed by	=
Greater than, is expressed by	>
Less than, is expressed by	<
Thus B is greater than A, is written	$B > A$

B is less than *A*, is written	$B < A$
A circle is expressed by	O
An angle is expressed by	L
A right angle is expressed by	R. L
Degrees, minutes and seconds are expressed by	° ′ ″
A triangle is expressed by	△
The term Hypothesis is expressed by	(Hy.)
The term Axiom is expressed by	(Ax.)
The term Theorem is expressed by	(Th.)
The term Corollary is expressed by	(Cor.)
The term Definition is expressed by	(Def.)
The term Perpendicular is expressed by	⊥
The difference of two quantities, when it is not known which is the greater, is expressed by the symbol	∼
Thus, the difference between *A* and *B* is written	$A \sim B$

GEOMETRICAL AXIOMS.

1. *Things which are equal to the same thing are equal to each other.*
2. *When equals are added to equals the wholes are equal.*
3. *When equals are taken from equals the remainders are equal.*
4. *When equals are added to unequals the wholes are unequal.*
5. *When equals are taken from unequals the remainders are unequal.*
6. *Things which are double of the same thing, or equal things, are equal to each other.*
7. *Things which are halves of the same thing, or of equal things, are equal to each other.*
8. *The whole is greater than any of its parts.*
9. *Every whole is equal to all its parts taken together.*
10. *Things which coincide, or fill the same space, are identical, or mutually equal in all their parts.*
11. *All right angles are equal to one another.*
12. *A straight line is the shortest distance between two points.*
13. *Two straight lines cannot enclose a space.*

Problems in Geometrical Drawing.

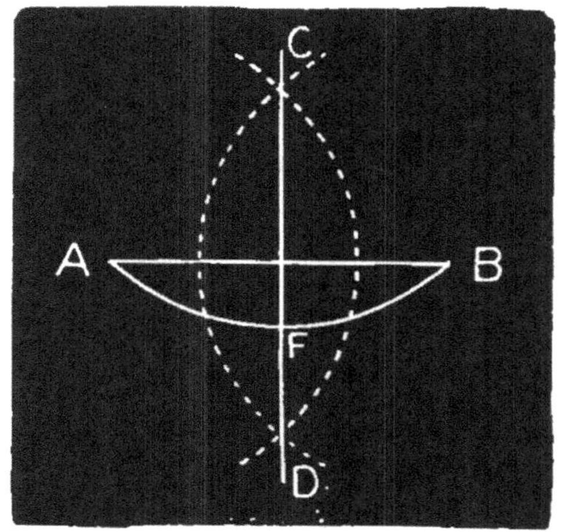

Fig. 99.

EXAMPLE 1.—*To bisect* (cut in two) *a straight line or an arc of a circle*, Fig. 99. From the ends of *A B* as centers, describe arcs cutting each other at *C* and *D*, and draw *C D*, which cuts the line at *E* or the arc at *F*.

EX. 2.—*To draw a perpendicular to a straight line, or a radial line to a circular arc*, Fig. 99. Operate as in the foregoing problem. The line *C D* is perpendicular to *A B*; the line *C D* is also radial to the arc *A B*.

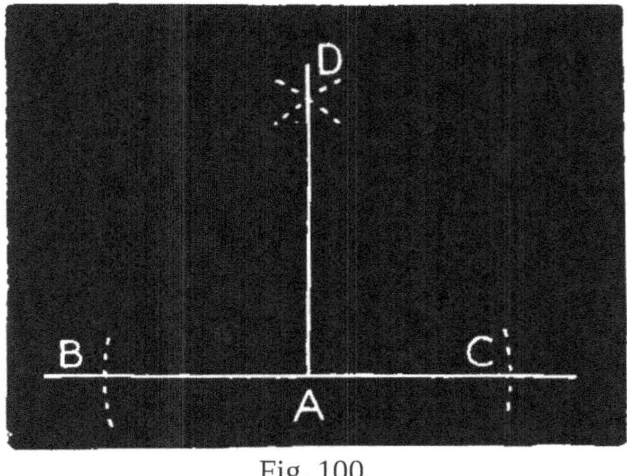

Fig. 100.

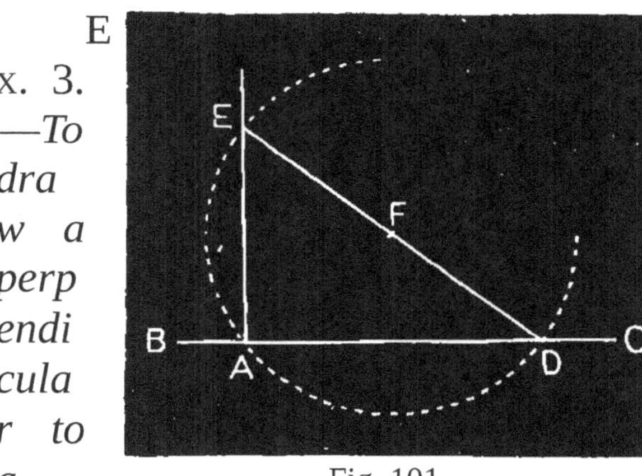

Fig. 101.

EX. 3.—*To draw a perpendicular to a straight line, from a given point in that line*, Fig. 100. With any radius from any given point *A* in the line *B C*, cut the line at *B* and *C*. Next, with a longer radius, describe arcs from *B* and *C*, cutting each other at *D*, and draw the perpendicular *D A*.

Second Method, Fig. 101. From any center *F* above *B C*, describe a circle passing through the given point *A*, and cutting the given line at *D*; draw *D F*, and produce it to cut the circle at *E*; and draw the perpendicular *A E*.

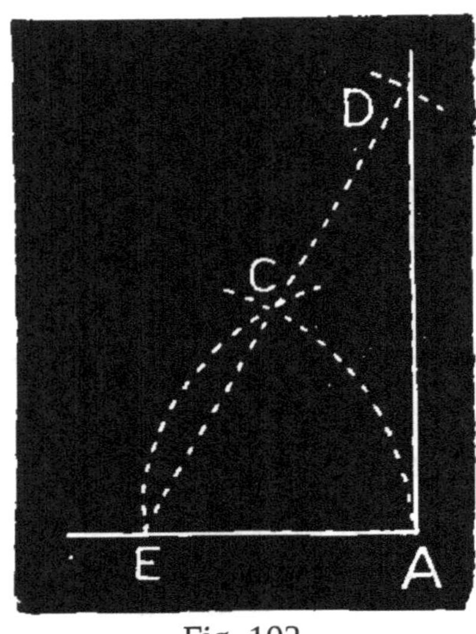

Fig. 102.

Third Method, Fig. 102. From *A* describe an arc *E C,* and from *E,* with the same radius, the arc *A C* cutting the other at *C;* through *C* draw a line *E C D* and set off *C D* equal to *C E,* and through *D* draw the perpendicular *A D.*

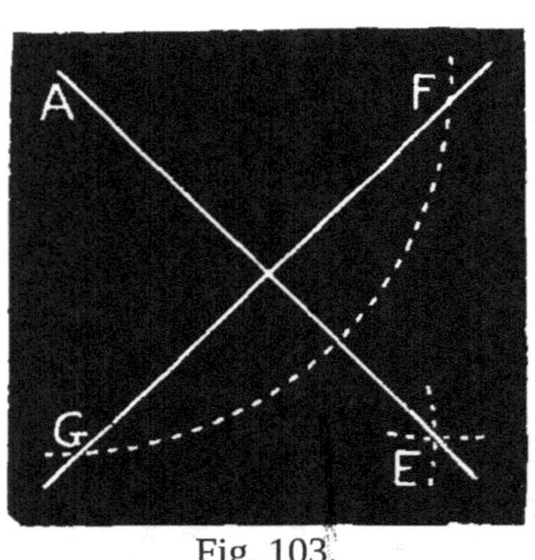

Fig. 103.

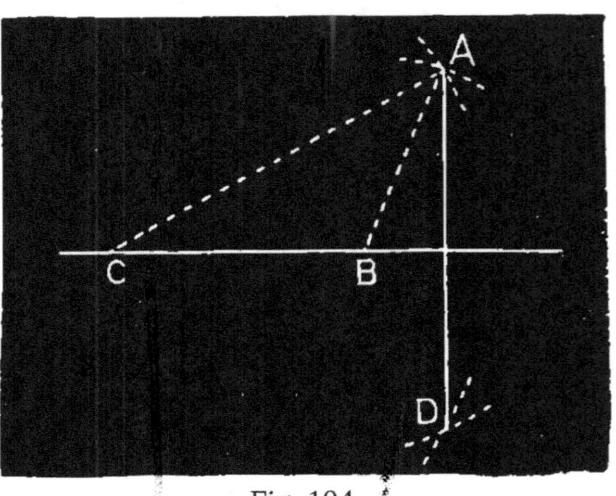

Fig. 104.

Ex. 4.—*To draw a perpendicular to a straight line from any point without it,* Fig. 103. From the point *A* with a sufficient radius cut the given line at *F* and *G;* and from these points describe arcs cutting at *E.* Draw the perpendicular *A E.*

If there be no room below the line, the intersection may be taken above the line; that is to say, between the line and the given point.

Second Method, Fig. 104. From any two points *B C* at some distance apart, in the given line, and with the radii *B A, C A,* respectively, describe arcs cutting at *A D.* Draw the perpendicular *A D.*

Ex. 5.—*To draw a parallel line through a given point,* Fig. 105. With a radius equal to the given point *C* from the given line *A B,* describe the arc *D* from *B,* taken considerably distant from *C.* Draw the parallel through *C* to touch the arc *D.*

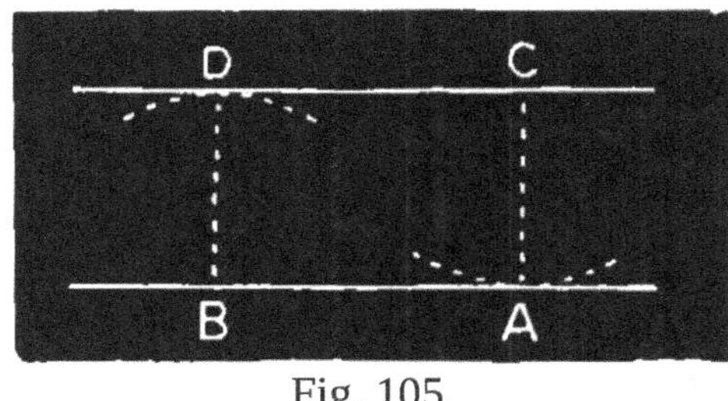

Fig. 105.

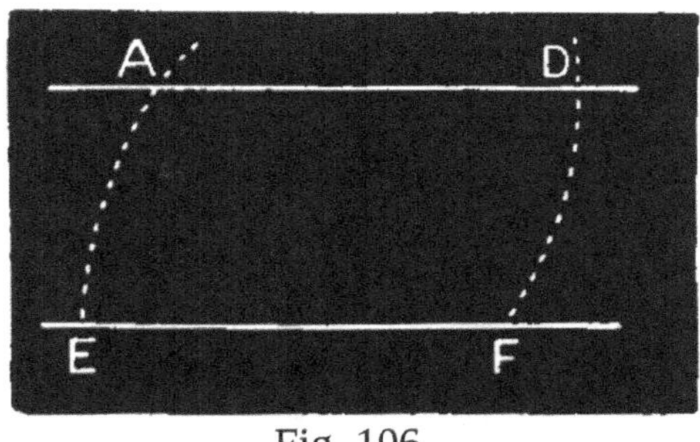

Fig. 106.

Second Method, Fig. 106. From *A*, the given point, describe the arc *F D*, cutting the given line at *F*; from *F*, with the same radius, describe the arc *E A*, and set off *F D*, equal to *E A*. Draw the parallel through the points *A D*.

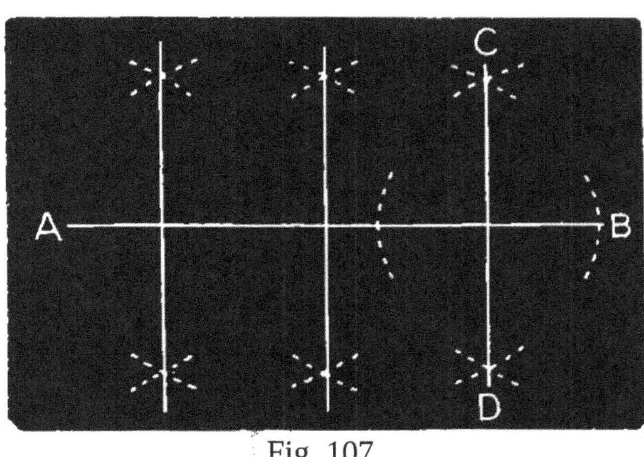

Fig. 107.

When a series of parallels are required perpendicular to a base line *A B*, they may be drawn as in fig. 107 through points in the base line set off at the required distances apart. This method is convenient also where a succession of parallels are required to a given line *C D*, for the perpendicular may be drawn to it, and any number of parallels may be drawn on the perpendicular.

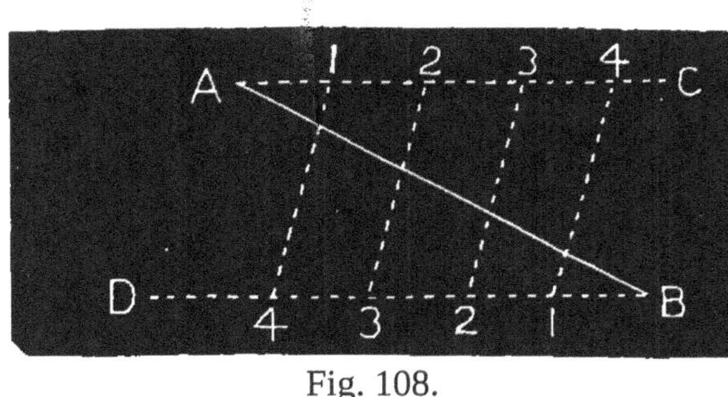

Fig. 108.

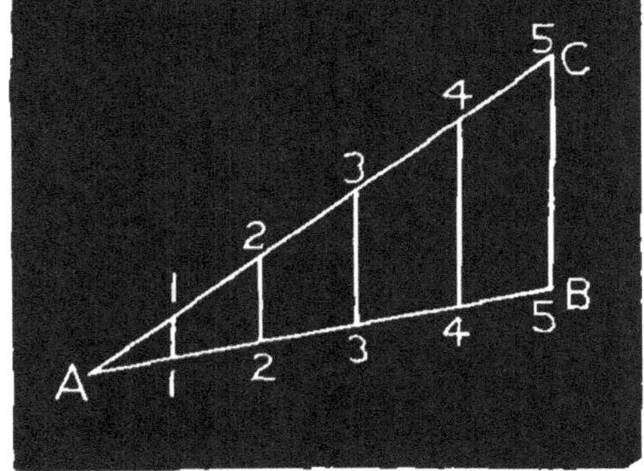

Fig. 109.

Ex. 6.—*To divide a line into a number of equal parts,* Fig. 108.

To divide the line *A B* into, say, five parts. From *A* and *B* draw parallels *A C*, *B D* on opposite sides; set off any convenient distance four times (one less than the given number), from *A* on *A C*, and on *B* on *B D*; join the first on *A C* to the fourth on *B D*, and so on. The lines so drawn divide *A B* as required.

Second Method, Fig. 109. Draw the line at *A C*, at an angle from *A*, set off, say, five equal parts; draw *B* 5, and draw parallels to it from the other points of division in *A C*. These parallels divide *A B* as required.

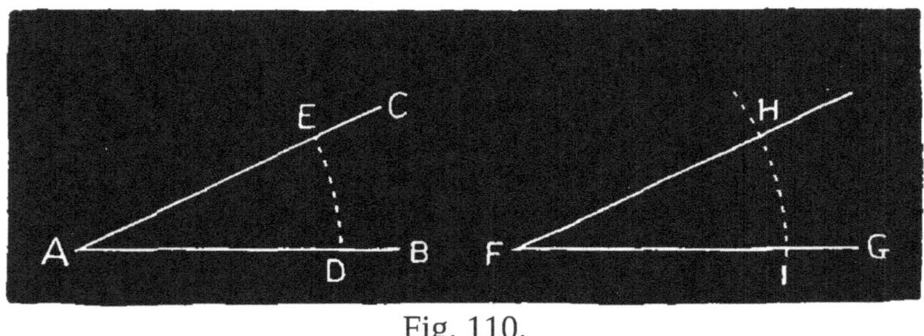

Fig. 110.

Ex. 7.—*Upon a straight line to draw an angle equal to a given angle*, Fig. 110. Let *A* be the given angle and *F G* the line. With any radius from the points *A* and *F*, describe arcs *D E, I H*, cutting the sides of the angle *A* and the line *F G*.

Set off the arc *I H*, equal to *D E* and draw *F H*. The angle *F* is equal to *A* as required.

Ex. 8.—*To bisect an angle*, Fig. 111. Let *A C B* be the angle; on the center *C* cut the sides at *A B*. On *A* and *B* as centers describe arcs cutting at *D* dividing the angle into two equal parts.

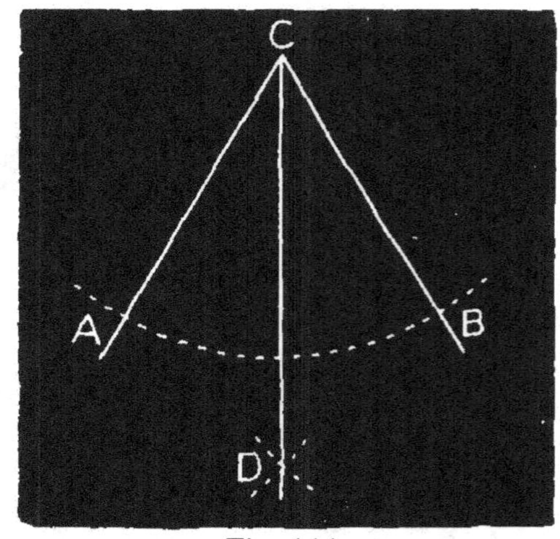

Fig. 111.

Ex. 9.—*To find the center of a circle or of an arc of a circle.* Fig. 112. Draw the chord *A B*, bisect it by the perpendicular *C D*, bounded both ways by the circle; and bisect *C D* for the center *G*.

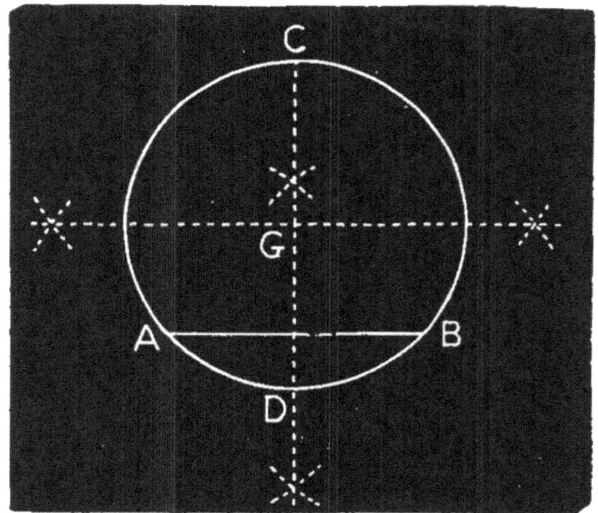

Fig. 112.

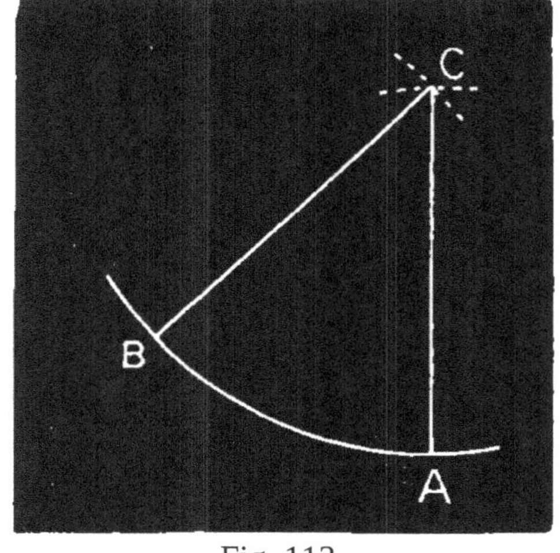

Fig. 113.

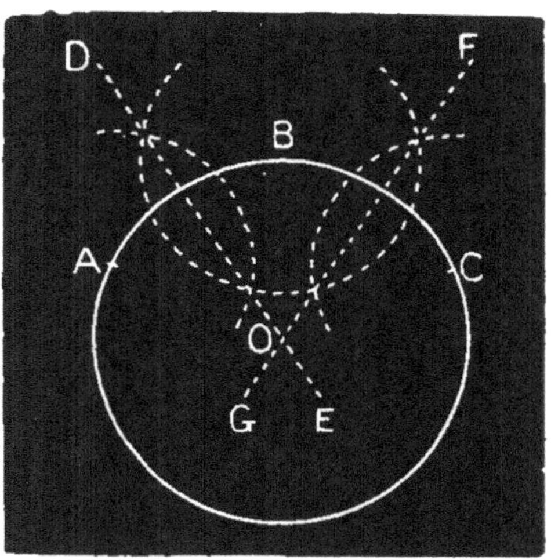

Fig. 114.

Ex. 10.—*Through two given points to describe an arc of a circle with a given radius*, Fig. 113. On the points *A* and *B* as centers, with the given radius, describe arcs cutting at *C*; and from *C*, with the same radius, describe an arc *A B* as required.

Second, for a circle or an arc, Fig. 114. Select three points *A*, *B*, *C* in the circumference, well apart; with the same radius describe arcs from these three points cutting each other, and draw two lines *D E*, *F G*, through their intersections according to Fig. 107. The point where they cut is the center of the circle or arc.

Ex. 11.—*To describe a circle passing through three given points*, Fig. 114. Let *A*, *B*, *C* be the given points and proceed as in last problem to find the center *O*, from which the circle may be described.

This problem is variously useful; in finding the diameter of a large fly-wheel, or any other object of large diameter when only a part of the circumference is accessible; in striking out arches when the span and rise are given, etc.

Ex. 12.—*To draw a tangent to a circle from a given point in the circumference,* Fig. 115. From *A* set off equal segments *A B, A D*, join *B D* and draw *A E*, parallel to it, for the tangent.

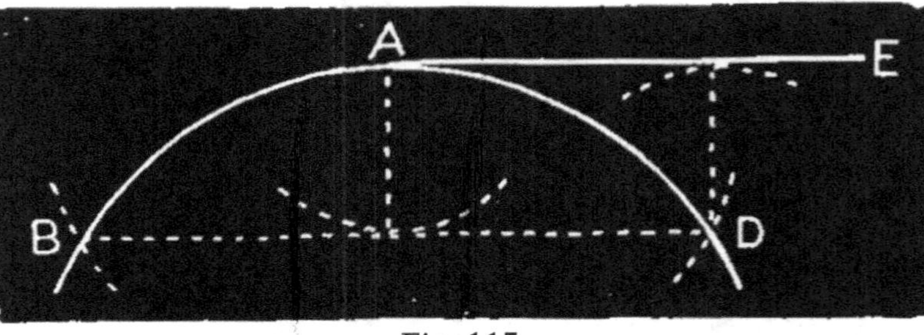

Fig. 115.

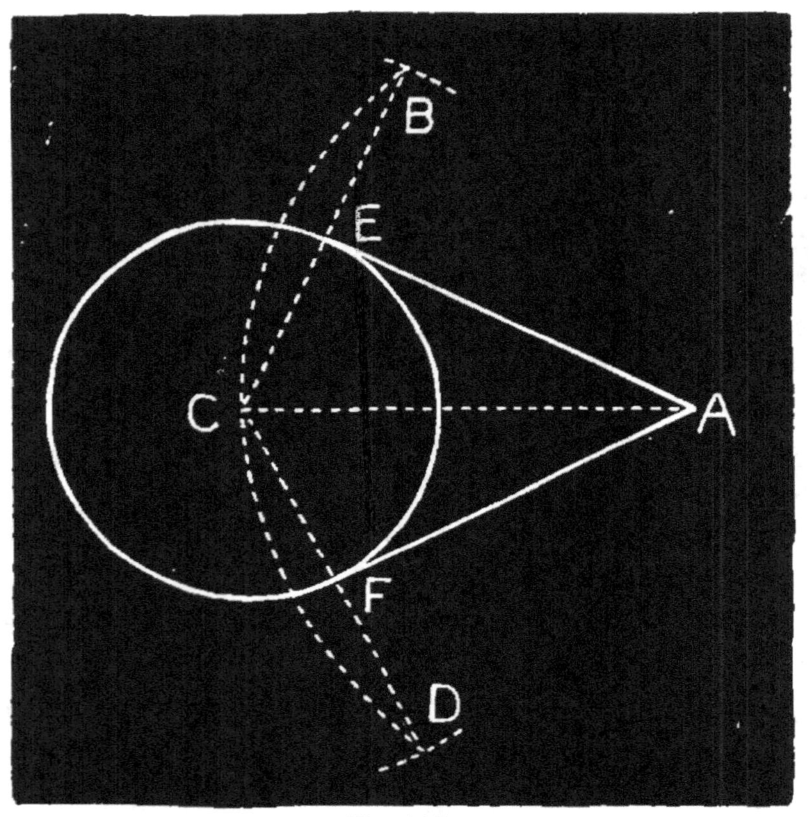

Fig. 116.

Ex. 13.—*To draw tangents to a circle from points without it,* Fig. 116. From *A* with the radius *A C* describe an arc *B C D*, and from *C* with a radius equal to the diameter of the circle, cut the arc at *B D*, join *B C, C D*, cutting the circle at *E F*, and draw *A E, A F*, the tangents.

Ex. 14.—*Between two inclined lines to draw a series of circles touching these lines and touching each other,* Fig. 117. Bisect the inclination of the given lines *A B, C D* by the line *N O*. From a point *P* in this line draw the perpendicular *P B* to the line *A B*, and on *P* describe the circle *B D*, touching the lines and cutting the center lines at *E*. From *E* draw

E F perpendicular to the center line, cutting *A B* at *F*, and from *F* describe an arc *E G*, cutting *A B* at *G*. Draw *G H* parallel to *B P*, giving *H*, the center of the next circle, to be described with the radius *H E*, and so on for the next circle, *I N*.

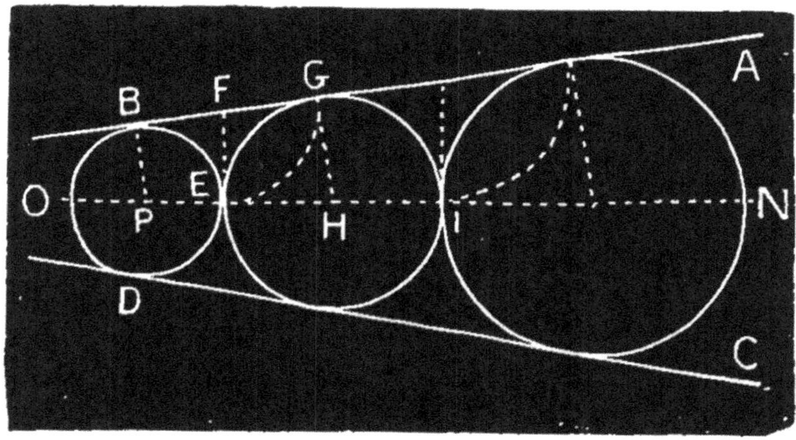

Fig. 117.

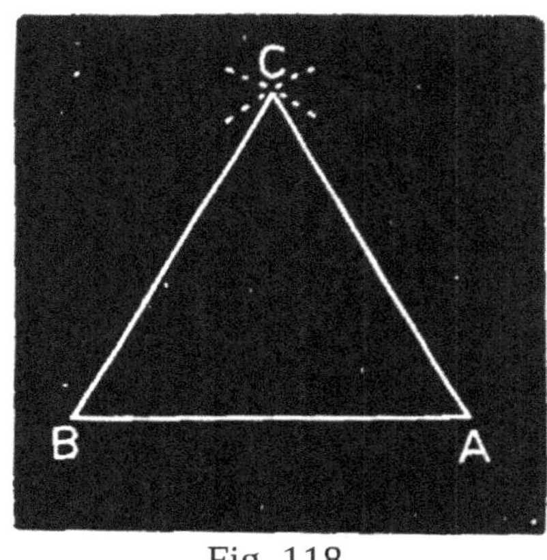

Fig. 118.

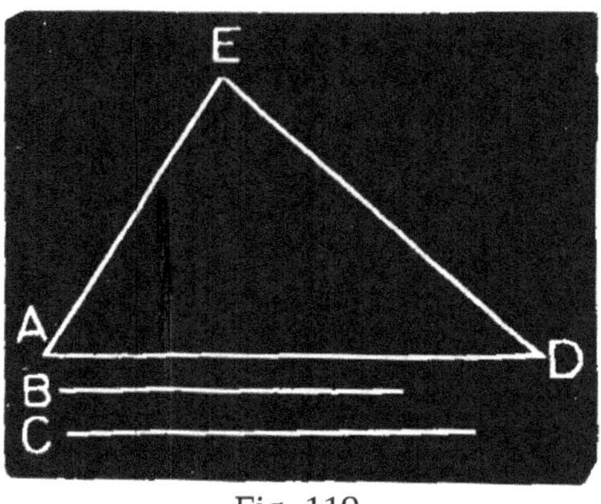

Fig. 119.

Ex. 15.—*To construct a triangle on a given base, the sides being given.*

First. An equilateral triangle, Fig. 118. On the ends of a given base *A B*, with *A B* as a radius describe arcs cutting at *C*, and draw *A C, C B*.

Second. Triangle of unequal sides, Fig. 119. On either end of the base *A D*, with the side *B* as a radius describe an arc; and with the side *C* as a radius, on the other end of the base as a center, describe arcs cutting the arc at *E*; join *A E, D E*.

This construction may be used for finding the position of a point *C* or *E* at given distances from the ends of a base, not necessarily to form a triangle.

Ex. 16.—*To construct a square rectangle on a given straight line.*

First. A square, Fig. 120. On the ends *B A* as centers, with the line *A B* as radius, describe arcs cutting at *C*; on *C* describe arcs cutting the others at *D E*; and on *D* and *E* cut these at *F G*. Draw *A F, B G* and join the intersections *H I*.

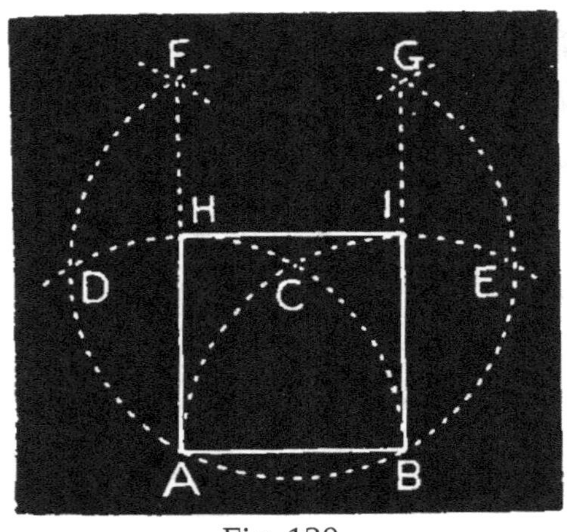

Fig. 120.

Second. A rectangle, Fig. 121. On the base *E F* draw the perpendiculars *E H, F G*, equal to the height of the rectangle, and join *G H*.

Fig. 121.

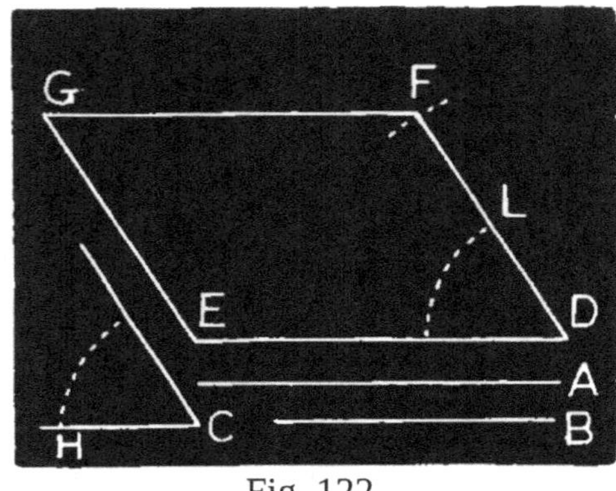

Fig. 122.

parallels to *D E, D F*.

Ex. 17.—*To construct a parallelogram of which the sides and one of the angles are given*, Fig. 122. Draw the side *D E* equal to the given length *A*, and set off the other side *D F* equal to the other length *B*, forming the given angle *C*. From *E* with *D F* as radius, describe an arc, and from *F*, with the radius *D E* cut the arc at *G*. Draw *F G, E G*. Or, the remaining sides may be drawn as

Ex. 18.—*To describe a circle about a triangle*, Fig. 123. Bisect two sides *A B, A C* of the triangle at *E F*, and from these points draw perpendiculars cutting at *K*. On the center *K*, with the radius *K A* draw the circle *A B C*.

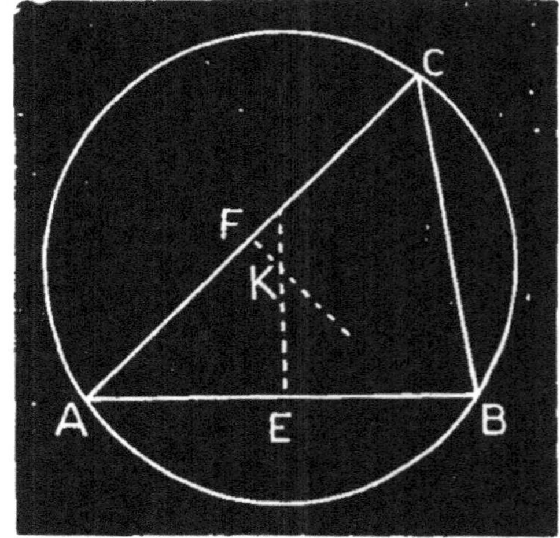

Fig. 123.

Ex. 19.—*To describe a circle about a square, and to inscribe a square in a circle*, Fig. 124.

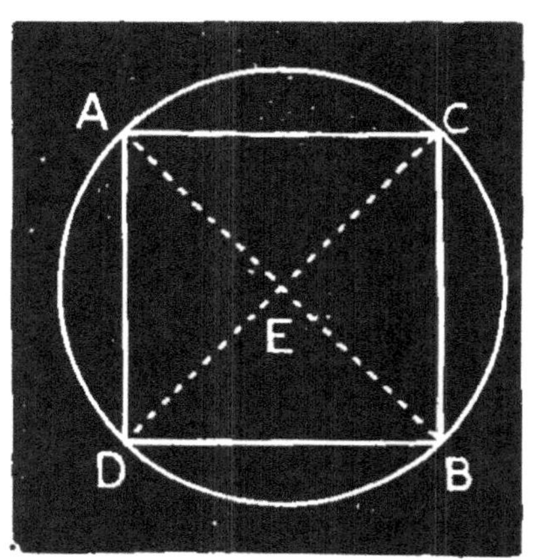

Fig. 124.

First. To describe the circle. Draw the diagonals *A B*, *C D* of the square, cutting at *E*; on the center *E* with the radius *E A* describe the circle.

Second. To inscribe the square. Draw the two diameters *A B*, *C D* at right angles and join the points *A B*, *C D* to form the square.

In the same way a circle may be described about a triangle.

Ex. 20.—*To inscribe a circle on a square, and to describe a square about a circle*, Fig. 125.

First. To inscribe the circle. Draw the diagonals *A B*, *C D* of the square, cutting at *E*; draw the perpendicular *E F* to one side, and with the radius *E F* describe the circle.

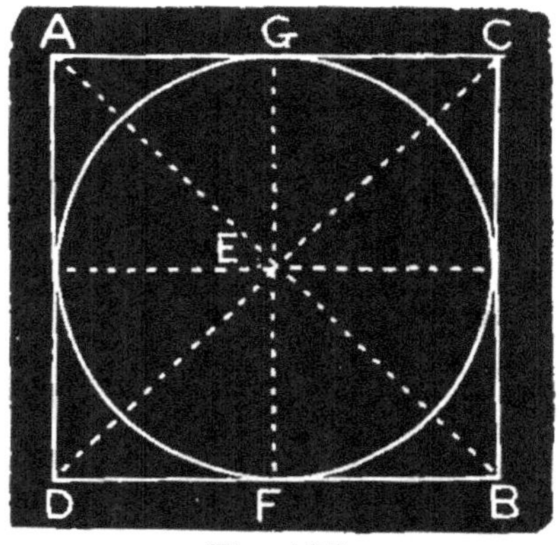

Fig. 125.

Second. To describe the square. Draw two diameters *A B*, *C D* at right angles, and produce them; bisect the angle *D E B* at the center by the diameter *F G*, and through *F* and *G* draw perpendiculars *A C*, *B D*, and join the points *A D* and *B C* where they cut the diagonals to complete the square.

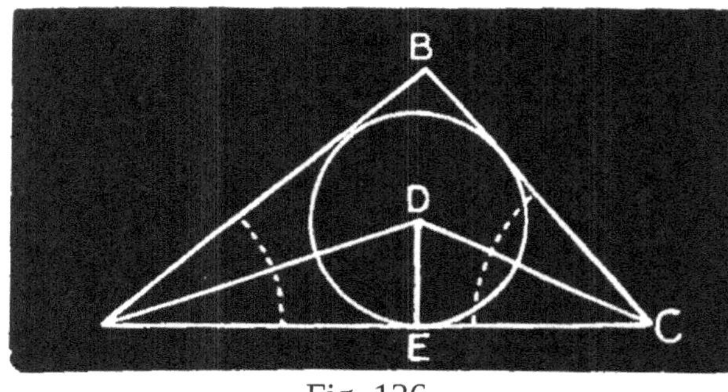

Fig. 126.

Ex. 21.—*To inscribe a circle in a triangle*, Fig. 126. Bisect two of the angles *A C* of the triangle by lines cutting at *D*; from *D* draw a perpendicular *D E* to any side, and with *D E* as radius describe a circle.

Ex. 22.—*To inscribe a pentagon in a circle*, Fig. 127. Draw two diameters *A C*, *B D* at right angles cutting at *O*; bisect *A O* at *E*, and from *B* with radius *B E* cut the circumference at *G H* and with the same radius step round the circle to *I* and *K*; join the points to form the pentagon.

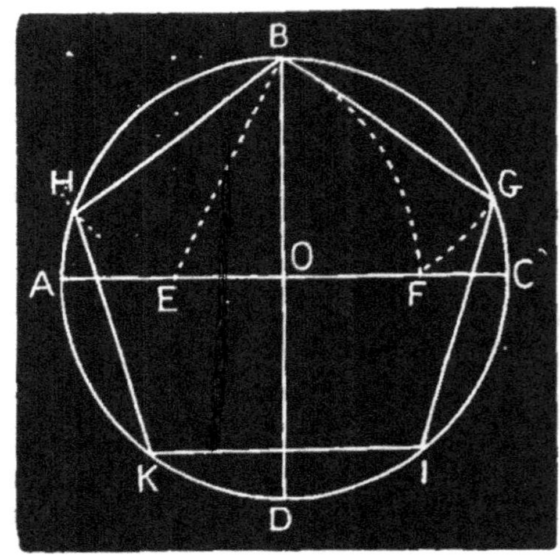

Fig. 127.

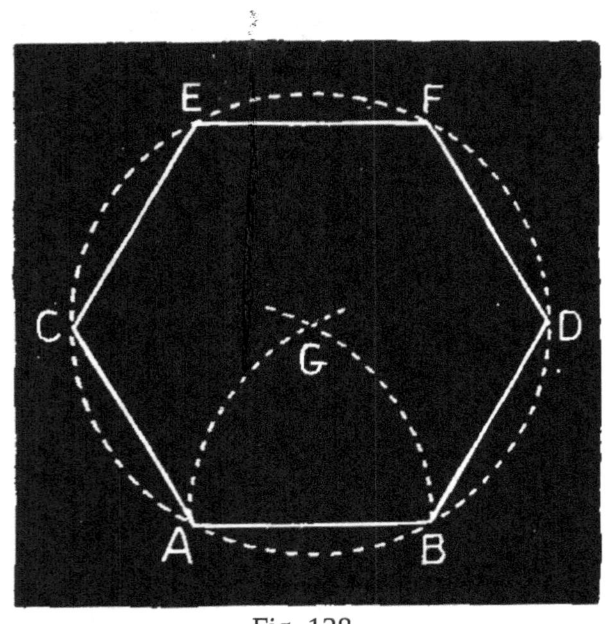

Fig. 128.

Ex. 23.—*To construct a hexagon upon a given straight line,* Fig. 128. From *A* and *B*, the ends of the given line, describe arcs cutting at *G*; from *G* with the radius *G A* describe a circle. With the same radius set off the arcs *A C*, *C F* and *B D*, *D E*; join the points so found to form the hexagon.

Ex. 24.—*To inscribe a hexagon in a circle,* Fig. 129. Draw a diameter *A C B*; from *A* and *B* as centers, with the radius of the circle *A C* cut the circumference at *D, E, F, G*, and draw *A D, D E*, etc., to form the hexagon. The points *D E*, etc., may be found by stepping the radius (with the dividers) six times round the circle.

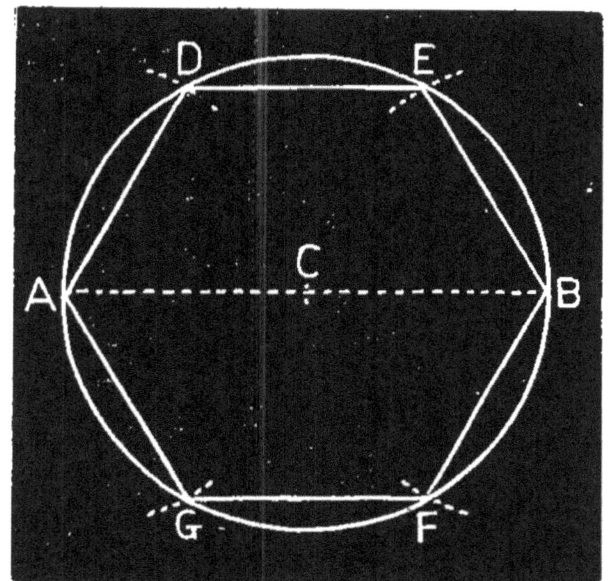

Fig. 129.

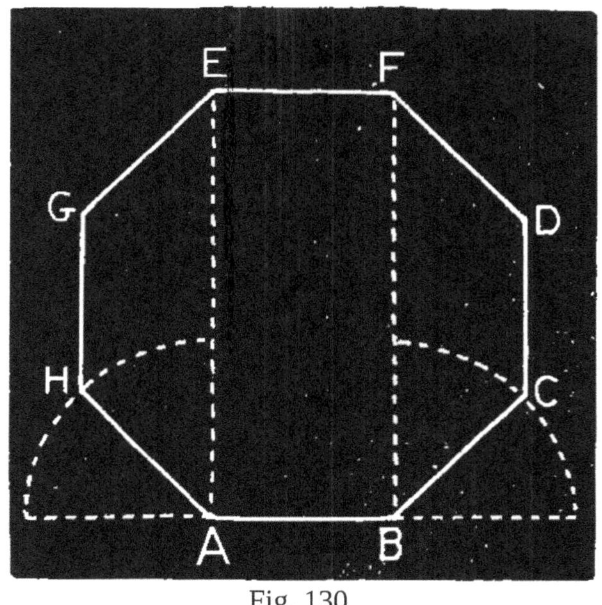

Fig. 130.

Ex. 25.—*To describe an octagon on a given straight line*, Fig. 130. Produce the given line *A B* both ways and draw perpendiculars *A E*, *B F*; bisect the external angles *A* and *B* by the lines *A H*, *B C*, which make equal to *A B*. Draw *C D* and *H G* parallel to *A E* and equal to *A B*; from the center *G D*, with the radius *A B*, cut the perpendiculars at *E F*, and draw *E F* to complete the hexagon.

Ex. 26.—*To convert a square into an octagon*, Fig. 131.—Draw the diagonals of the square cutting at *E*; from the corners *A*, *B*, *C*, *D*, with *A E* as radius, describe arcs cutting the sides at *G*, *H*, etc., and join the points so found to complete the octagon.

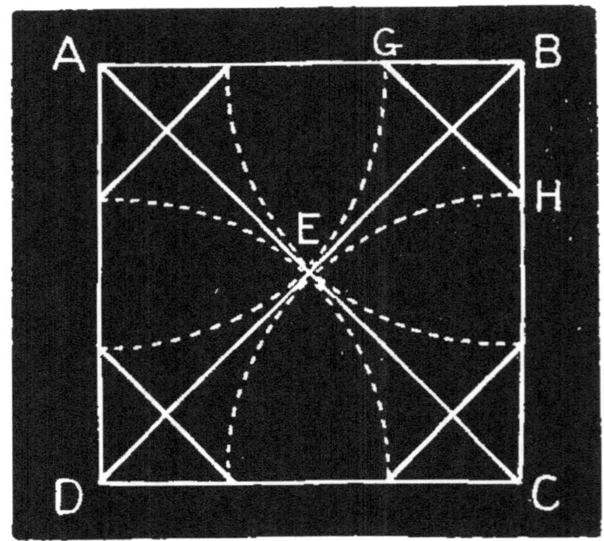

Fig. 131.

Ex. 27.—*To inscribe an octagon in a circle*, Fig. 132. Draw two diameters *A C, B D*, at right angles; bisect the arcs *A B, B C*, at *E, F*, etc., to form the octagon.

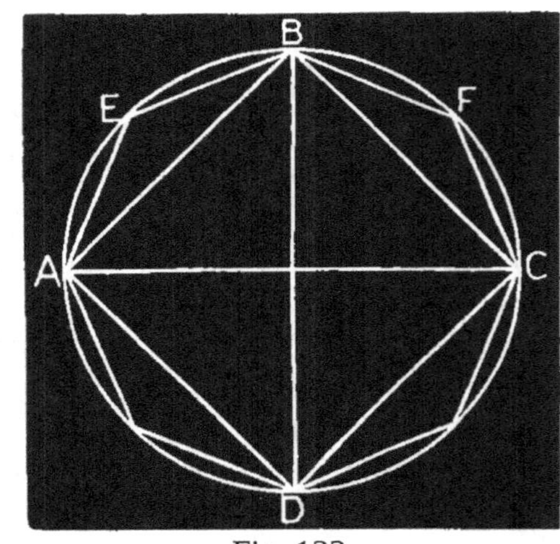

Fig. 132.

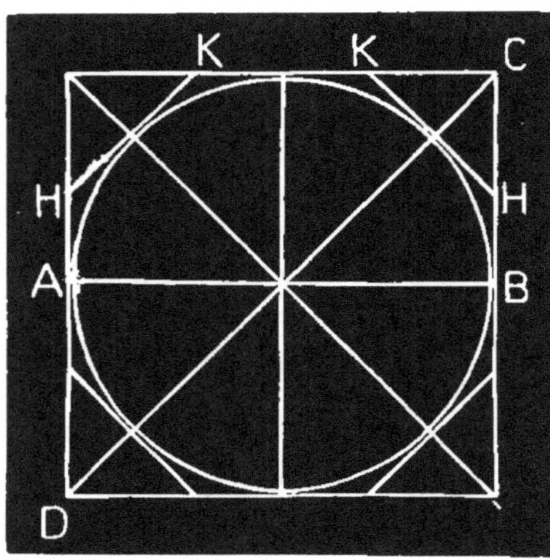

Fig. 133.

Ex. 28.—*To describe an octagon about a circle*, Fig. 133. Describe a square about the given circle *A B*, draw perpendiculars *H* and *K*, to the diagonals, touching the circle to form the octagon. Or, the points *H, K*, etc., may be found by cutting the sides from the corners, by lines parallel to the diagonals.

Ex. 29.—*To describe an ellipse when the length and breadth are given*, Fig. 134. On the center *C*, with *A E* as radius, cut the axis *A B* at *F* and *G*, the foci, fix a couple of pins into the axis at *F* and *G*, and loop on a thread or cord upon them equal in length to the axis *A B*, so as when stretched to reach the extremity *C* of the

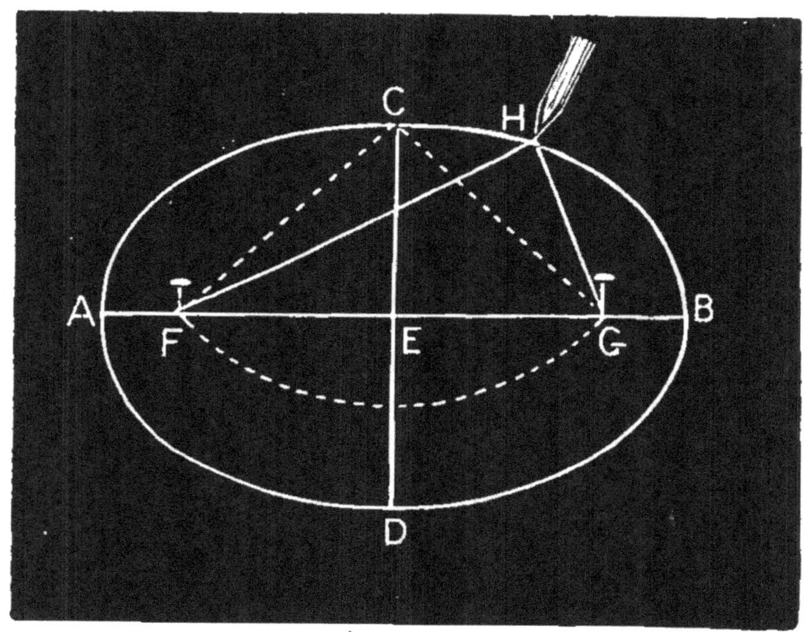

Fig. 134.

conjugate axis, as shown in dot-lining. Place a pencil or drawpoint inside the cord, as at *H*, and guiding the pencil in this way, keeping the cord equally in tension, carry the pencil round the pins *F*, *G*, and so describe the ellipse.

Note.—The ellipse is an oval figure, like a circle in perspective. The line that divides it equally in the direction of its great length is the *transverse axis*, and the line which divides the opposite way is the *conjugate axis*.

Second Method. Along the straight edge of a piece of stiff paper mark off a distance *a c* equal to *A C*, half the transverse axis; and from the same point a distance *a b* equal to *C D*, half the conjugate axis. Place the slip so as to bring the point *b* on the line *A B* of the transverse axis, and the point *c* on the line *D E*; and set off on the drawing the position of the point *a*. Shifting the slip, so that the point travels on the transverse axis, and the point *c* on the conjugate axis, any number of points in the curve may be found, through which the curve may be traced. See fig. 135.

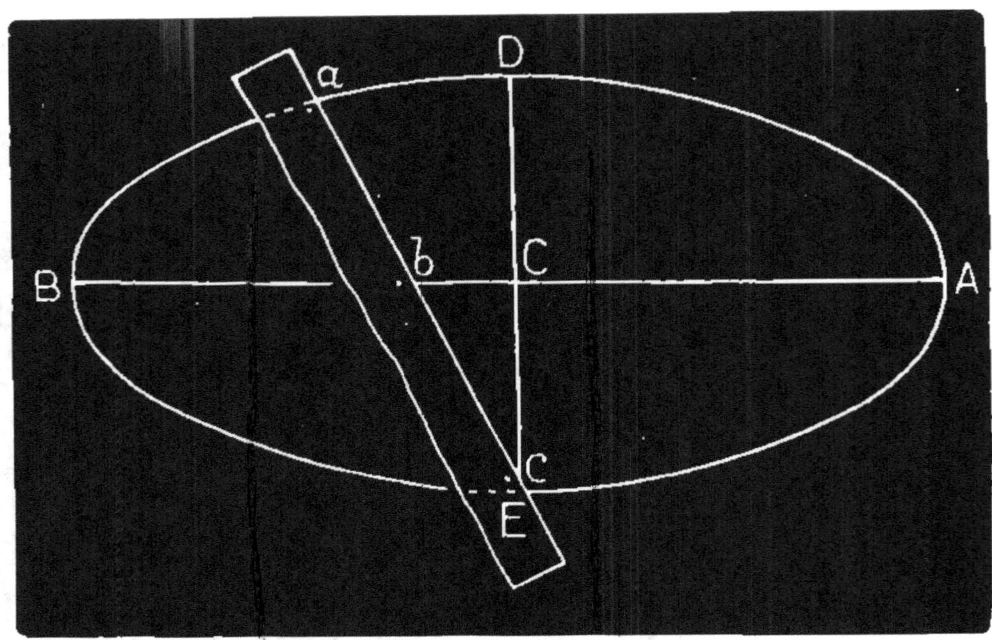

Fig. 135.

Trigonometry.

Trigonometry is that portion of geometry which has for its object the measurement of triangles. When it treats of plane triangles, it is called *Plane Trigonometry*; and as the engineer will continually meet in his studies of higher mathematics *the terms* used in plane trigonometry, it is advantageous for him to become familiar with some of the principles and definitions relating to this branch of mathematics.

The circumferences of all circles contain the same number of degrees, but the greater the radius the greater is the absolute measures of a degree. The circumference of a fly wheel or the circumference of the earth have the same number of degrees; yet the same number of degrees in each and every circumference is the measure of precisely the same angle.

The circumference of a circle is supposed to be divided into 360 degrees or divisions, and as the total angularity about the center is equal to four right angles, each right angle contains 90 degrees, or 90°, and half a right angle contains 45°. Each degree is divided into 60 minutes, or 60′; and for the sake of still further minuteness of measurement, each minute is divided into 60″. In a whole circle there are, therefore, 360 × 60 × 60 = 1,296,000 seconds. The annexed diagram, fig. 136, exemplifies the relative positions of the

Sine,

Co-sine,

Versed Sine,

Tangent,

Co-Tangent,

Secant and

Co-secant

of an angle.

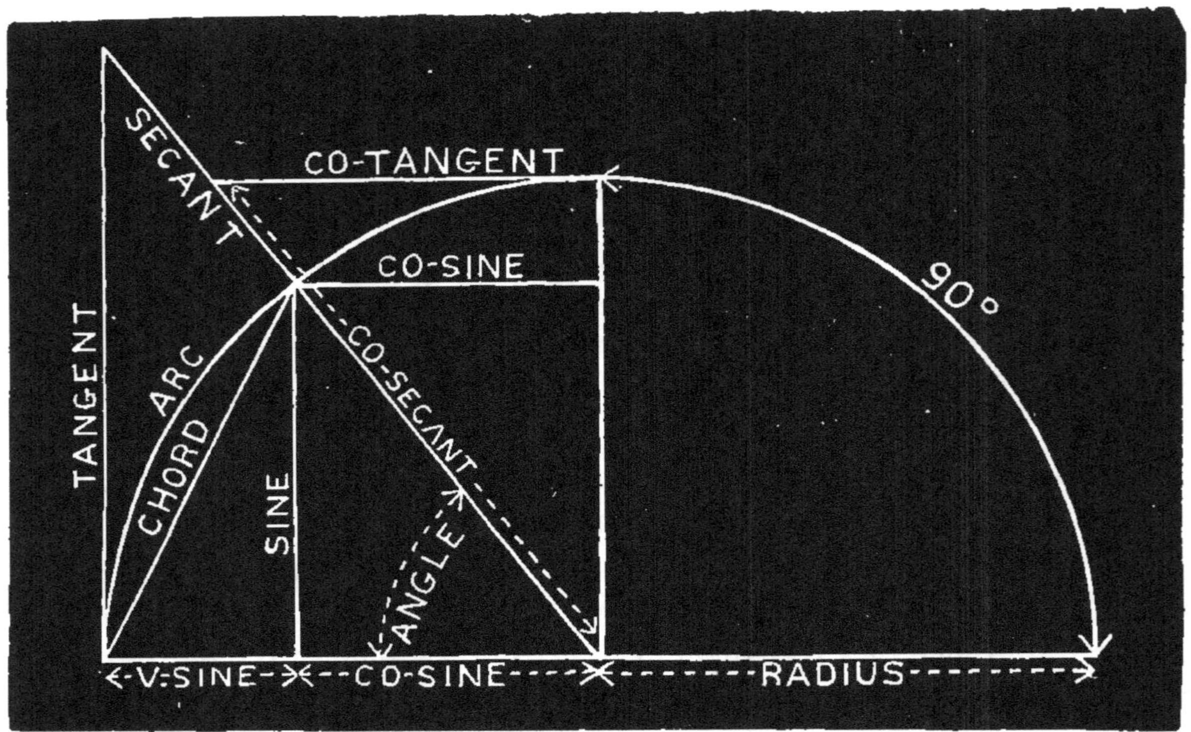

Fig. 136.

These may be defined thus:

DEFINITIONS.

1. The *Complement* of an arc is 90° minus the arc.

2. The *Supplement* of an arc is 180° minus the arc.

3. The *Sine* of an angle, or of an arc, is a line drawn from one end of an arc, perpendicular to a diameter drawn through the other end.

4. The *Cosine* of an arc is the perpendicular distance from the center of the circle to the sine of the arc; or, it is the same in magnitude as the sine of the complement of the arc.

5. The *Tangent* of an arc is a line touching the circle in one extremity of the arc, and continued from thence, to meet a line drawn through the center and the other extremity.

6. The *Cotangent* of an arc is the tangent of the complement of the arc. The *Co* is but a contraction of the word complement.

7. The *Secant* of an arc is a line drawn from the center of the circle to the extremity of the tangent.

8. The *Cosecant* of an arc is the secant of the complement.

9. The *Versed Sine* of an arc is the distance from the extremity of the arc to the foot of the sine.

For the sake of brevity, these technical terms are contracted thus: for sine *A B*, we write *sin. A B*; for cosine *A B*, we write *cos. A B*; for tangent *A B*, we write *tan. A B*, etc.

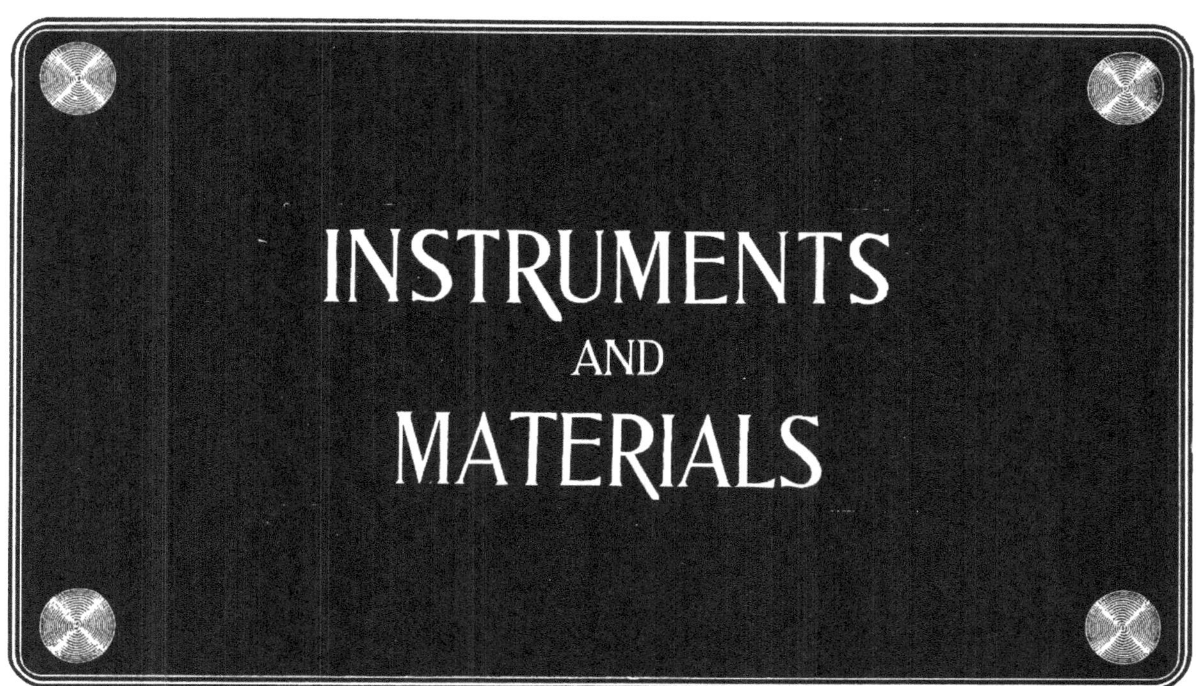

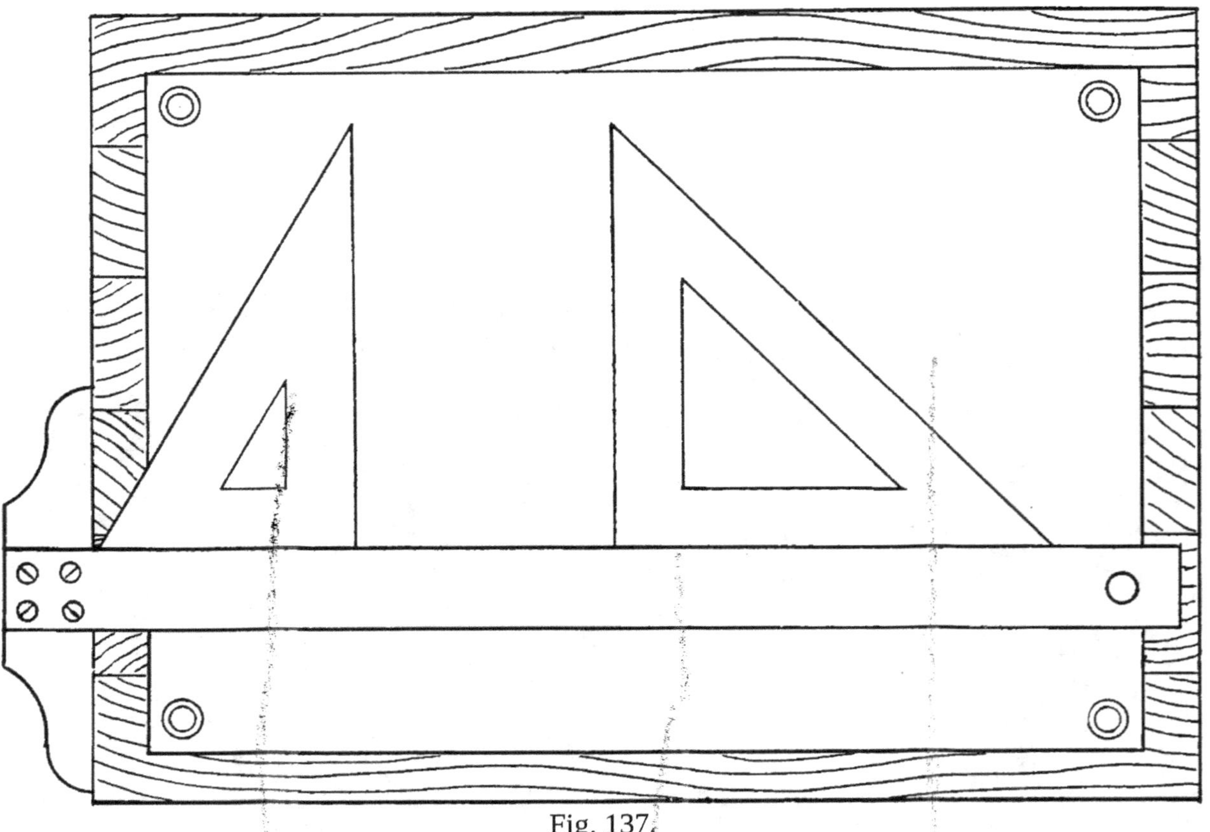

Fig. 137

Drawing Materials and Instruments.

Drawing tools or instruments are contrived solely for mechanical drawing; aside from this use they are perfectly worthless, hence the quality of these special utensils is a matter of the first consideration to the earnest student.

There are several degrees of excellence to be found in the make-up of drawing instruments and materials; it may be remarked with truth that "any kind are good enough, and the best none too good," i. e., a learner in this delightful art should not stop at the lack of goodness or the low grade existing in his "tools," but rather do the best work possible with the means at hand.

However, in order that acceptable work may be accomplished, fairly good instruments should be procured. The advice of some one experienced in the use and care of draughting tools should be sought before purchasing. A drawing board, a single sheet of paper and a pencil is the simplest "outfit" to be thought of; to this small beginning may be added, soon afterwards, an inexpensive pair of compasses, a T-square and a couple of triangles; a vast range of work can be executed with these few tools.

Nothing else will be needed to do fine work except, perhaps, one or two pairs of better compasses and a few sweeps or means of drawing irregular curves; all these had best be purchased separately; for in buying a "box of instruments," it may contain some articles which are not desired, or that are of a wrong size, or even duplicates of those already possessed.

An outfit recommended by the author of "Reed's Hand Book" is as follows.

Large compasses with movable leg.

A pair of dividers.

Bow pencil.

Bow pen.

Pencil leg for large compasses.

Pen leg for large compasses.

Drawing pen.

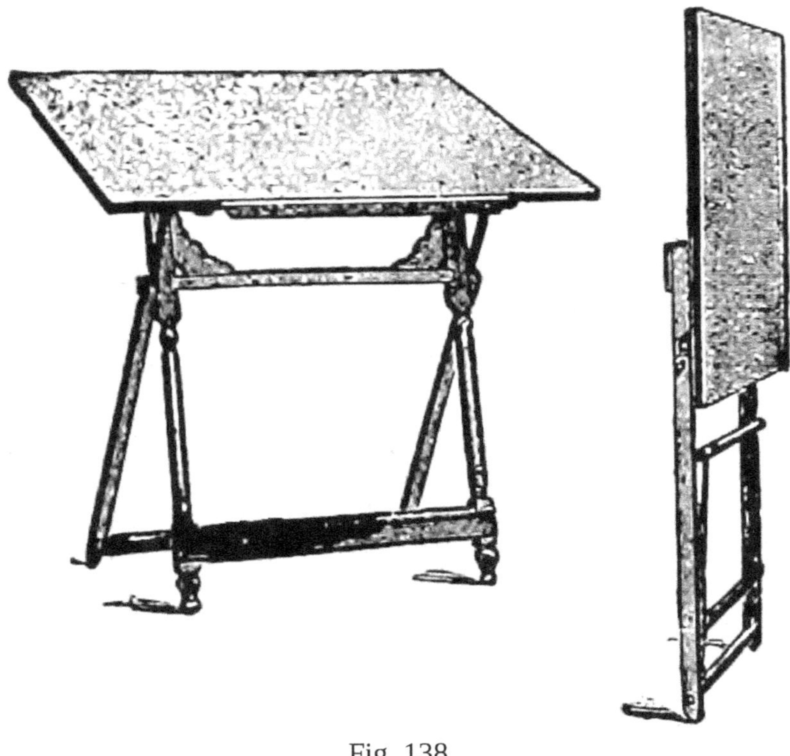

Louis Rouillon, B. S., Instructor of Drawing in Pratt Institute, New York, recommends the following:

Compasses, 5½ inches, with needle point; pen pencil and lengthening bar.

Drawing pen, 4½ inches.

T-square, 24-inch blade.

45-degree triangle, 9 inches.

30 and 60 degree triangle, 9 inches.

1 Scroll.

Fig. 138.

Dixon's V. H. pencil.

12-inch boxwood scale, flat, graduated $\frac{1}{16}$ inch the entire length.

Bottle of liquid India ink, four thumb-tacks, pen and ink eraser.

20 sheets drawing paper, 11 × 15 inches, and a drawing-board about 16 × 23 inches will also be necessary; students can usually make the board themselves for less money than it can be bought.

NOTE.—The purchasing of drawing tools is one of the most difficult points to settle that can present itself to a person about to buy a drawing outfit for the first time. Nothing can be so productive of distress to a person drawing as to have his tools getting out of order, joints one day too tight, next day too slack, points getting blunt or perhaps turning up altogether; if needle points, then the needles slip up, and drawing spoiled; in fact, the purchaser can be annoyed in numberless different ways.— W. H. THORN.

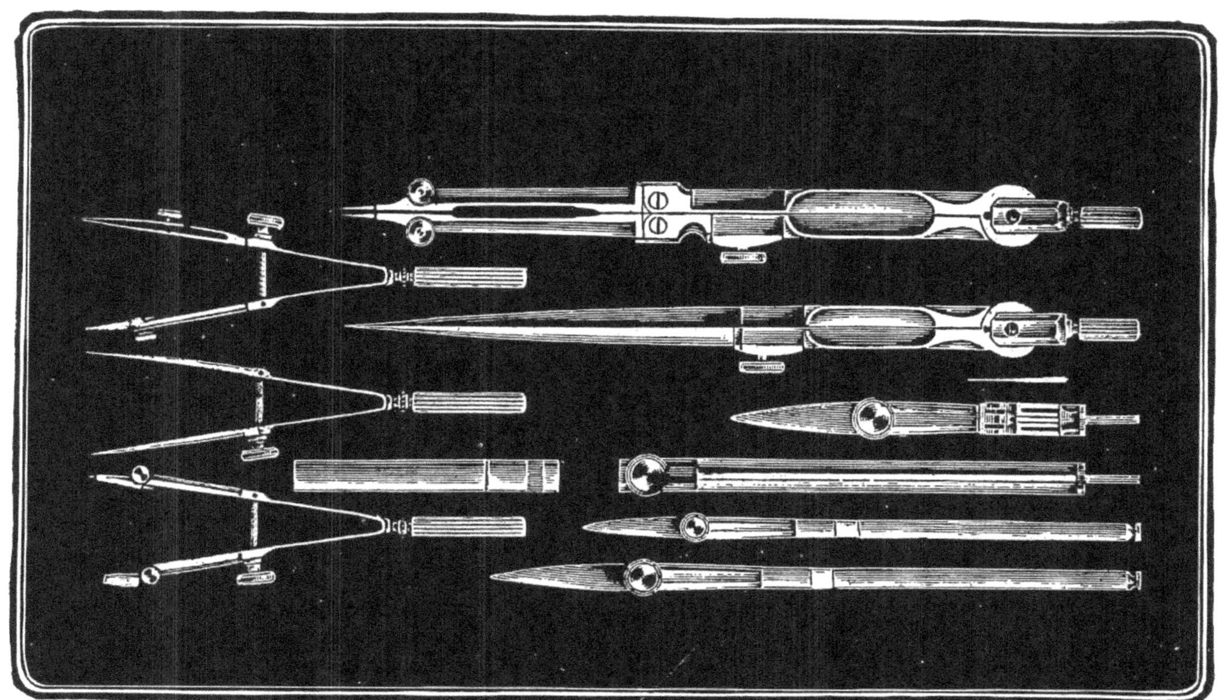

Fig. 139.

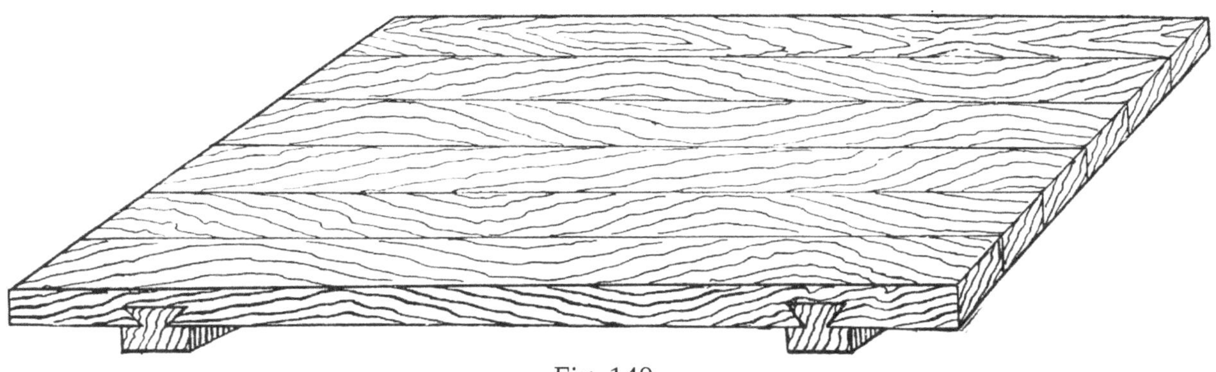

Fig. 140.

THE DRAWING BOARD.

A drawing-board should be made of well seasoned pine of a convenient size, say 23 × 16, which will take half a sheet of imperial paper, leaving $\frac{1}{2}$-inch margin all around.

The working surface of the board—or its front side—should be perfectly smooth, but instead of being flat it should have a very slight camber, or rounding, breadthways, this latter feature in its construction being to prevent the possibility of a sheet of paper when stretched on its surface having any vacuity beneath it.

The *four edges* of the board need not form an exact rectangle, as much valuable time is often wasted in the attempts to produce such a board; but it will answer every purpose of the draughtsman so long as the adjacent edges at the lower left-hand corner of it are at right angles, or square to each other.

An English authority recommends the use of two drawing-boards, 42 inches long and 30 inches wide, made of plain stuff, without cleets, 1¼ inches thick—seasoned—with edges perfectly straight and at right angles to each other. *With two boards, one may be used for sketching and drawing details and the other for the finished drawing.*

The board should be ¾ inch in thickness, and fitted at the back, at right angles to its longest side, with a couple of hardwood battens, about 2 inches wide and ¾ inch thick; the use of these battens being to keep the board from casting or winding and to allow of its expansion or contraction through changes of temperature. This latter purpose, however, is only effected by attaching the battens to the back of the board in the following manner: ... At the middle of the length of each batten—which should be one inch less than the width of the board—a stout, well-fitted wood screw is firmly inserted into it, and made to penetrate the board for about ½ inch, the head of the screw being made flush with the surface of the batten; on either side of the central screw, two others, about 3½ inches apart, are passed through oblong holes in the battens, and screwed into the body of the board until their heads are flush with the central one; fitted in this way the board itself can expand or contract lengthwise or crosswise, while its surface is prevented from warping or bending.

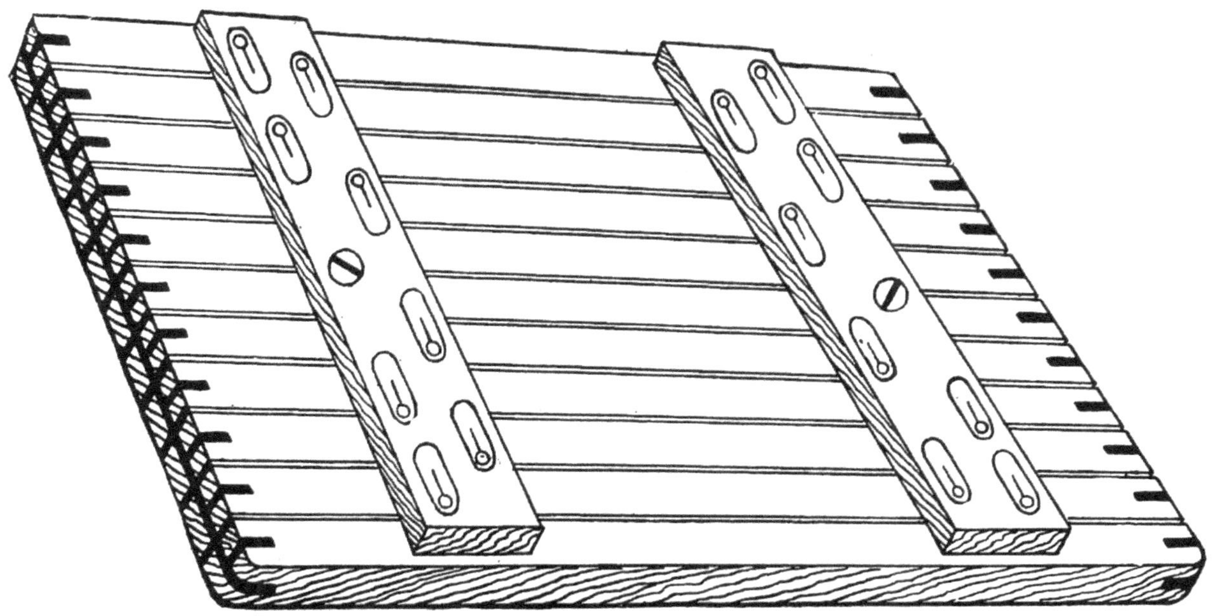

Fig. 141.

A further improvement in such a drawing board as above shown is made by cutting lengthwise along its ends a narrow groove and inserting an ebony or hardwood strip; this is cut or sawn apart at about every inch to admit of contraction; this strip serves as a guide to the stock of the drawing square, allowing an easy sliding movement.

To produce really good work in the shape of a mechanical drawing, one perfect straight edge only is required on a drawing board, and that the left one, which is always known as the *working-edge*; but for the convenience of being able to draw a long line across the board at right angles to its lower edge, this edge is made truly square with that on the left side of the board.

The details for building these drawing boards are given, because they are easy to be made by one who understands the use of a few wood-working tools; while the boards themselves are difficult of transportation—in case of the change of residence of their owners—quite unlike the instruments which are to accompany them.

Fig. 141 represents the board which has been described in the text, with provisions for the contraction and expansion; the very dark lines are intended to represent the ebony insertions—as described. Fig. 140 represents a plain pine board with dovetailed battens.

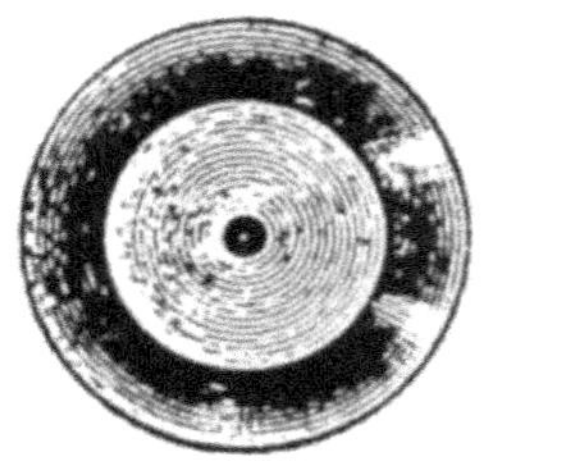 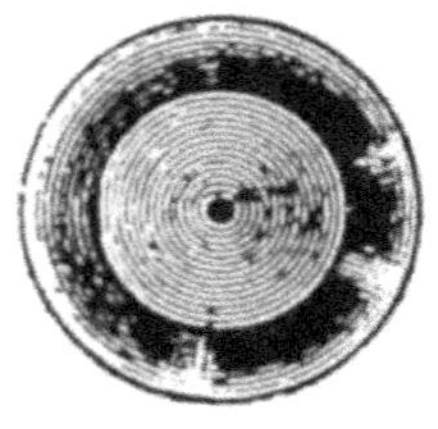 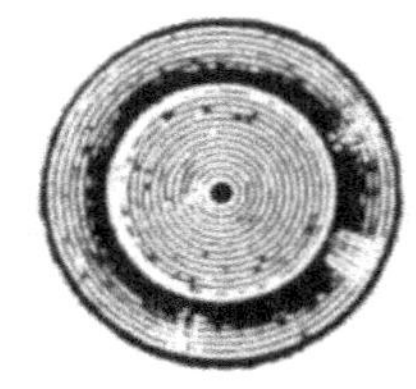 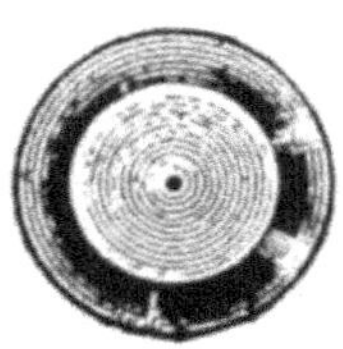 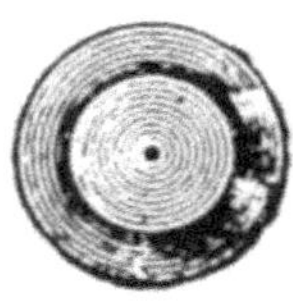

Fig. 142.

Fig. 142 represents the common means used to attach or secure slightly or temporarily the drawing paper to the drawing board; these are called thumb-tacks, and are usually forced through the paper into the wood by the hand, whence they are easily detached. These are made to have as slight a projection as may be, so as not to interfere with the free movement of the tee-square.

For mechanical drawing the invariable practice is to secure the paper on which the drawing is to be made to the drawing board by pinning it; this is effected by various kinds of *drawing pins* or *thumb-tacks*.

The best kind for this purpose have a head as thin as possible without cutting at its edges, slightly concave on the under side next the paper, and only so much convex on its upper side as will give it sufficient thickness to enable the pin to be secured to it; better use four or more small pins along the edge of a sheet of paper, than use one clumsy, badly made pin at each end.

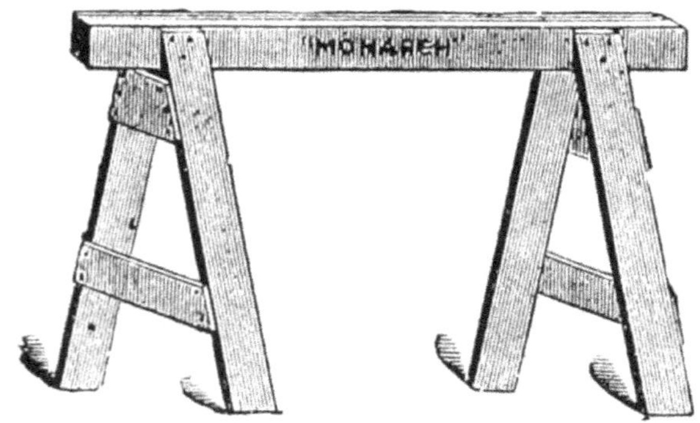

Fig. 143.

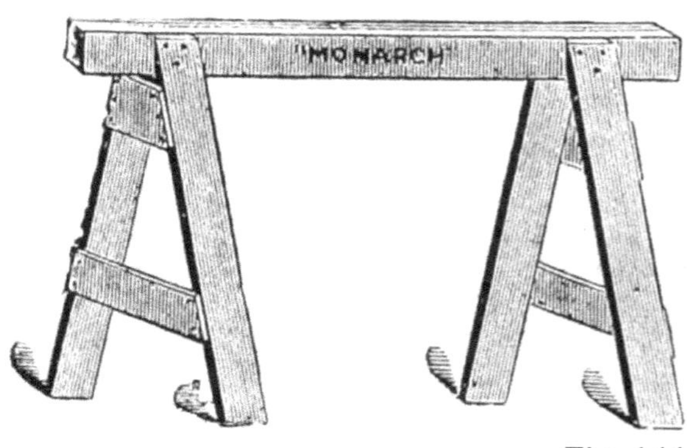

Fig. 144.

Fig. 143 and fig. 144 represent a pair of plain trestles or horses in common use for supporting large size drawing boards. This pattern is found frequently in the laying-out shop. Fig. 145 and fig. 146 represent *adjustable* horses or trestles—these are designed, primarily, for office use. As will be seen by viewing the illustration, the upper part is supported by two hardwood sliding pieces; these are provided with strong pins and numerous holes, and pass through the frame of the trestle, as shown, so that the upper portions can be arranged at any angle convenient to the draughtsman, as he lies over his work or stands by it.

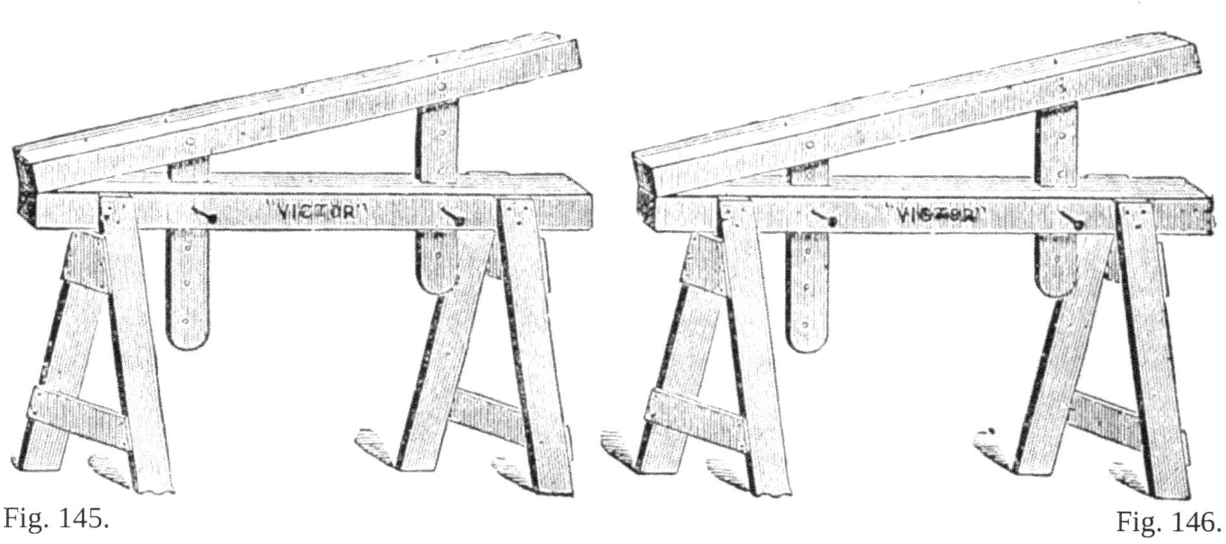

Fig. 145.   Fig. 146.

Fig. 137 is introduced to exhibit the paper attached to the drawing board with the thumb-tacks, and with the T-square and set-squares arranged to commence work; the paper should not extend to the edges of the board; three, four or more tacks may be used on each edge of the sheet of paper, instead of two, as shown in illustration.

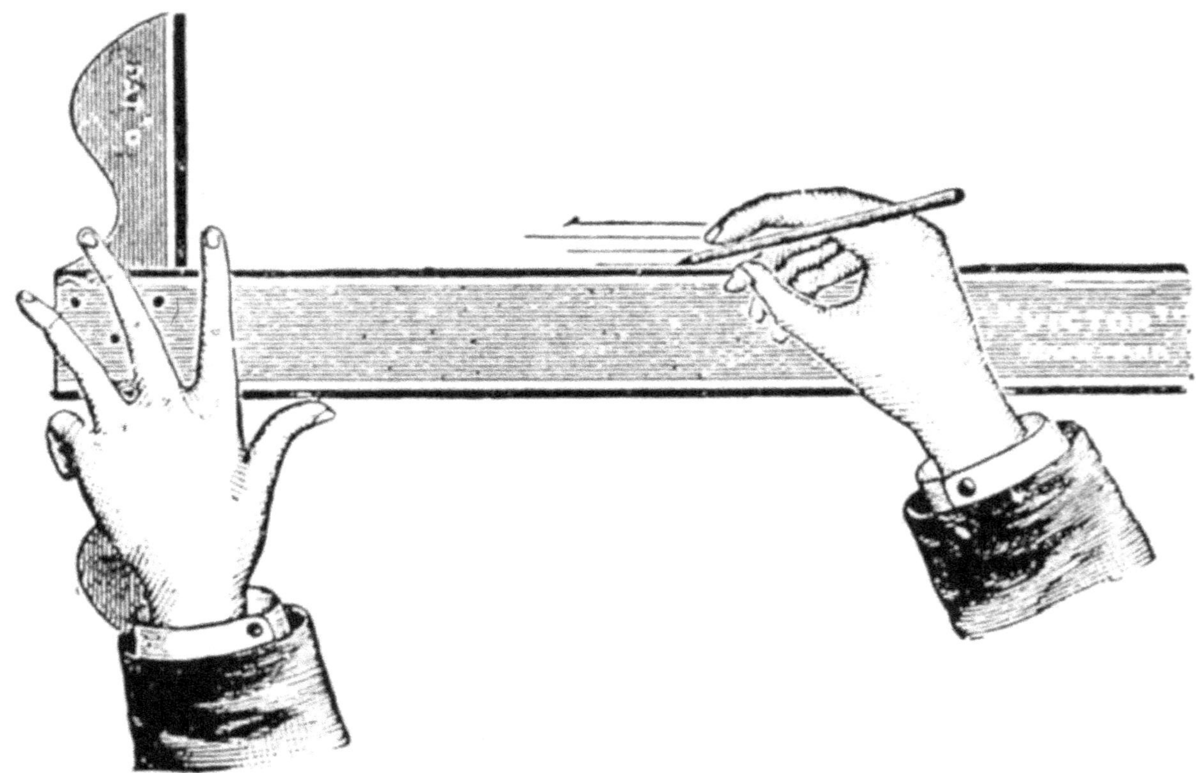

Fig. 147.

A most convenient—and except for its extreme lightness, which is not good in a drawing stand—a most admirable device is shown in fig. 138. The drawing table is simply a drawing board with folding legs; these are made from hard-wood, while the top is made of soft, seasoned pine, with square corners; while the device is strong and well braced, it can be folded and easily carried about—all as shown in the illustration.

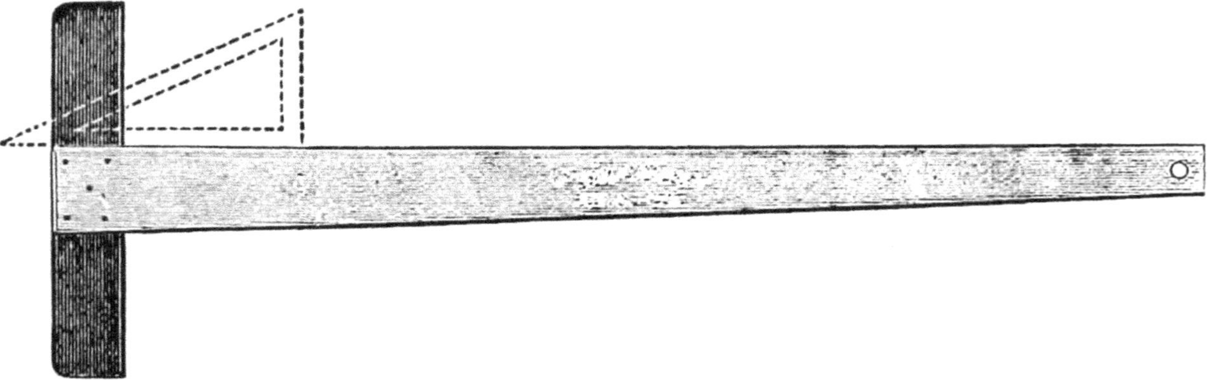

Fig. 148.

THE TEE-SQUARE.

This is an instrument in the form of a letter T, as shown in the figures 149 and 150; the two parts are known as *stock* and *blade*; the horizontal part of the letter (T) is the stock, and the vertical part the blade—hence the name, T-square; to form the square, the two parts are joined together in such a way as to make them exactly at right angles to each other; the stock, which is applied to the working edge of the drawing board, being about one-third the length of the blade, and about three times its thickness.

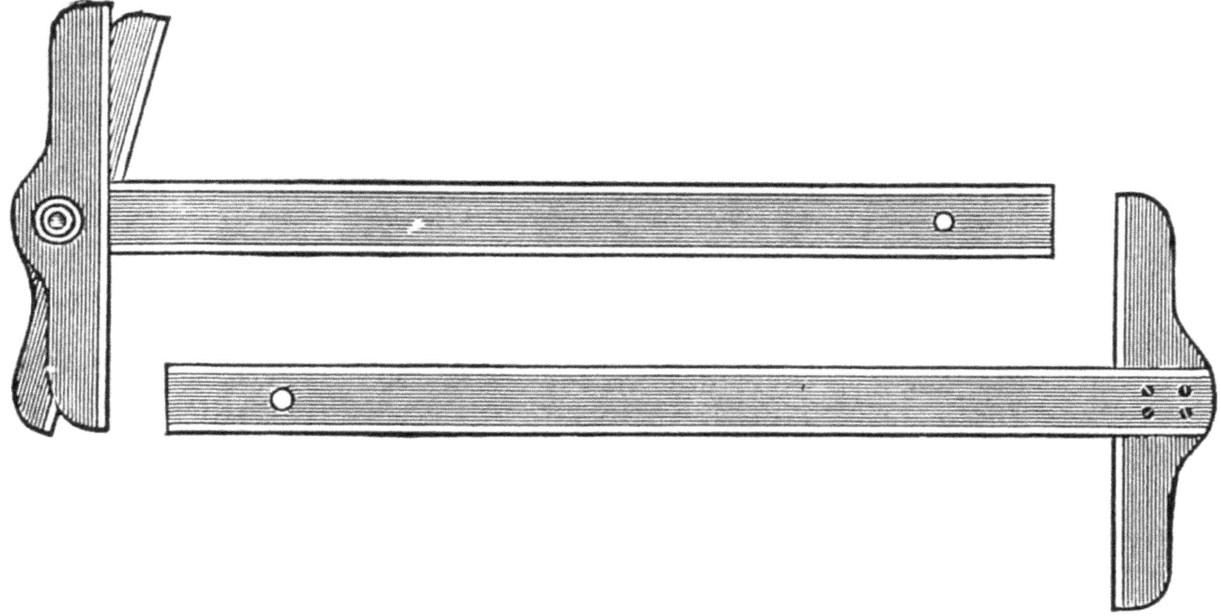

Figs. 149 and 150.

To be perfect in construction, a tee-square should be as light as is consistent with its necessary strength and stiffness of parts; it should be made of suitable material easily manufactured, put together, and repaired, and withal as truly correct as is possible to be made. Such a square is represented in fig. 148; it has a taper blade, which is generally about double the width where secured to the stock as it is at the end.

The manner in which the stock is united to the blade determines its adaptability or otherwise to the use made of it; in some the stock is rectangular in section, and the blade mortised into it; in others the blade is dovetailed and let into the stock for the whole of its thickness.

ADJUSTABLE BLADED SQUARE.

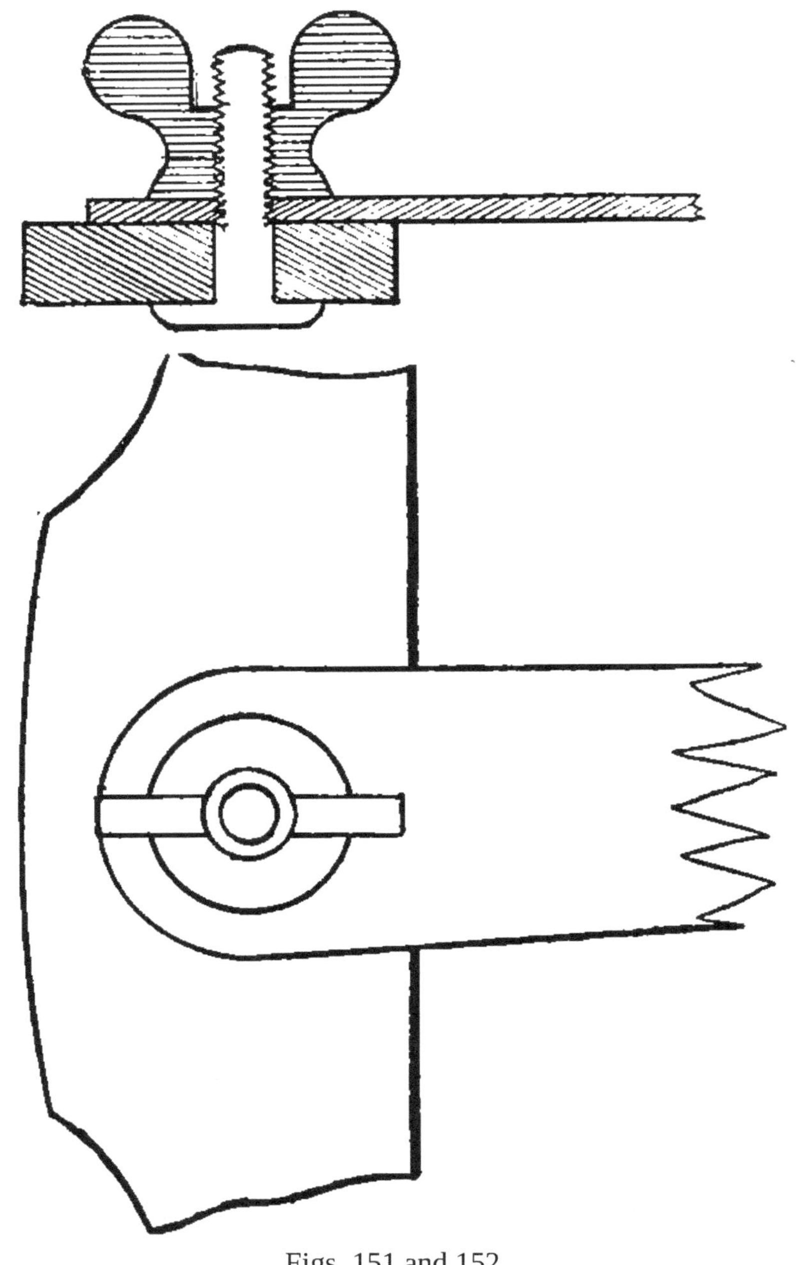

In cases where many parallel lines have to be drawn, of lengths beyond the capabilities of ordinary set-squares, and in directions other than square with or parallel to the working edge of the drawing board it is convenient to have for use an *adjustable* bladed tee-square, or one whose blade can be set at any desired angle. The blade of such a square should be tapered as in illustration, but shaped at its wide end as shown, and having a stock wide enough to allow for the surface required in the washers of the fittings necessary to make the blade adjustable. These fittings, though requiring to be well made and neatly finished, are not expensive or difficult to make, as they consist merely of two washers, a square-necked bolt, and a fly nut.

Figs. 151 and 152.

The tee-square, as shown, has four parts: 1, blade; 2, fixed head; 3, shifting head; 4, swivel. The head is held firmly by the left hand to the left edge of the drawing board, and the blade serves as a straight-edge for horizontal lines that may extend the whole length of the paper. It can be used for either horizontal, or, by reversing to the bottom of the board, for vertical lines; and, by turning it over, so that the shifting head is against the edge of the drawing board instead of the fixed head, lines at different angles may be drawn. The length of the blade should be the length of the drawing board; if it is shorter, inconvenience will be experienced when lines the whole length of the board are wanted.

TRIANGLES, OR SET-SQUARES.

Set-squares are invariably used in connection with the tee-square, as shown in fig. 148. The illustrations below show several patterns of the device; by these, vertical lines, triangles, squares and hexagonal, octagonal and twelve-sided figures, diagonal section lines, etc., can be easily drawn. For ordinary purposes, a triangle or set-square with angles of 45° may be 4 inches long and the other 8 inches in length, but a six-inch set-square having angles 90°, 45° and 45°, and an eight-inch one having angles of 90°, 60° and 30°, will be found sufficient for all purposes; there are other triangles used specially for making letters.

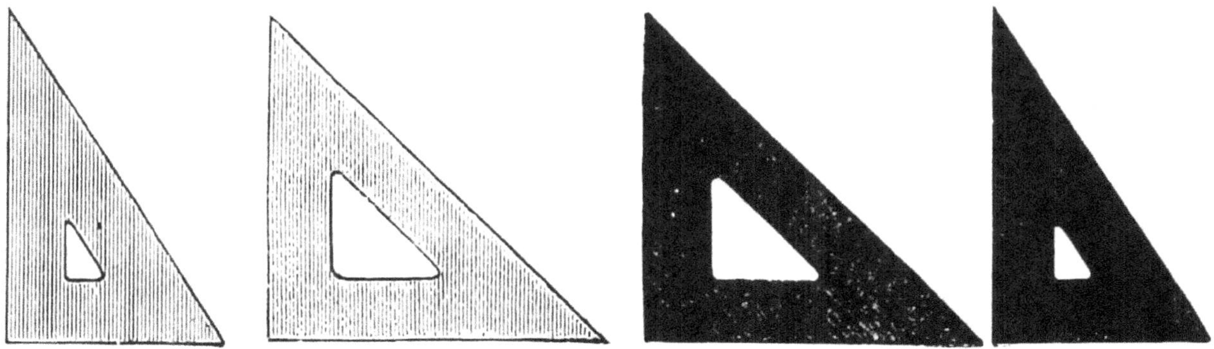

Fig. 153.—Fig. 154.—Fig. 155.—Fig. 156.

In practice the triangles or set-squares are slid along the edge of the blade, and need not be any thicker than it.

PARALLEL RULE.

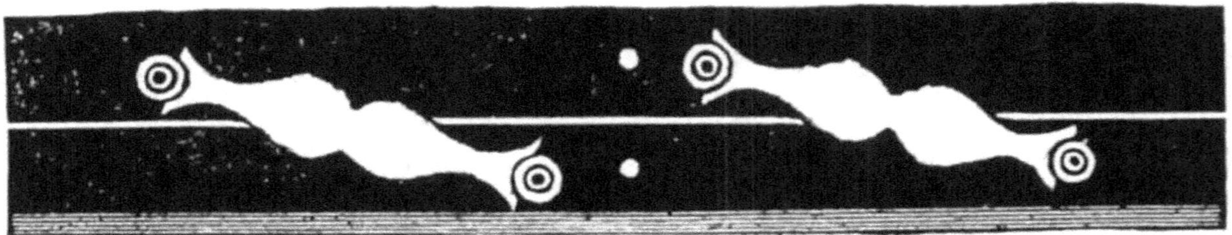
Fig. 157.

This instrument is used to mark lines which are neither horizontal nor vertical (usually these are drawn by the square and set-square), and which are parallel to one another; by adjusting the edge of the parallel ruler to a line, it can be extended or opened out (or vice-versa closed), and the line or lines drawn will be parallel or equally distant from the base or first line it was set by. See fig. 157.

Fig. 158 is a parallel ruler, constructed with two rollers fixed on a rod so that they move the same distance, carrying the ruler parallel to the starting line.

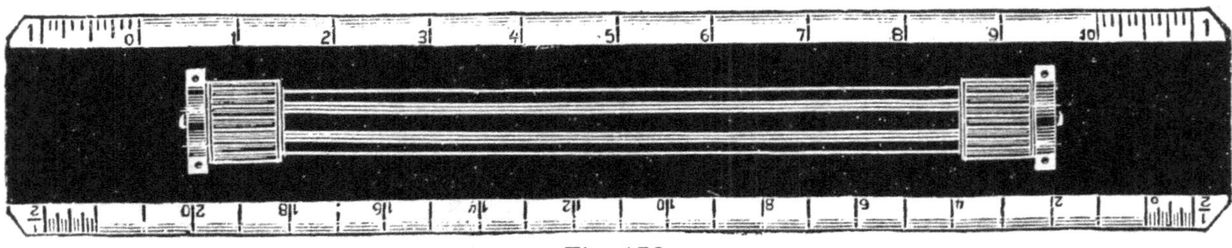
Fig. 158.

Note.—It has been said that "a workman may be known by his tools," but the statement must be taken with a good deal of allowance. Some workmen may possess a very fine set of tools and never use them, because they have not the ability or inclination to learn how; especially is this the case with drawing instruments.

If all the fine sets of drawing instruments that are owned by workmen were put to frequent use the owners would find a marked improvement in their abilities in other lines as well as drawing; for it is a noticeable fact that when a person's mind has been trained in a business that requires close calculation and a knowledge of materials, he is capable of showing good qualifications in other lines, and the more skilled he is in one the easier can he acquire skillfulness in another, if he applies the same amount of energy, thought and interest as he did to acquire skill in the first.

SECTION LINER.

Fig. 159 shows an improved section liner which can be adjusted to any angle, and will space the parallel lines at any desired regular distance.

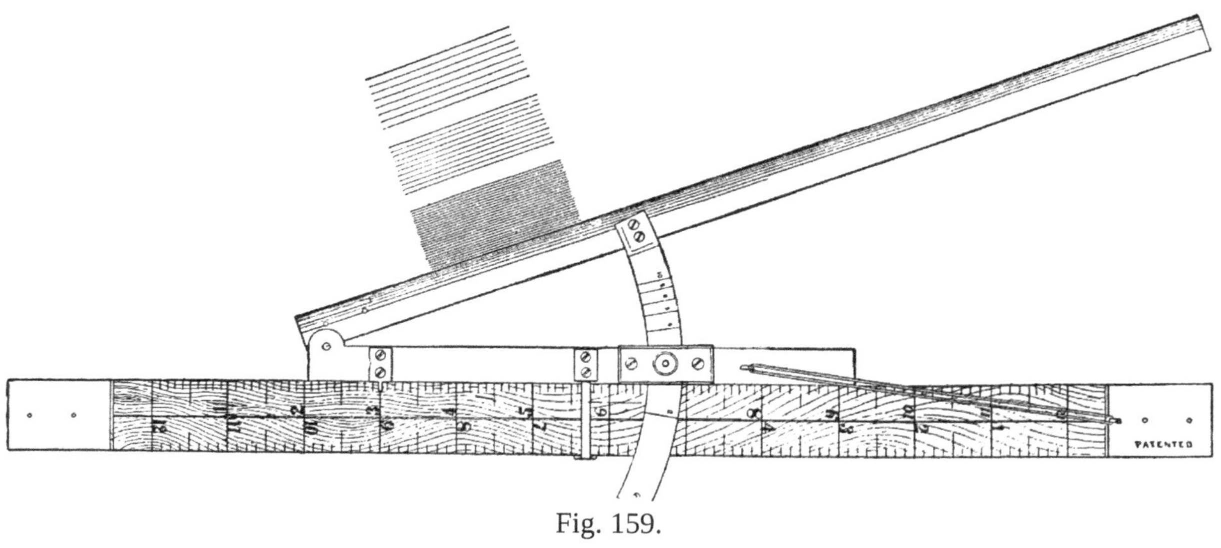

Fig. 159.

IRREGULAR CURVE OR SCROLL.

Irregular curves, or, as they are sometimes termed, sweeps, represented by figs. 160-166, are used for curves that cannot be put in by the other instruments. They are very useful when elliptical or parabolic curves are desired, in preference to circles or arcs of a circle. They are much used in design and architectural drawing. They are made of thin hardwood or rubber, and sometimes of horn.

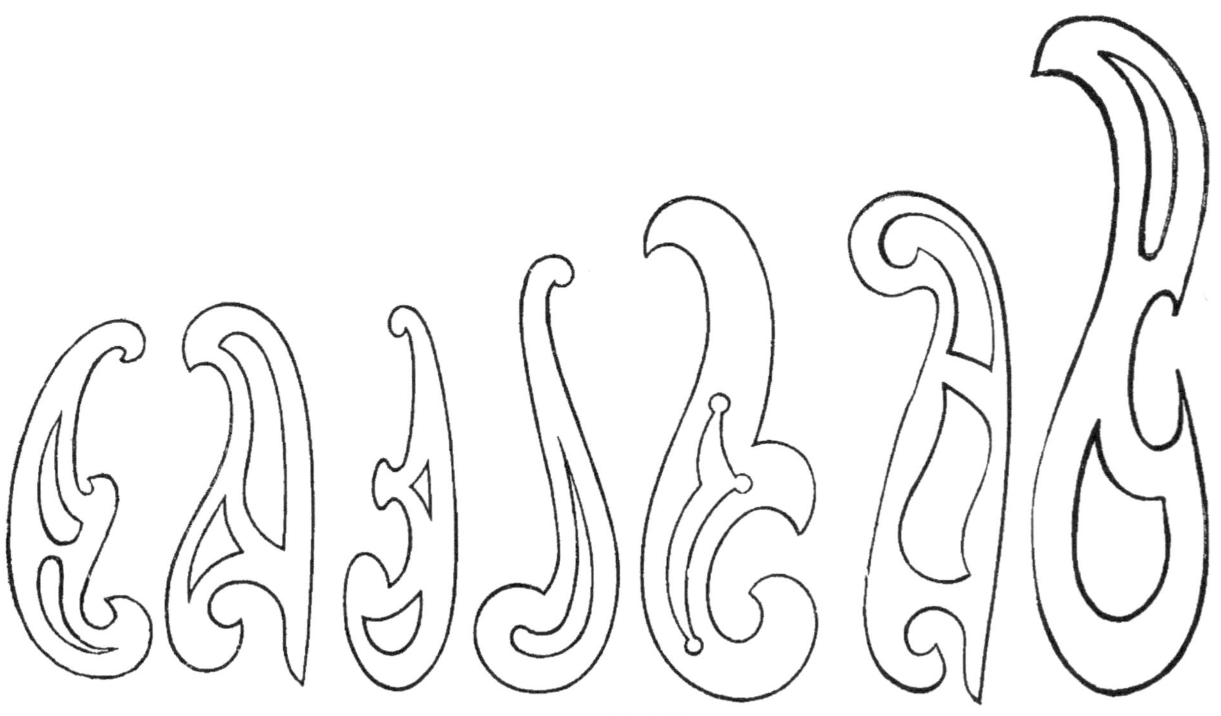

Figs. 160-166.

Curves are irregular lines; a circle is a regular line. If a curve is to be passed through a number of predetermined points it should be first sketched in lightly, free-hand; a section of the scroll is then applied to the curve so as to embrace as many points as possible; only the central points of those thus embraced should be inked in; this process is continued until the desired curve is completed.

Curves are made of various material, pearwood, cardboard, xylonite, hard rubber, and a strip of soft lead is sometimes used, which may be easily adjusted to the curve required.

The curves generally used in mechanical drawing are shown on previous page.

Fig. 208, page 134, is a logarithmic *spiral* curve. It is mathematically constructed and contains every curve within the limit of its size.

ELLIPSES.

An ellipse is a geometrical figure, and can be drawn as described in geometrical problem 29, page 96; many drawing offices keep sets of hard rubber ellipses, to economize time constructing them.

DRAWING PENCILS.

These are instruments for marking, drawing or writing, formed of graphite, colored chalk or materials of similar properties, and having a tapering end, inclosed, generally, in a cylinder of softwood. Fig. 167 represents a ruling pencil; its point is a parallelogram or of a wedge shape. In ruling, the length view rests against the square; its shape gives considerable strength to the lead and allows the making of a very fine line. Fig. 168 differs in the point of the pencil shown, as may be observed in the illustration.

A pencil that is hard is best for mechanical drawing; one that will retain a good point for some considerable time. Pencil lines should be made as light as possible; the presence of lead on the surface of the paper tends to prevent the ink passing to the paper, and in rubbing out pencil lines the ink is reduced in blackness, and the surface of paper is roughened, which is a disadvantage. As little erasing or rubbing out as possible should be done.

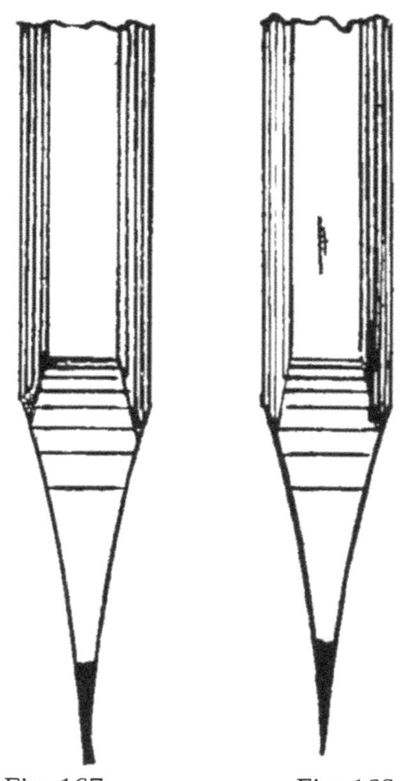

Fig. 167.   Fig. 168.

Fig. 169.   Fig. 170.

DIVIDERS AND COMPASSES.

These instruments, while they appear alike, have a separate use: the dividers are used to space off distances and dimensions; especially are they necessary in reading drawings made to scale. *Compasses* are used for describing circles, curves, etc., *dividers* are used for marking out spaces.

Two forms of the dividers are shown in figs. 169 and 170; the simplest, plainest form is shown in fig. 169; these are used for rough spacings; fig. 170 represents a pair of dividers fitted with an adjustable screw controlled by a steel spring in one leg; by this a very exact measurement can be made. Fig. 170 is intended to exhibit what is called a "hair-spring divider."

PROPORTIONAL DIVIDERS.

These dividers differ from the ordinary ones shown in figs. 169 and 170 in that they are provided with four steel points, one pair of which being set to the full dimension will be reproduced by the other pair, but in a smaller, or reduced size.

Fig. 171 are "bisecting" dividers, being proportional dividers, which, when open, one end measures double the distance of the other.

Fig. 172 are proportional dividers; the points at one end are capable of being changed, to measure practically any desired proportion at the other end, by altering the position of the pivot where the legs cross one another. The lower connecting link is a micrometer adjustment, for minute measurements.

Fig. 173 are proportional dividers which are marked for the proportions of lines and radii of circles, being provided with a rack movement for adjustment.

Fig. 174 represents three-leg dividers, used for taking the position of three points; this instrument is very useful in finding the position of a point in a figure.

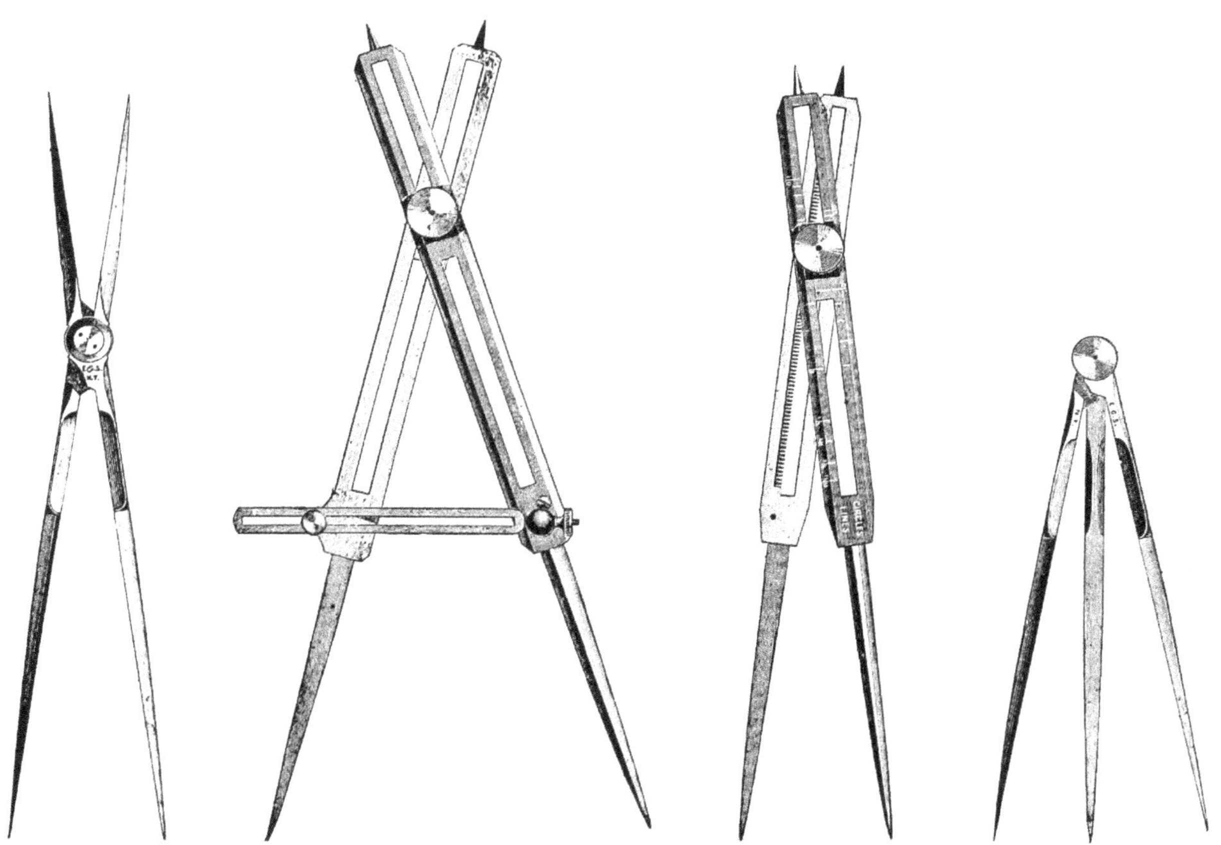

Fig. 171.—Fig. 172.—Fig. 173.—Fig. 174.

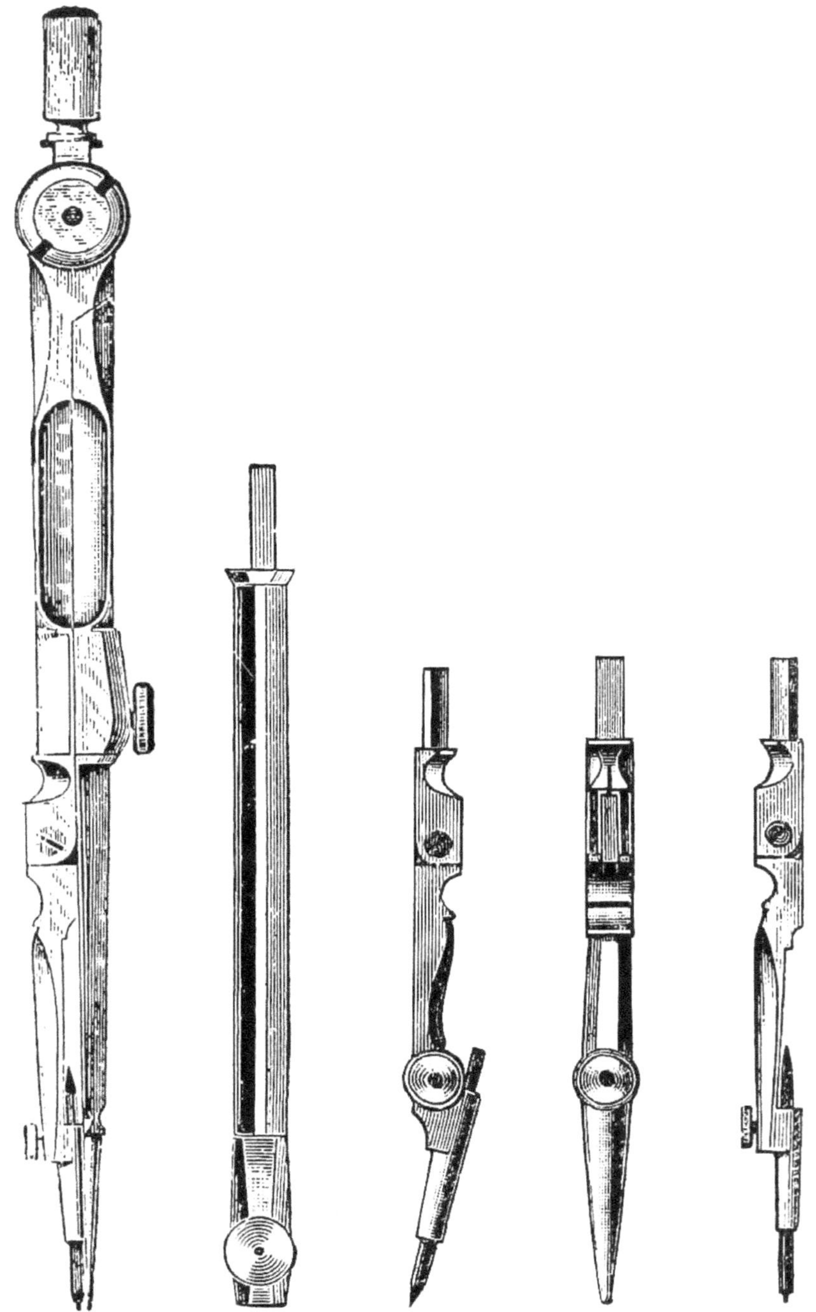

Fig. 175.—Fig. 176.—Fig. 177.—Fig. 178.—Fig. 179.

COMPASSES.

Compasses consist of two pointed legs; they are instruments for describing circles or for—sometimes—measuring figures, in absence of dividers. Fig. 175 represents compasses fitted as dividers.

Compasses should have jointed legs, which will allow the points to be placed at right angles to the paper, whatever the size of the circle to be drawn. Compasses should not be used for circles which are too large to allow the points to be thus placed; a lengthening bar is generally provided, which greatly increases the diameters of circles which may be drawn by this attachment; it is shown in fig. 176.

One leg of the compasses is usually provided with a socket to which are fitted three points: a divider point, fig. 179; a pencil point, fig. 177; and a point, fig. 178, carrying a special pen for the inking of circles. Each of these points is generally provided with a joint, so that it may be placed at right angles to the paper.

The other leg should be jointed; it is often provided with a socket which receives two points, one a divider point, and the other carrying a needle point. Such an instrument may be used as dividers for spacing, or as compasses for penciling or inking circles.

The joint at the head of the compasses (see fig. 175) is the most important feature. It should hold the legs firmly in any position, so that in going over a circle several times only one line will result. It should allow the legs to move smoothly and evenly, and should be capable of adjustment.

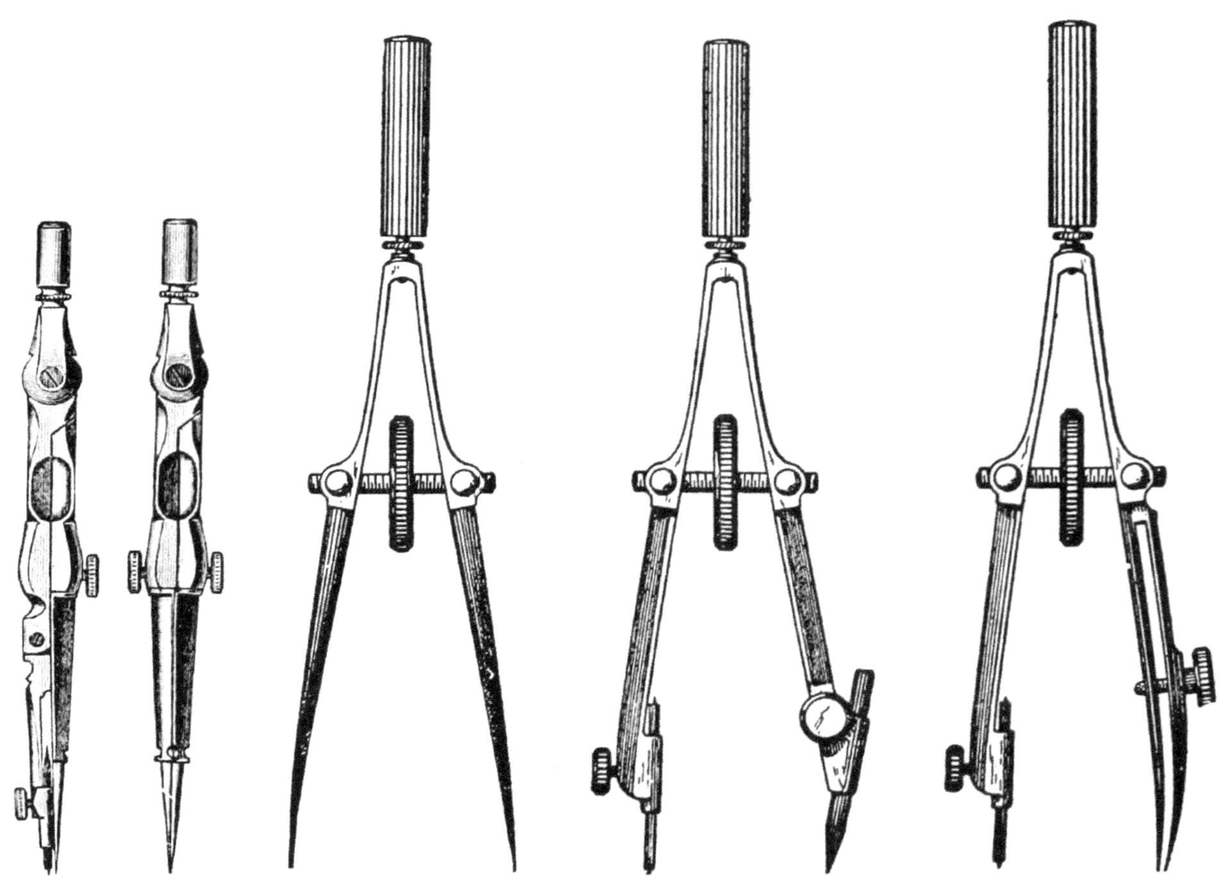

Fig. 180.—Fig. 181.—Fig. 182.—Fig. 183.—Fig. 184.

As shown in fig. 174, one leg has a hinge or joint, and a needle point, which can be regulated by a thumb screw; the other leg has a socket or recess into which interchangeable parts can be inserted. The four figures to the right of the compasses show the parts which are provided with shanks or insertion pieces. Fig. 180 and fig. 181 represent compasses specially used for making small circles, and work too minute for the larger instruments described above.

To do work of this nature easily a pair of spring dividers are frequently used. This instrument has one point attached to a spring, which is regulated by a screw, so that very slight changes in the space may be made with ease.

Compasses specially used for putting in fine circles and dimensions are called "bows." When a pen point it is a "bow pen," with a pencil point a "bow pencil," and if with needle point a "bow dividers." Fig. 180 is a "bow dividers", this fitted with screw for fine adjustment in one leg, fig. 181, is called a "hair-spring bow dividers"; for small details, bows with steel spring legs without any joint are used; these are called "steel-spring bows."

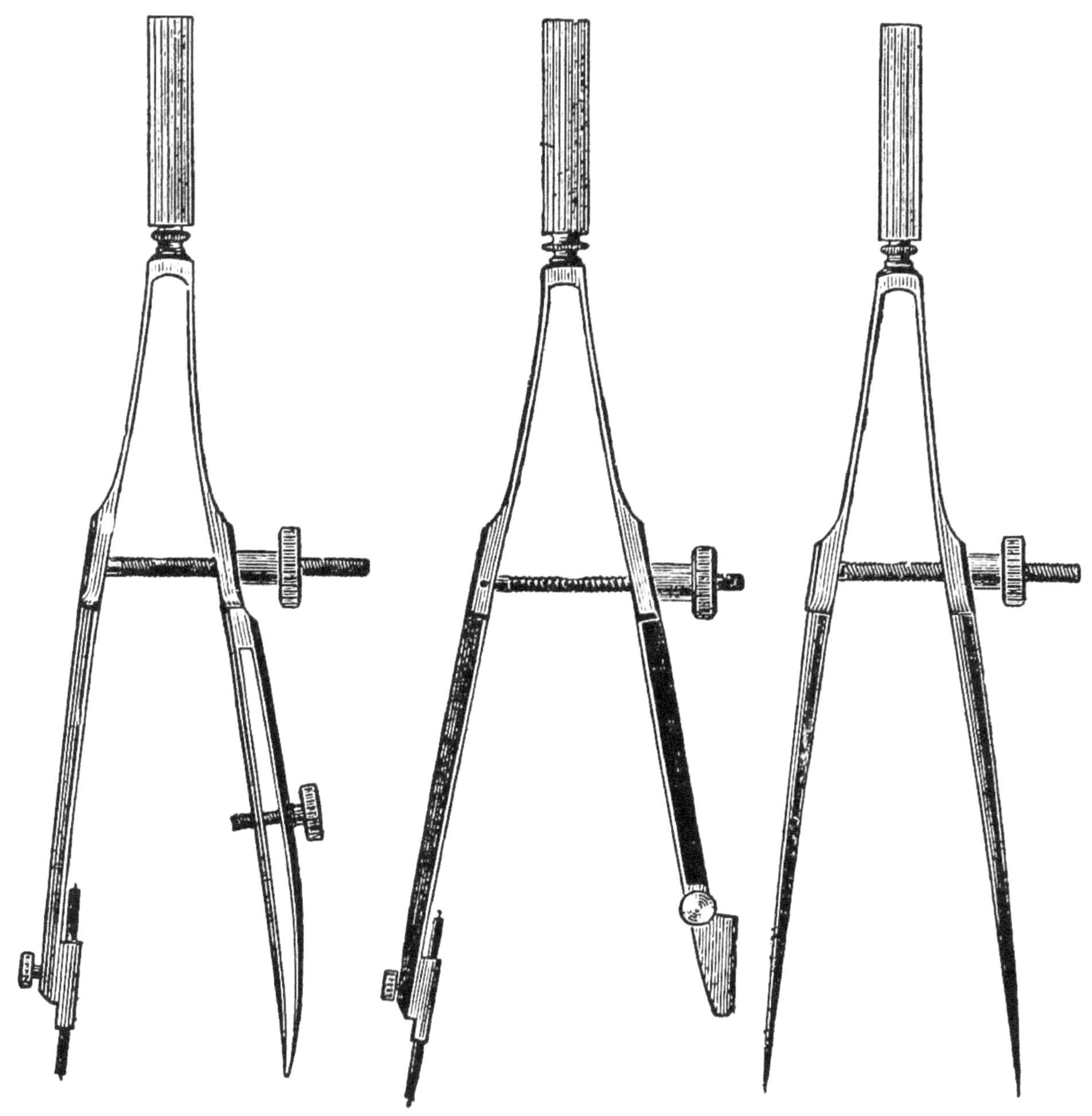

Fig. 185.—Fig. 186.—Fig. 187.

SPRING BOWS.

These were originally developed from the common form of compasses, with a single spring leg; later, the demand for smaller sizes made changes necessary, and spring bows are now made symmetrical, both sides of the bow being made to "spring."

Fig. 182 are spring dividers.

Fig. 183 is a spring pencil.

Fig. 184 is a spring pen.

In these figures it will be seen that the two threads, a right and a left, are moved with one central thumbscrew; in the figs. 185 to 187 a single screw is used.

In choosing spring bows, care must be exercised to select a sufficiently strong, stiff spring, as the relation between spring pressure and thumbscrew is important.

BEAM COMPASSES AND TRAMMELS.

In fig. 188 is shown a set of beam compasses, together with a portion of the wooden rod or beam on which they are used.

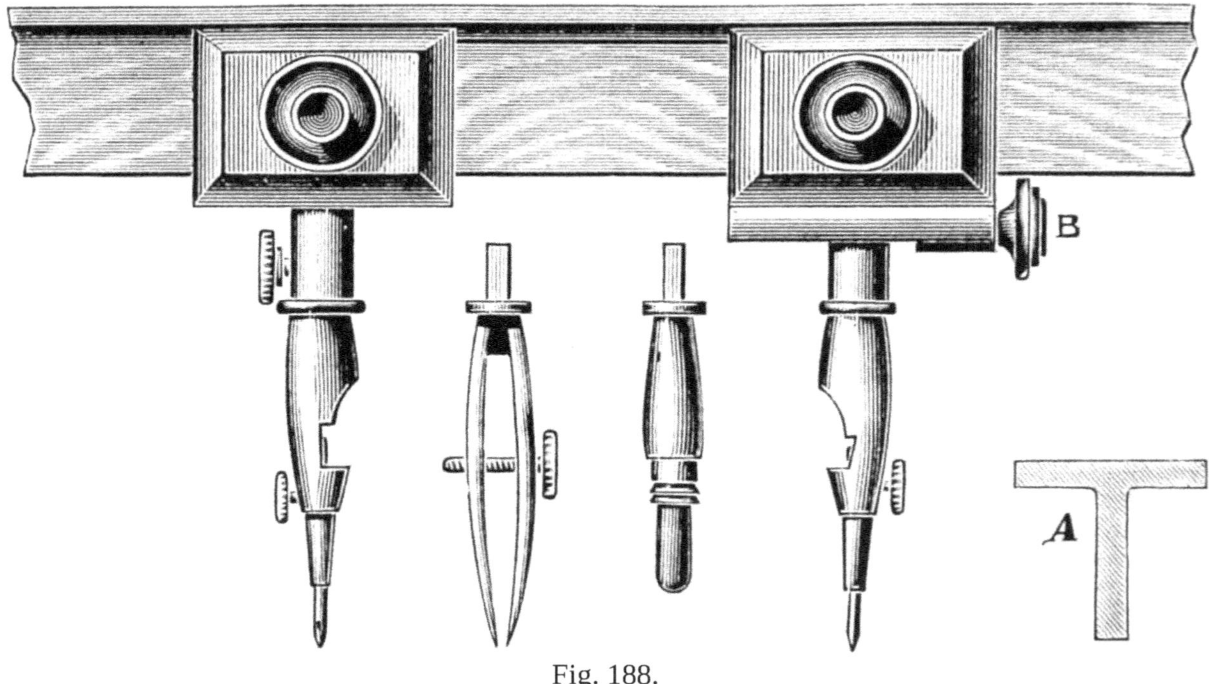

Fig. 188.

The latter, as will be seen by the section drawn to one side, *A*, is in the shape of a T. This form has considerable strength and rigidity. Beam compasses are provided with extra points for pencil or ink work, as shown.

While the general adjustment is effected by means of the clamp against the wood, minute variations are made by the screw, *B*, shifting one of the points, as shown in the figure.

This instrument is quite delicate, and, when in good order, is very accurate. It should be used only for fine work on paper, and never for scribing on metal.

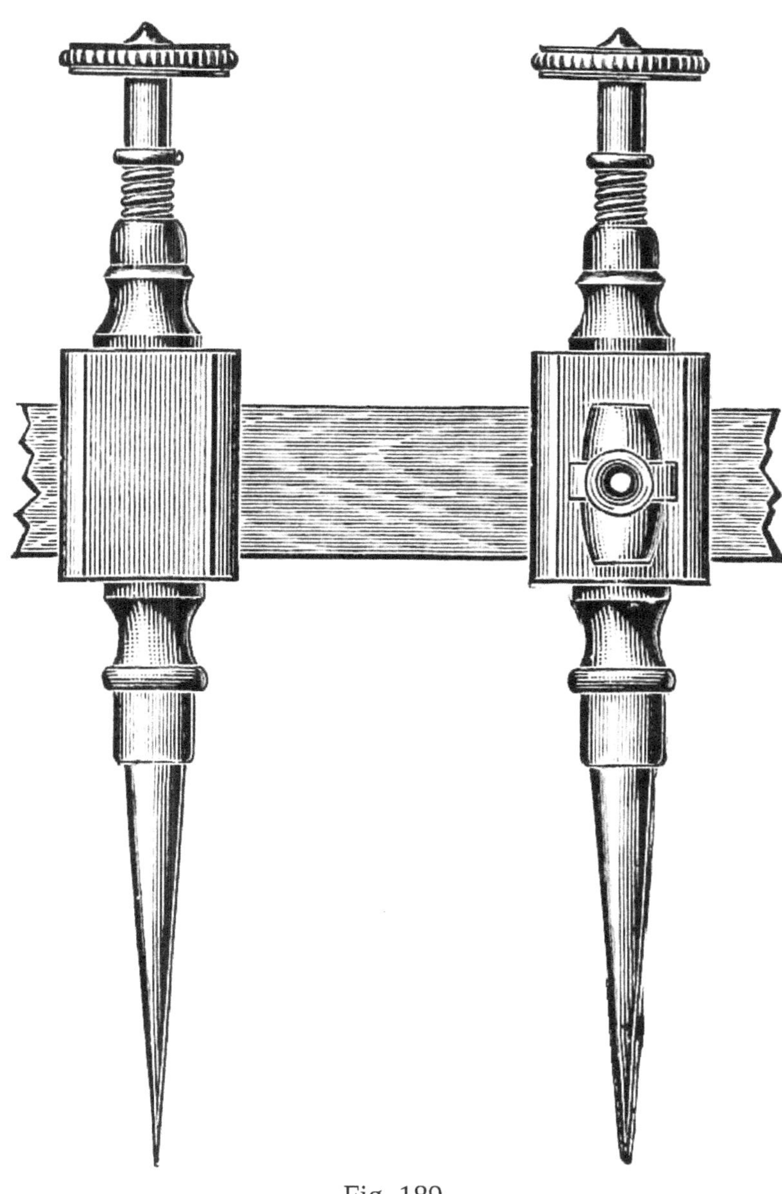

Fig. 189.

A coarser instrument, and one especially designed for use upon metal, is shown in fig. 189, and is called a trammel. There are various forms of this instrument, all being the same in principle. The engraving shows a form in common use. A heavier stick is used with it than with the beam compasses, and no other adjustment is provided than that which is afforded by clamping against the stick.

In the illustration, a carrier at the side is shown, in which a pencil may be placed. Some trammels are arranged in such a manner, that either of the points may be detached and a pencil substituted.

A trammel, by careful arrangement, can be made to describe very accurate curves, and hence can be used in place of the beam compasses in many instances. For all coarse work it is to be preferred to beam compasses. It is useful for all short sweeps upon sheets of metal, but for curves of a very long radius a strip of sheet iron or a piece of wire will be found of a more practical service than even this tool.

The length of rods for both beam compasses and tramels, up to certain limits, is determined by the nature of the work to be done. The extreme length is determined by the strength and rigidity of the rod itself. It is usually convenient to have two rods for each instrument, one about 1½ or 2 feet in length and the other considerably longer—as long as the strength of the material will admit.

DRAWING SCALES.

Scales are proportioned rules or mathematical instruments of wood, metal, etc., on which are marked lines and figures for the purpose of measuring sizes and distances. It is usual to make scales in the proportion of parts of an inch equalling a foot; the most generally adopted scale for machine drawing is one and a half inches, equalling one foot; that is, twelve-eighths of an inch (each eighth of an inch representing one inch); there is no fixed rule in the choice of a scale, as they are varied according to the coarseness or fineness of the parts of the machine to be drawn and the space or surface of paper to be utilized.

When objects are of moderate proportions they may be represented full size; but when large, the drawings must be smaller. Standard scales for mechanical drawings are ½, ¼, ⅛ and ¹⁄₁₆ full size. These scales are often written 6″ = 1 ft.; 3″ = 1 ft.; 1½″ = 1 ft., and ¾″ = 1 ft.

Instead of selecting one of the scales named or one found upon the ordinary scales used by draughtsmen, drawings may be made to any scale whatever. Thus, if any object is to be represented in a certain space, a scale should be constructed which will cause the whole of the object to be shown.

Drawing to Scale.—The meaning of this is, that the drawing when done bears a definite proportion to the full size of the particular part, or, in other words, is precisely the same as it would appear if viewed through a diminishing glass.

The two-foot rule shown in fig. 192 is the most useful instrument for the comparison of linear dimensions—it can be used as a scale of one-twelfth, or 1 inch equal to a foot, 12 inches = 12 feet, it being divided into portions or spaces, each of which is subdivided into halves, quarters, eighths and sixteenths; frequently in the latter class of two-foot rules there are graduations of scales, and it is then also called a draughting scale.

Fig. 190 represents a flat scale, graded so that one inch represents a foot—¹⁄₁₂th size—etc., as shown.

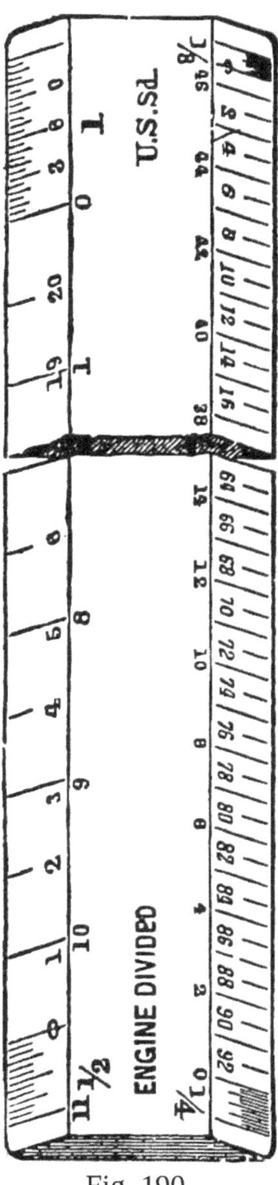

Fig. 190.

Fig. 191 represents a triangular scale (broken). The triangular scale should read on its different edges as follows: Three inches and $1\frac{1}{2}''$ to one foot, $1''$ and $\frac{1}{2}''$ to one foot, $\frac{3}{4}''$ and $\frac{3}{8}''$ to one foot, $\frac{1}{4}''$ and $\frac{1}{8}''$ to one foot, $\frac{3}{16}''$ and $\frac{3}{32}''$ to one foot, and one edge read sixteenths the whole $12''$ of its length.

Fig. 190 shows such a scale broken. An explanation of the $1''$ and $\frac{1}{2}''$ side will suffice for all. Where it is used as a scale of $1''$ to one foot, each large space, as from 0 to 12 or 0 to 1, represents a foot, and is a foot at that scale. There being $12''$ in one foot, the twelve long divisions at the left represent inches; each inch is divided into two equal parts, so from 0 to one division at the left of 9 is $9\frac{1}{2}''$ and so on. The $1''$ and $\frac{1}{2}''$ scales being at opposite ends of the same edge, it is obvious that one foot on the $1''$ scale is equal to two feet on the $\frac{1}{2}''$ scale, and conversely, one foot on the $\frac{1}{2}''$ scale is equal to six inches on the $1''$ scale; and $1''$ being equal to one foot, the total feet in length of scale will be 12; at $\frac{1}{2}''$ to 1 foot the total feet will be 24.

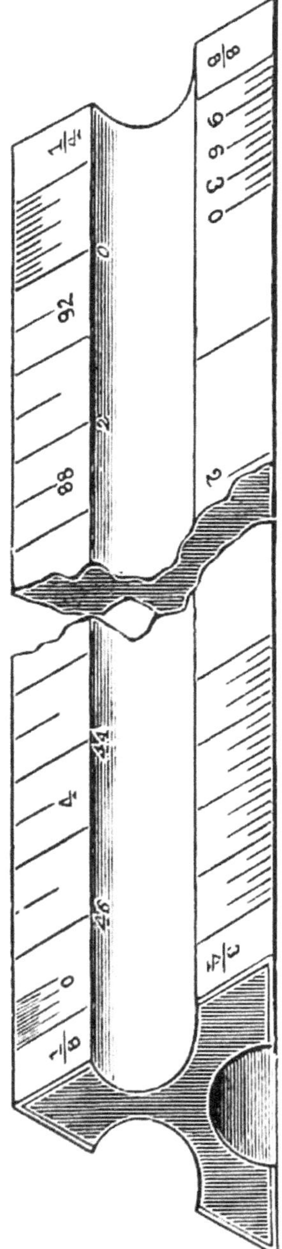

Fig. 191.

In working to regular scales, such as $\frac{1}{2}$, $\frac{1}{8}$, or $\frac{1}{16}$ size, a good plan is to use a common rule, instead of a graduated scale. There is nothing more convenient for a mechanical draughtsman than to be able to readily resolve dimensions into various scales, and the use of a common rule for fractional scales trains the mind, so that computations come naturally, and after a time almost without effort.

The protractor shown in fig. 193 is an instrument for laying down and measuring angles on paper; it is used in connecting with a scale to define the inclination of one line to another.

Protractors have the degrees of a half circle marked upon them; as the whole circle contains 360 degrees, half of it will contain 180, one-quarter 90, etc. Hence, protractors showing 180° exhibit all that is needed. To protract means to extend, so this instrument is also useful in "extending" the lines of inclination at the circle.

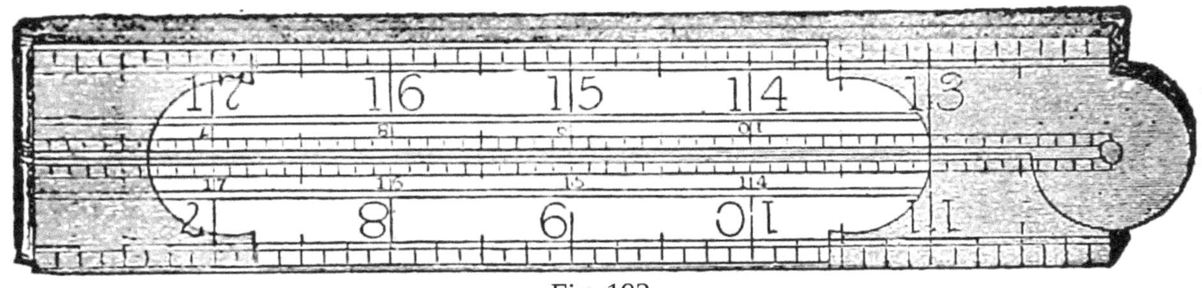

Fig. 192.

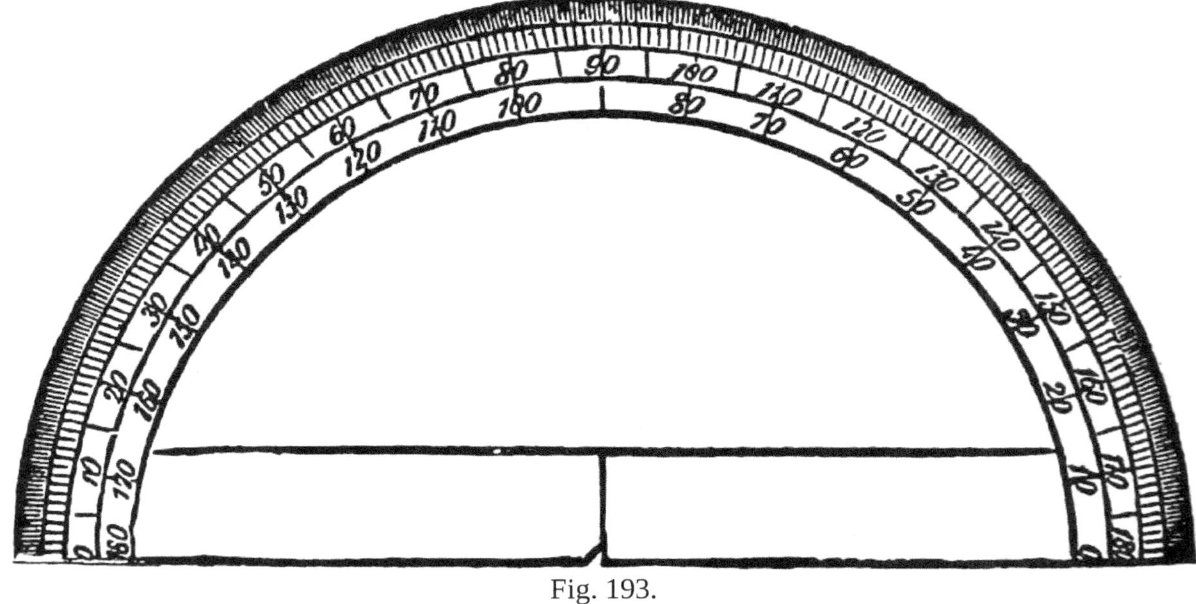

Fig. 193.

DRAWING-PENS.

A special pen called a drawing-pen, and also special ink, are required to ink a drawing; figs. 194 and 195 represent two sizes of drawing-pens— one being best adapted for fine work, and the other for coarse or heavy line work. The points, as will be observed in the illustration, are made of two steel blades which open and close as required for thickness of lines by a regulating screw.

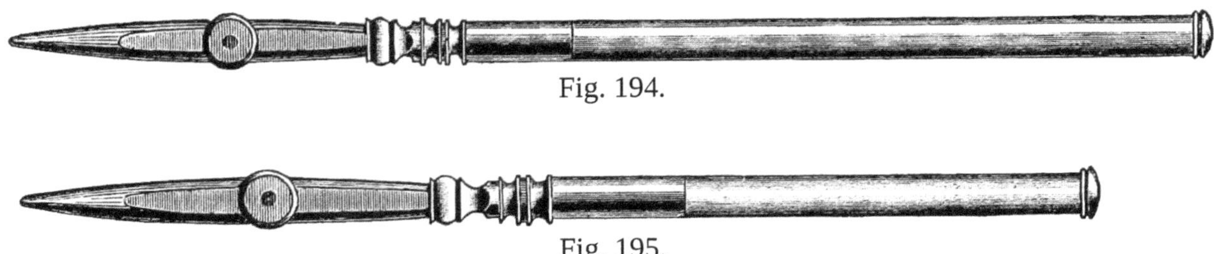

Fig. 194.

Fig. 195.

A good drawing pen should be made of properly tempered steel, neither too soft nor hardened to brittleness. The nibs should be accurately set, both of the same length, and both equally firm when in contact with the drawing paper. The points should be so shaped that they are fine enough to admit of absolute control of the contact of the pen in starting and ending lines, but otherwise as broad and rounded as possible, in order to hold a convenient quantity of ink without dropping it. The lower (under) blade should be sufficiently firm to prevent the closing of the blades of the pen, when using the pen against a straightedge.

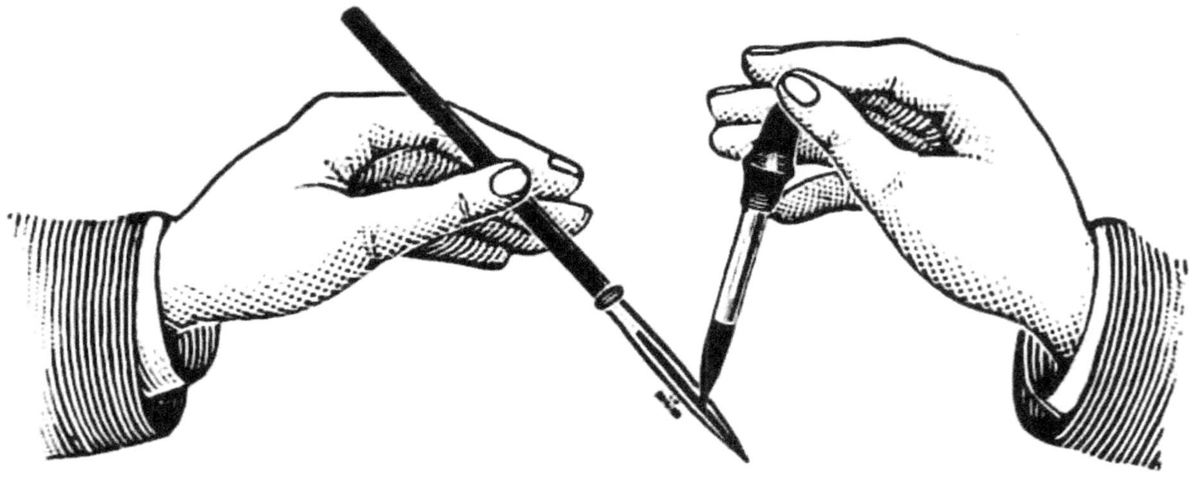

Fig. 196.

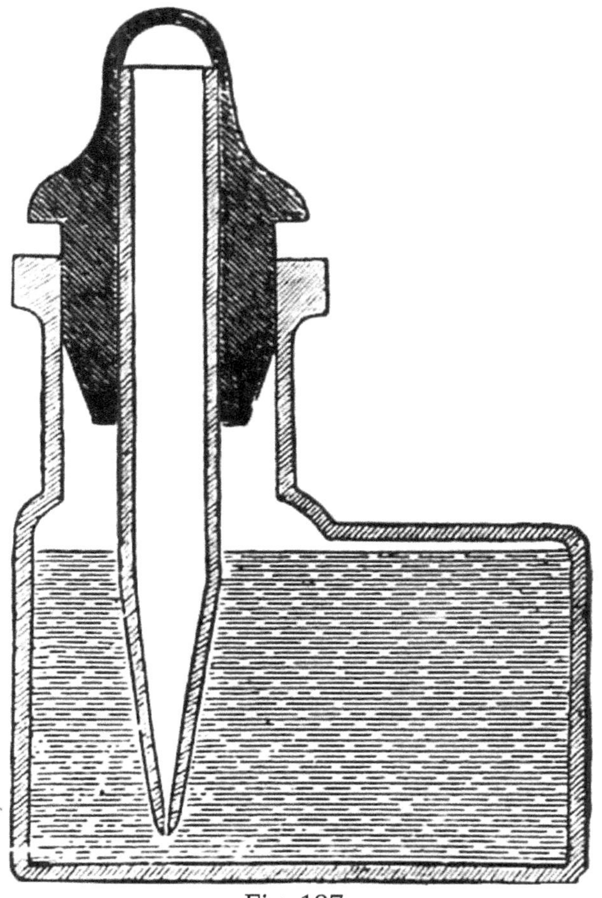

Fig. 197.

The spring of the pen, which separates the two blades, should be strong enough to hold the upper blade in its position, but not so strong that it would interfere with easy adjustment by the thumbscrew. The thread of the thumbscrew must be deeply and evenly cut so as not to strip.

An important requisite after the pencil lines have been put in is ink, with which to line the drawing. This should be of the best that can be procured. The pen is filled by dropping the ink between the blades, or nibs, while held in a nearly vertical position, as shown in fig. 196.

Liquid India ink can be procured in bottles with glass tube feeders, which are very good, and keep the hands and fingers free of the ink. Fig. 197 is a sectional view of such a bottle and "filler," or feeder. This generally answers all requirements, but the dry ink of good quality, in sticks or bars, cannot be surpassed, although it requires skill for its preparation. Fig. 198 represents a sloping dish or "tile" for mixing, which should be done with little pressure, in clean, filtered or distilled water, care being taken to keep the liquid free of dust, which obstructs the free flow of the ink in the pens.

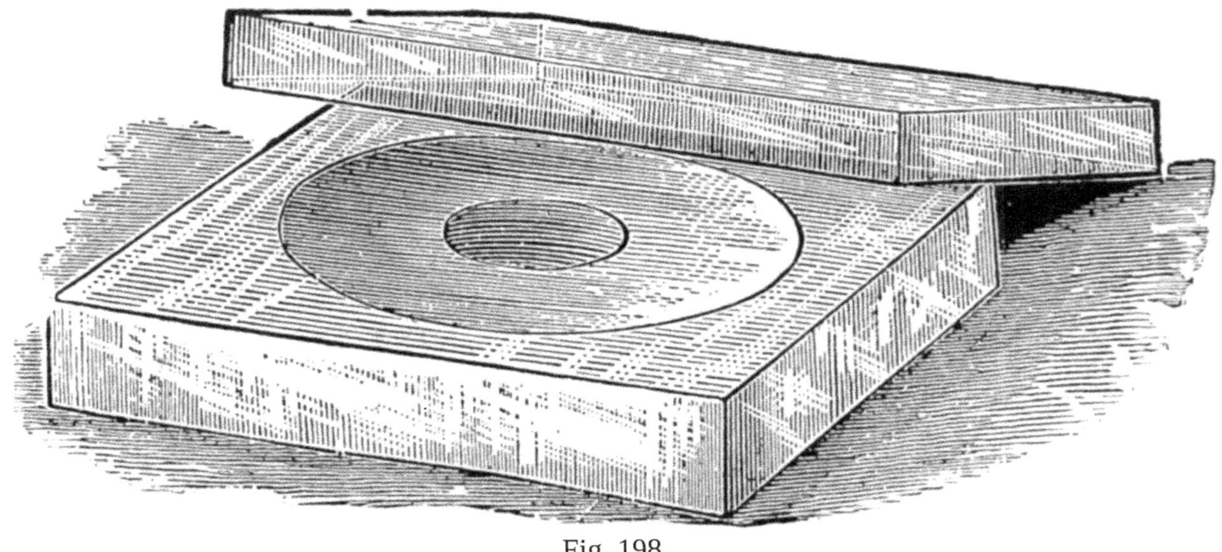

Fig. 198.

The bars of India ink are shown, as they are imported, in figs. 199 to 202.

Pure India or China ink is only made in those countries, because the special wood from which it is prepared is found only in those regions. So-called India inks, made of lampblack and animal glue, are only imitations; therefore India ink should be purchased from a reliable importing house—shape is little guarantee of quality.

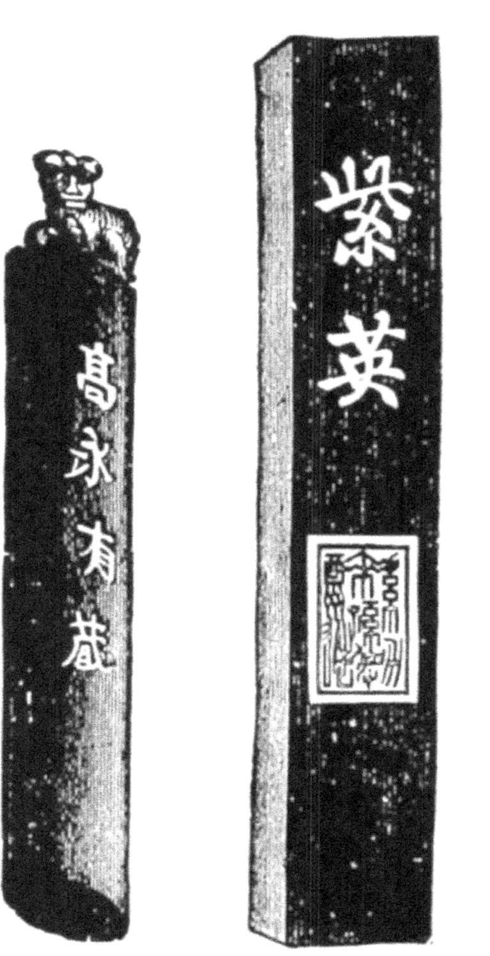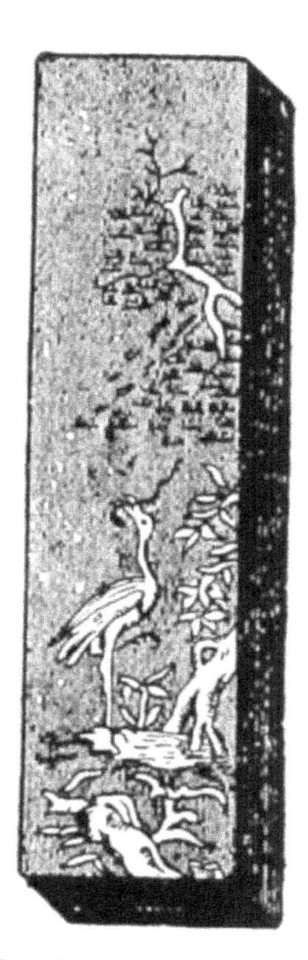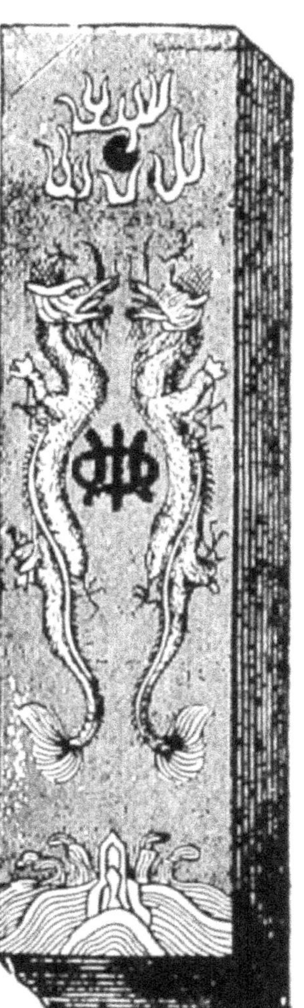

Fig. 199.—Fig. 200.—Fig. 201.—Fig. 202.

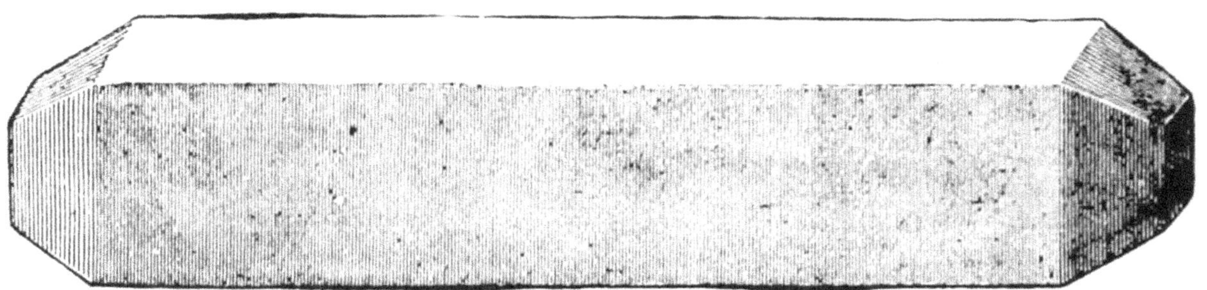

Fig. 203.

Soft gray vulcanized rubber (fig. 203) should be used for cleaning drawing paper; for erasing any portion of a line in pencil, a piece of prepared white vulcanized rubber is the best, small in size and of rectangular shape (see fig. 205).

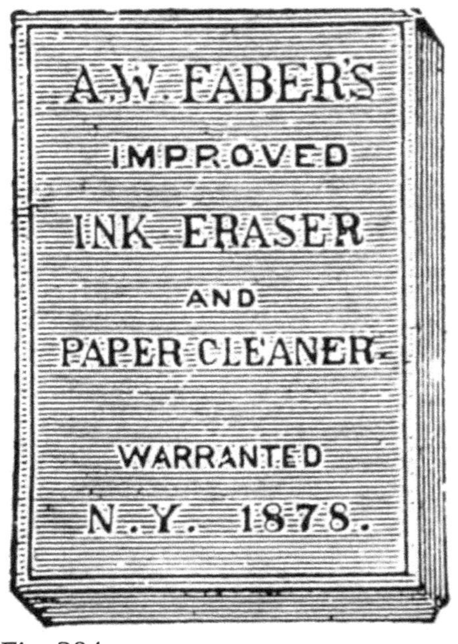

Fig. 204.

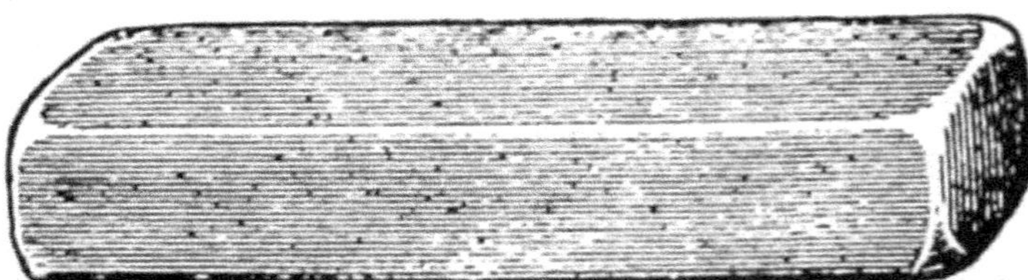

Fig. 205.

An ink eraser is made of a composition of rubber and ground glass, and it should be used as sparingly as possible on drawings, as it roughens the paper and removes the gloss from its surface (see fig. 204). Steel ink erasers are useful in removing defects, overrun lines, joint of lines if swollen, etc.; they have a fine point and can be used to advantage with a little practice; they are used with a scratching, not a cutting, motion (see figs. 206, 207).

DRAWING PAPER.

The first thing to be considered in selecting drawing paper is the kind most suitable for the proposed plan. Paper may be purchased in sheets 22 × 30 inches, that make four exercise sheets 11 × 15 inches; this may be of several grades and tints.

The qualities that constitute good paper are strength, uniformity of thickness and surface, neither repelling nor absorbing liquids, admitting of considerable erasing without destroying the surface, not becoming brittle nor discolored by reasonable exposure or age, and not buckling when stretched, or when ink or color is applied.

The sizes and names of paper made in sheets is as follows:

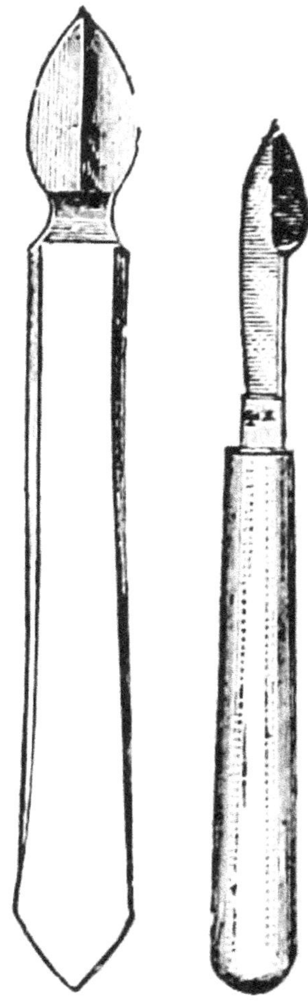

Cap	13×17 ins.
Demy	15×20 „
Medium	17×22 „
Royal	19×24 „
Super Royal	19×27 „
Imperial	22×30 „
Atlas	26×34 „
Double Elephant	27×40 „
Antiquarian	30×53 „

Fig. 206. Fig. 207.

For large drawings paper is made in rolls. "Detail paper" is especially made for marking out new designs; it is made in rolls 36, 42 and 54 inches wide; it has excellent erasing qualities and takes ink and color with facility.

When working by artificial light it is desirable that the paper be of a light-brown color, which is less trying to the eyes than a pure white.

If it is a shop drawing or sketch not to be preserved, use detail paper, which is the most economical and will stand a great deal of handling without becoming soiled. If it is a detailed plan, finished drawing or a picture, use the best white drawing paper to be obtained, so that your drawings can be preserved indefinitely without danger of fading, which is due either to the paper being poorly made and discoloring with age, or being of poor fiber and absorbing the ink or color, and the drawing consequently losing its brightness.

After deciding on the size of paper most suitable for the work, then carefully select the paper embracing the most qualities of value for the proposed drawing.

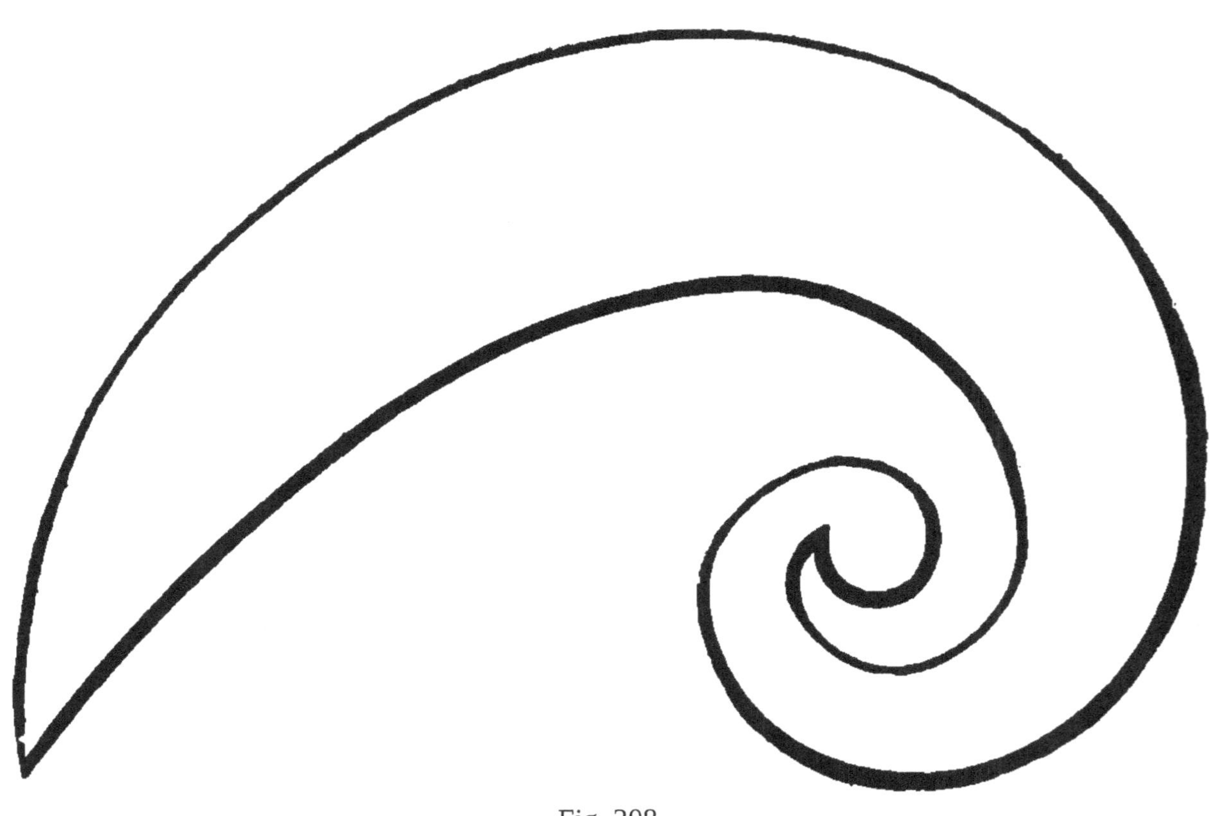

Fig. 208.

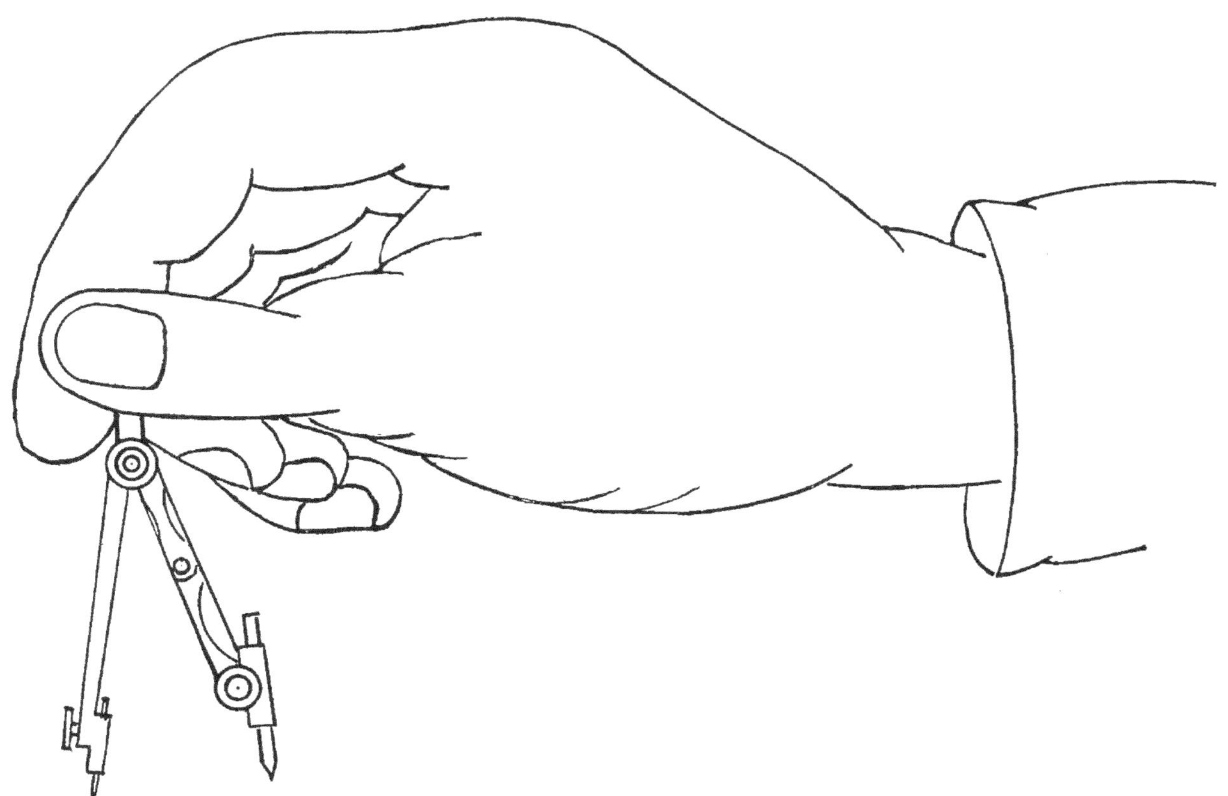

Fig. 209.

Mechanical Drawing.

In distinction to "free-hand," mechanical drawing is executed almost entirely by the use of the instruments previously described; hence its other term, instrumental drawing. To define it particularly it may be said that,—

Mechanical drawing is the correct reproduction of any figure or part of a machine, whether of full size or reduced in the proportion of one part to another; it also comprises the art of delineating the interior parts which are hidden from view in solid bodies.

A mechanical drawing is the vehicle for conveying the ideas of the designer to those who are to embody them in wood and metal, and the considerations which should govern its production are those which affect its clearness and legibility or those which facilitate reference to it.

Drawings consist of plans, elevations and sections; plans being views on the top of the object in a horizontal plane; elevations, views on the sides of the object in vertical planes; and sections, views taken on bisecting planes, at any angle through an object.

Drawings in true elevation or in section are based upon flat planes, and given dimensions parallel to the planes in which the views are taken.

Two elevations taken at right angles to each other fix all points, and give all dimensions of parts that have their axis parallel to the planes on which the views are taken; but when a machine is complex, or when several parts lie in the same plane, three and sometimes four views are required to display all the parts in a comprehensive manner.

A man must have either a natural talent for hand-drawing or years of experience, before he can produce a sketch and "dimension" it, fit to work from; hence the elementary character of the examples given for practice. A "pretty" drawing is not expected from a beginner; it should always be borne in mind, that correctness of dimensions and general clearness, rather than elaborate finish, are what will save the battle in the days of competition.

Mechanical drawings should be made with reference to all the processes that are required in the construction of the work, and the drawings should be responsible, not only for dimensions, but for adaptation to fitting, forging, pattern-making, moulding, and so on.

Every part laid down should have something to govern it that may be termed a "base"—some position which, if understood, will suggest size, shape and relation to other parts. Searching after a base for each and every part and detail, the draughtsman should proceed upon a regular system, continually maintaining a test of what is done.

A mechanical drawing consists chiefly of three views:

1. The plan or top view.

2. The side elevation.

3. The end elevation.

In addition to the above, drawings are used to show interior portions of the figure; these are termed "sections," and they may be taken where any plane crosses another.

NOTE.—The word *elevation*, as applied to mechanical drawings, means simply a view; hence a side elevation is a side view, or an end elevation is an end view.

The word *plan* is employed in place of the word top; hence a plan view is a top view or a view looking down upon the top of the piece.

A *general* view means a view showing the machine put together or assembled, while a detail drawing is one containing a detail, as a part of the machine or a single piece disconnected from the other parts of the whole machine.

Penciling.

It is very nearly true, as has been said, that every mechanical drawing is, in the first instance, penciled; if this is so, then more work is done with the pencil than with the pen; therefore the first attention of the student of mechanical drawing should be directed to the following instructions for penciling a drawing.

With all necessary materials in hand, and in good order for the beginning of a drawing, the first thing to do is to pin the paper on the board quite square.

To do this effectively, lay the paper flat and put on the T-square with its head at the left side of the board; slide the square up nearly to the top, and arrange the paper level with the blade; with the right hand hold the paper still and move the square down a little; now, pin the top of the paper with thumb-tacks.

Next, pressing the square lightly to the paper, slide it down to the bottom and pin that part of the paper to the board. The paper must not project outside or over the edges of the board, and the pins or tack-heads should be forced down flush with the paper, so as not to interfere with the free movement of the tee-square up and down the board as occasion may require.

The accuracy of the work depending upon their condition, it is first needful to see that the pencil and pencil compasses are properly sharpened. Reference is made to valuable directions contained on pages beginning with 55, under the heading of "Free-hand Drawing," to which may be added that—

All lines should be drawn with the pencil slightly inclined in the direction in which it is moved.

Fig. 211.

Any and all lines not needed in the finished drawing should be erased at one time after the final lines have been determined, for the surface of the paper is soiled very quickly when worked upon after erasures have been made.

The working lines and other lines that are to be removed should be erased when the drawing is ready to finish and before its outlines have been strengthened, in order that the final lines may be left in perfect condition.

To show where the lines meet or terminate it is needful that all pencil lines pass the actual ending place, making a distinct intersection. This does not apply to "inking in" the lines, but rather to prevent the over-drawing of the ink lines, because the edge of the rule and the pen itself obstruct or partly cover the view of the line, it is very liable to pass over or beyond the required point in inking the lines, which must not occur.

In the preliminary operation of producing a regular mechanical or instrumental drawing, it is necessary to make a "sketch," in pencil, of the object to be represented. The AMERICAN MACHINIST has given in a few words the order to be followed, in effecting the best results; we quote, as follows:

"In making a free-hand sketch of an object from the model it is well to observe the following order: Look the model over carefully and determine the number of views necessary to illustrate it fully, drawing the same, free-hand, in their proper relation to each other, on sketching paper. Look the sketch over carefully to see that nothing has been omitted, and put on dimension lines, after which scale the model carefully and put on dimensions. Do not put in the dimensions at the same time the dimension lines are drawn; have all the dimension lines in place before attempting to insert dimensions.

"Follow the same order in making the drawing with instruments as was used in making the sketch; that is, draw the views in their proper relation to each other, put in dimension lines, then dimensions, and lastly notes and title. If section drawing is made, do not draw section lines in pencil."

POINTS TO BE OBSERVED IN SKETCHING.

1. Especial attention is to be paid to outlines—edges of plane surfaces are lines; when a line is made it represents the edge or outside of something.

2. Learn to be accurate before being rapid.

3. A sketch should be intelligible to any one, even if they are unacquainted with drawing.

4. Horizontal and vertical lines and a few curves will enable one to make almost any simple sketch.

5. It must be also remembered in making drawings from actual measurement that the instruments are not in the first place employed; the rough sketch is first made and then it is converted into a drawing. The draughtsman makes a rough sketch entirely by the hand and eye, measures the various parts, and jots down the measurements in his sketch; after this he reduces the whole to the desired scale, and proceeds to make his mechanical drawing.

6. Let the sketch book be the constant companion of the student; it may be advantageously filled with outlines of machine or other work suitable for preservation, to be made into finished drawings, or for reference. Sketches are often valuable for reference as aids in originating new designs.

7. A sketch, when possible, should have all the dimensions written upon it, but—

8. Sketches in shop practice should not take the place of working-drawings; the latter have a check upon them in being drawn to a scale—hence the figures written upon them and dimensions by scale must agree.

9. Place title and date on each sketch—no matter how seemingly unimportant—for future reference.

10. Practice sketching at every favorable opportunity. There is no necessity for detail at first—simply the outlines of the article and its parts.

11. Sketch-books, with paper bound in cloth covers, are utilized for bold, off-hand sketches by experienced draughtsmen, but a single sheet of paper, used on both sides, is not unworthy of service in an emergency—or even the blank side of a letter may be available. Sketching-blocks, or paper "pads," 4×6, or more, in size, and containing 48 sheets, are sold by stationers, and are found to be most convenient to have in hand and for practical use. Portfolio-envelopes, made of extra length paper (manila) are useful in filing away sketches and drawings. The size $10\frac{1}{2} \times 15$ is used for United States Patent Office drawings.

The function of the pencil—in mechanical drawing—is to make a path for the pen to follow. If it were possible to make a drawing with all its lines ending at the proper place, at the first time, there would be no necessity for using the pencil. One is obliged, however, so to use the pencil that all lines pass beyond the actual ending place, thus making a distinct point for the drawing pen to stop at.

The pencil should be pressed to the paper just enough to make a clean, fine line, and no more; once over the path is sufficient, if the line is visible and true.

To sharpen drawing pencils, 1, use a fine file, after taking off enough of the wood with a knife; 2, make a conical point for the free-hand drawing pencils and a chisel point for ruling and marking distances.

Pencil compasses are instruments where one leg is provided with a pencil point. Fig. 209 shows the mode of manipulation of those shown in fig. 180 and fig. 181.

The pencil compass is held by the projection above the joint between the thumb and first finger, which enables it to be rotated by a movement of the finger without causing any undue pressure on the points. Should much pressure be applied, there is a tendency to force the point or center through the paper, making an ugly center mark; at the same time the pressure tends to break off the pencil point.

These few illustrations from fig. 212 to fig. 219 are made designedly simple, so that they may be utilized in "free-hand" work, for which they are good practice, as well as serving for examples in mechanical drawing.

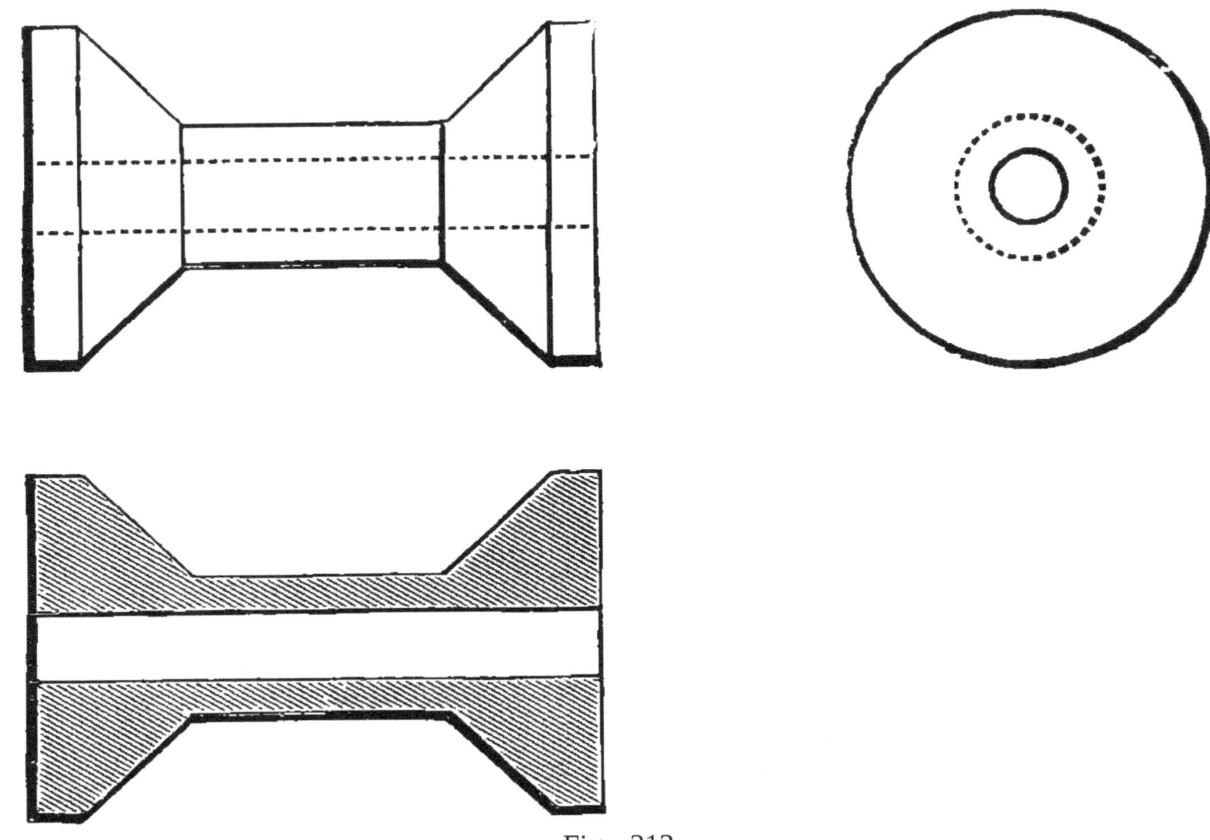

Figs. 212.

Figs. 212, showing a spool or bobbin, exhibit three views, viz.: front elevation or plan, and section; both are drawn with simple lines, the end elevation by circles.

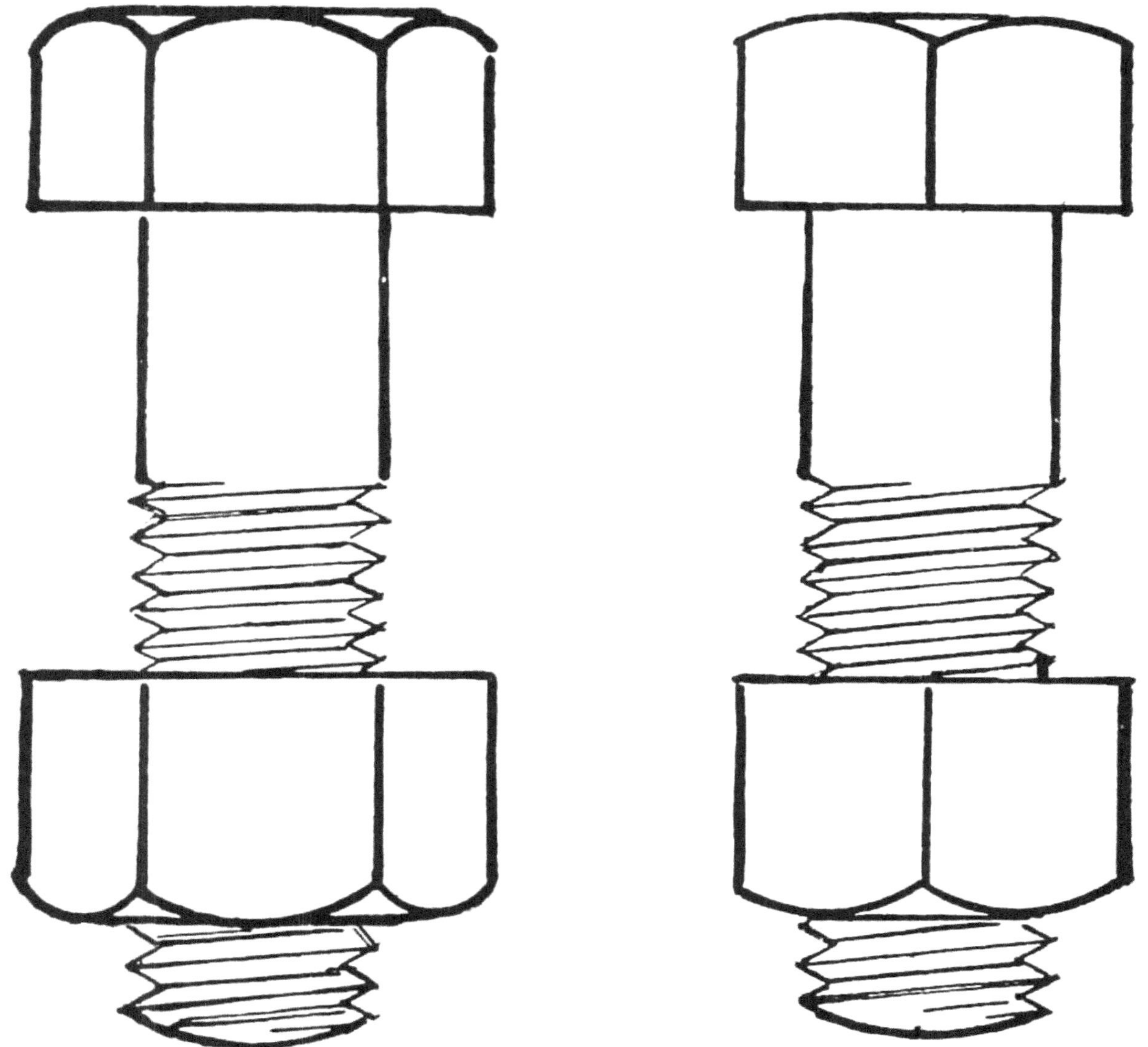

Fig. 213.—Fig. 214.

Figs. 213 and 214 are two side views of a hexagon head bolt. Figs. 216 and 217 are a square head bolt—two side views and end view. Figs. 218 and 219 are a front and edge view of a forked or double joint.

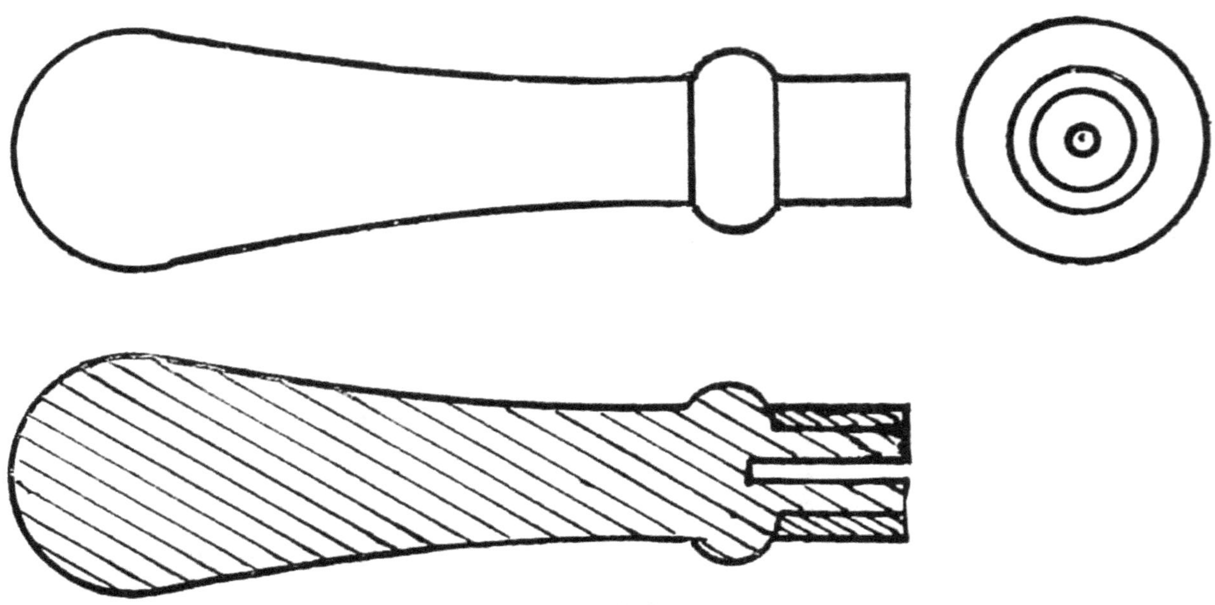

Figs. 215.

Figs. 215 show three views of a file handle; the front view and section are practice for compound curves and curved lines meeting straight ones; all these are capable of being produced by instruments.

Moreover, many of the views and illustrations used to instruct and explain machine tools and other devices in other parts of the volume, are drawn so that they may be used also as examples in advanced instrumental practice. This is a "hint" to the diligent and painstaking student worthy of remembering.

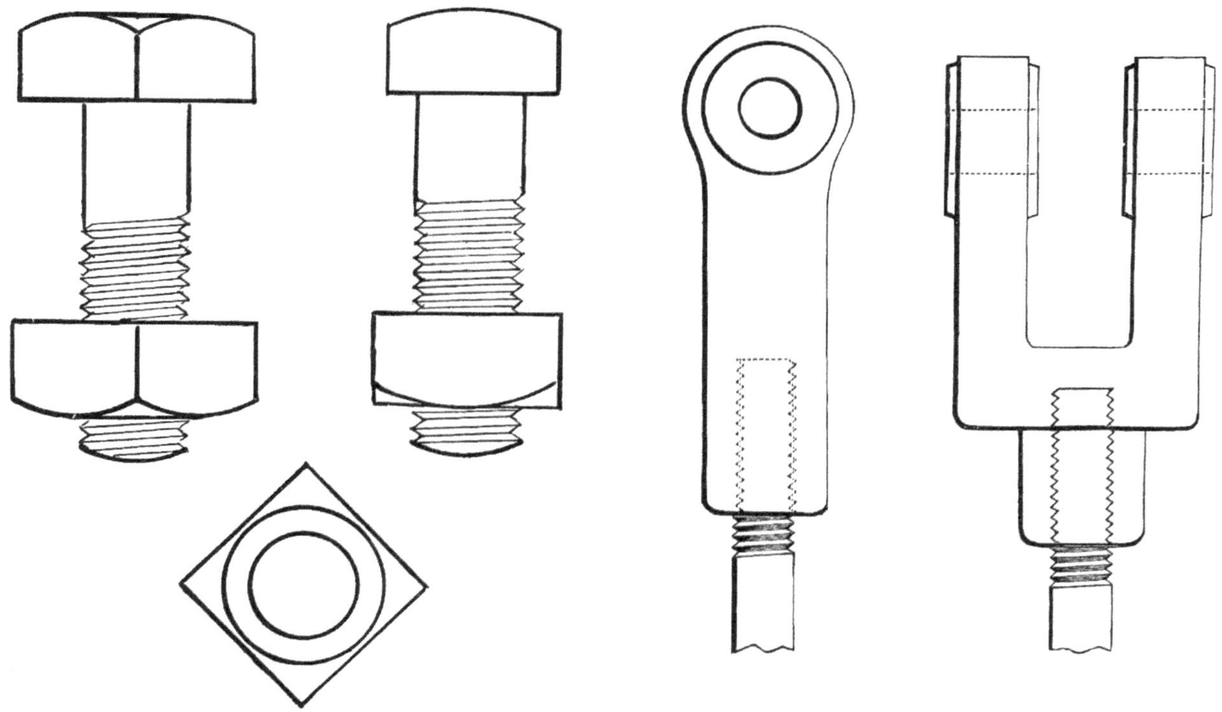

Fig. 216.—Fig. 217.—Fig. 218.—Fig. 219.

The designing and drawing of arcs and whole circles occupy a large proportion of space in nearly all mechanical drawings. The making of a complete circle is a matter of no great difficulty, but the beginning and termination of parts of circles require both judgment and considerable practice.

To aid the student these two illustrations of circles are introduced. To draw fig. 220 with a pencil, using the upper edge of the blade of the T-square as a guide, draw a center line, *A B*, mark on it a distance of 4 inches, space this into half inches, using the dividers and making the points with it; then with the pencil compasses or bow pencil, which must be held as shown on page 209, and rotated from left to right, or clockwise, draw a series of circles through these points, tangent to one another or all touching at *A*, care being taken that the pencil lines exactly meet at *A*, and also cut the divided points as shown in the illustration. For fig. 221 divide the center line as before, and draw the semi-circles on it *A B*, *B C*, meeting at *B*, and *C D*, *D E*, etc.

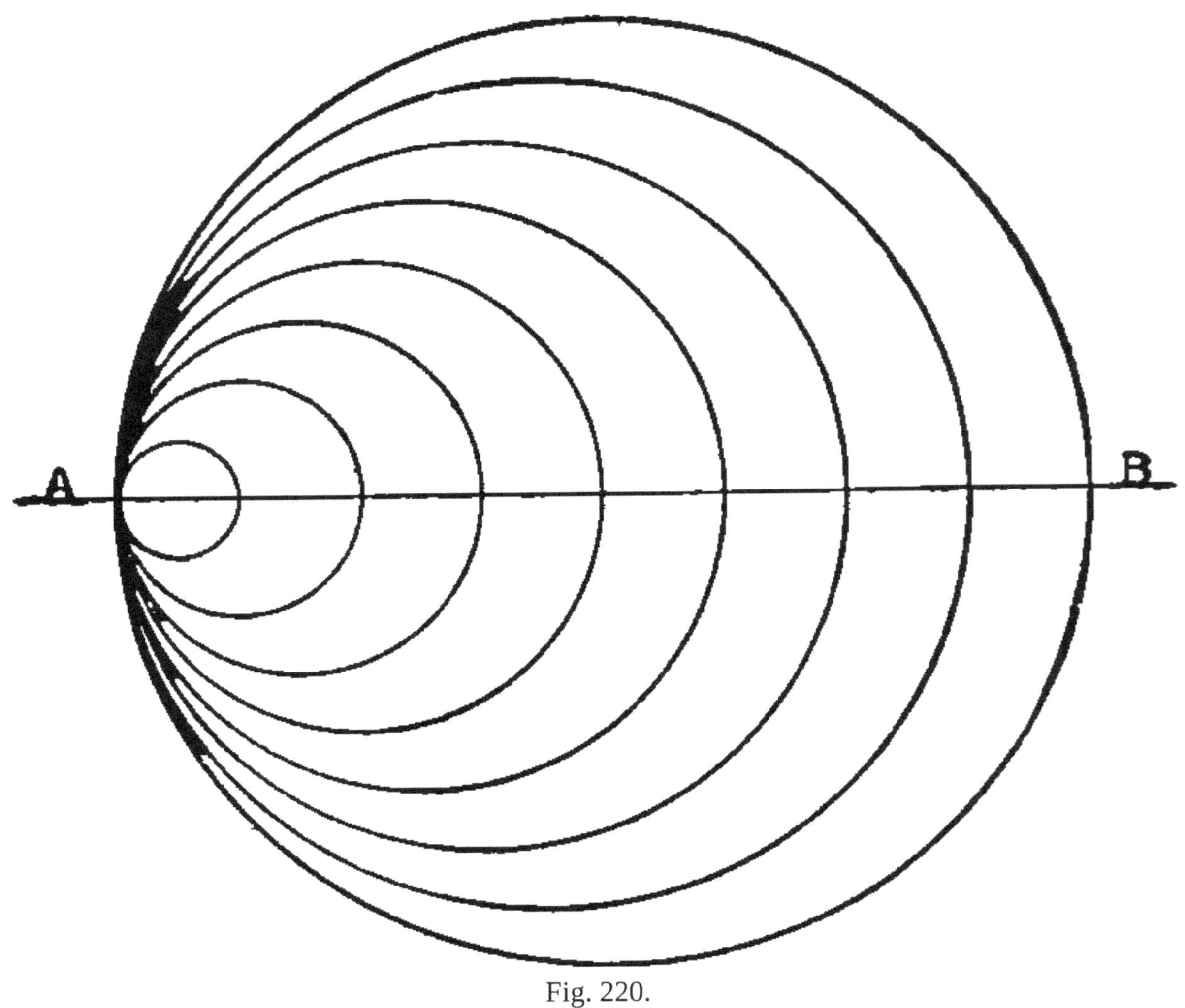

Fig. 220.

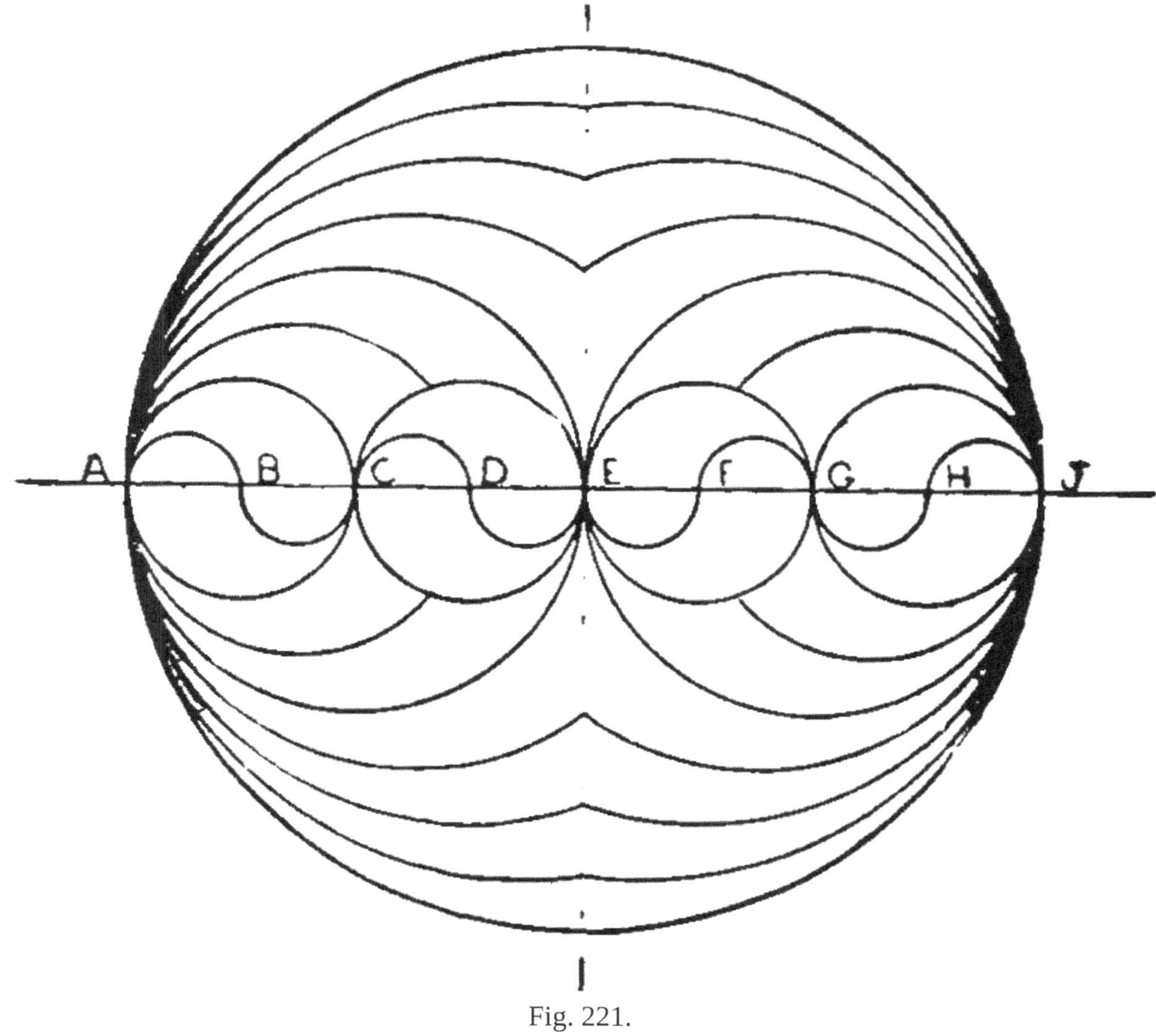

Fig. 221.

Now from center *B* draw circles *A C, C E*, meeting in *C*, and so on with the circles, arcs or segments; success in drawing this figure depends on the correct spacing of the center line in the first instance into equal parts.

The T-square should be used for drawing horizontal lines only. Its head should always be placed upon the left edge of the board. Vertical lines should be drawn by the use of a triangle placed upon the T-square and not by means of the T-square only; because the edges of a board are seldom at right angles to each other, and the blade of the T-square is often not at right angles to the head, so that lines at right angles to each other will not result from the use of the T-square upon all edges of the board. Only the upper edge of the T-square should be used, as the edges are often not quite straight or parallel.

The 45° triangle has two angles of 45° and one of 90°. The 30° and 60° triangle has an angle of 30°, one of 60°, and one of 90°. By placing these triangles upon the T-square, lines at any of these angles with a vertical or horizontal line may be drawn.

Drawings finished in ink are much more effective and desirable than pencil drawings; but as a good inked drawing cannot be made except upon an accurate pencil drawing, students should begin with the pencil, and should not use ink until they are able to produce satisfactory results in pencil.

Projection.

The word projection means to throw forward, and in ordinary machine drawing it is the projecting or throwing forward of one view from another view.

In drawings the lines in one view or plan may be availed of to find those of others of the same object, and also to find their shape or curvature as they would appear in the other representations; this is called projection-drawing.

Fig. 222 is the illustration as shown in fig. 212 on page 143, with the addition of dotted projection line, which illustrates the method of throwing forward the section and the end view of the object; these two views are procured from the plan or first figure, as shown in fig. 222.

Fig. 224 represents the square bolt and nut shown in fig. 216, and the mode of projecting is similarly shown by dotted lines.

Fig. 223 shows file handle shown in fig. 215 and the mode of projecting.

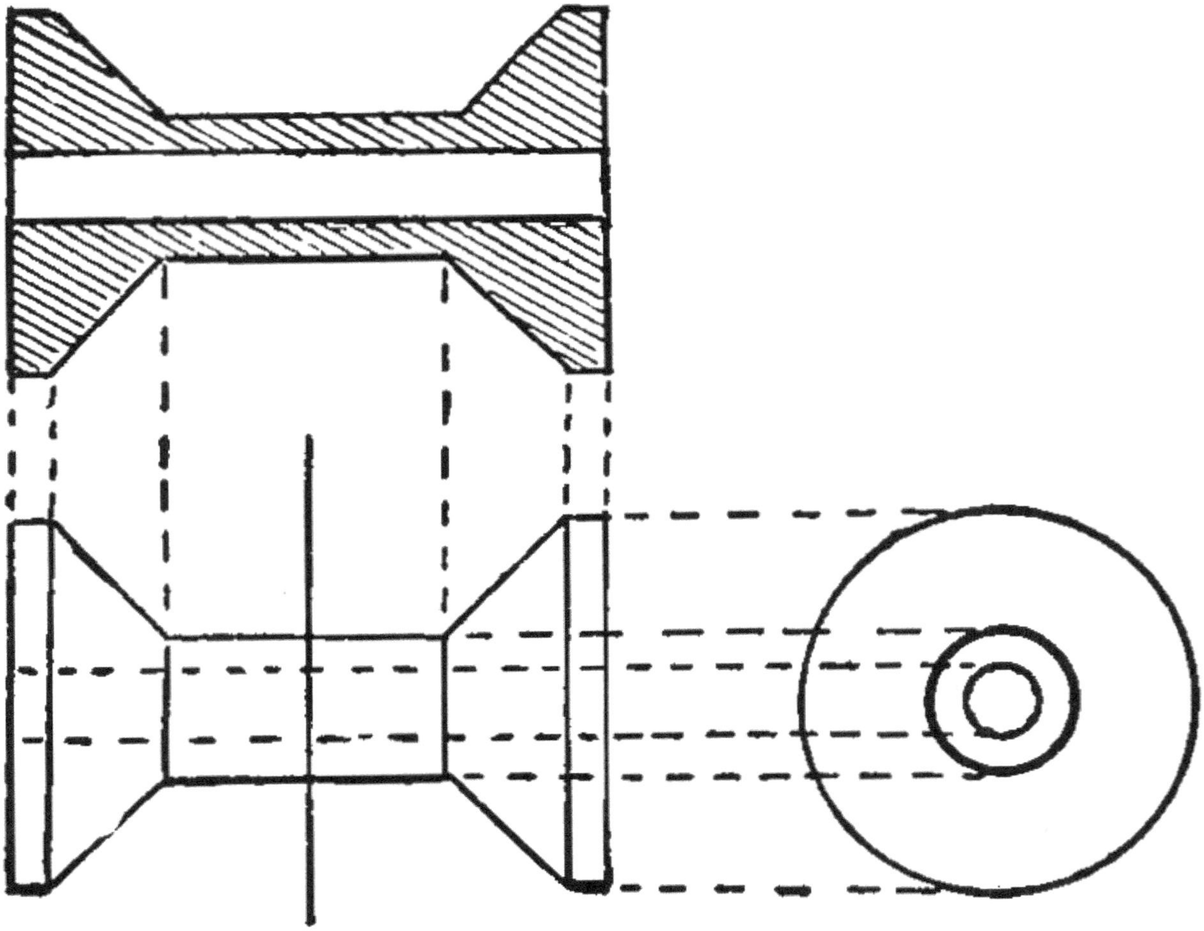

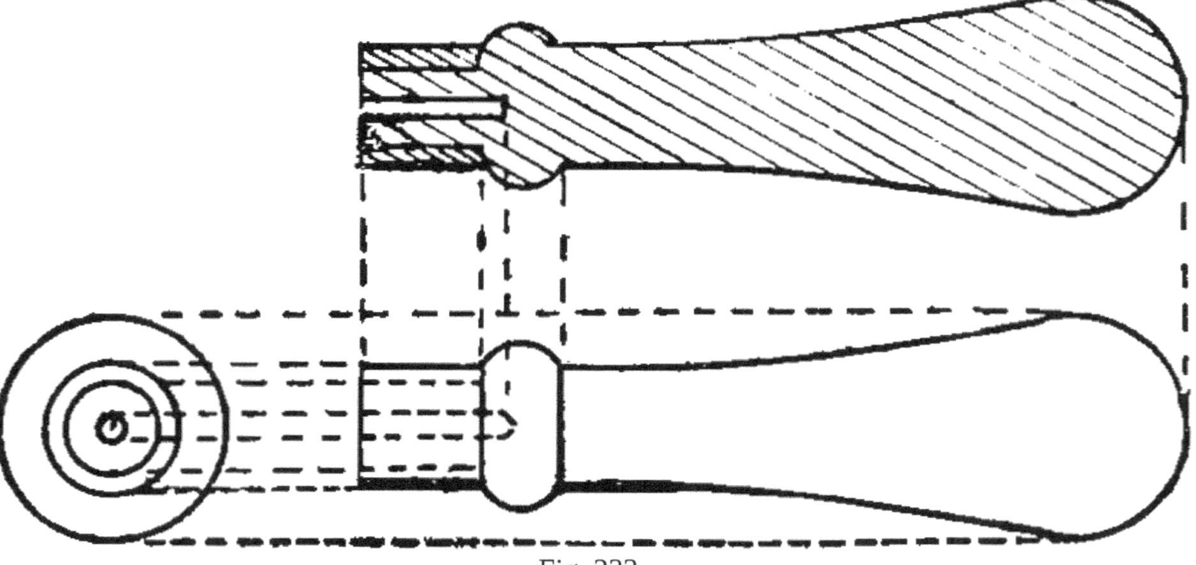

Fig. 222.

Fig. 223.

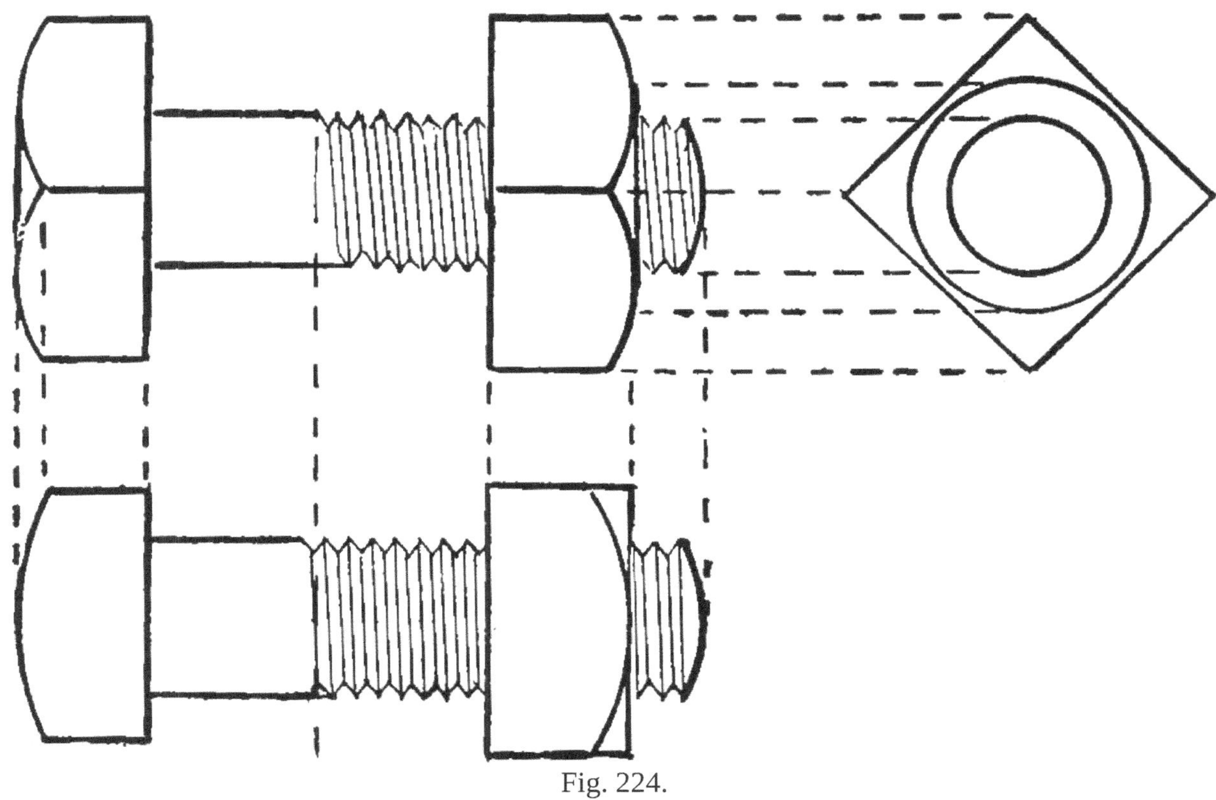

Fig. 224.

The principles upon which "projection" in drawing is based, are illustrated in the following examples and text: As a real object can be scaled with a foot rule, so a drawing must permit of scaling and measuring. This measuring may take place as with the real object in full size or the drawing may, for the sake of convenience, be reproduced and measured in a reduced scale, as half, or in still smaller sizes. Sometimes it may prove convenient to enlarge the drawing to twice the natural size of the object, as a means of making it stand out more clearly than the real size would accomplish.

For practical purposes, it is productive of economy of time to mark the dimensions of height and width or depth on the drawing in figures, to avoid the scaling. This marking of the dimensions is best done at the time of making the drawing, while the conception of the object is clear.

To convey a correct impression of the object, all lines that are marked to be of equal length should appear equally long on the drawing and be capable of being scaled to such equal length; for this, it must be assumed that the eye of the observer is equally distant from all points of a plane through the nearest point, or one of the axes of the object, and that the lines of sight are all parallel to each other and square to this plane.

In fig. 225 these lines of sight are seen as directed toward one side of a cube or block; it will be readily understood, however, that in this way nothing is visible and accessible for scaling and dimensioning except this front face of the block, thus, a determination of the dimensions of only height and width would be possible, while the dimension of depth is entirely undetermined.

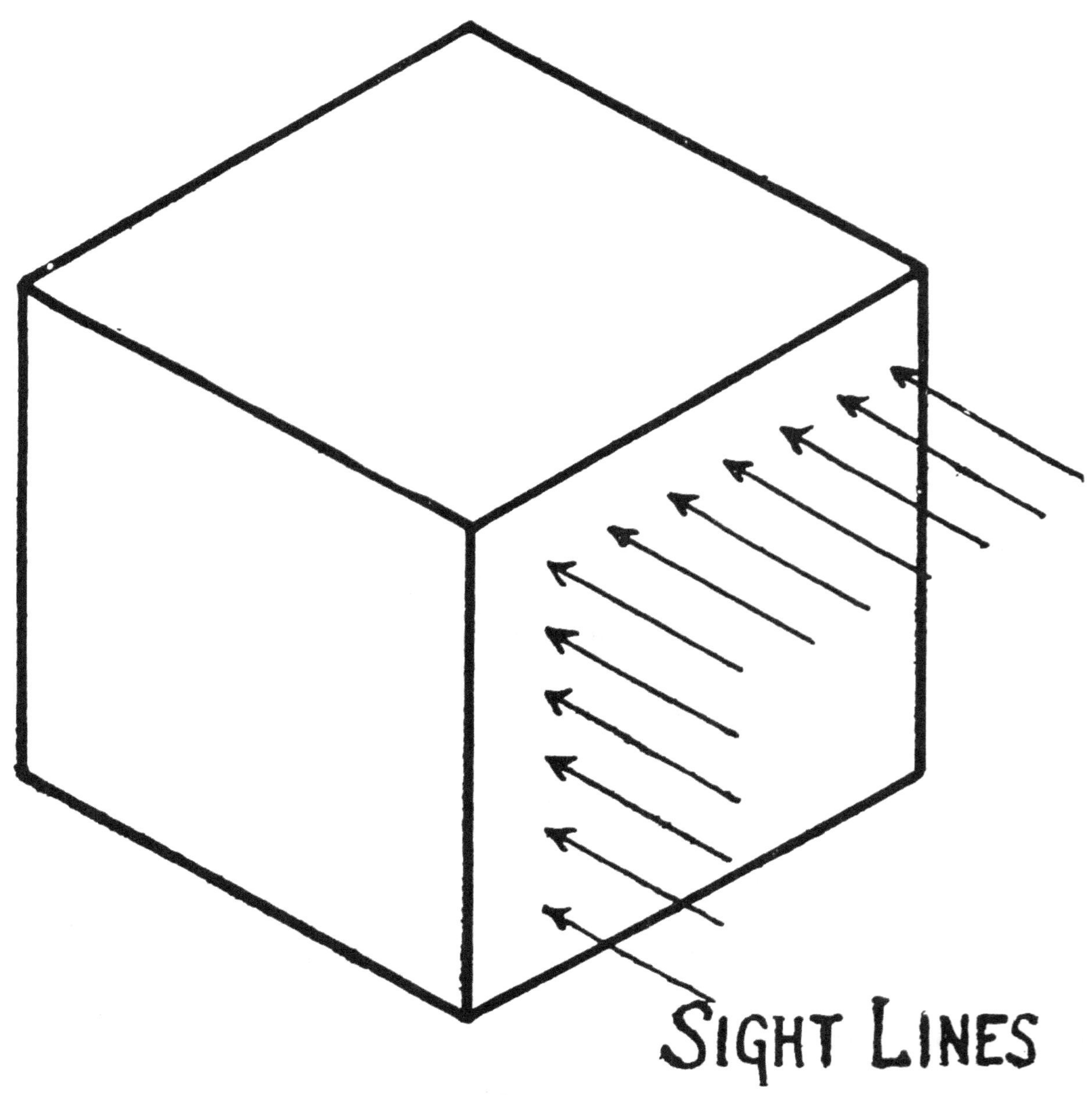

Fig. 225.

It is thus necessary to get a view of the block from another side; the direction in which it will be most instructive to obtain additional views is in the direction of the breadth and of the length and square to the lines of sight of the first view.

Fig. 226 shows how the lines of sight would strike the object in the three directions. If these lines should be rays of light, some of them would pass by the body until they squarely strike the large plane surfaces, *I, II, III*; naturally the rays of light on the faces of the object will be retained, and cannot strike the plane surfaces, thus leaving dark shadows of exactly the same outlines as the block; these would be exact drawings of the faces, and if by some means they can be fixed and retained on the plane they can be completely measured and dimensioned.

This throwing forward of the outline of the object in different views on the planes is called projection of the object, and furnishes a highly important means of fixing the outlines and dimensions in the three main directions of height, width and depth; evidently, the light rays passing by the front face may not all reach the plane of projection, but they may be retained by protruding parts of the object behind the front face. These protruding parts naturally would also be projected on the plane in the same manner as the main body of the block.

These projections of the protruding part are plainly visible in plane *II* and plane *III*, while the part would not be drawn in outline in plane *I*. It may be imagined, however, that the greater thickness of the body in the direction of the protruding part would intensify also the shadow, thus outlining the face of the protruding part in plane *I*.

It is apparent that these three projections are all needed, but as drawing is all done in one single plane, the three projections will for the sake of convenience have to be brought into a single plane. This can be realized if plane *II* is swung around axis *O Z* and plane *III* around axis *O Y*, until all three surfaces are in one single plane, which would then appear as shown in fig. 227.

It is also possible to assume transparent planes in front of the body and extend the parallel lines of sight forward instead of backward. Thus an outline picture will be created on each of the three planes *I, II, III* in fig. 228, in a manner similar to fig. 226. For drawing purposes, all three views again have to be brought into a single plane, which is done by swinging *II* around *O Z*, and *III* around *O Y* in the same manner as fig. 227 was evolved from fig. 226.

It will be noted that in fig. 229 plane *III* is now above *I* and plane *II* on the left-hand side of *I*, while in fig. 227 they were below and at the right-hand side of plane *I*. As the swinging of the top and side planes takes place around the edges of the front plane *I* two systems may thus be distinguished, according to the position of plane *I* in regard to the object. Fig. 226 thus represents the system of backward projection, while fig. 228 represents the system of forward projection.

Either system can have, however, the plane *II* at the right- or left-hand side edge, while plane *III* may be attached to the top or bottom edge of plane *I*; it is readily understood that a number of combinations are possible for each system, as it is not necessary to adhere absolutely to one rule. The system of forward projection is the one generally practiced and further examples are all executed by this system, meaning that the planes are always between the observer and the object.

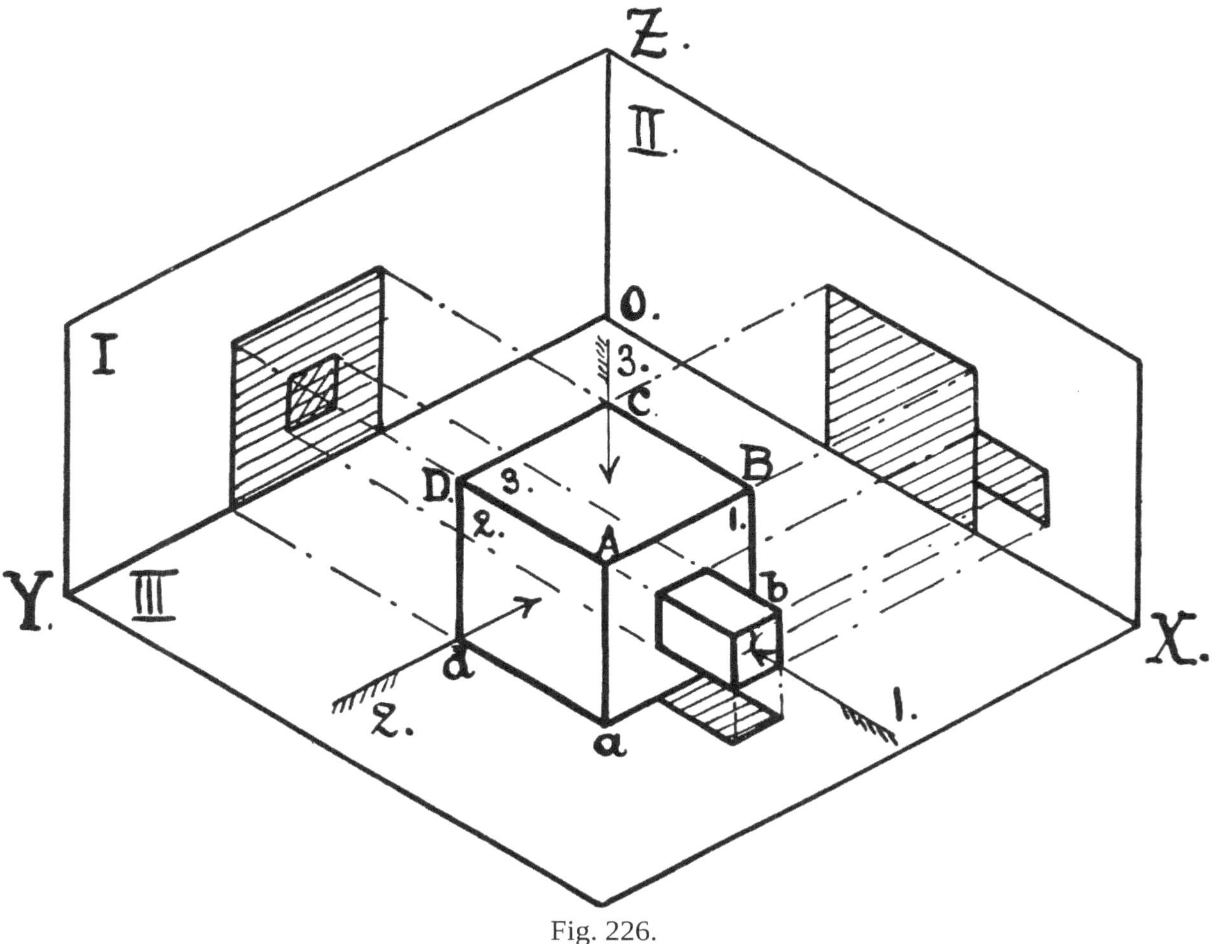

Fig. 226.

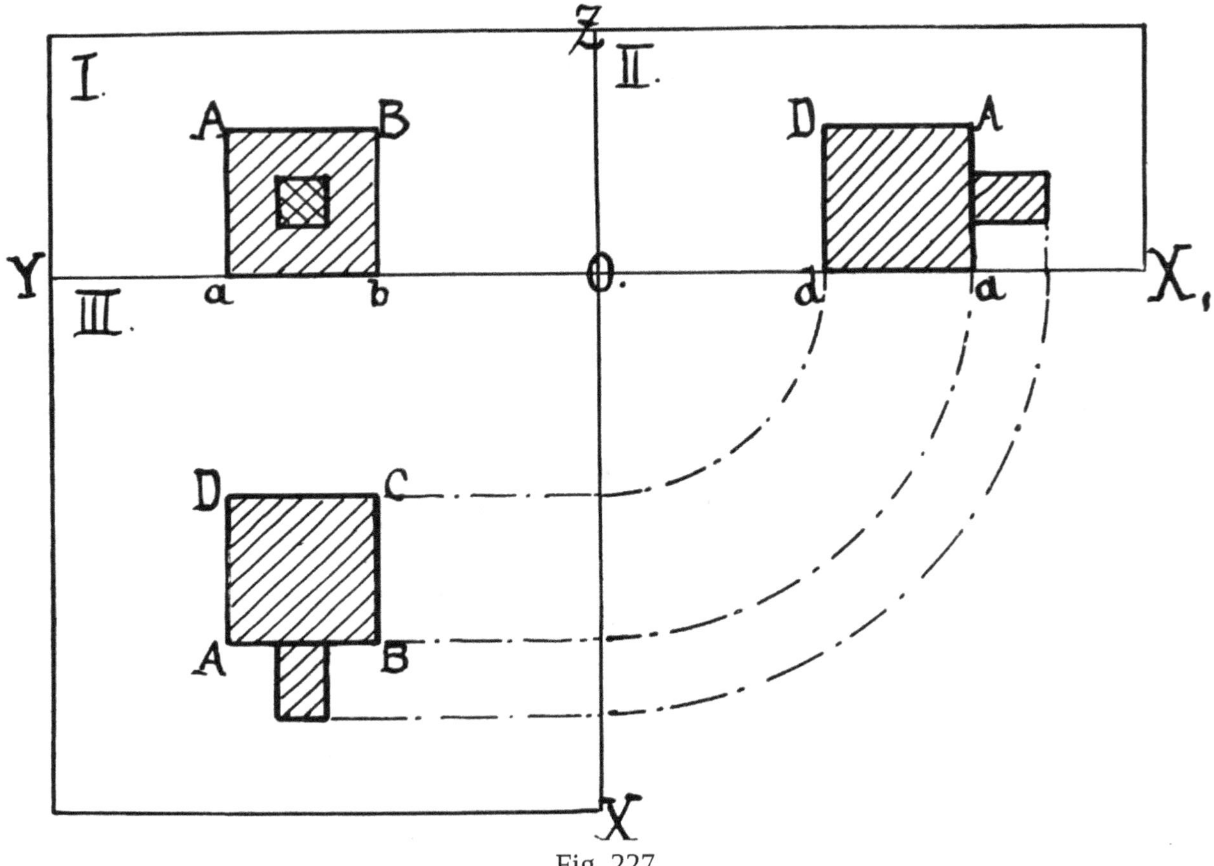

Fig. 227.

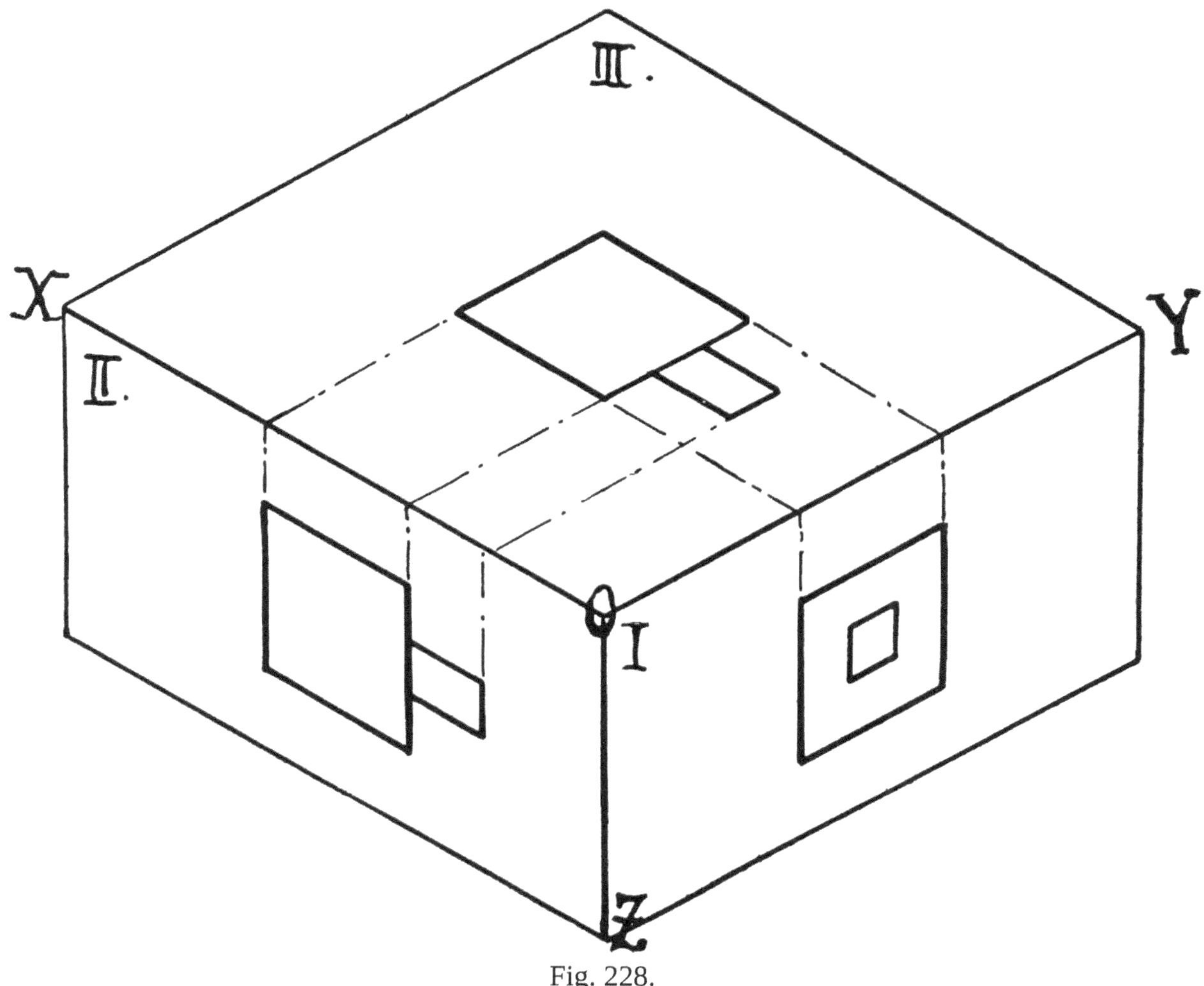

Fig. 228.

For the clearness of the drawing, it is desirable to have all corners, edges and outlines appear in such solid lines as they appear to the eye. If, therefore, certain sharply defined outlines occur on one side more than on the opposite one, it is most desirable to take the view against the side that has the most definitely marked outlines.

If the opposite side should show a number of wholly different features, it may prove even desirable to show this side also, thus gaining four views instead of the usual three, and so obtain a more complete understanding of the shape of the object, besides giving increased facilities for dimensioning each part of the body.

This additional view may be taken from the sides, as well as up or down, thus making a maximum of five views possible by which the outside of the object may be delineated.

Fig. 230 shows why it may be desirable to take five views of a block that has a receding space of different outlines in each of the side and top and bottom faces.

It is not necessary, however, to resort to five views in such a case as is represented in fig. 230, as the only differing feature, the circular space in *III* bottom, might be shown in *III* top by dotted lines, and the difference of *II* right might be shown in *II* left, also by dotted lines. It is desirable to show four or five views only where great complication and consequent lack of clearness through numerous dotted lines would result from having a less number of views.

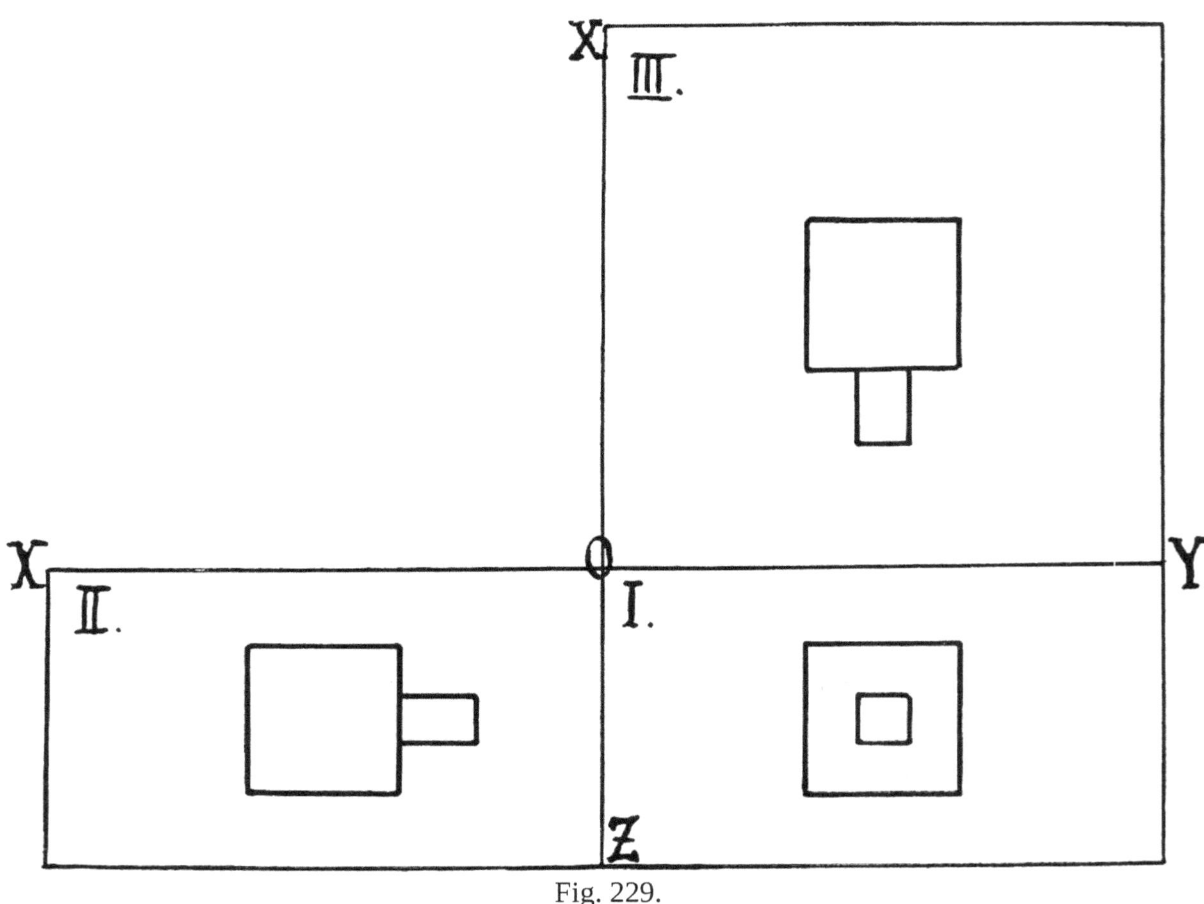

Fig. 229.

So far the projections and views have only represented the outlines of the object; it may often be desirable, however, to show central holes or other perforations or variations of sections; in this case it is possible to imagine the object cut in slices, by planes, through certain well defined axes, or other lines of distinctive importance, and then take a view of this sectional plane with its newly created intersections or sharply marked outlines; thus, a section may often take the place of the third, fourth or fifth view to great advantage.

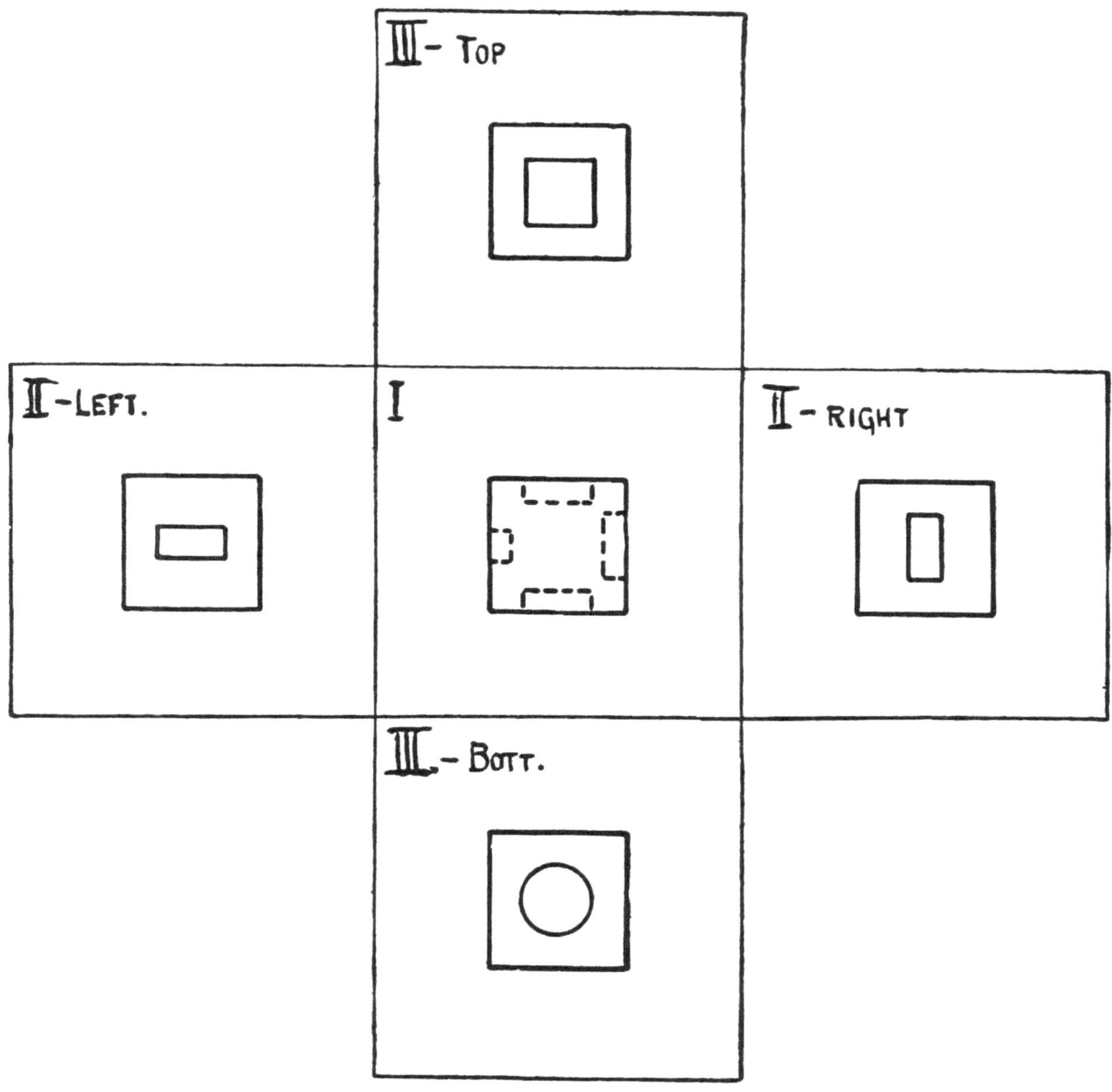

Fig. 230.

It is not always possible to get a view against a face or side of the object, but, with irregularly shaped bodies or under special conditions, it may be necessary to take a view of corners, sloping planes, curved or irregularly shaped surfaces.

Fig. 231 shows a hexagonal nut in the three normal projections; from the top view it is readily seen that the front view shows the side of the hexagon in a contracted scale, and that therefore the scaling and dimensioning for the horizontal direction have all to be done in the top or plan view; the front and side views convey, however, the dimension of height correctly, and these are therefore the right places for scaling and dimensioning in the vertical direction.

Fig. 231 shows how a cylindrical outline appears in the three views; the hole in the nut presents itself as circular in the top view, while it appears in the front and side views as a rectangle. For simple objects, it is unnecessary to show the edges of the planes, and the three views are grouped, as regards distances and positions, as most convenient for the execution of the drawing.

Where sloping surfaces are of irregular form, it may be necessary to employ help lines for their full determination in the three views. Fig. 232 shows how the surface that is produced by a slanting cut through a cylinder would appear in the three views. The help lines are placed in the top view in eight equal divisions around the circumference of the cylinder. These division lines are shown by dotted lines on the cylinder in the front and side views. Their intersections, with the sloping cut in the front view, furnish also the height of the corresponding points for the side view.

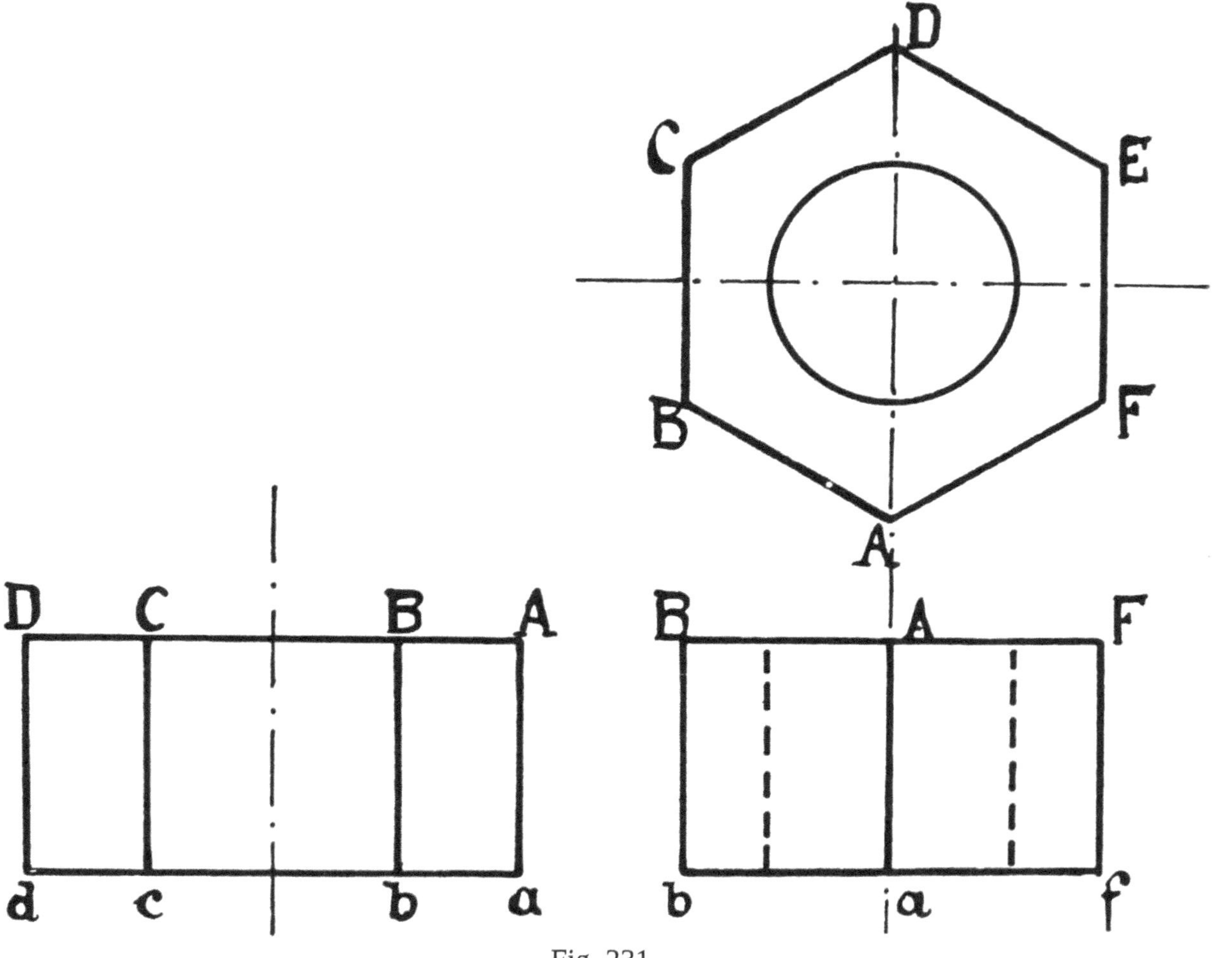

Fig. 231.

By progressive determination of points, lines and surfaces, even the most complicated bodies can be completely represented for their reproduction in any application to mechanical or industrial purposes.

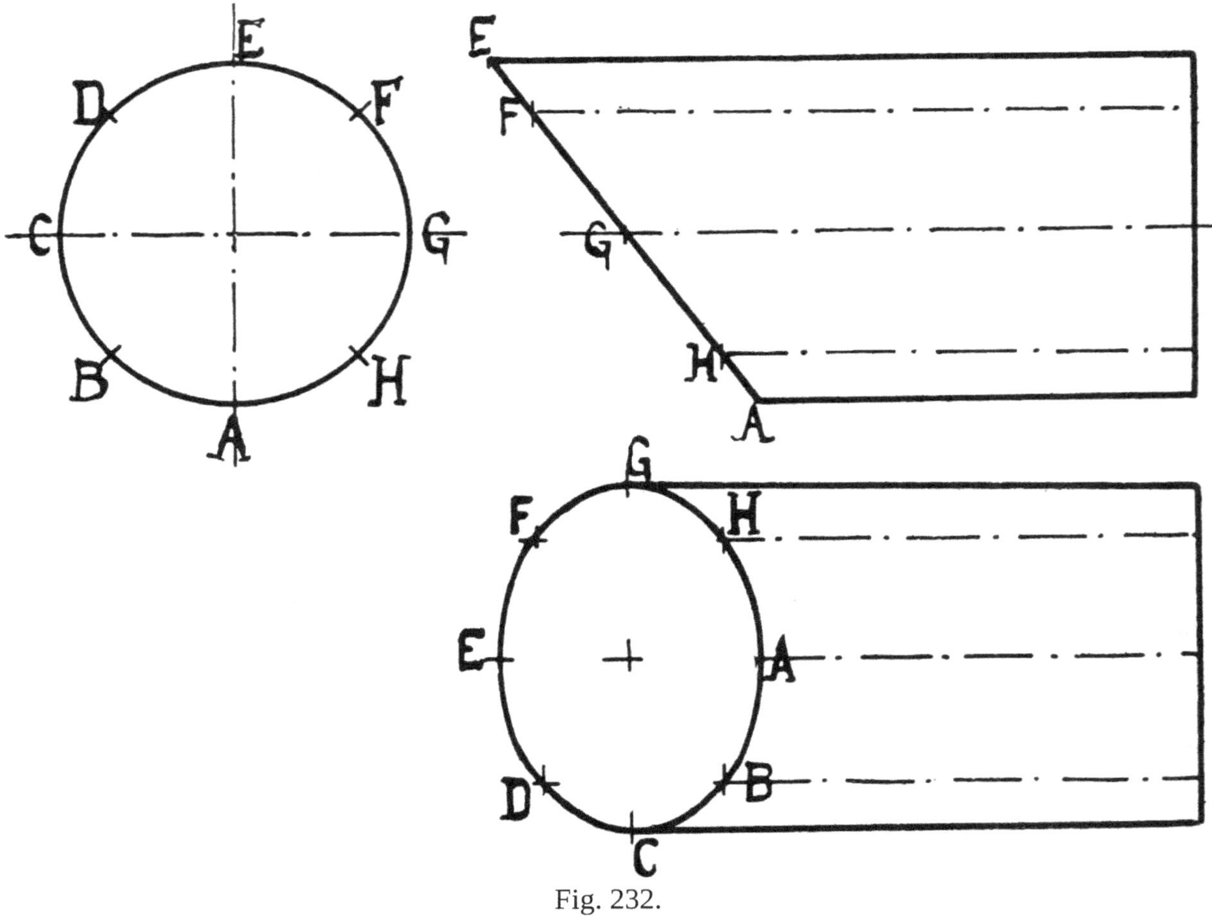

Fig. 232.

The spur wheel shown on page 163 is an example of projection drawing.

The wheel is illustrated in three views: fig. 235 is a side view, or elevation; fig. 234 is a front elevation; fig. 233 is a section view on *C D*. The section is projected from the front elevation by drawing parallel lines from the points in front elevation where the lines are intersected by the center line *C D*, cutting the plane of view and showing the interior shape at *C D*.

The side elevation, fig. 235, is projected from the front elevation, fig. 234, by drawing parallel lines from the edges in the front view across its face.

In actual drawing practice the figures should be made about three times larger than the example, and as follows:

For the front elevation draw the center lines *A B*, *C D*, and from their point of intersection as a center, with the compasses draw the inner circle or hole, also the pitch line *E E*. With the dividers space this line into nineteen equal divisions; each point on this line will be the center of a tooth, and the distance from one point to the next one is the pitch of the tooth.

Now, with the dividers mark off the thickness of tooth at each side of these points on pitch line; with the compasses draw the outer circle for points of teeth, the inner circle for the root of teeth, and circles for thickness of rim and hub; also circles representing the fillets at rim and hub. For clearness and to prevent confusion these lines are shown on one-half the wheel only, terminating in center line *C D*; all the lines of the front elevation are now complete excepting the teeth.

In the drawing office it is unusual to delineate all the teeth in a gear wheel, the lines without the teeth as now completed being deemed sufficient, giving all particulars; however, to prevent the error of mistaking the circles it is well to represent one or two teeth on the drawing.

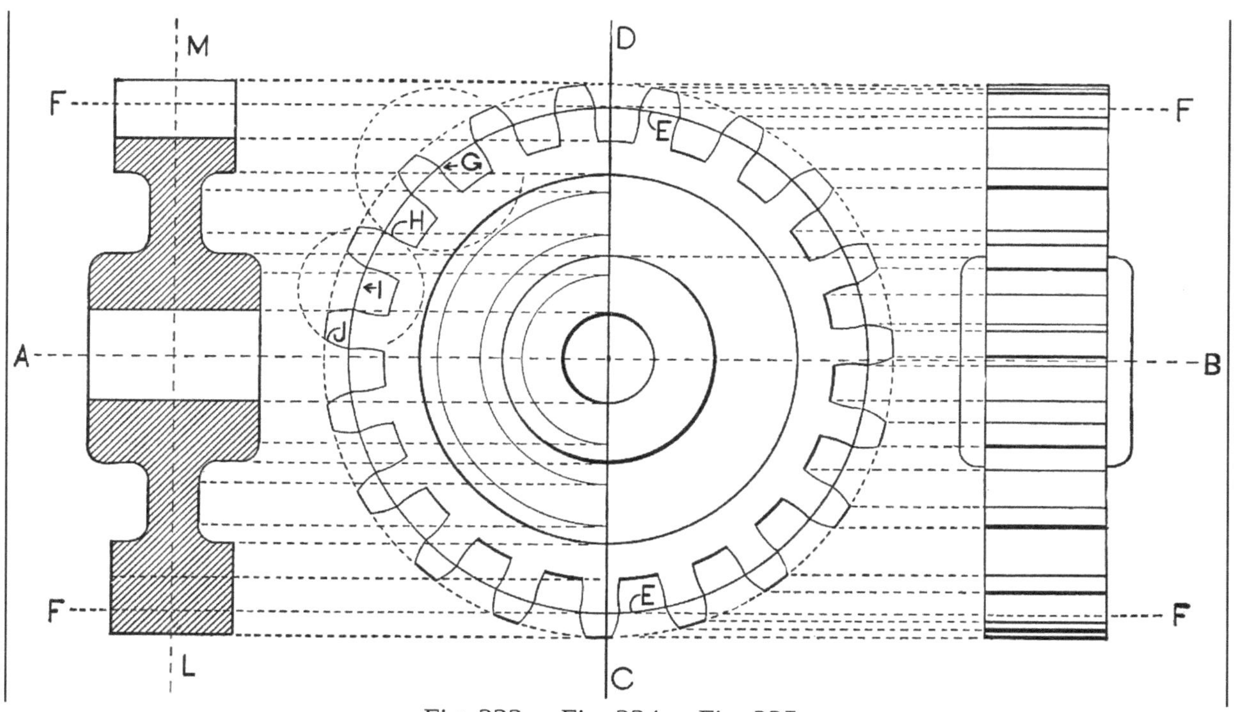

Fig. 233.—Fig. 234.—Fig. 235.

In the example, proceed and complete the entire wheel, taking on the compasses a radius equal to the pitch of the tooth; set them on the pitch line at the point *G*, already spaced for thickness of tooth, draw line *H* from pitch line to root of tooth; proceed similarly all around the circle, completing one side. Next, reverse the operation and draw the corresponding side of the root of tooth. Now take a radius equal to half the space between teeth and the thickness of tooth on pitch line, and, with center in pitch line, as shown at *I*, draw the outside or addendum of tooth, *J*; it will be apparent that the reverse addendum of the tooth next adjoining can be formed at the same time, with one setting of the compasses; finish all the teeth similarly; the front elevation will thus be completed.

Fig. 233 is an excellent example of sectional drawing, to be executed as follows:

First draw the center line *L M* of fig. 233, lay off at each side of it half the breadth of face and of the hub; now project, from center line *C D*, in the front elevation, fig. 234, with the T-square the upper and lower teeth, the fillets, the chamfers, the hub and center hole, also dot in the pitch line *F F*, take the radii and draw the fillets and chamfers; draw section lines and the view will appear as shown in fig. 233.

Fig. 235 is a side elevation of fig. 234, and is a fine sample of projection, to be executed as follows:

Proceed similarly as for fig. 233, projecting the lines from the outside edges of the front elevation, instead of from the center line *C D* as in last figure, and the end elevation will be as shown in fig. 235.

The student will be assisted in understanding this working drawing by consulting the pages under the heading of "Gearing."

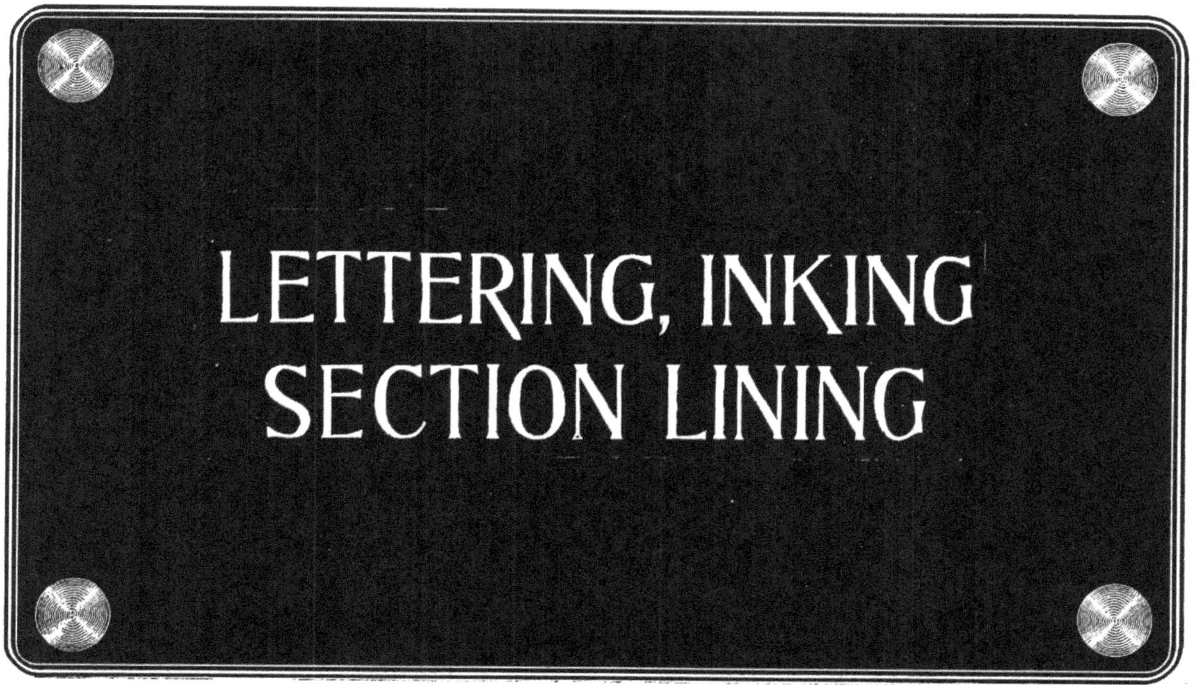

LETTERING, INKING
SECTION LINING

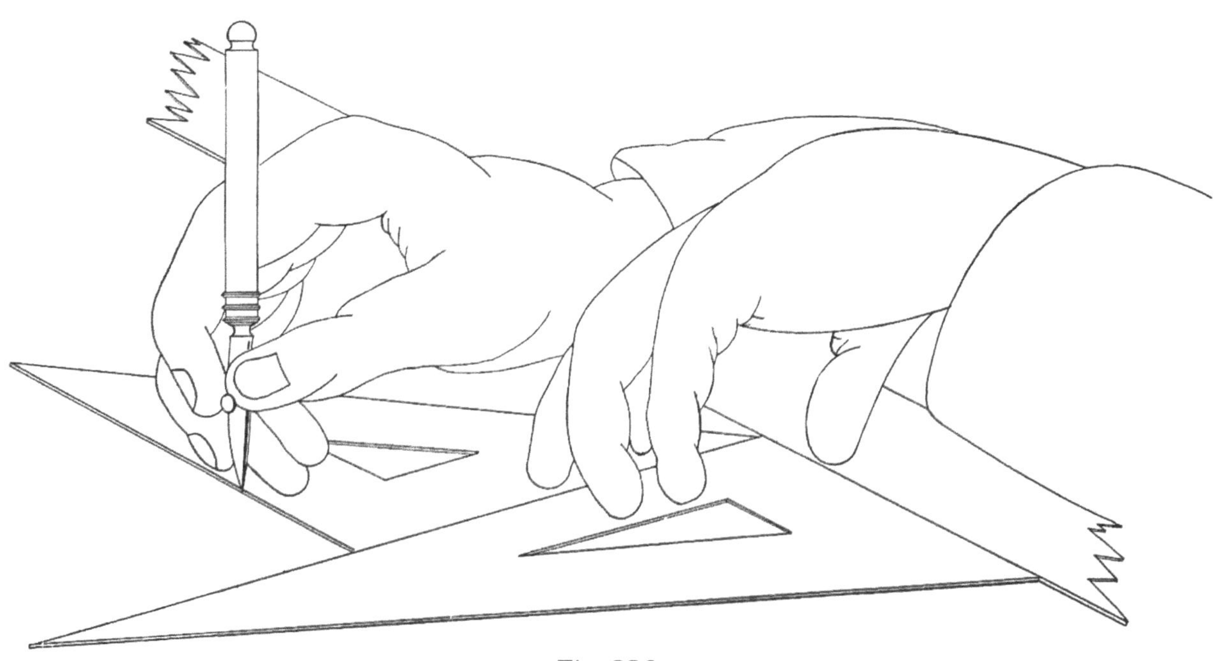

Fig. 236.

"Inking In" Drawings.

When a drawing is completely finished in penciling, it should next be "inked in" for preservation.

Care should be used that the pen may be perfectly clean; the pen should be held nearly vertical, leaning just enough to prevent it from catching on the paper; the pen should be held between the thumb and first and second fingers, the knuckles being bent, so that it may be at right angles with the length of the hand.

The ink should be rubbed up fresh whenever it is about to be used, for it is better to waste a little time in preparing ink slowly than to be at a continual trouble with pens, which will occur if the ink is ground too rapidly or on a rough surface.

To test ink, a few lines can be drawn on the margin of a sheet, noting the shade, how the ink flows from the pen, and whether the lines are sharp. After the lines have dried, cross them with a wet brush; if they wash readily, the ink is too soft; if they resist the water for a time and then wash tardily, the ink is good.

Care must be exercised not to overload the pen with ink, and, like the pencil, the pen should always be moved from left to right and from the bottom to the top of the board. When inking, both "nibs" of the pen point must rest evenly on the paper and the pen be pressed only lightly against the T-square. Never ink any portion of a drawing until the penciling is complete.

In inking long, fine lines it is well to go over each line twice, without moving the T-square, trying not to widen the line on the second passage; also see that the pen contains ink enough to finish a line, as it is difficult to continue with the same width of line after re-filling.

To produce finished drawings, it is necessary that no portion should be erased, otherwise the color applied will be unequal in tone; thus, when highly finished mechanical drawings are required, it is usual to draw an original and to copy it. Where sufficient time cannot be given to draw and copy, a very good way is to take the surface off the paper with fine sandpaper before commencing the drawing; if this be done, the color will flow equally over any erasure it may be necessary to make afterwards.

The rules of procedure in drawing the lines in "inking" are, 1, ink in the small circles and curves; 2, ink in the larger circles and curves; 3, then all the horizontal lines, beginning at the top of the drawing and working downward; 4, next ink in all the vertical lines, commencing at the left and moving back to the right; 5, draw in the oblique lines; 6, all the center lines and dimension and reference lines. The figuring and lettering should be always done with India ink, thoroughly black; the last lines to be drawn are the section lines. The reason why irregular curves and arcs of circles are inked in first is, that it is easier to draw a straight line up to a curve than to take a curve up to a straight line.

In practice, the flat side of the drawing-pen is laid against the tee-square or ruler; the taper of the blade of the pen is sufficient to throw the point enough away from the edge to prevent blotting; the pen is drawn from left to right and from the bottom to the top of the board.

This is shown in fig. 237, intended to represent "short work" with the drawing-pen. The wrist is shown resting upon the blade of the square.

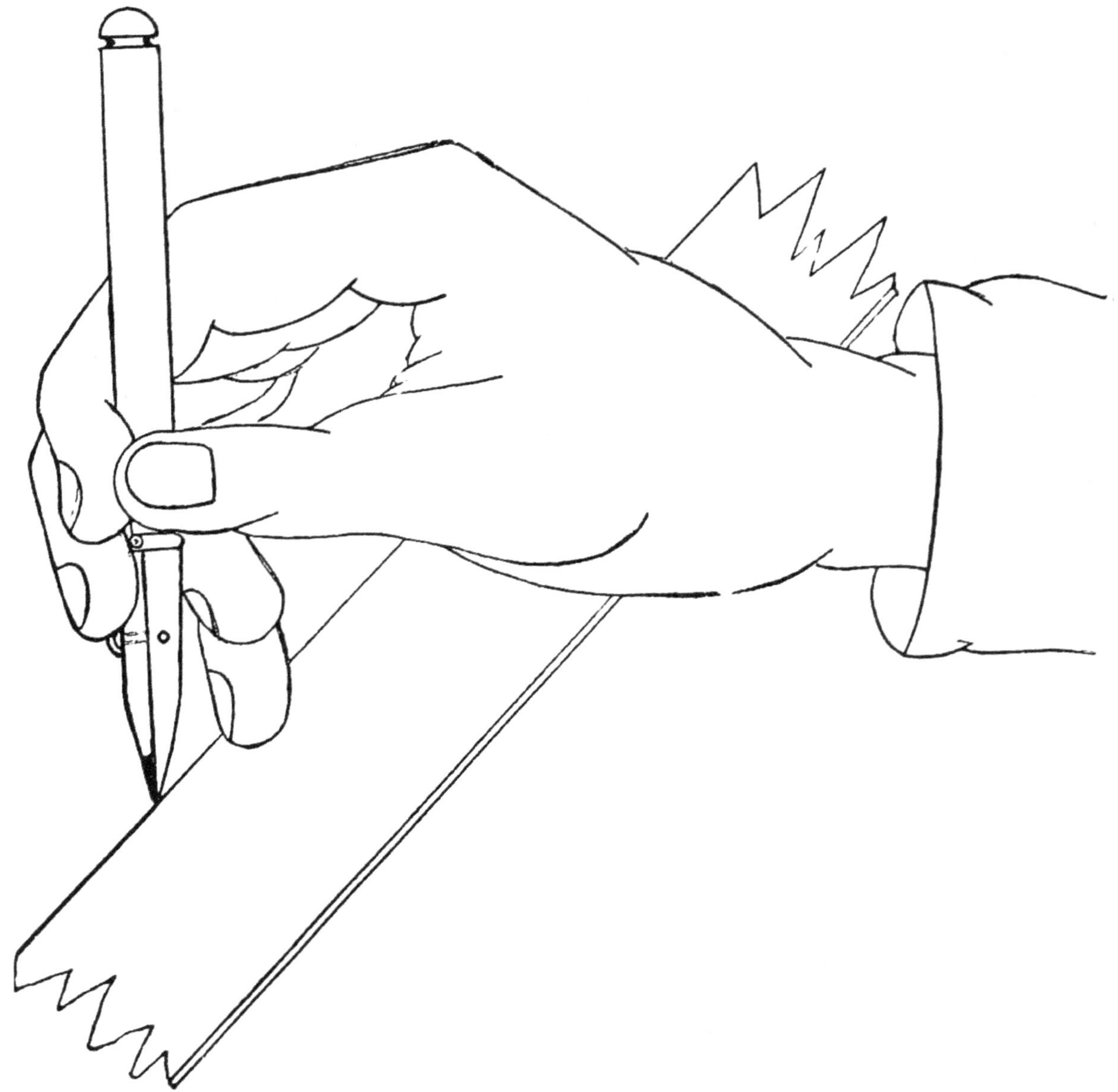

Fig. 237.

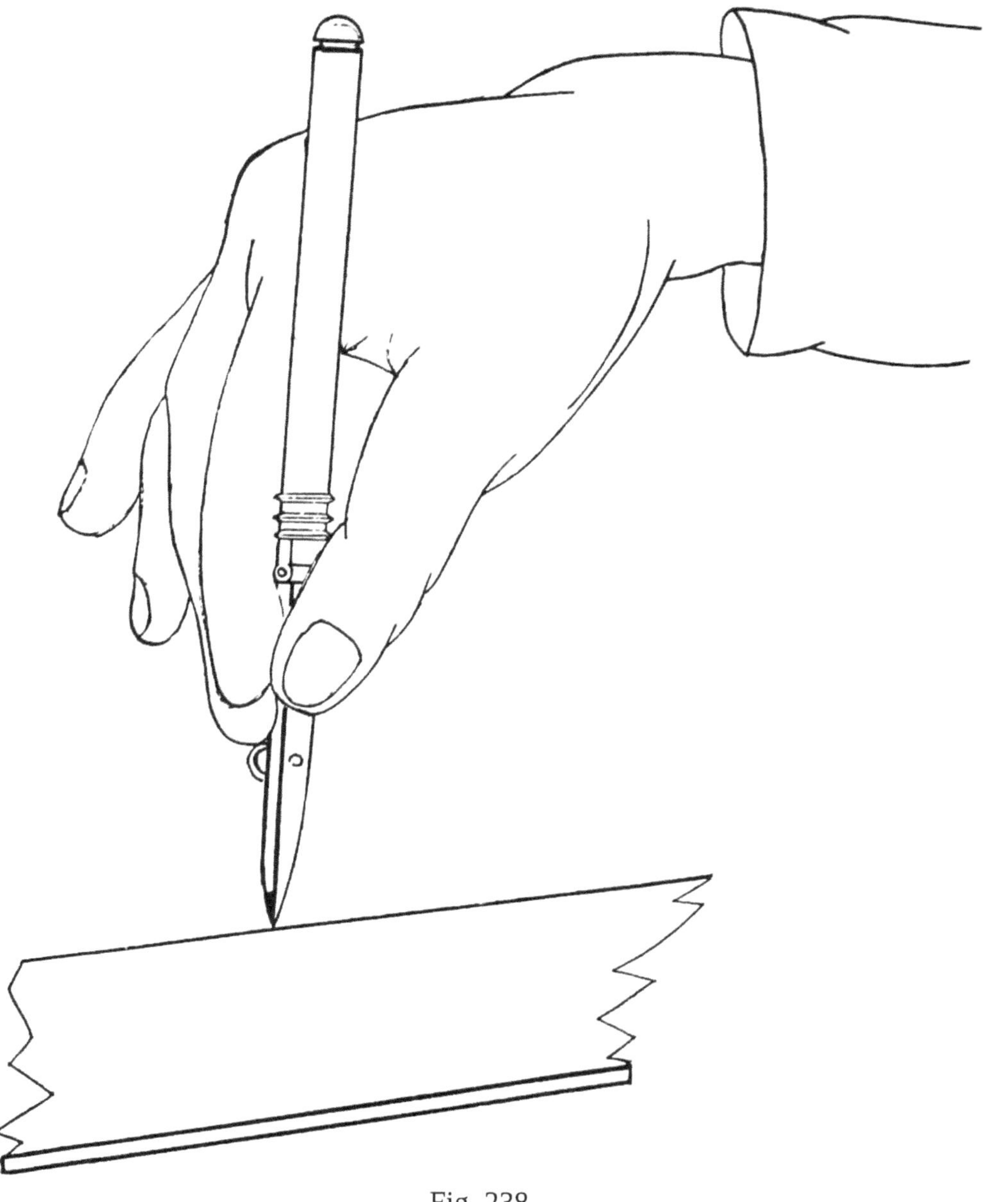

Fig. 238.

In a similar figure, 238, the position of the hand holding the pen indicates the best relative posture for inking long lines. In one of these illustrations the work is executed principally by the wrist—in the other by the arms and fingers working together.

The pen should be held with even pressure against the straight-edge or curve. If the pressure varies, the blades will spring and the width of the line will change. The blades should be of such length that both will bear equally upon the paper when the pen is inclined slightly, so as to bring the inner blade near the straight-edge; the angle of the pen should not be changed while drawing any line.

When the inking is finished, the whole drawing may be cleaned by rubbing it with bread which is not greasy or so fresh as to stick to the paper. If the paper is much soiled it may be necessary to use an eraser. A soft pencil eraser should be used and great care taken that the ink lines are not lightened and broken by it.

To avoid the necessity of using an eraser upon a finished drawing, instruments and paper must be kept free from dust and dirt. The triangles and T-square should be cleaned often, by rubbing them vigorously upon rough, clean paper.

Pounce is a powder used to prevent blotting in rewriting over erasures; it is held in a bag or small box with a perforated lid for convenience in sprinkling on paper; when used it should be distributed evenly with a piece of chamois, and the surplus or loose particles removed before applying the ink.

A drawing is made to be read, and the skill in inking, as in "free-hand" and in penciling, does not consist so much in the fineness of the lines as in their clearness.

Lettering Drawings.

Lettering is an important part of making drawings, the object aimed at being to identify any portion by reference letter or letters; thus in fig. 239 the line *A C* describes the line extending from

Fig. 239.

Any information which cannot be expressed in the drawing is always expressed by lettering, and it is desirable to confine the lettering of drawings to one or two standard alphabets that are plain and distinct, and the principles of which are easily acquired. These conditions are fulfilled in the Gothic fonts shown on page 173.

Both letters and figures must be carefully made and of uniform proportion; it is well to "lay out" these by regular measurement before permanently inking them. Letters should not be less than one-eighth of an inch in height and penciled carefully before inking.

On page 173 are printed two forms of numerals and letters of the alphabet; it is recommended that these be used both for practice in free-hand and for regular office work.

For easy reference, letters should not be crowded nor allowed to interfere with one another; they should be drawn neatly, avoiding all lines of the drawing; plain letters are always used on mechanical drawings, whether for title, scale, reference, etc.

Arrow-heads, figures and letters should be in black, and made with a writing pen. A pen with a ball point is preferable, giving an equal thickness of line, no matter in which direction the stroke is made.

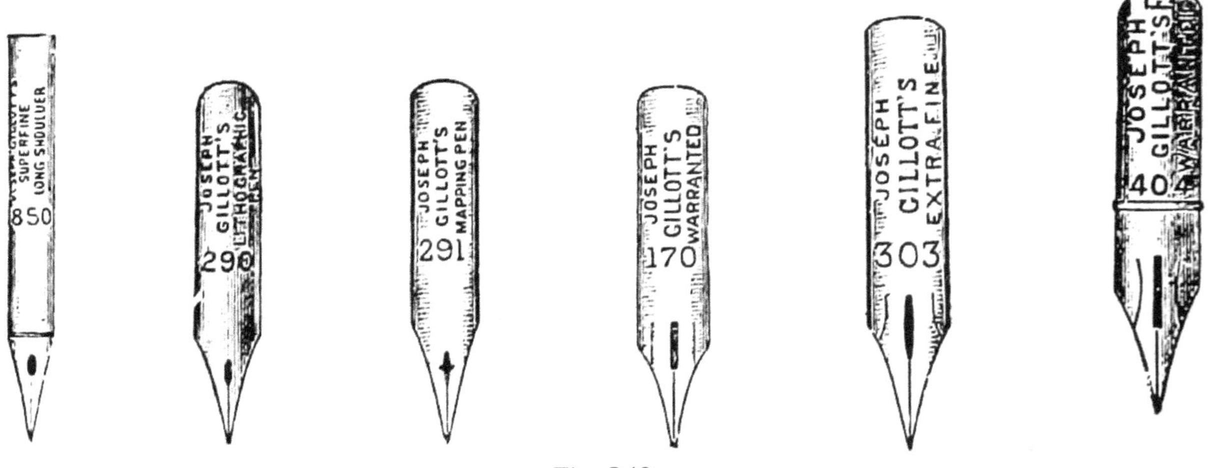

Fig. 240.

Neat, well-lettered drawings go far towards establishing a high standing for the aspiring draughtsman. All lettering should be done free-hand, first with the pencil, sharpened to a fine round point, and afterwards written in ink. For this purpose common writing pens are best to be used; fig. 240 represents the several numbers of the approved Gillott's pens adapted to this purpose.

In lettering, it is well, for a guide for size and location, to draw, with a round-pointed pencil, two horizontal lines just the height the letters are to be; the letters are also best made with careful use of the instruments, rather than free-hand.

In order to letter systematically, it is a good plan to start with the middle letter of the inscription and work in both directions; making too prominent letters should be avoided, plain and distinct letters being most desirable.

Finally, with an ordinary writing pen, trace over the penciling in ink; the pencil guide lines being erased after the letters are inked in completes the operation.

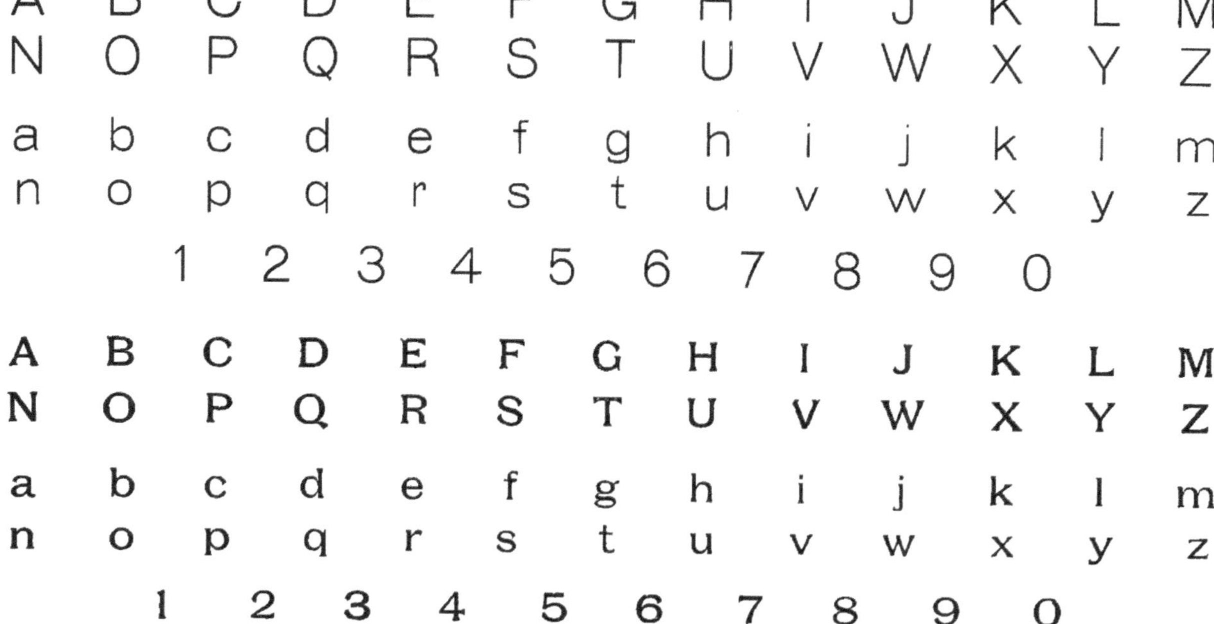

An important matter in connection with lettering a drawing is the location of the letters; these should be so placed as not to interfere with the lines of the drawing and should clearly point out the part intended to be described. When single letters are used, they should be inked in before the shade or section lines are drawn.

Fig. 241 is an example introduced to show the method of lettering a descriptive mechanical drawing.

The figure shows a "blow-off valve" of approved design drawn in section; the letters designate the several parts; the reading to accompany the lettering is as follows:

A—Inlet communicating with annular passage (*C*) to admit steam, which blows off scale and sediment from seat (*E*) before disc (*L*) comes in contact with same.

B—Plug to permit passage of rod to clean out blow-off pipe.

C—Annular steam passage around casing (*D*) and communicating with inlet (*A*).

D—Removable bronze casing, in which plug (*L*) fits snugly.

E—Removable bronze seat ring, which also holds casing (*D*) in place.

J—Slot in casing (*D*) arranged to discharge sheet of steam from *C*, which, blowing across seat (*E*), cleans off scale and sediment before contact with disc (*L*).

K—Non-rotating washer to prevent loosening of locknut (*H*) when opening
   valve.
L—Reversible disc, having two Babbitt-metal seating faces (*F*) (*F*).

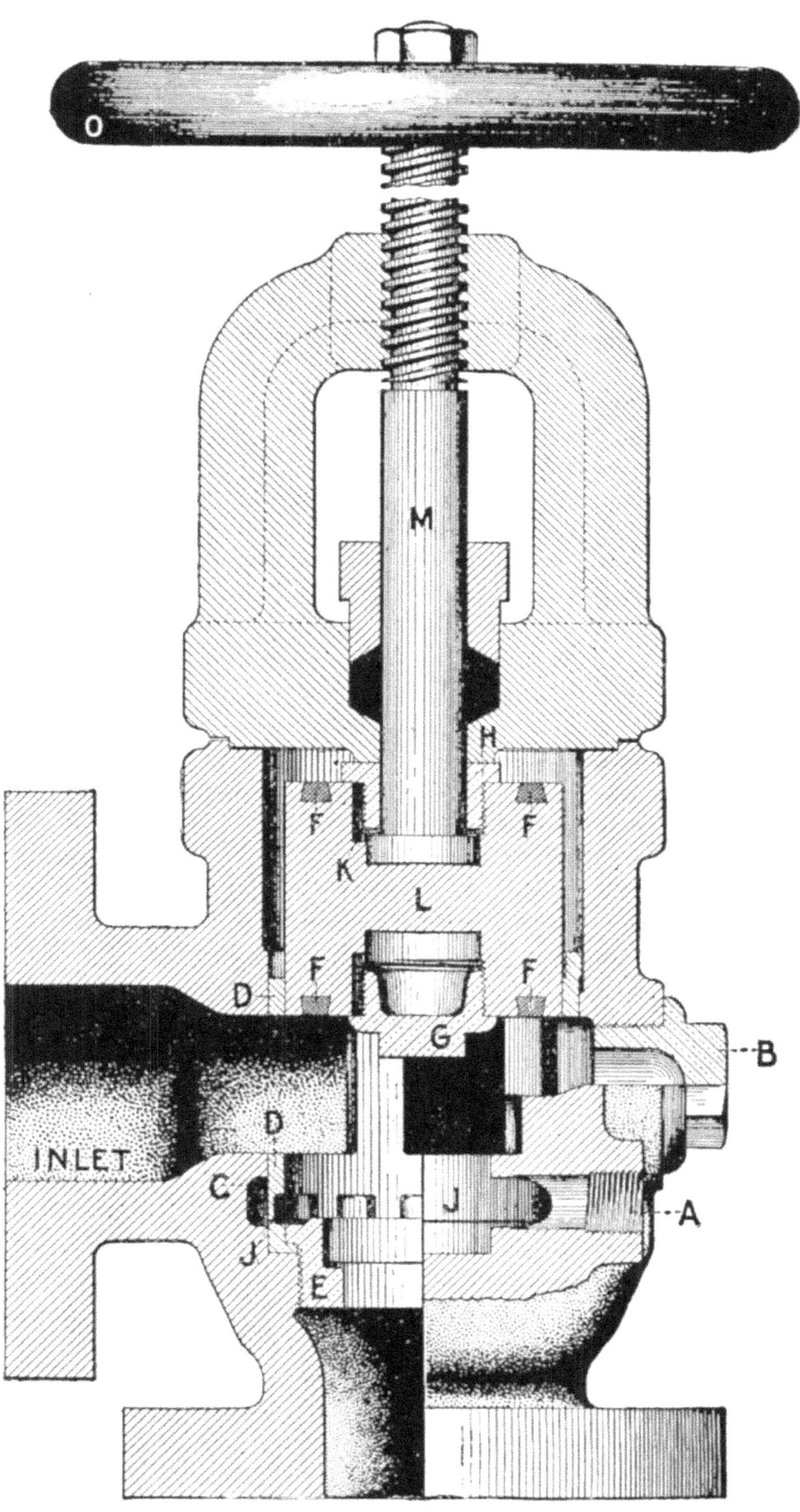

O
M
H
F
F
K
L
F
F
D
G
B
INLET
D
C
J
J
A
E

Fig. 241.

Dimensioning Drawings.

To "dimension" working drawings is to place measurements upon the parts represented, to enable the workman to proceed without measuring the drawing itself.

These dimensions should be placed so as not to interfere with nor crowd the lines of the drawing, nor yet interfere with one another.

Arrow-heads are used at the extreme points of measurement, the figures are generally inserted midway between the arrows; a dot and dash line reaches from the figure to the arrow-heads, as shown below.

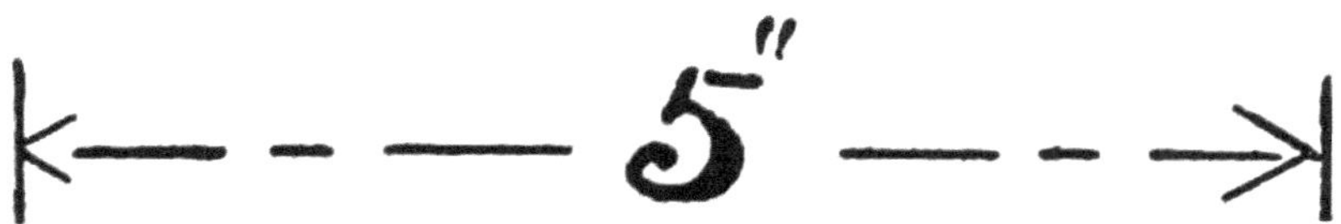

When the dimension is short these lines are omitted and the dimension is placed outside the drawing, thus and connected by a curved line; at other times it is found needful to place arrow-heads outside the drawing and the measurement inside.

When the dimension is long and narrow it is usual to carry the dimensions under the drawing by dotted and dash lines, as shown below.

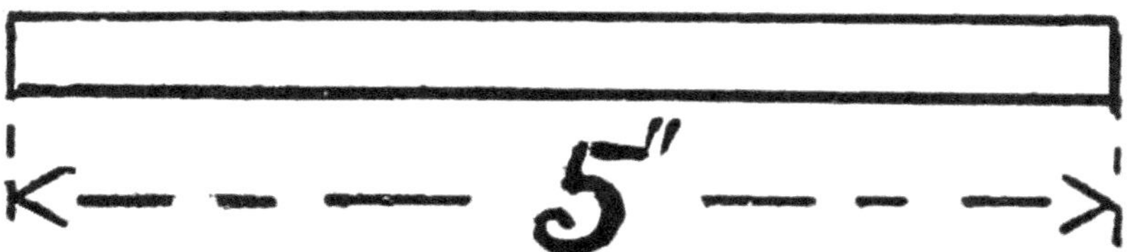

Arrow-heads and figures should be drawn free-hand with a common writing pen.

Usually dimensions are given in inches, up to 24 inches, as it is found less confusing; for instance, if written 1′ 1″ it may be mistaken for 11″; if written 13″ no mistake could be made.

Again, 1′ 0″ may be mistaken for 10″; if written 12″ it would not; in addition to being more distinct, it occupies less space on the drawing. In large measurements there is more room for the figures, and, therefore, they can be spaced further apart—in feet and inches.

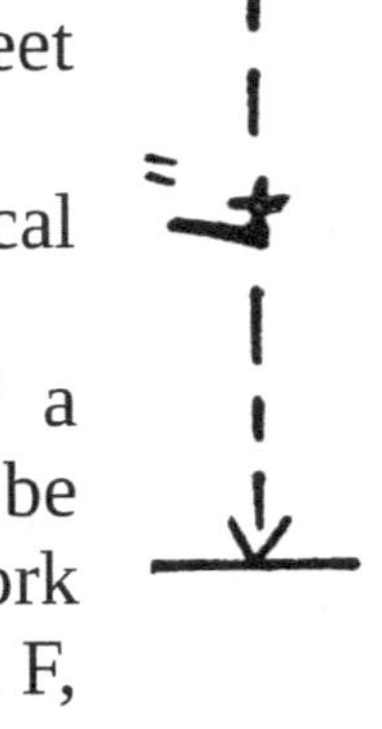

All figures should be made of a fairly large size. Vertical dimensions should read from the right hand, thus, as shown:

Measurements of importance, such as the diameter of a circle, the pitch or distance apart of rivets and bolts, etc., should be marked in figures on the drawing. When rough or unfinished work is mixed with machined or finished portions, it is usual to mark F, or "fin.," after the latter dimension.

In practice, at times, instead of dimensions reference letters are used, thus:

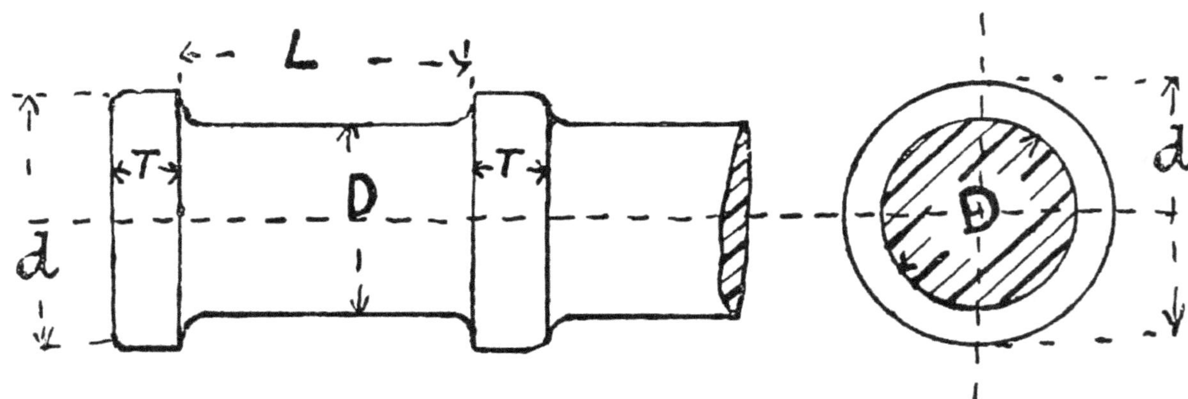

D = diam. of shaft, 2½ inches.
L = length of bearing, 3¾ inches.
T = thickness of collar, ⅞ inch.
d = diam. of collar, 3½ inches.

Generally it is preferable to give the diameters of turned and bored work on a section, instead of an end drawn separately; confusion is sometimes caused by a number of radial dimensions.

Fig. 242 and fig. 243 are introduced to show the principal measurements required in practical work, and the usual way in which such dimensions are marked when ordering parts of machinery.

Fig. 242 is a pedestal, or metal frame; three views are shown, the center figure being an elevation, the lower figure is the plan of the base, the upper figure is a view of the top, on which is bolted the bearing block, it being on the outside of the center figure. The essential measurements are marked by letters. *H* is the vertical height from base to the seat of bearing block: *L* being the length, and *W* the width of the base; *P* is the length between checks, and *B* the width of seat for bearing block; *C* is the distance from center to center of the holding down bolt holes, and *T* is the depth of the holes in the base; *K* is the distance from center to center of the bolt holes in the top for bearing block.

Fig. 243 is a hanger, or metal bracket, and shows the center figure or elevation, the plan of the top and the plan of the seat for bearing block, which is bolted on the interior of the center figure. *H* is the vertical distance from the top to the seat for bearing block; the other measurements required are marked by letters similar to figure 242.

Now, one of the important matters in connection with dimensioning a drawing is the location of the figures. One rule, whose utility cannot be gainsaid, is that they should be so located that they can be altered or erased without damage to the lines of the drawing, as changes may be necessitated either by original errors in writing down the figures or by changes in the design being found desirable during the construction of the machine.

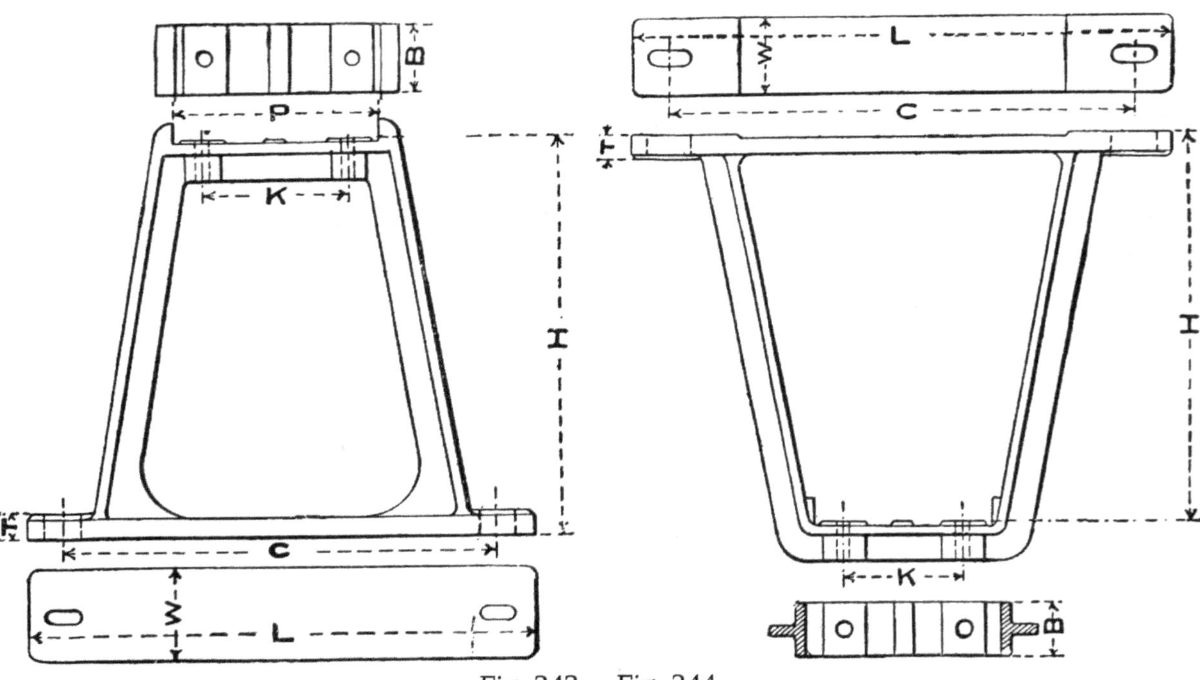

Fig. 243.—Fig. 244.

Shading Drawings.

To produce an effect, drawings are shaded; that is, shadow lines about twice the width of the regular line are drawn according to a recognized rule, which always represents the same peculiarity of form in the same way.

In working drawings light lines only are permitted; shade lines are wider than the working lines, and in reading scale measurements the extra thickness of line would make a difference.

Instead of representing the shadow as it is really cast by the object, the edges which cast the shadow are determined, and all the views are treated as if the light came from behind and from the left, downwards, at an angle of 45° to the horizontal line, as shown by the arrows in figs. 245 to 248.

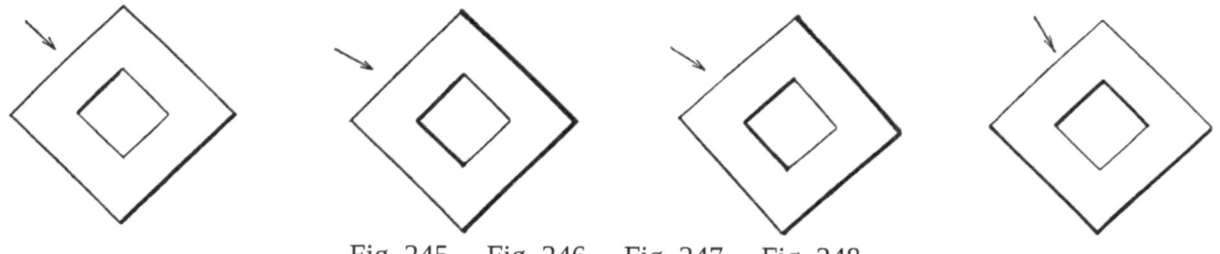

Fig. 245.—Fig. 246.—Fig. 247.—Fig. 248.

The lower and right-hand outlines of projecting parts will cast shadows, and the student should make them of extra width.

Fig. 249: In shading curves, divide the center line as before (see page 146) and describe circles from center, *D*; these lines are not to be shaded in penciling, but when inking. The figures represent two rings, *A* and *C*, and spaces, *B* and *D*. The outside of a surface is shaded according to circle 1, and the inside surface according to circle 2. This will give the desired shading, but it makes a drawing incorrect, and therefore shading is not used in working drawings.

This shading is accomplished by inking the circle first with regular width of line; then with the same radius remove the point of compasses from the *true center*, placing it outside, according to the desired position of the shaded line, and describe an arc of a circle.

In fig. 250 divide center line as before; with the 45° triangle or set square, draw through the center the diagonals shown by dotted lines; and through the points *A*, *B*, *C*, etc., draw the perpendiculars, cutting the diagonals; from the points of intersection draw the horizontal lines, completing the squares.

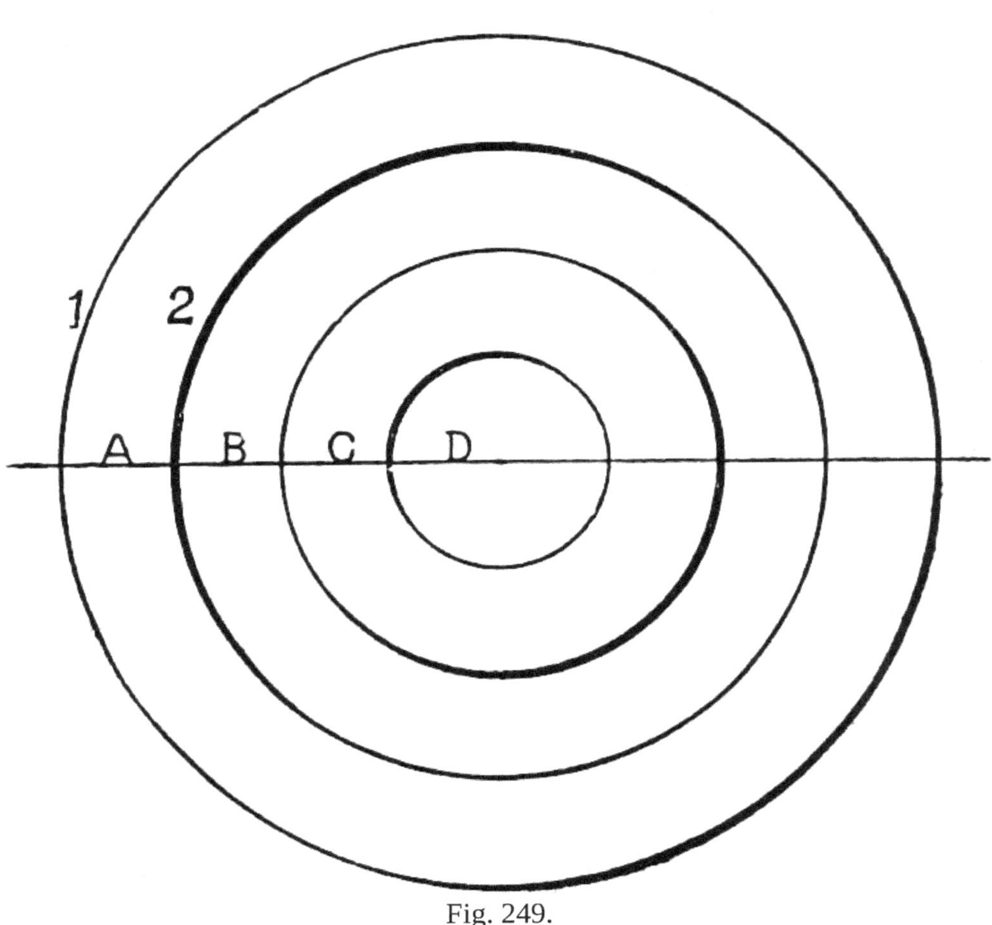

Fig. 249.

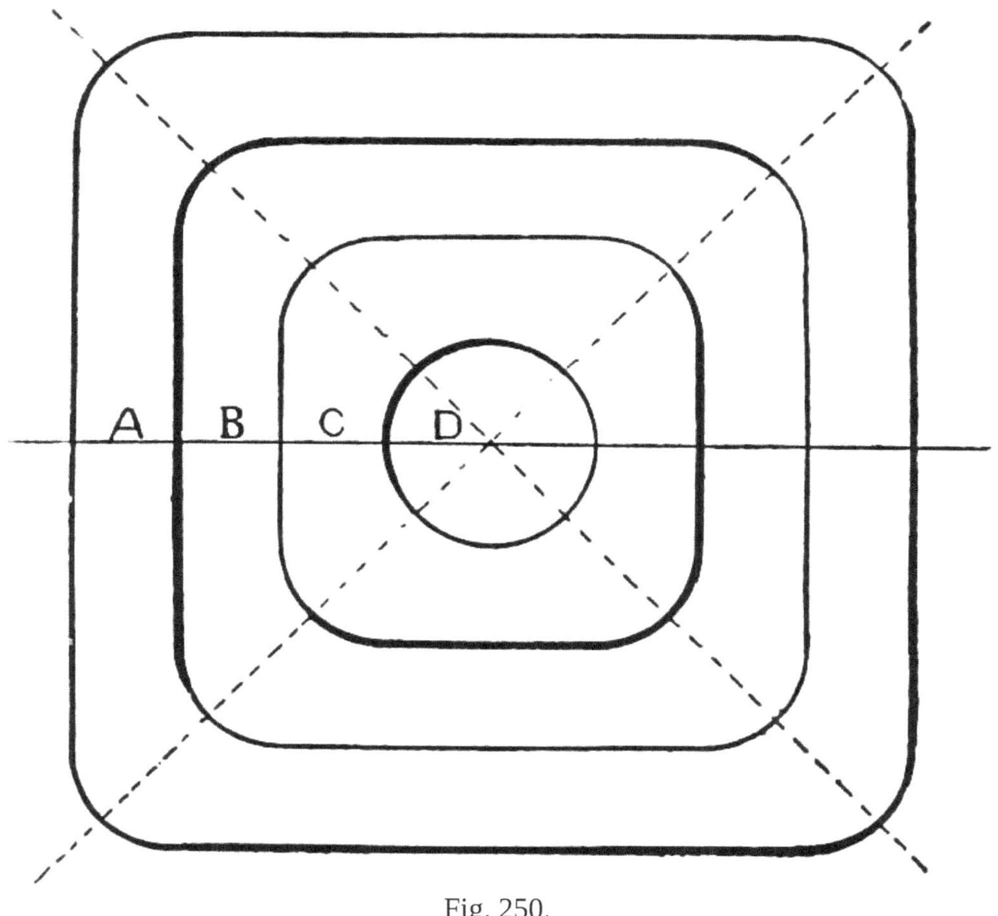

Fig. 250.

Now, take a radius of half an inch, and in the corner of each square draw with the bow-pencil a circular arc meeting the pencil lines exactly; with the bow-pen *ink in the arcs* first, then ink carefully the lines joining with the arcs; all lines must be of the same width; put in the shade on arcs and lines as in fig. 249; and, finally, erase the pencil lines at corners, etc.

Section-Lining.

Cross-hatching has been defined in the "preliminary definitions" to drawing; this term represents the practice of drawing diagonal lines representing the interior of an object, shown as a piece cut in half or when a piece is broken away. This is done to make more of the parts show, or to exhibit more clearly the nature of the materials; hence section lining and cross-hatching tell the same thing, *i. e.*, the drawing of diagonal lines, usually at an angle of 45°, to show that the object is broken away and the interior designed to be represented.

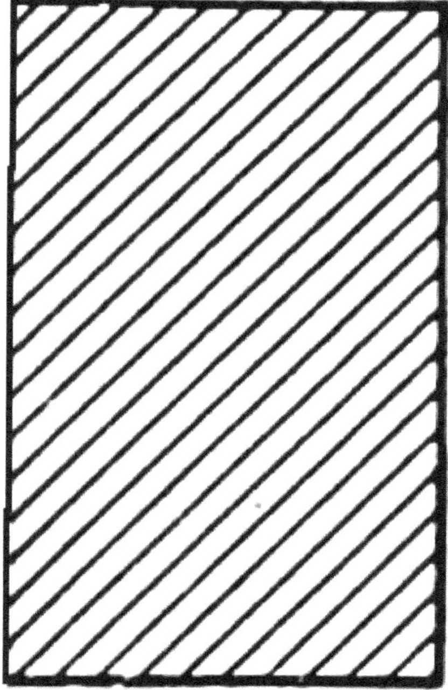

Cast iron.
Fig. 251.

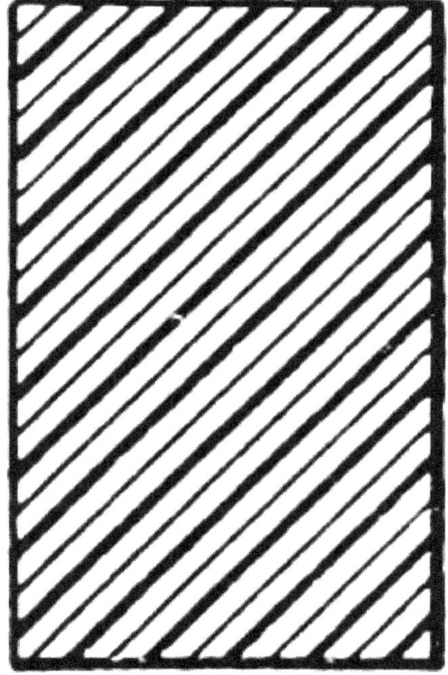

Wrought iron.
Fig. 252.

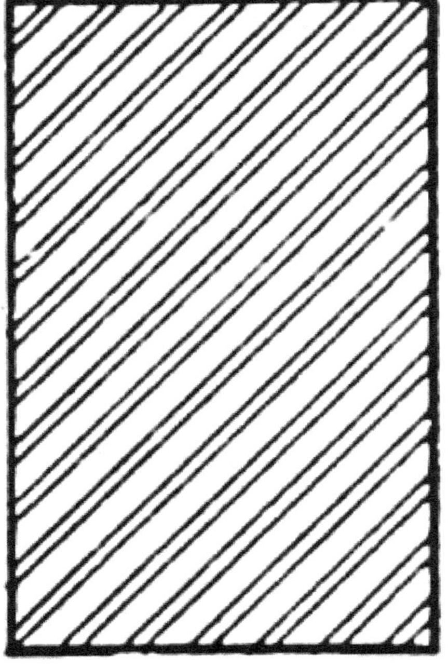

Steel.
Fig. 253.

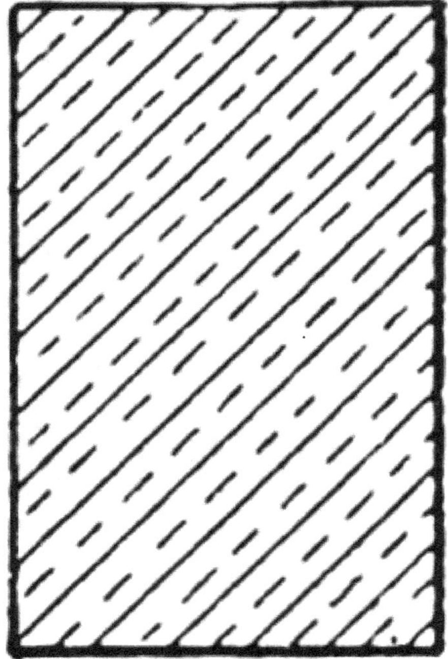

Composition.
Fig. 254.

Vulcanite.
Fig. 255.

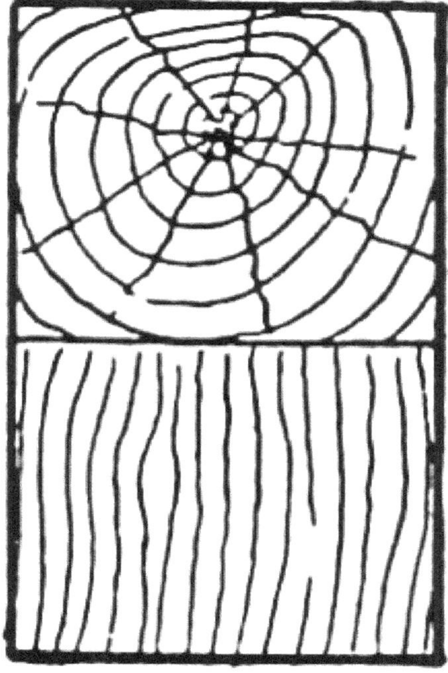

Wood.
Fig. 256.

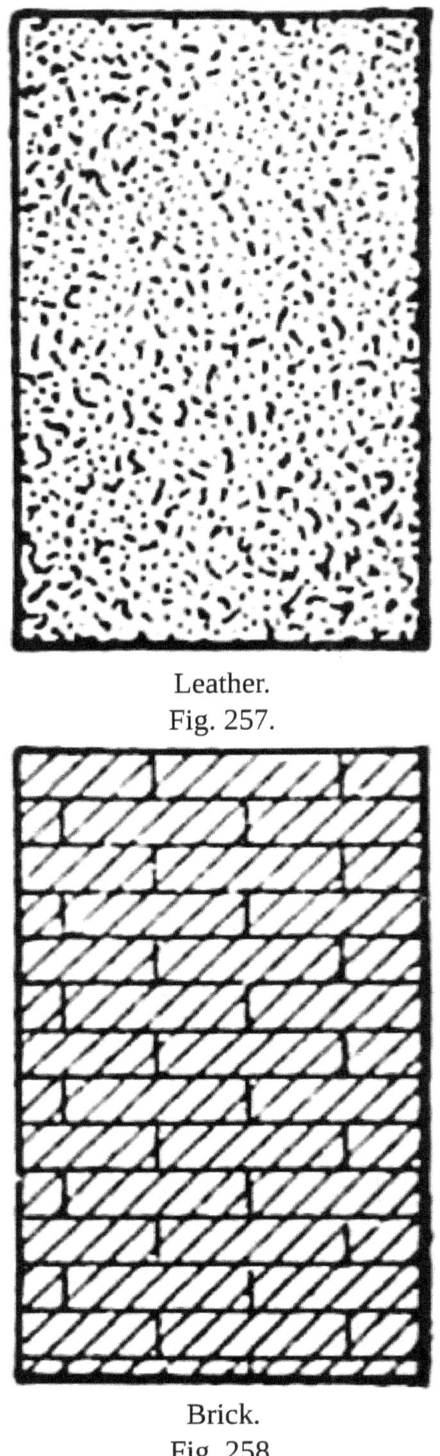

Leather.
Fig. 257.

Brick.
Fig. 258.

Figs. 251 to 258, inclusive, show the section lining and cross-hatching by which it is customary to represent the various materials entering into a construction.

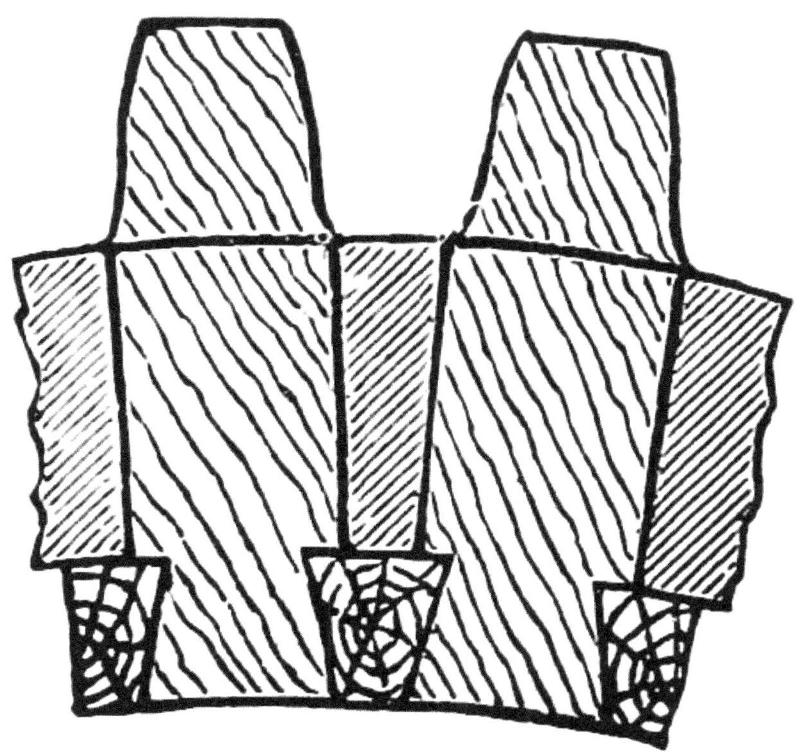

Fig. 259.

In fig. 259 is outlined a representation of a section of a cog-wheel; section 1 being the wood cogs; 2, the iron wheel, and 3 the wedges at the root of the gear. It would be impossible to convey the same ideas by ordinary plan or elevation drawing; all the objects on the same page are more clearly represented by the use of section lines or cross-hatching.

Sectioning is executed by drawing a series of parallel lines about $\frac{3}{32}$ inches apart. Lay the 45° triangle on the upper edge of the T-square and draw the top-most line of the sectioning. Then slide the triangle along the T-square for each successive line. The sectioning should be inked in without previous penciling and the lines should be finer than the lines of the general drawing.

Various devices are in use for mechanically equalizing the distances in section lining, but the trained eye is the most practical method. When two abutting pieces are sectioned, the section lining on one piece slants in an opposite direction to that on the other.

To draw an object to be sectioned on both sides of its center line, only one side is sectioned, while the other side is drawn in full.

Sections are necessary in nearly all machine drawings; they are usually taken horizontally or vertically, but they may be taken in any direction; the position of a section should be shown by a line upon the object; this line is called the cutting plane.

In fig. 261 is shown the hub of a wheel, it is also a sample of work for practice.

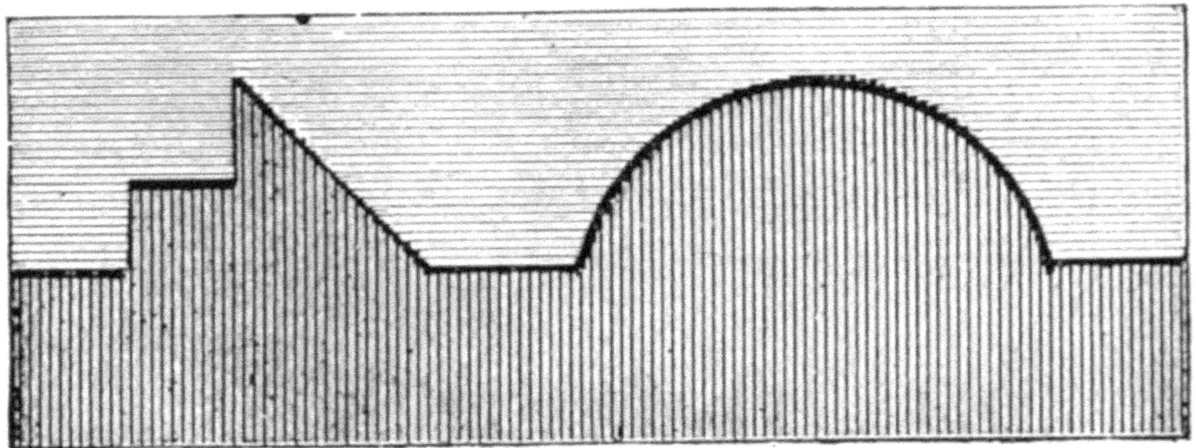

Fig. 260.

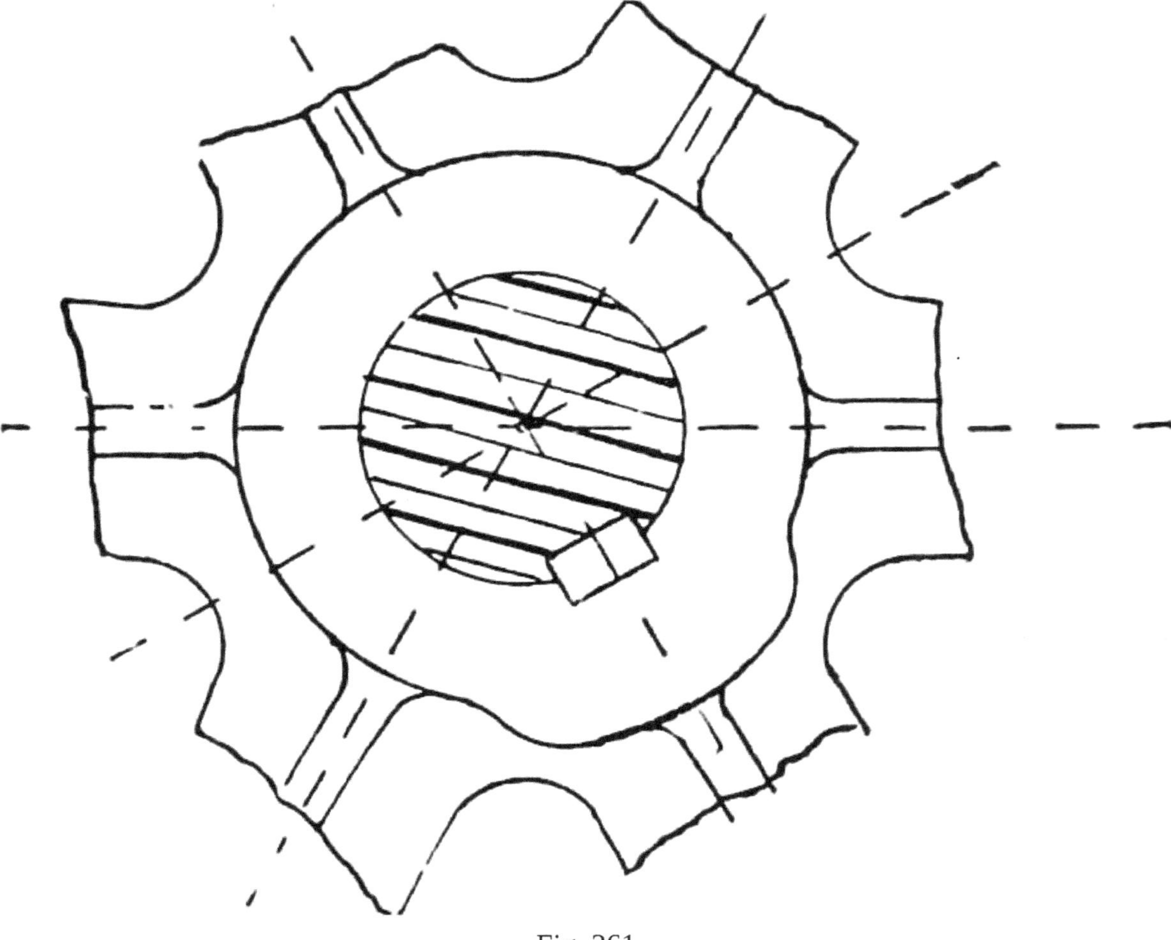

Fig. 261.

Fig. 260 shows the mode of representing two different materials in one plane, or a section may be represented by the darker portion, and the lighter shaded portion being a surface resting on the section.

Fig. 261 shows the section of a shaft surrounded by the surface of a wheel.

TINTS AND COLORS.

For special purposes of illustration drawings are made which must be tinted. In such cases the paper must be expanded and stretched evenly all over its surface; otherwise when the moist tint is applied the paper will wrinkle and get out of shape; to do this cut the paper at least half an inch less in size than the drawing board; lay the paper face down, turn up a margin or edge of about three-fourths of an inch all round, then dampen the paper with a sponge and clean water; allow it to soak for a few minutes until it is evenly dampened or moistened all over, turn the paper upside down (face up).

Apply strong paste to the under side of the margin all round; rub down, on the drawing-board, working from the center of the board outwards so as to exclude the air and prevent creases or furrows. The board is then inclined and left to dry slowly; make sure that the paper is all well pasted and every part of the edges attached to the board.

If tracings are required to be tinted or shaded, the color may be applied before the tracing is cut off, or what is more usual, the color may be applied on the back of the tracing; then there is no liability to wash out the lines.

Mechanical drawings are seldom tinted, but are mainly produced in India ink. Where, however, a fine effect is desired, working drawings are colored, so as to show at a glance the material of which the different parts are to be made.

The colors required are few but should be of the best quality. Besides India ink the following water-colors are generally used:

1, Neutral-tint. 2, Prussian Blue. 3, Chrome Yellow. 4, Gamboge. 5, Raw Sienna. 6, Carmine. 7, Vermillion. 8, Venetian Red. 9, Sepia. 10, Indigo. These come in hard cakes.

Certain colors and tints represent different metals and materials as follows:

Wrought Iron—Prussian Blue.

Steel—Carmine and Prussian Blue, mixed to give a purple shade.

Steel Casting—Same as the above darkened by Venetian Red.

Cast-Iron—Neutral Tint made of India Ink, indigo, mixed with a little carmine.

Brass—Gamboge or Chrome Yellow.

Babbitt—Emerald Green; sometimes light mixture of India Ink.

Copper—Purple Lake.

It is sometimes found necessary to prepare a highly finished and shaded drawing of the work in hand. Such elaborations, in fact, are much admired by the uninitiated, although the complete shading of the drawing is no criterion as to the scientific value of the machine. An illustration of this is told in the note.

NOTE.—A consulting engineer had to lay before a board of directors plans of horizontal engines for their consideration. One of these drawings was of a very superior machine, but being only depicted lineally was at once rejected by them, for a highly finished representation of a very inferior apparatus. The engineer, wishing to induce the board to decide for the best, suggested that the matter should be postponed to a future day, and in the meantime had the drawing of the superior machine highly colored and finished. At the next meeting the directors unanimously decided that this was the very one which they preferred and had chosen.

Reproducing Drawings.

When once finished, one or more copies of drawings are frequently required; these are produced, 1, by blue printing, as described before; 2, by tracing. A tracing is a mechanical copy of a design or drawing, made by reproducing its lines as seen through a transparent medium—as tracing-cloth or tracing-paper.

Tracing-cloth is a thin linen fabric, coated with size; this is called *tracing-lines*; *tracing-paper* is so prepared as to be transparent, so that it will receive marks either in pencil or with pen and ink.

Tracing-cloth must be fastened to the board, over the drawing, by pins or other tacks; moisture or dampness should be carefully avoided and the drawing done on the smooth side of the cloth.

When tracing cloth will not take ink readily a small quantity of pounce may be applied to the surface of the cloth and distributed evenly with a piece of cotton waste, chamois, or similar material, but the pounce should be thoroughly removed—by washing—before applying the ink.

In making tracings the same order is followed as described under the section "Inking"—to repeat: 1, ink in the small circles and curves; 2, ink in the larger circles and curves; 3, then all the horizontal lines, beginning at the top of the drawing and working downward; 4, next ink in all the vertical lines, commencing at the left and moving back to the right; 5, draw in the oblique lines; 6, all the center lines red (carmine), and dimension and reference lines in blue (Prussian blue) or *vice versa*. The figuring and lettering should always be done with India ink, thoroughly black.

BLUE PRINTING.

Copies of drawings or parts representing details and measurements are frequently needed for the office, pattern shop, machine and blacksmith shop, etc. These copies are best made by printing on sensitized or specially prepared paper, from tracings drawn on transparent cloth or paper, as hereabove described. The original design may be guarded with the utmost care for long preservation, but the blue prints, so called, are for ready reference and use without much regard to the length of time they are to be in existence.

The usual practice is to carefully trace from the drawing on transparent cloth or paper an exact reproduction of it, filling in all detail lettering and sizes or figured dimensions.

This tracing is fixed in a frame similar to a picture frame, with the side on which the drawing is made next to the glass: 1, place the sensitized side of the paper (which has been prepared previously) against the back of the tracing; 2, fix soft padding against the back of the paper and fasten it up so that both paper and tracing are compressed firmly against the glass, permitting no creases or air spaces between them.

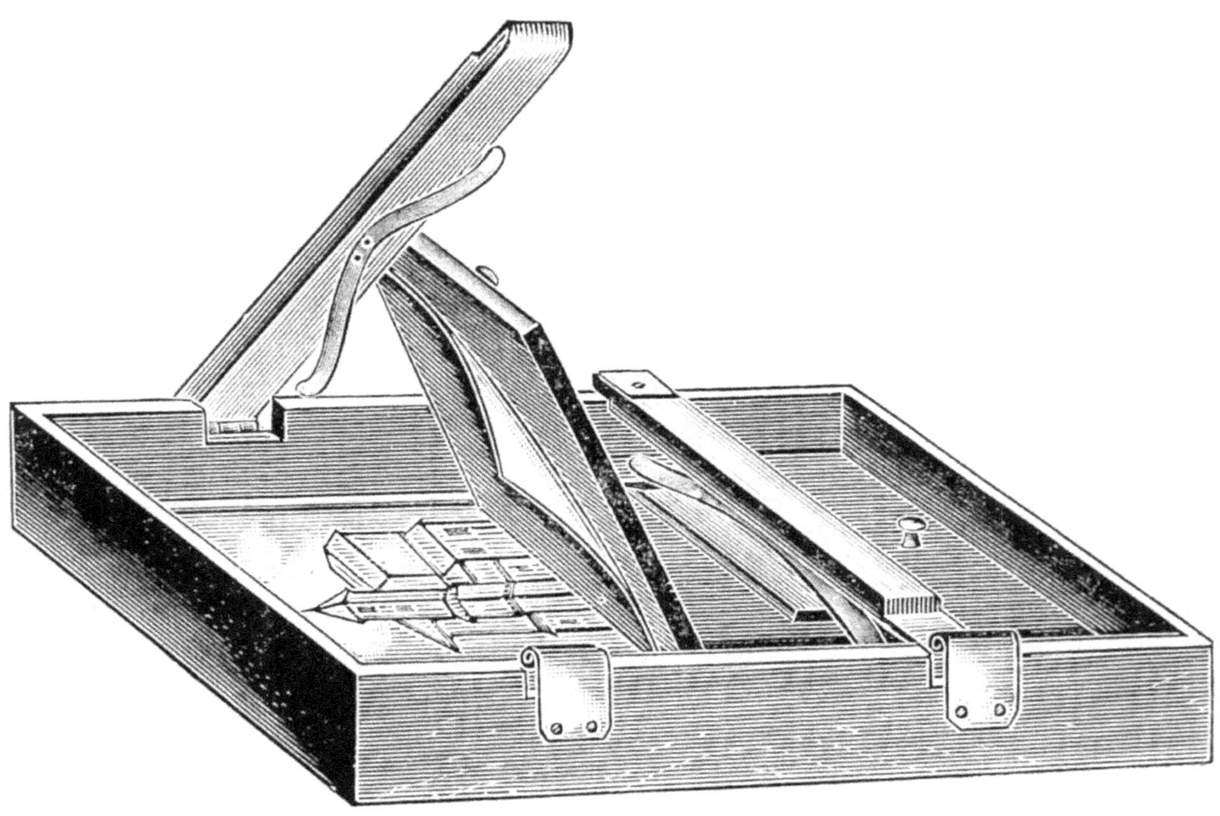

Fig. 262.

This should be done in a darkened room; 3, expose for three to six minutes, according to the intensity of the sun; 4, take the sensitized paper out of the frame and quickly wash well in clean running cool water, and the drawing will appear in white lines on blue ground; 5, hang the print up by one edge so that the water will run off and the print will soon dry and be ready for use.

TEST-PIECES.

To make good blueprints, being guided only by the appearance of the exposed edge of sensitized paper, requires considerable experience. Very often, especially on a cloudy day, the edge looks just about right, but when taken out of the frame and given a rinsing, it is only to find that the print looks pale because it should have been allowed to remain exposed for a longer period.

Now simply take a small test-piece of the same paper (say about 4 inches square) and a piece of tracing cloth with several lines on its surface and lay these small pieces out at the same time the real print is being exposed, and cover these samples with a piece of glass about 4 inches square. As a general rule, we can find a place on top of the frame for the testing-piece, and by having a small dish of water at hand for testing the print by tearing off a small bit and washing same to note its appearance, the novice can get just as good results as the experienced hand without danger of failure.

BLACK PROCESS COPYING.

This is accomplished by specially sensitized paper by which a fac-simile of the original drawing can be made; that is, black lines upon white ground. It also avoids the objection to the blue print paper of shaded drawings which show light and shade reversed.

The prints made by the process are said to be absolutely permanent and can be altered, added to or colored the same as original drawings.

The sensitized paper is sold ready for use, but it can be prepared by dissolving two ounces of citrate of iron and ammonium in eight ounces of soft water; keep in a dark bottle, also, one and one-third ounces of red prussiate of potash in eight ounces of water; keep in another dark bottle; when about to use mix an equal quantity of each in a cup and apply in a dark room with a soft brush or sponge to one side of white rag paper, similar to envelope paper, let it dry and put away in a dark place until required for use.

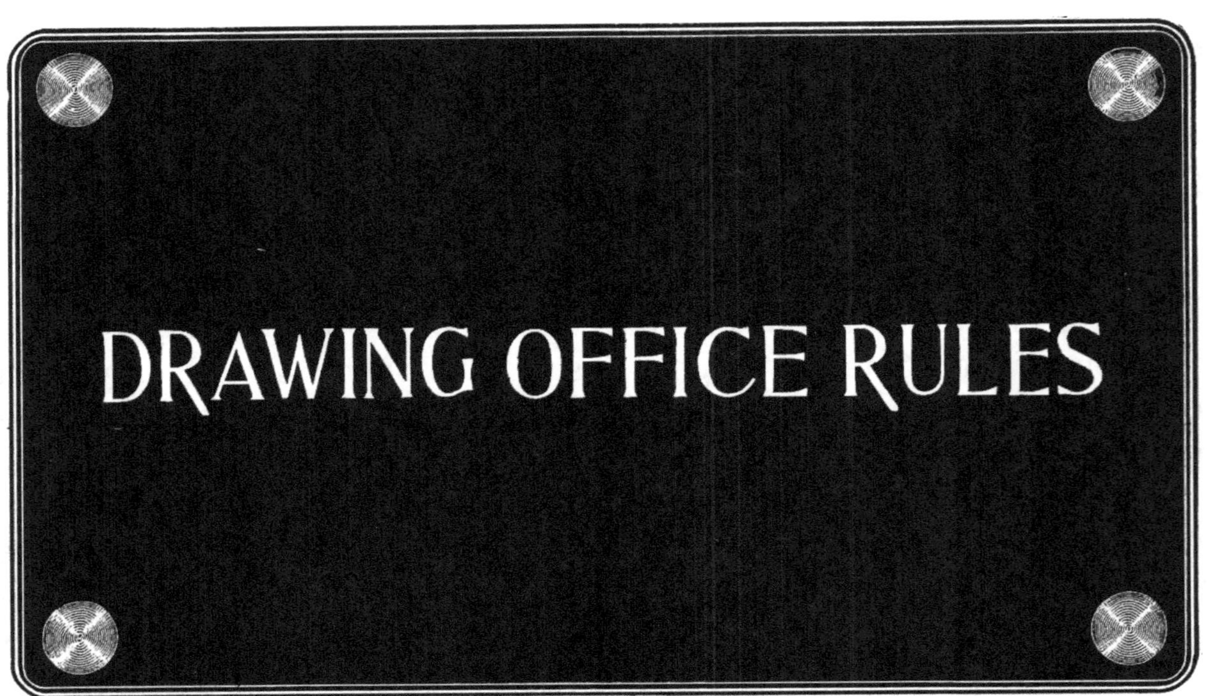
DRAWING OFFICE RULES

Drawing Office Rules.[1]

[1] Note.—A. W. Robinson, M.E., Montreal, must have all credit for these admirable rules and regulations. They bring into a single focus the whole science and art of mechanical drawing.

There are drawing offices where from ten to nearly one hundred people are busily employed in making new plans and sketches by the hundreds, and where thousands of completed drawings are filed for reference or for changes, as these are needed in the shop management.

To be introduced for the first time into such a company is a trial for the "new man" both of nerve and manners, and a test as well of skill; nothing helps more at such a time than an acquaintance with the rules and routine of the office, for the old saying holds good in a drawing office, of "doing in Rome as the Romans do." The author of this book has felt this strangeness in a new position and so adds the following model-rules for the guidance of the student when first entering a regular position in an office where many are employed and where success depends upon a systematic ordering of the work in hand.

SIZE OF DRAWINGS.

1. The standard size shall be 23 inches by 36 inches, subdivided into half, quarter and eighth sheets.

2. Full-size drawings shall be reserved, as far as possible, for general views and parts not capable of being shown on smaller sheets.

3. All shop detail shall, as far as possible, be shown on quarter and eighth sheets.

CHARACTER OF DRAWINGS.

4. Detail drawings shall, as far as possible, classify the different kinds of works, such as castings, forgings, shafts, levers, piping, etc. Different kinds of work shall not be shown on the same detail drawing.

5. All shop drawings liable to repetition shall be traced and blue-printed. All temporary details, requiring only one copy, may be made on

sketch sheets and press copied.

6. A shop drawing is to be considered as an order or instruction to the shop, and not merely as a statement or illustration. For this purpose it must convey clearly and distinctly all the information necessary to make the article.

7. Every dimension necessary to the execution of the work is to be clearly stated by figures on the drawing, so that no measurements need to be taken in the shop by scale. All measurements to be given with reference to the base or starting point from which the work should be laid out, and also with reference to center lines.

8. All figured dimensions on drawings to be plain, round vertical figures, not less than one-eighth inch high, and formed by a line of uniform width and sufficiently heavy to insure printing well. No thin, sloping, or doubtful figures, or diagonal-barred fractions will be tolerated. All figured dimensions below two feet to be expressed in inches.

9. All center lines to be alternate dot and dash in fine black line. All dimension lines to be double dot and dash, with a central space for the figure, and of such strength as to show on blue-print more faintly than lines of drawing. Lines of drawing to be bold and clearly defined in proportion to the scale, and may be shade-lined by making the right-hand and bottom lines heavier. No ornamental shading or other "frills" allowed on shop drawings.

10. Every drawing, whether whole or half-sheet, shall have the title, date, scale and number of the sheet stamped in lower right-hand corner, and the quarter and eighth sheets printed on top.

11. The name of the drawing, as given in the title, is invariably to consist of two divisions in one line separated by a hyphen. The first division is to state the general name of the thing or machine, and the second name is to clearly designate the part or parts represented (or if a general view should so state). The wording of titles should be submitted to the chief engineer or head draughtsman for approval.

12. Each drawing shall bear the name of the draughtsman and examiner, the surname being used without initials.

13. Drawings of piping details shall be made in diagram form, using standard symbols.

14. All detail parts for standard or repetition work shall be shown unassembled as far as possible.

DRAWING SYMBOLS.

15. Detail shop drawings should state:

(a) The pattern number of every casting in plain figures of larger size than the dimension figures.

(b) The material of which the parts are made, using symbols as follows: C.I.—Cast iron. W.I.—Wrought iron. M.S.—Machinery steel. H.S.—Hammered steel. Bs.—Brass. Bbt.—Babbitt. Bz.—Bronze. C.R.S.—Cold rolled steel.

Other materials write full name.

(c) Finished surfaces will be indicated by "f" written on the line or surface to be finished. When not so marked it is understood that the part is to be left black or rough. In cases where finish might be presumed but not required, follow the figured dimensions by the word "cast," if a casting, and "rough," if a forging.

STANDARDS.

16. The following standards shall be strictly adhered to as given in the tables noted:

(1.) Table of standard diameters of shafting and key seats.
(2.) Table of standard stock sizes of rounds.
(3.) Table of standard stock sizes of flat steel.
(4.) Table of standard clearance fits.
(5.) Table of standard symbols for notation of riveting.
(6.) Table of standard symbols for pipe fittings.
Also such other standards as may be adopted from time to time.

NUMBERING OF DRAWINGS.

17. Drawers and filing cases shall be numbered consecutively. Drawers shall contain 100 sheets each, and filing cases 200 sheets each, and to be fully indexed. Drawings shall be numbered by a number indicating both drawer number and serial number in the drawer—thus, 7,604 is the fourth sheet in drawer 76, etc.

18. Drawing numbers shall be checked off the index as required, and the index posted up in uniform handwriting by the clerk.

19. Standard size drawings shall be kept in drawers and quarter and eighth sheets in filing cases. All drawings shall be indexed by an index

sheet kept in each drawer or case.

CHECKING.

20. All drawings must be approved before being traced. When tracing is completed it will be given immediately to the chief draughtsman, who will have a preliminary print made and carefully checked, before being used.

PATTERNS.

21. All patterns shall bear the number of the drawing on which they are first detailed, followed by a serial letter, according to the number of patterns on the drawing.

22. Standard patterns used repeatedly and liable to be ordered from in repairs must not be changed. Other patterns may only be changed when absolutely necessary and by order. When so changed they will bear the original number and letter, followed by A for the first change, B for the second change, and so on thus: 4860 AB is the second change in pattern 4860 A.

SKETCH BOOKS.

23. Each draughtsman will be supplied with a sketch book by the company, in which he shall make all his notes, calculations and data referring to his work, and under no circumstances shall notes of value be made on loose sheets. Each entry should invariably be commenced with the subject and date, and full notes made of data on which the calculations were based, and the results obtained clearly stated. These books are to remain the property of the company.

IN GENERAL.

24. Changes in drawings, sketches or order lists issued to the shop shall only be made when authorized by the chief engineer, or, in his absence, by the chief draughtsman, and when so authorized shall be made by the order clerk.

25. The names of all similar parts in order lists and drawings are to be uniform.

26. Tracings must be kept in safe, for blue-printing purposes only. Office copies of blue-prints must be used for references.

27. No drawing, print or photograph shall be taken from office without permission.

NUMBERING WORKING DRAWINGS.

There are a great many different systems used in indexing drawings, most of which have some good points, but very few are sufficiently elastic to cover a wide field. A plan based upon the decimal system of notation is very simple, and, as there is no practical limit to the number of subdivisions, it can be expanded indefinitely. Following are the main outline features of the system as adapted to the needs of drawing offices belonging to large works.

The main division numbers, 000, 100, 200, 300, etc., are used respectively for all plans and general sheets referring to the division concerned. 100 includes general plans covering more than one department, and all small-scale plans with cross references to departments covered.

The class or tens divisions contain general drawings of the subdivisions, the subclasses or units divisions being limited to details only. Further subdivisions would probably be necessary in some cases. A card index with cross references and written by someone who knew what to do is an essential part of the system.

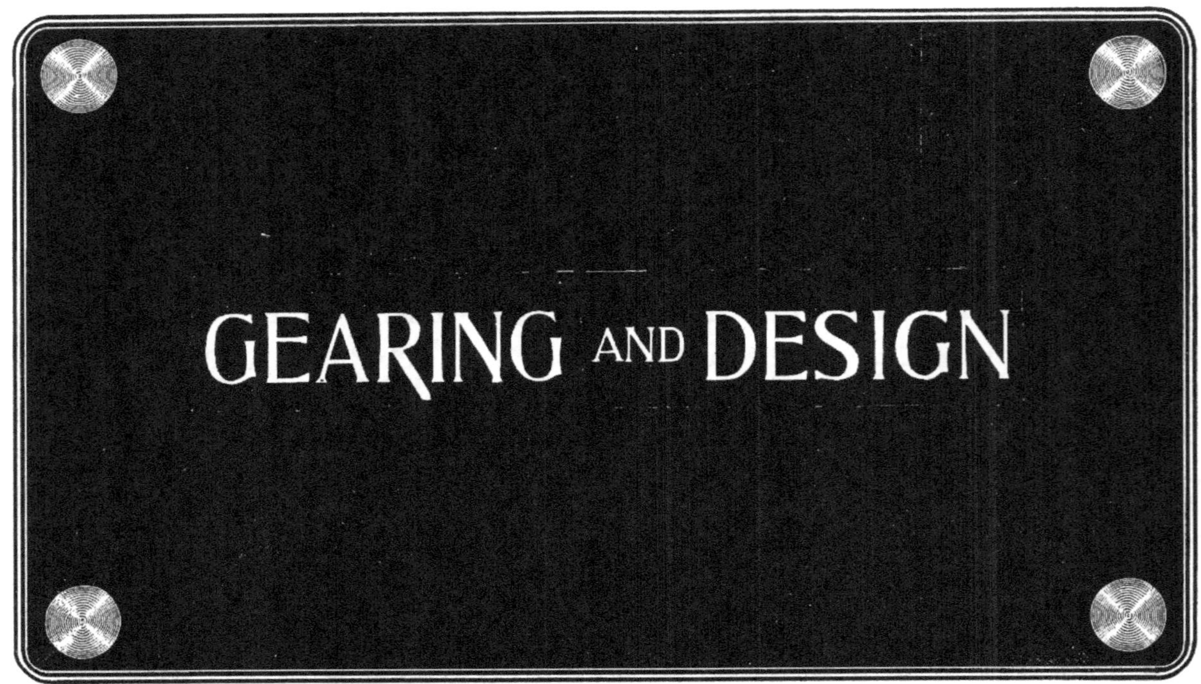

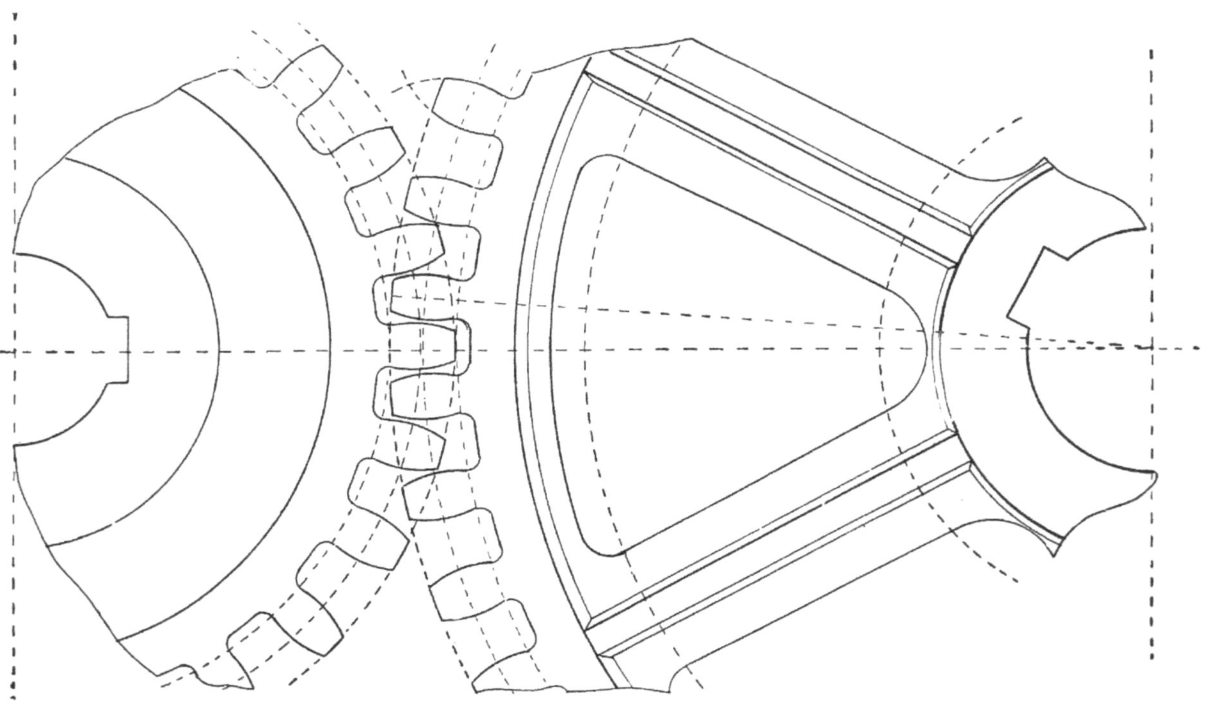

Fig. 263.

Gearing.

Under this heading the author has grouped some information relating to a subject of wide interest and one sure to interest a student of mechanical drawing.

The diagrams are intended for exercises in drawing, *i. e.*, to be redrawn as parts of practice; the text is to be studied not only for the good to be gained from the study of gearing, but as an example of the way in which written or printed descriptions are necessary to explain a subject illustrated by drawings.

A gear is primarily a toothed wheel; gearing is a train of toothed wheels for transmitting motions; there are two chief sorts of toothed gearing, viz., spur gearing and bevel gearing.

A spur wheel has teeth around the edge pointing to the center; commencing at the center, a spur wheel may be said to consist of a hole, square, octagonal or round, for its axle or shaft; a hub; the web, body or arms; a rim, and the teeth; see fig. 263.

A spur wheel has teeth on its circumference which run parallel to its shaft; wheels as shown in fig. 271 are termed *helical wheels*; these are similar to spur wheels except their teeth are arranged upon different angles to the shaft.

A bevel is a slant or inclination of a surface from a right line, hence a bevel wheel is one whose teeth stand beveling or at an oblique angle to the shaft, or towards the center; see fig. 267.

Miter wheels are bevel wheels of the same size, working at right angles with one another; see fig. 268.

The diameter of both spur and bevel wheels is measured and calculated neither from the outside nor from the bottom of the teeth, but on the pitch circle. When we speak of the diameter of a spur or bevel wheel, we mean the diameter of the pitch circle, without any reference to the form of tooth.

The addendum circle of a toothed wheel is as shown in illustration, fig. 264; *addendum* means "something added," and, as shown in the figure, it is the part added beyond the pitch "line" or circle.

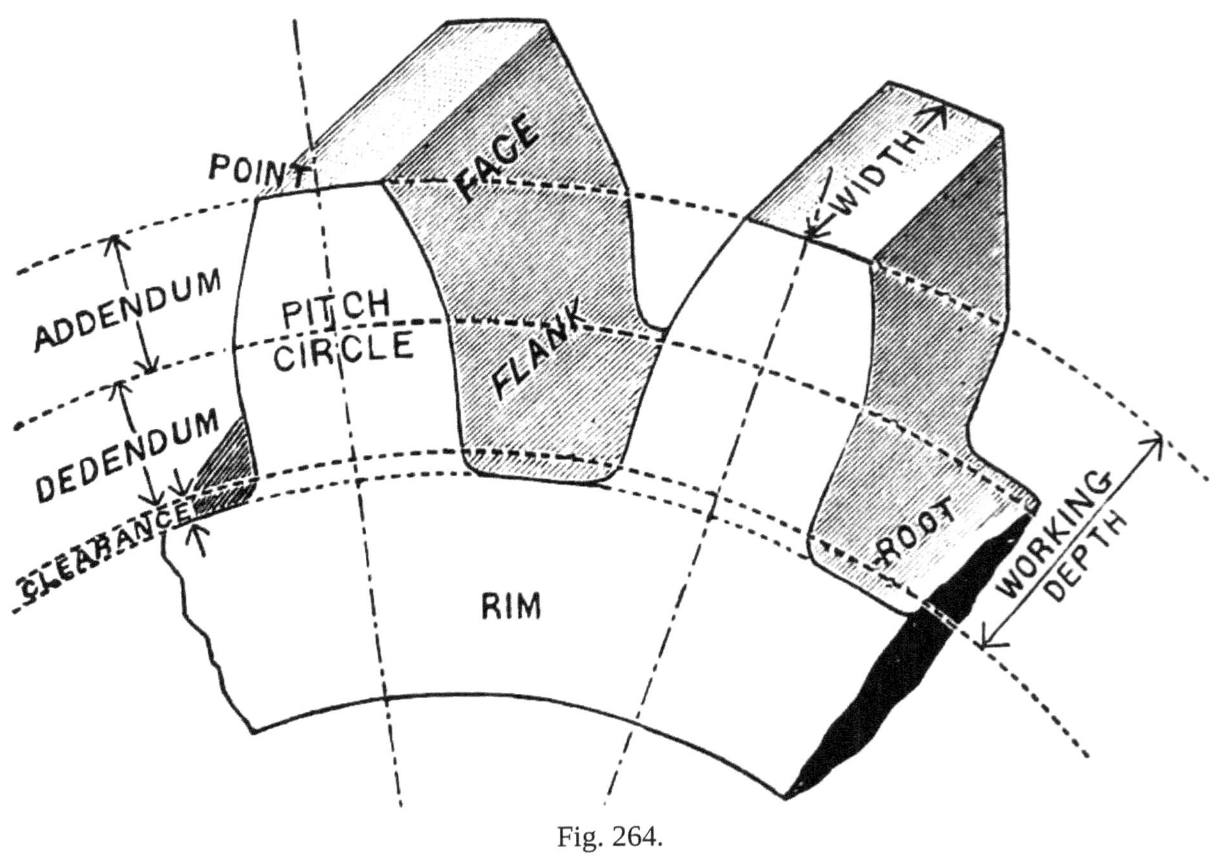

Fig. 264.

The pitch line is the most important one in gearing; the "pitch line" or "pitch circle" is supposed to be the working circle. This is shown in P—P in fig. 274.

The periphery of a wheel is the extreme circumference, as N in fig. 274.

All parts of gear-wheels consist of portions, to which have been given generally accepted names. Fig. 264 shows the "addendum circle" and the "pitch line" as marked. The teeth and rim are shown in white, and the other portions are indicated by the names.

The circular pitch line, as opposed to the diametral pitch, is the same as the pitch circle. It is a line which bisects all the teeth of a toothed wheel.

The rolling circle is the same as the circular pitch line.

Diametral means pertaining to a diameter or the length of a diameter; hence a diametral pitch is a system of measures or enumeration based upon the diameter instead of the circular pitch line; it is used very generally in spacing for fine tooth gear. Wheels of this description usually have their teeth cut in a gear-cutting machine, *i. e.,* medium and fine tooth gears.

A cog wheel is the general name for any wheel which has a number of cogs placed around its circumference.

When the teeth of a wheel are made of the same material and formed of the same piece as the body of the wheel, they are called *teeth*; when they are made of wood or some other material and fixed to the circumference of the wheel, they are called *cogs*; see fig. 265.

A pinion is a small wheel. When two toothed wheels act upon one another, the smaller is generally called the pinion. The terms *trundle* and *lantern* are applied to small wheels having cylindrical bars instead of teeth. The teeth in pinions are sometimes termed *leaves*; in a trundle, *staves*. See fig. 273.

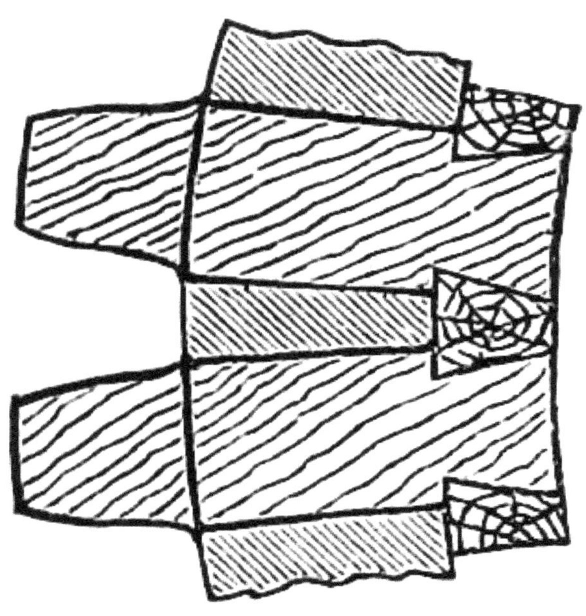

Fig. 265.

The wheel which acts is called a *leader* or *driver*; and the wheel which is acted upon by the former is called a *follower* or the *driven.* When a screw or *worm* revolves in the teeth of a wheel, the latter is termed a *worm wheel* or *worm gear*; see fig. 270. When a pinion acts with a rack having teeth, we speak of *rack* and pinion. When the teeth are on the inside of the rim, and not on the periphery, the wheel is termed an *internal gear*; see fig. 272.

Two wheels acting upon one another in the same plane are called *spur gear*; the teeth are parallel with the axis. When wheels act at an angle, they are called *bevel gear.*

Friction gear-wheels are those which communicate motion one to the other by the simple contact of their surfaces.

In frictional gearing the wheels are toothless and one wheel drives the other by means of the friction between the two surfaces which are pressed together.

Grooved friction wheels are used to give greater cohesion than can be obtained by the plain surface.

Fig. 263 shows a pair of spur-wheels in gear. The dotted circles which meet are the rolling circles, called the "pitch line" or "pitch circle."

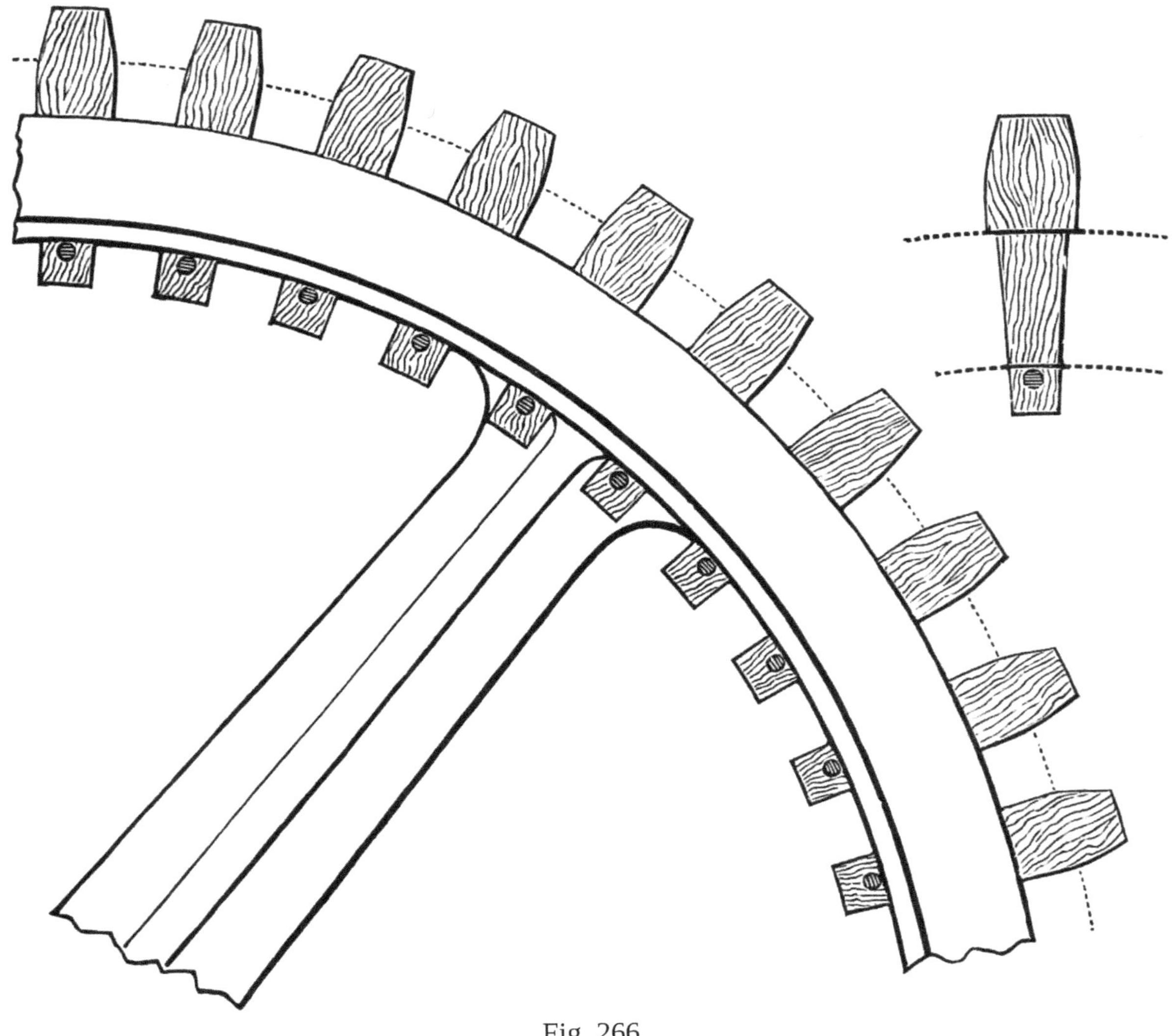

Fig. 266.

A spur mortise wheel is similarly shown in fig. 266; it is very like in appearance to a spur wheel; it differs essentially in that the teeth are separate cogs, fixed in singly to the rim; see also fig. 265, page 201.

NOTE.—The teeth of spur wheels cast from a pattern must of necessity be larger at one side than at the other, because the teeth must have taper to permit the extraction of the pattern from the mould; therefore, in fixing wheels to gear, the large side of one should meet the smaller side of the other; should the two large sides come together the teeth will meet only at the large side, and the teeth will probably break away from the excessive strain on that point.

Skew gearing are bevel wheels working out of center; the teeth do not form radial lines from the wheel center.

Fig. 267 shows a pair of bevel wheels in gear as described on page 199. A bevel mortise wheel, *i. e.,* one having cogs inserted in its rim instead of teeth.

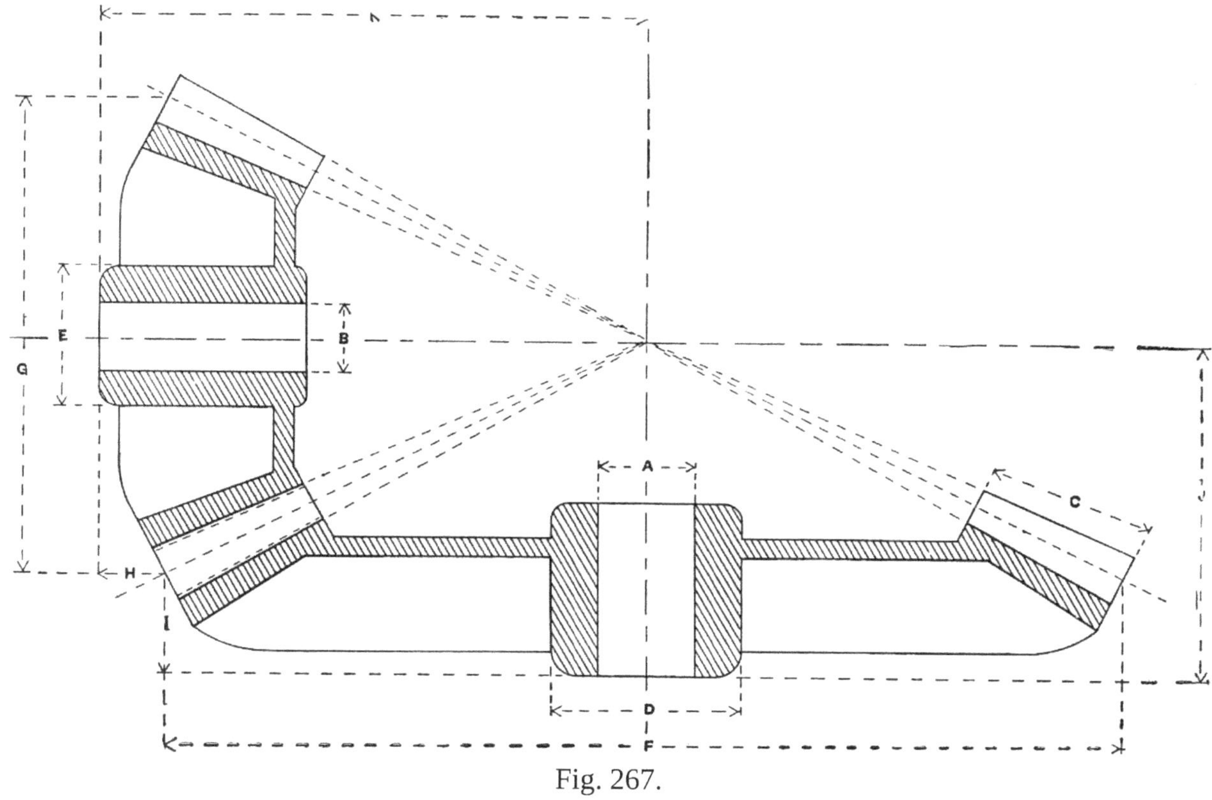

Fig. 267.

A bevel wheel and pinion must be made to suit one another by both having teeth forming together an angle of 90°, therefore they are pairs, or proportioned in the number of teeth one to the other. Any other proportion used would not exactly gear and would be termed a "bastard" gear.

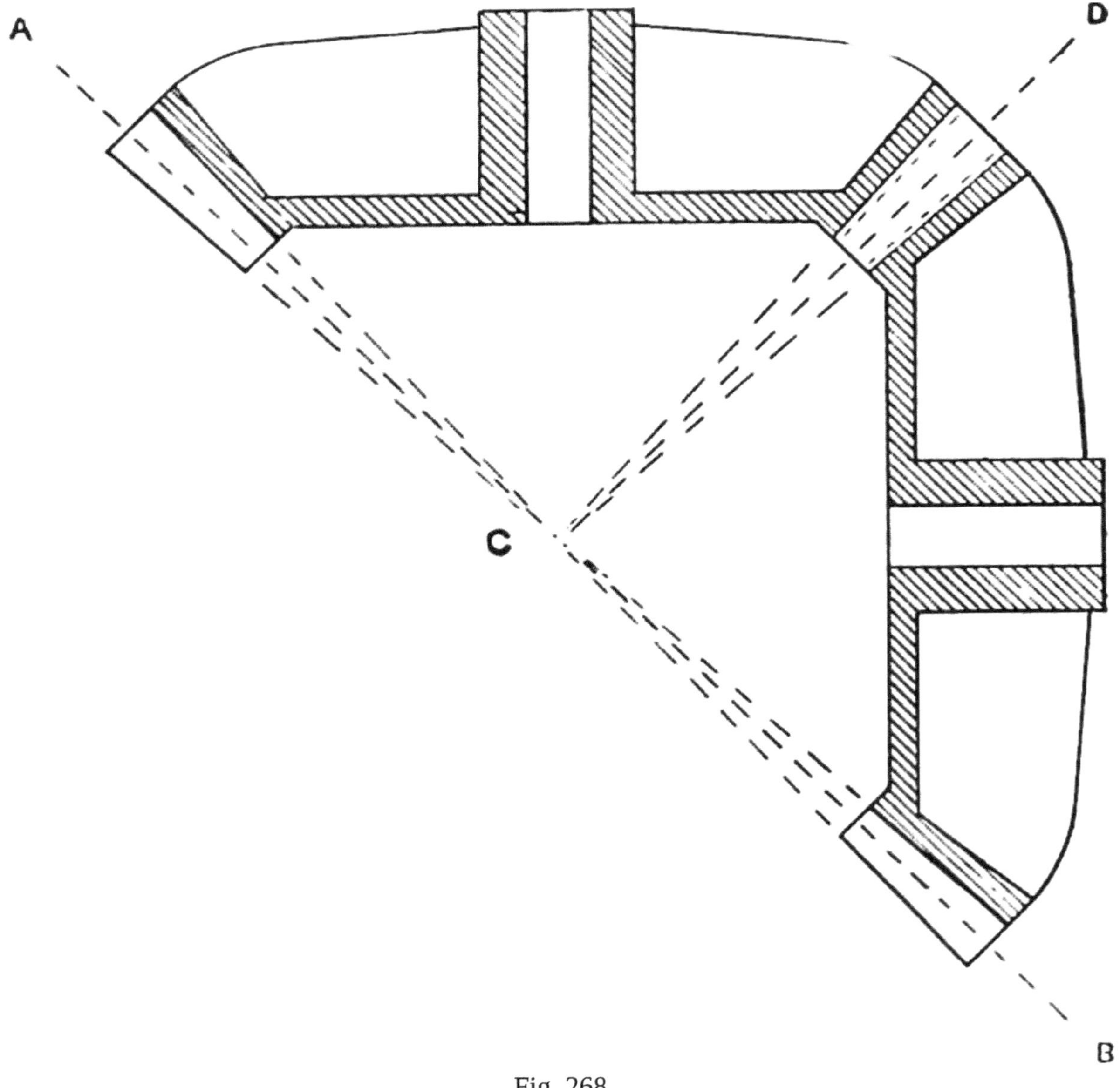

Fig. 268.

Fig. 268 represents a pair of miter wheels in gear; it will be noted that the shafts, when connected, will be at right angles to each other, the wheels being in all particulars of the same dimensions; the figure answers the purpose of a much longer description, if given in words.

A miter-wheel can easily be known by putting a square upon the face of the teeth, which are always at an angle of 45° with one another, irrespective of size.

A miter-wheel is a particular kind of bevel-wheel, the bevel being limited to an angle of 45° in each wheel.

The curve of the teeth in bevel-gears, when correctly formed, changes constantly from one end of the tooth to the other, therefore bevel-gears whose teeth are produced with a forced cutter are not theoretically correct.

Fig. 269 represents a rack and pinion: the teeth in this form of gear are shaped similarly to those in the spur wheel, shown on page 198, with the difference that the teeth of one are on a circle and on the rack are made on a straight line.

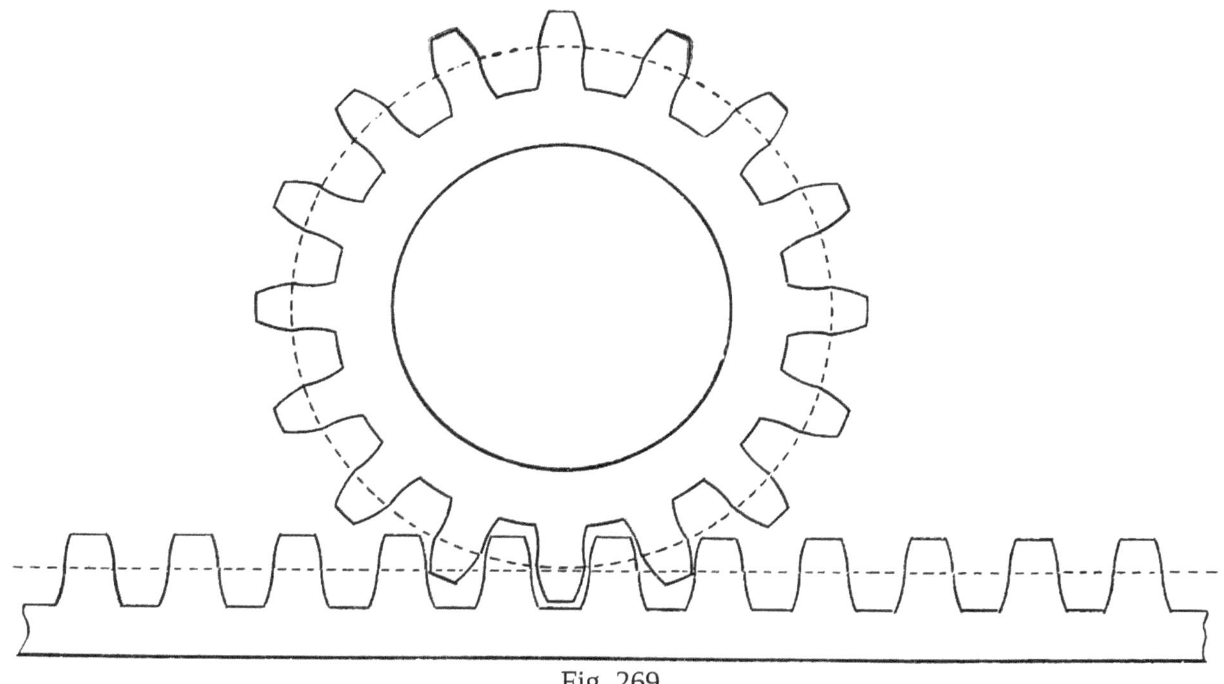

Fig. 269.

A flange or addition to the end of a tooth and the rim connecting them together is used to strengthen the teeth. This extends from the root to pitch line when the wheel and pinion are both flanged: if only one is flanged it extends from the root to the addendum.

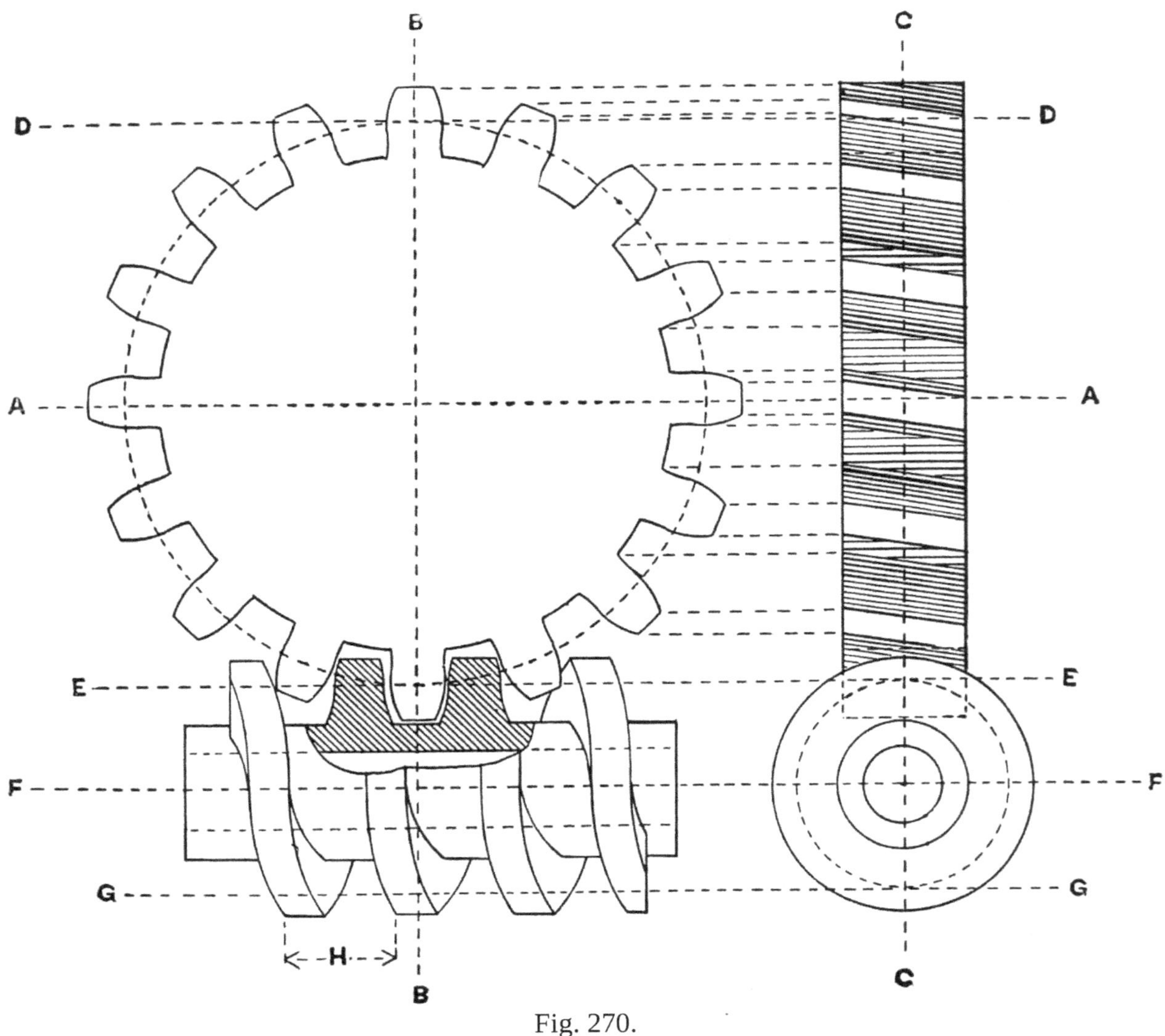

Fig. 270.

Fig. 270 illustrates a worm and a worm wheel, sometimes called screw gears. This is a slow but powerful method of transmitting power, one revolution of the worm only moving the wheel the distance of one tooth and space.

A worm gear is a spur wheel with teeth at an angle to the axis, so as to work with a worm which is a *screw,* or has teeth shaped in the form of a spiral wound round its circumference; the screw or worm is called an endless screw, because it never comes to a stopping place in the circumference of the wheel.

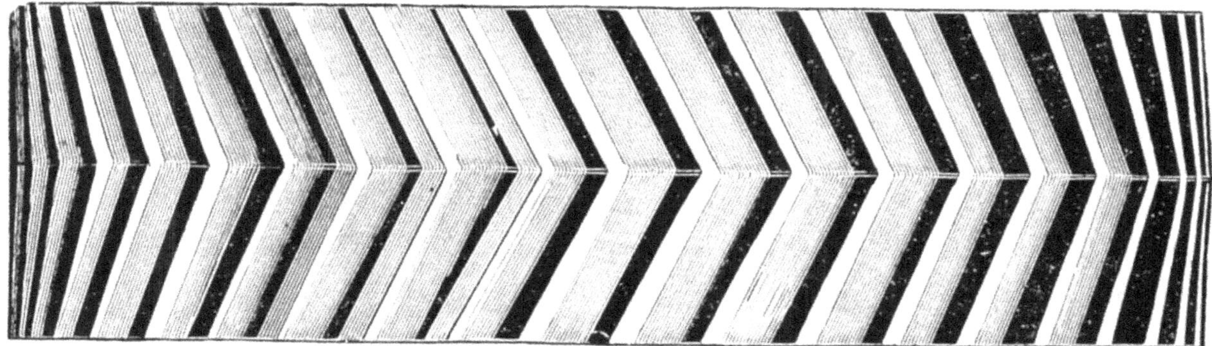

Fig. 271.

Fig. 271 represents a gear with helical teeth. It is similar to a spur wheel, and is used in place of same in heavy and slow moving machinery, the formation of teeth preventing—in large measure—the jar or concussion noticeable in common spur gears.

In recent years the speed at which gearing is run has been greatly increased. A striking instance is that of a pair of *cast-iron* helical wheels, 6 ft. 3 in. diameter, 12 in. wide, making 220 revolutions per minute, the speed of the pitch line being 4,319 feet per minute; these wheels are running continuously and with little noise. There is also a *cut* gear in a mill in Massachusetts, 30 feet in diameter, and the speed of pitch line is 4,670 feet per minute.

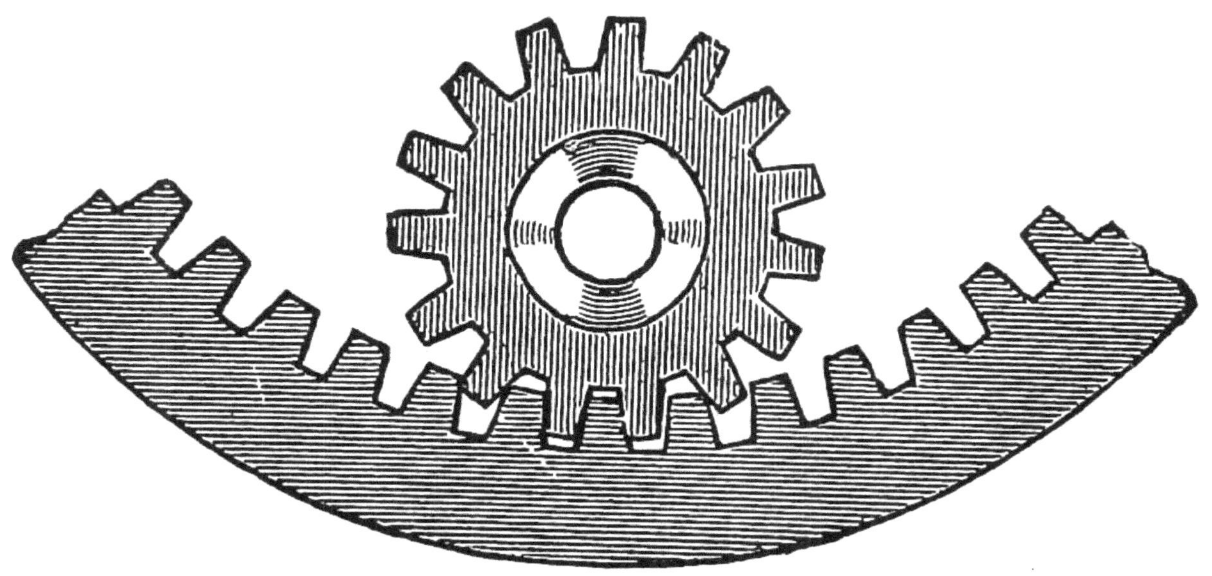

Fig. 272.

An internal or annular gear wheel is one in which the faces of the teeth are within and the flank without the pitch circle, hence the pinion operates within the wheel. See fig. 272.

In internal geared wheels there is almost an entire absence of friction and consequent wear of the teeth, as compared to ordinary spur gearing.

Fig. 273 shows a *crown-wheel* which has pin teeth which are fixed by one end only, on its side face and gear into a trundle wheel.

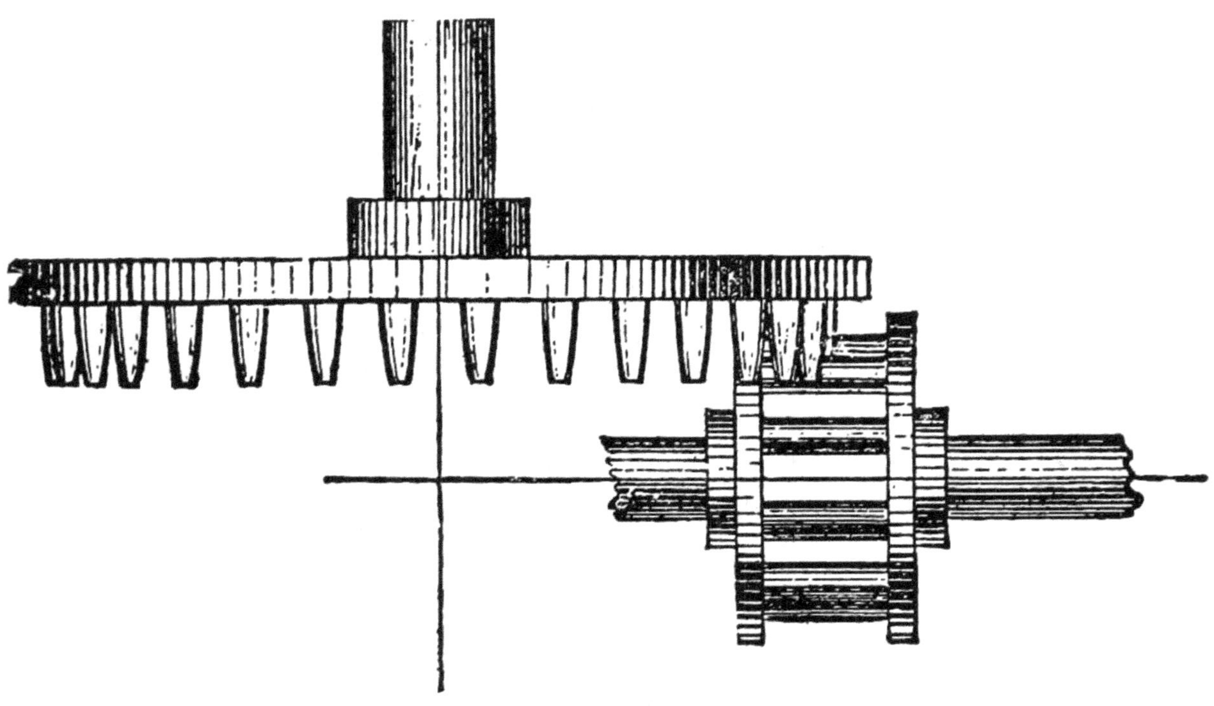

Fig. 273.

A trundle wheel has no teeth, properly speaking. Instead of teeth, it has pins as shown on illustration, fig. 273, arranged like the rungs of a ladder between two walls. See page 201.

Trains of Gears.—When two wheels mesh—that is, engage with each other—as in fig. 263, one axle revolves in the opposite direction to the other; but when internal gears mesh as shown in fig. 272, the shafts revolve in the same direction; three or more gears running together are often called *a train of gears.*

Maximum speed of gears under favorable conditions for safety is comparatively—

Ordinary cast-iron wheels,   1,800 feet per minute.
Helical cast-iron wheels,   2,400 feet per minute.
Mortise wood cog wheels,   2,400 feet per minute.
Ordinary cast-steel wheels,   2,600 feet per minute.
Helical cast-steel wheels,   3,000 feet per minute.
Cast-iron machine cut wheels, 3,000 feet per minute.

It is not, however, advisable to run gears at their maximum speeds, as great noise and vibration are caused.

Designing Gears.

This section is introduced into the work for a double purpose; 1, as an exercise in drawing; 2, as a study in accurate measurements. It is a sample of the work that the advanced student in mechanical drawing will be confronted with as he puts in practice the theory of the art of drawing.

Some sample rules are given in the following pages to aid in calculations relating to gears, and still others are given under the section "Useful Rules and Tables" at the end of the volume; these are to be carefully studied.

To accurately divide the pitch circle of a gear wheel by hand requires both patience and skill. On the accuracy of spacing lies the essential requisite of a good gear wheel.

The drawing in plate, fig. 274, illustrates a pair of spur wheels, shown in gear, the office instructions for which being:

"Required, *a detail plan* of a pair of spur wheels; dimensions: wheel, 76 teeth, 3½ inches pitch, 7-inch eye, 6 arms; pinion, 19 teeth; scale, 1½ inches = 1 foot."

The drawing, as illustrated, is the result of the above instructions, all pencil lines being removed, and this result is worked out as follows:

76 teeth × 3½ inches, pitch = 266 inches in circum. = 7 ft. $0^{11}\!/_{16}$ in. diam. = 3 ft. $6^{11}\!/_{32}$ in. radius; with this measurement as represented on scale, draw line *P P* on drawing. This is called the pitch line.

Draw next diameter line, produce or extend this diameter line for pinion, and with radius of $10^{19}\!/_{32}$ (19 teeth × 3½) from pitch line of wheel, draw pitch line of pinion.

Take any point in this pitch line of wheel, mark off 3½ inches as represented on scale, mark this around the pitch line, it will be the center of each of the 76 teeth; then the breadth of thickness of each tooth (= pitch × 0.475) must be marked from these centers, then mark from *P L*, length of tooth to point (= pitch × 0.35) and *P L* to root (= pitch × 0.4), draw circles for outside of teeth *N* and root of tooth *O*; now with compass set to the pitch (3½) of the wheel, draw the outer portion from pitch line of tooth.

The radius will center in the pitch line of next tooth where thickness of tooth has been marked; after finishing outer portion of both sides of teeth, set the compass from *center* of tooth with radius to the thickness marked on pitch line and draw the portion of tooth from pitch line to root.

Now mark off with dividers and draw thickness of rim (= pitch × 0.5), divide this line into six parts, draw radii for centers of arms; draw the bore hole 7″ and the thickness of metal for hub same as pitch.

On radii lines of arms, draw the breadth of arm at rim (= pitch and thickness of tooth), increase in breadth approaching the center (1″ per foot), draw the thickness of feather of arm (= pitch × 0.35); draw web on inside of rim (= pitch × 0.375); fill in arcs for the joining of arms in rim and hub (radii = pitch × 0.8) and feather to rim and hub (radii = pitch × 0.37).

Proceed in similar manner, completing the teeth of pinion, and when pencil lines are all in, ink the drawing, erasing all needless lines.

P P shows the pitch line; *B*, thickness of tooth; *c*, breadth of space; *A*, the pitch; *E*, clearance at root; *N*, the addendum of tooth; *O*, the root of tooth; *H*, length of tooth from pitch line to point; *I*, length of tooth pitch line to root; *G*, whole length of tooth; *F*, thickness of rim; *J*, web or feather on rim; *K*, breadth of arm; *L*, thickness of feather; *M*, hub, or thickness round the eye.

NOTE.—It must be remembered that no fixed standard has ever been agreed upon for these proportions, and workshops differ considerably in practice.

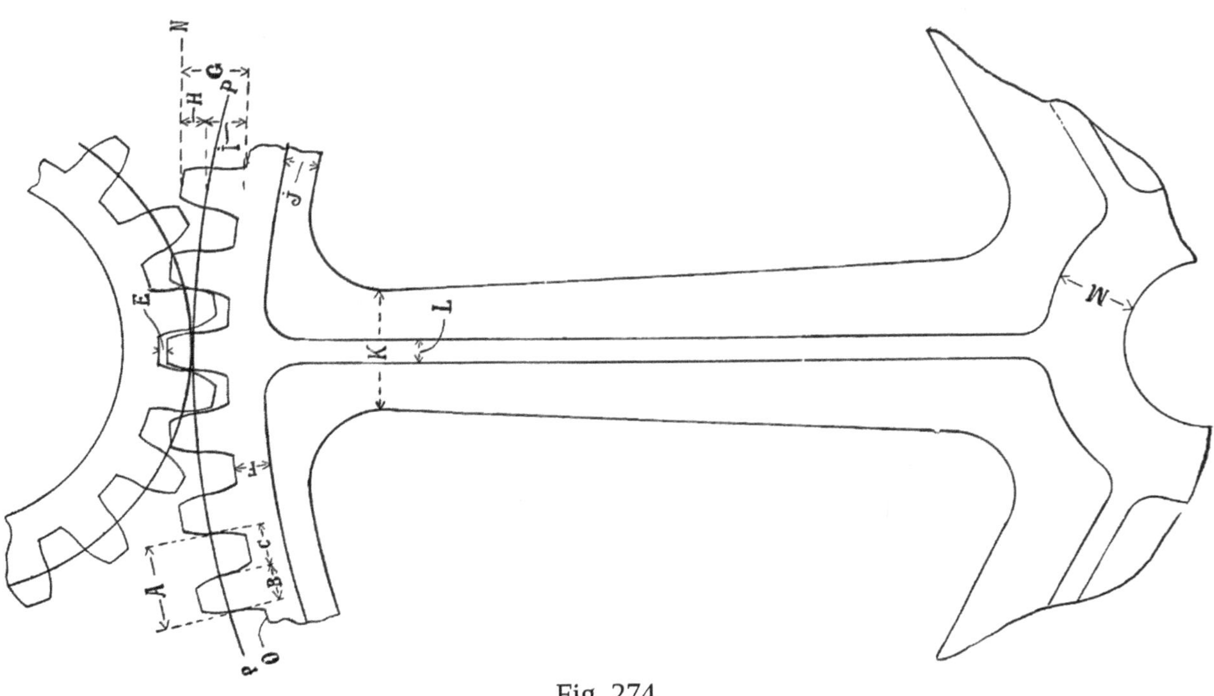

Fig. 274.

The number of teeth, their proportions, pitch and diameter of pitch circle are frequently determined on the "Manchester" principle. This system originated in Manchester (Eng.), and is now generally used in the United States for determining diameters and number of teeth, which, of course, regulate speeds. The principle is not applicable to large wheels, but is limited in its application to small wheels, or wheels having "fine pitch," as will be seen in the following explanation, which is introduced as very useful and indispensable knowledge for the acquisition of the student in mechanical drawing.

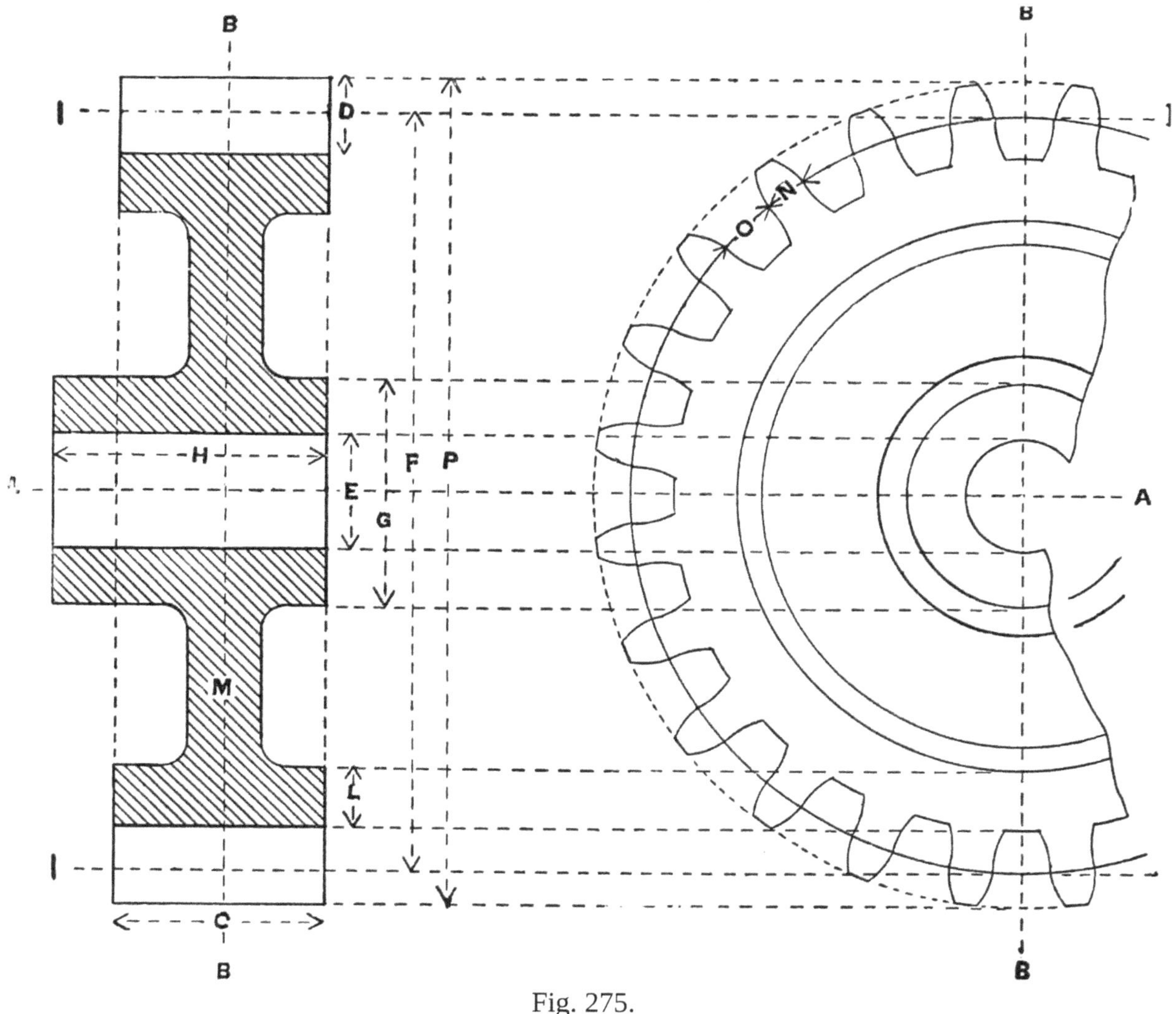

Fig. 275.

The "pitch" of teeth has already been stated to be the distance from center of one tooth to the center of another on the "pitch line," measured on the chord of the arc. In determining the number of teeth or pitch of wheels on this principle, the pitch is reckoned on the *diameter* of the wheel, *in place of the circumference,* and distinguished as wheels of "4 pitch," "6 pitch," "8 pitch," etc. In other words, this means that there are four, six, or eight teeth in the circumference of the wheel for every inch of diameter.

In designing gears to transmit power the stress on a tooth is calculated; it determines the breadth or width and also the thickness of the tooth on pitch line; the space between the teeth is in proportion to the thickness of tooth, and the thickness of both combined (one tooth and one space), measured on the pitch line or circle, is the pitch of the wheel.

From the pitch all the proportions and measurements for the sizes and strength of the parts of the wheel are taken *by rule,* and a symmetrical form is produced.

In machine drawing the practice is to represent wheels by circles only; the teeth are never shown except on enlarged details and then only in very rare instances; the circles drawn are always the *pitch lines* or the rolling points of contact of the wheels.

The addendum circle is seldom if ever used in practical drawing. Should it be necessary to show it in an exceptional case, the circle would be represented by "dotted" line.

The shape of tooth and mode of constructing it, as practiced in drawing offices, differs from the true theoretical curve of the tooth, although very minutely.

In all calculations for the speed of toothed gears the estimates are based upon the pitch line, the latter standing in the same place as the circumference of a pulley.

To find the *diameter of a gear-wheel* multiply the number of teeth by the pitch, divide by 3.1416.

To find the *pitch of a gear-wheel* multiply the diameter by 3.1416 and divide by the number of teeth.

To find the *number of teeth in a gear-wheel* multiply the diameter by 3.1416 and divide by the pitch.

The *breadth of wheels,* where practicable, should be at least three times the pitch.

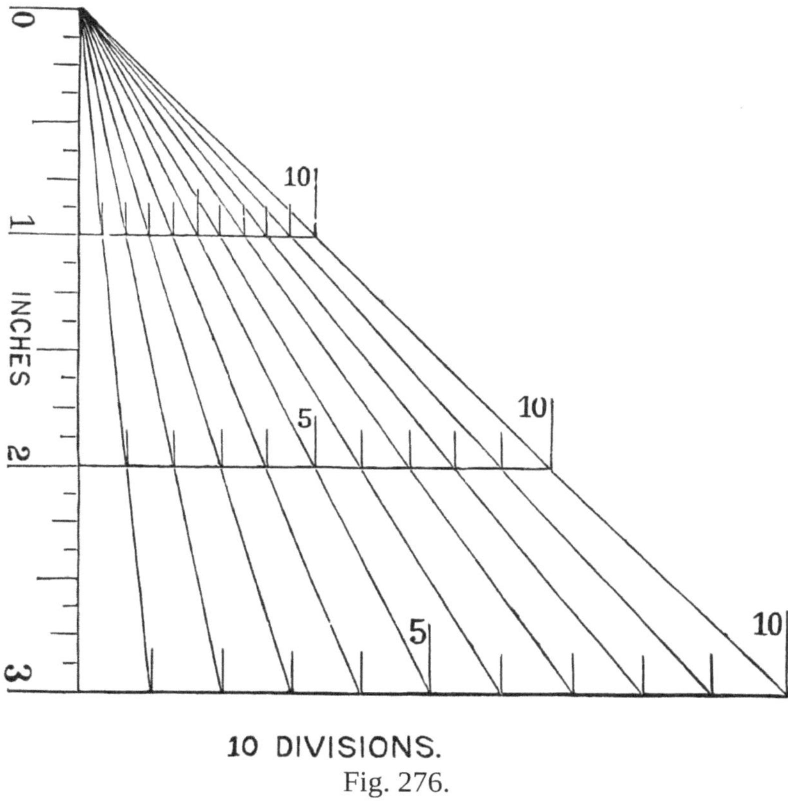

Fig. 276.

Fig. 276 shows a scale for proportions of teeth; it is divided into tenths and used thus:

Say wheel is 2″ pitch, then from pitch circle to addendum will be 3½ tenths, and from pitch circle to root of tooth will be 4 tenths measured at the 2″ line on scale, and so on.

The decimal proportions already given in example, page 210, are adopted in many workshops. Many others use the proportions approved of by Sir William Fairbairn, which are:

Table of proportion of gears:

Depth of tooth above pitch line	.35 of the pitch.
Depth of tooth below pitch line	.40 of the pitch.
Working depth of tooth	.70 of the pitch.
Total depth of tooth	.75 of the pitch.
Clearance at root	.05 of the pitch.
Thickness of tooth	.45 of the pitch.
Width of space	.55 of the pitch.

The diameter of a wheel or pinion is invariably the diameter measured on pitch circle, except it is specially described otherwise, thus the diameter "over all," etc.

The shape of the curved face of the teeth of gears extending from the root to the addendum is the curve conforming to the passage of the teeth described on its fellow entering and leaving, as they rotate or roll together on their pitch circles.

The curve of teeth outside the pitch circle is called "the face," and the curve from pitch circle to root is called "the flank."

The difference between the width of a space and the thickness of a tooth is called clearance or side clearance.

The play or movement permitted by clearance is called the backlash; clearance is necessary to prevent the teeth of one wheel becoming locked in the spaces of the other.

Wheels are in gear or geared together when their pitch lines engage, *i. e.*, when the pitch circles meet.

Wheels to be geared together must have their teeth spaced the same distance apart, or in other words, of the same pitch.

The teeth of spur wheels are arranged on its periphery parallel to the wheel axis, or shaft on which it is hung.

The teeth of a bevel wheel or bevel gears are always arranged at an angle to the shaft.

When the *teeth* of bevel gears form an angle of 45° they are called miter wheels.

Miter wheels to gear must be of equal sizes.

A crown wheel is a disc that has teeth which are on its side face; that is, teeth on a flat circular surface all parallel to the axis of the wheel.

A rack has teeth on a flat surface or plane all parallel to one another.

A gear cut by machine is called a *cut gear*. It has teeth with less clearance than cast wheels, which are not so true or perfect, and therefore require more clearance.

A worm with even a light load is liable to heat and cut if run at over 300 feet of rubbing surface travel. The wheel teeth will keep cool, as they form part of a large radiating surface; the worm itself is so small that its heat is dissipated slowly.

A worm throws a severe end thrust or strain on its shaft.

Steel Gears.—There is great economy in the use of cast-steel over cast-iron in gears; the average life of the former is nearly twice as great as of cast-iron gears. And, apart from their longer life and efficiency, there is less danger of breaking.

The most accurate teeth, strongest and most uniform in wearing, are to be found in steel gears cut from solid stock, or made by cutters of proper shape.

Fig. 275 shows an elevation and a vertical section of a spur wheel. From these views the various parts in spur gears can be better understood, as they are represented here in combination, and the wheel in its entirety.

AA is the horizontal center line, *BB, BB* the vertical center lines, *II* and *II* the pitch lines, *N* thickness of tooth, *O* space of tooth, *D* total depth of tooth, *C* breadth of face, *F* diameter on pitch line, *P* diameter over all, *G* diameter of hub, *E* diameter of hole, *H* depth of hole, *L* thickness of rim, *M* thickness of web.

Much has been and still is being written on gearing. No general rule is followed by the writers; the elementary principles given will enable the student to master spur gearing, and bevel and combinations of many kinds of wheels will afterwards be found easier to delineate than the numerous lines seem to indicate.

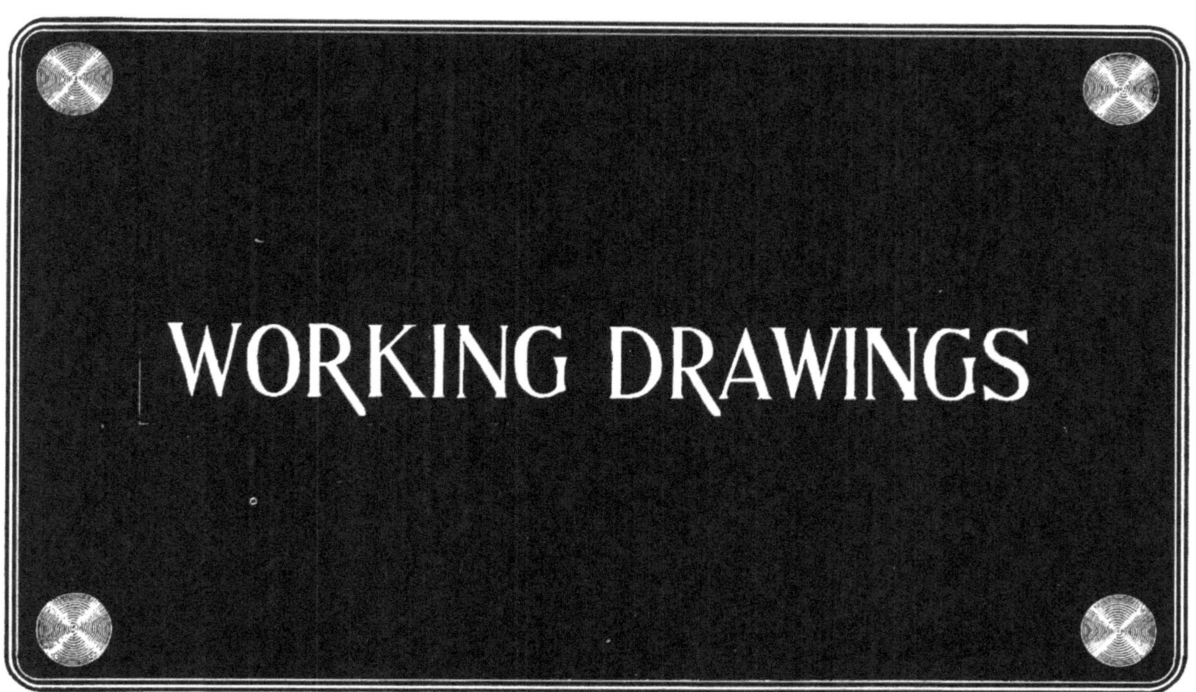

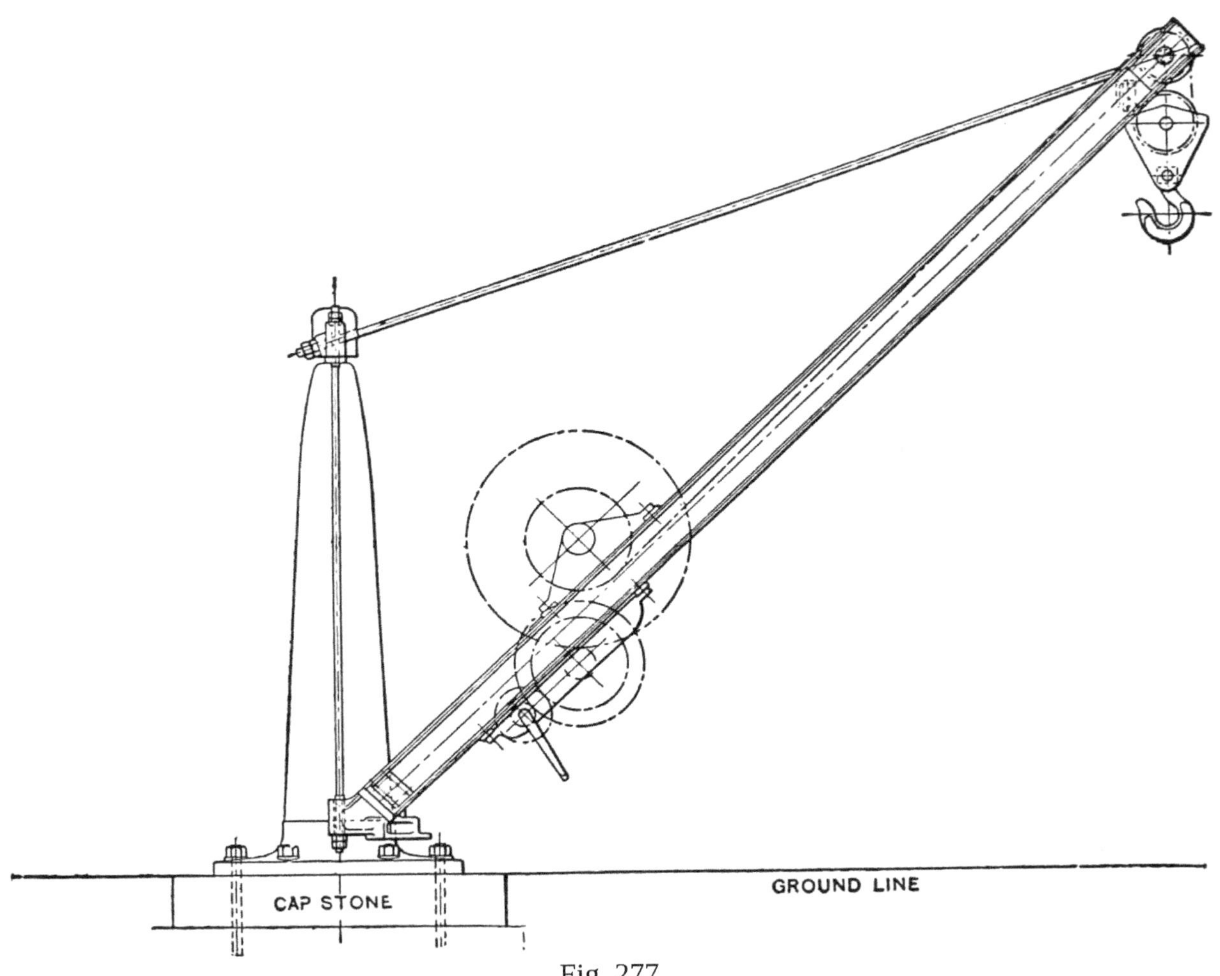

Fig. 277.

Working Drawings.

From the "plans" made in the office are produced "working drawings"—which represent in detail the work to be done to exact measurement and of material, as indicated, by the pattern-maker, the foundry, the forge, the shop, and finally, by the erector of the completed mechanism.

How to satisfactorily fulfill the directions contained in these drawings, representing only a part of the work, so that it will fit, with needed accuracy, to all other parts of the design, is the task before each separate worker.

It is by means of this division of the process of manufacture through these drawings, that scores and hundreds of men can be employed at the same time upon a single engine or machine; thus, while handwork has been superseded by machines in many quarters, the art of drawing has not been narrowed nor diminished, for no drawings or designs have yet been made by machinery, nor are they likely to be.

It is thus that a good designer and draughtsman "projects" or extends himself, to the advantage of many fellow workers.

The drawing, fig. 277, shows a simple form of pillar crane: it consists of an upright cast-iron pillar, which is bolted on a cap stone, under which is the foundation plate not shown in the drawing; the boom is of rolled steel, supported by steel tie rods, and provided with rollers at the base; the hoisting gear is shown in broken lines and circles; all as seen in the drawing.

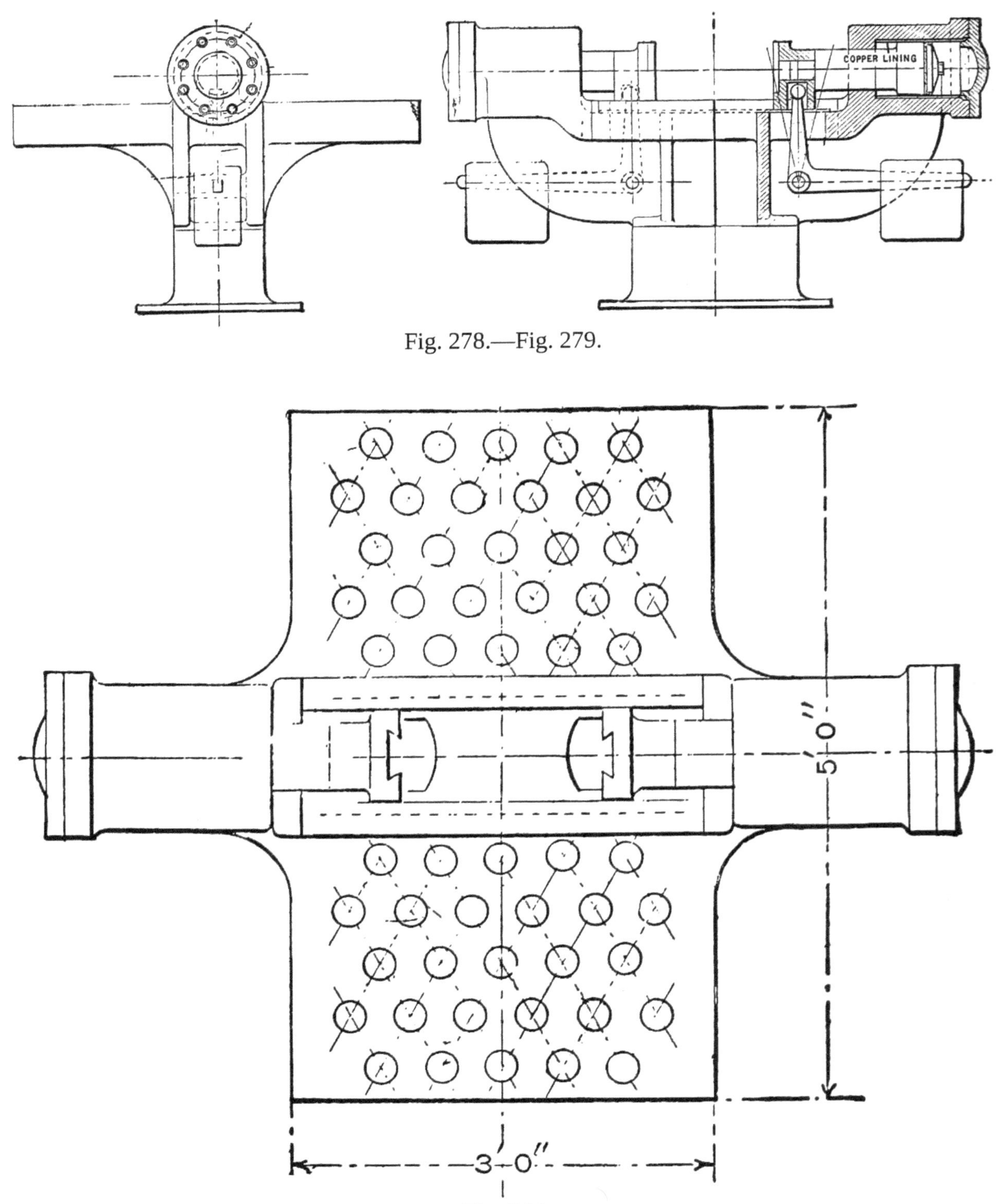

Fig. 278.—Fig. 279.

Fig. 280.

Figs. 278, 279 and 280 show a drawing of a "hydraulic beam bending machine" in three views; fig. 280 is a plan, fig. 278 is an end elevation, and fig. 279 a side elevation, and a portion of the latter in section shows the interior construction.

NOTE.—These three views are a practical illustration of drawings for a machine of the following dimensions: this machine has a bed 3 × 5 feet in area, with 27 holes in each side for the bending pins. The frame and cylinders are made of cast iron, the rams of machinery steel, and the slides for holding the bending blocks, of steel casting. The distance between the bending blocks is 17 inches. The cylinders are copper lined, 8 inches diameter, and the rams have a 6-inch stroke. The rams, which are independent and single acting, are returned by counterweights placed as shown under the table. The cylinders can be operated independently from either side of the machine by an arrangement of valves and levers. The machine complete weighs about 7,500 lbs.

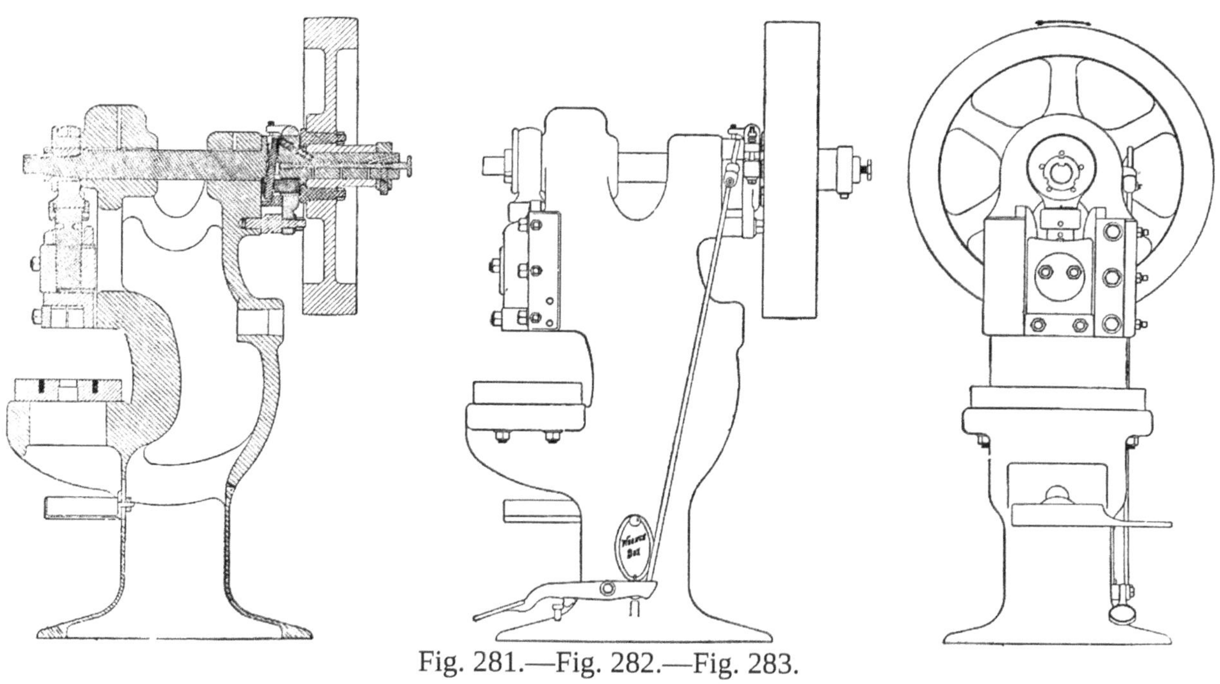

Fig. 281.—Fig. 282.—Fig. 283.

The drawing, page 222, shows three views of a power punching press.

Fig. 282 is a side elevation.

Fig. 283 a front elevation.

Fig. 281 a vertical sectional view; from these views the proportion, general arrangement and disposition of the automatic devices can be easily understood; it may be well to call particular attention to the automatic clutch on the top shaft and the tripping device.

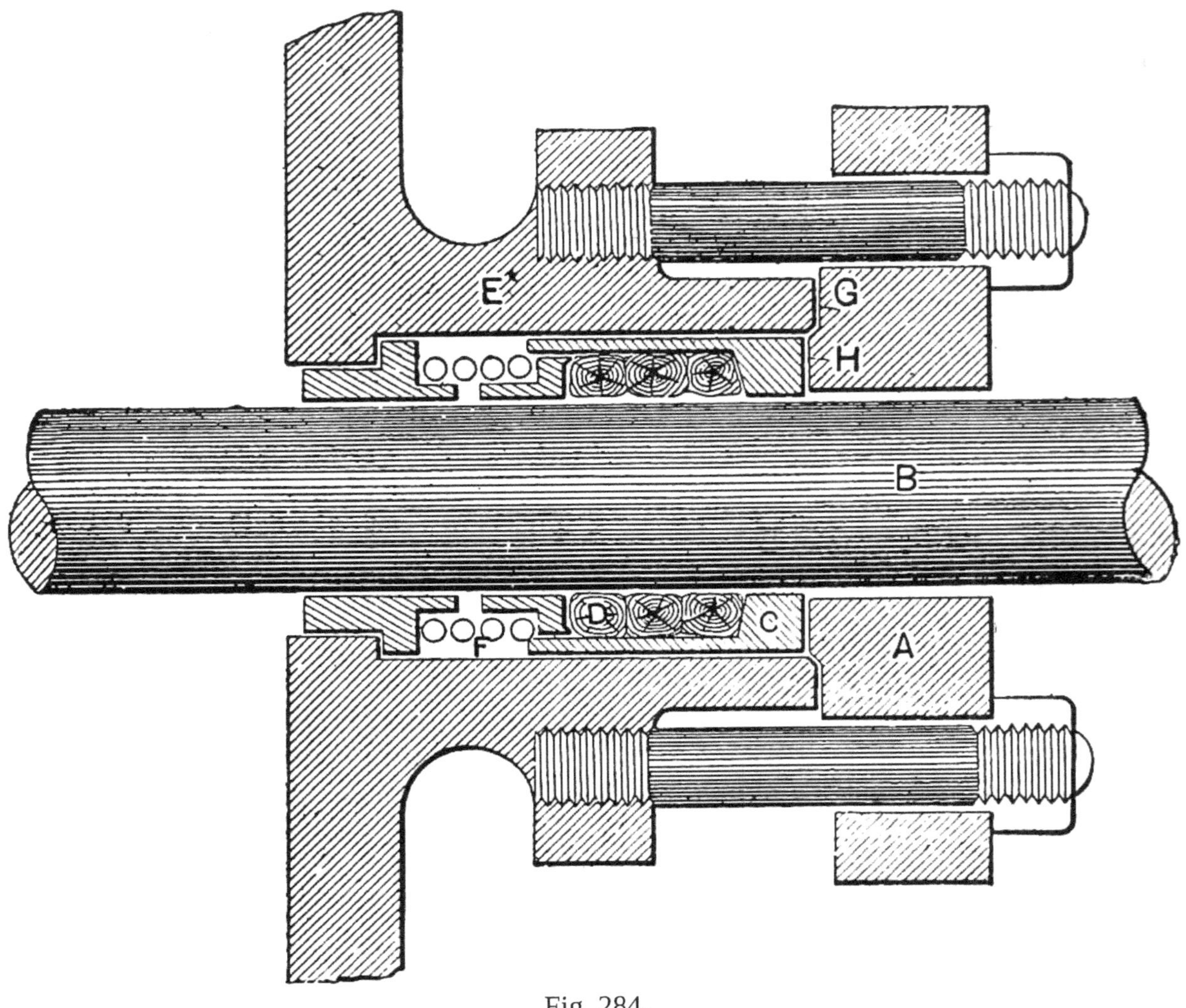

Fig. 284.

This drawing, fig. 284, shows a side elevation in section of a self-adjusting piston-rod packing.

A is the gland, *B* is the piston rod, *C* is a brass sleeve which contains the packing *D*, *E* is the cylinder cover, *F* is a coil spring. It will be seen that the spring *F* abuts on a bushing in the bottom of the stuffing box and is prevented from scoring the piston rod by stepping over the ends of the bushing and follower. All as shown in the drawing.

The drawing, fig. 285, shows a sectional view of a large pulley fixed on a "quill," or hollow shaft: the driving shaft passes through the hollow shaft and is attached to the friction clutch shown at the right-hand end; this friction clutch drives the hollow shaft and pulley.

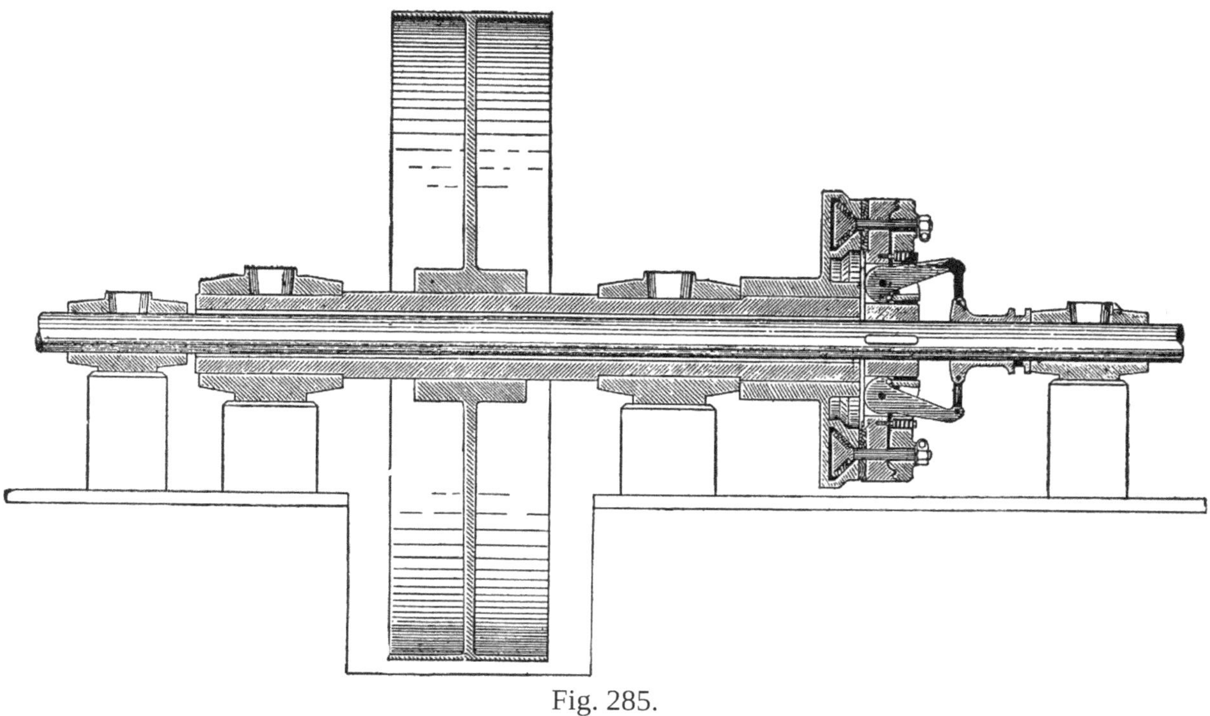

Fig. 285.

Fig. 286 shows the mechanism, called the link-motion, employed to reverse an engine, or to enable it to be run in either direction. Many forms of link-motion have been devised, but the Stephenson form, as shown in the figure, is, however, the one in almost universal use.

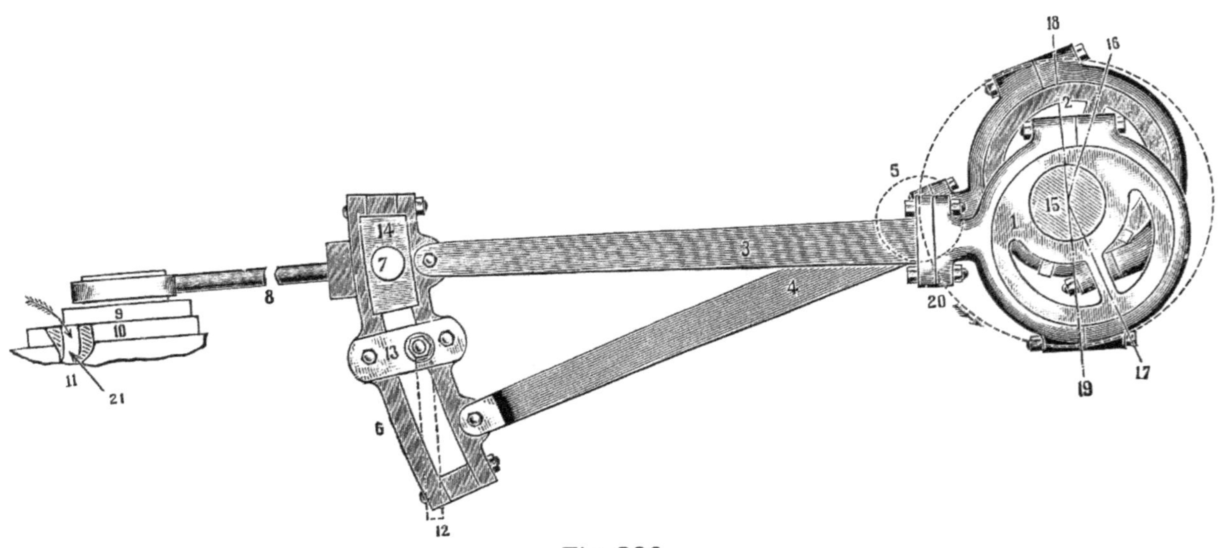

Fig. 286.

This drawing shows shading and the mode of figuring the parts for identification.

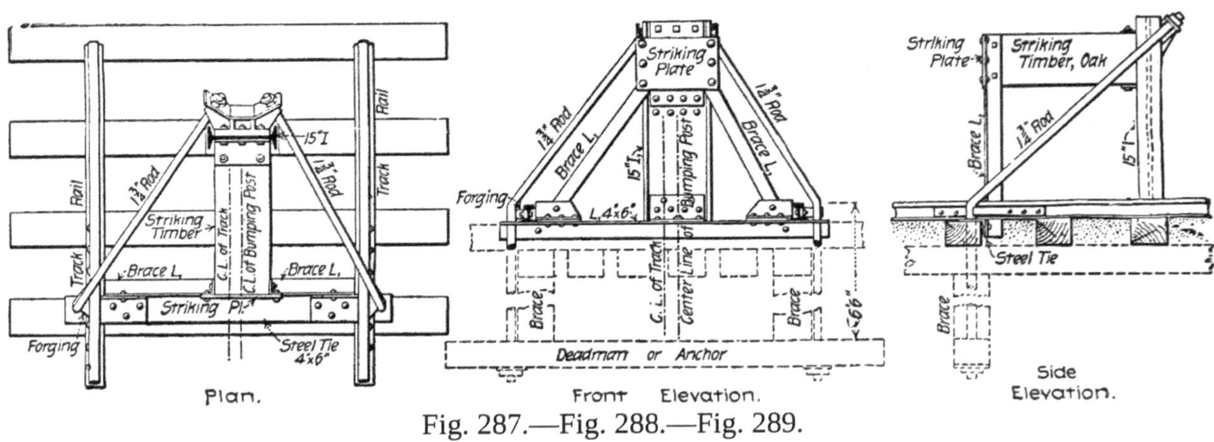

Fig. 287.—Fig. 288.—Fig. 289.

Figs. 287 to 289 represent a bumping-post for the end of railway tracks, reproduced on an enlarged scale from the columns of the *Engineering News.*

In addition to the lettering and dimensions, admirably shown in the drawings, the following description is appended to show how printed text and mechanical drawings mutually aid in practical—or commercial—usage.

The unique feature of the arrangement shown, is that the center line of the post does not coincide with the track, thus adapting itself to the nature of the blows of a car-bumper, as received in the single-post style of the mechanism.

BUMPING POST FOR RAILWAY TRACKS.

The post is a 15-in. steel I-beam, resting on a base plate ¾-in. thick, and supported by anchor rods 1¾ ins. diameter, with upset ends held by nuts on a heavy forging bolted to the top of the post. These rods extend forward and outward to clear the rails, and then pass vertically through a 4 × 6-in. angle iron crosstie, and an ordinary wooden tie, extending down to an anchor block or deadman buried in the ground 6½ ft. below the top of the rail.

Vertical braces or spreaders are fitted between the anchor timber and a longitudinal timber under the ties, so as to prevent the loosening of the anchor rods when the post is struck. The rods are held in position against the rails by steel forgings bolted to the rail with 1-in. turned bolts. An oak striking block, 12 × 12 ins., 3 ft. long, is bolted between angle iron brackets on the face of the post.

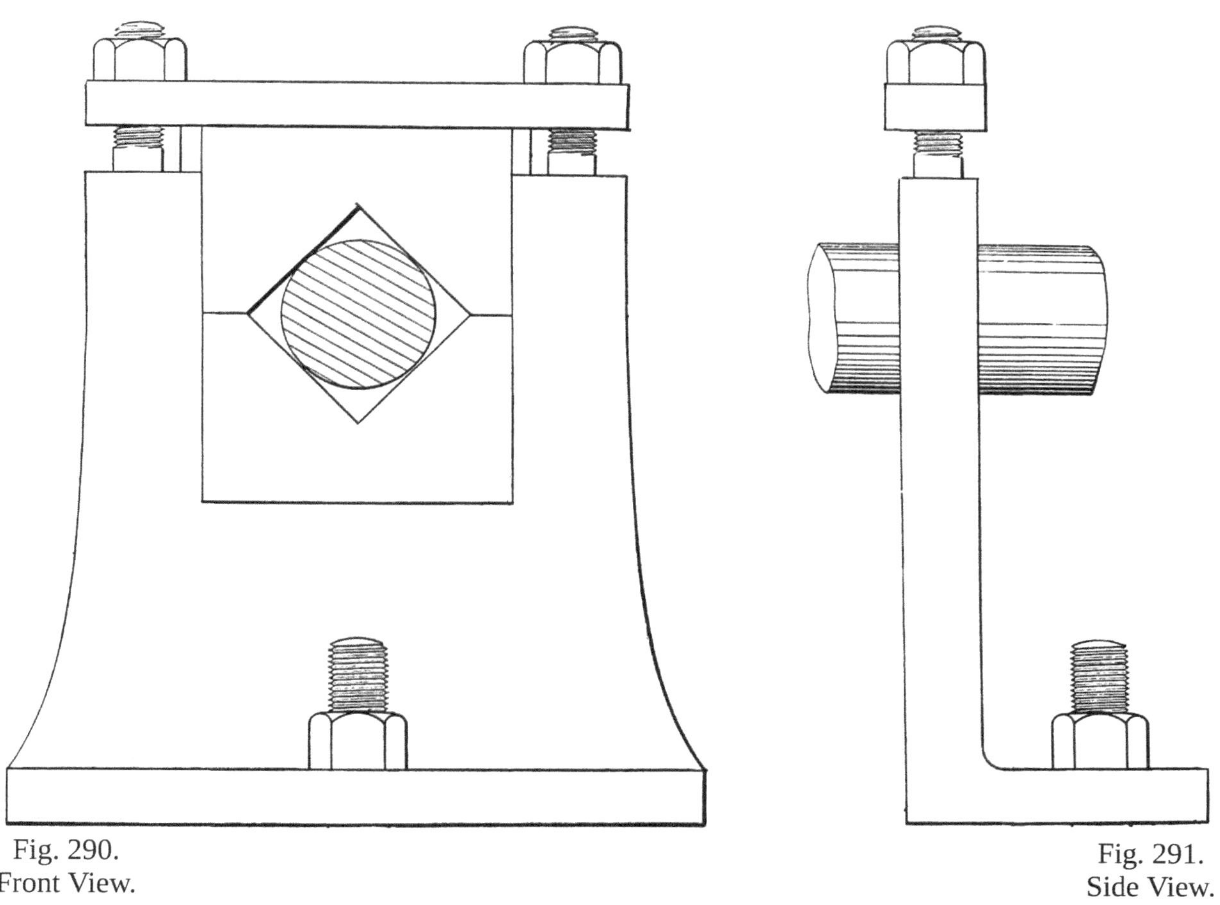

Fig. 290.
Front View.

Fig. 291.
Side View.

Scale, 3 in. = 1 ft.

To Read Working Drawings.

One of the advantages resulting from a knowledge of practical draughting is, that it enables a mechanic to *read* a drawing when given him as a guide for his work. It is getting every day more general among draughtsmen to figure exactly and minutely every part of their drawings which are made to a scale.

Drawings are almost always made "finished size," that is, the dimensions are for the work when it is completed. Consequently all the figures written on the different parts indicate the exact size of the work when finished, without any regard to the size of the drawing itself, which may be made to any reduced and convenient scale.

Even in full size drawings this system of figuring is not objectionable. It is a system which should be followed whenever a drawing is made "to work to," for it allows the workman to comprehend at a glance the size of his work and the pieces he has to get made. Figuring makes a drawing comprehensible even to those who cannot make drawings.

A working drawing should be made, primarily, as plain as possible by the draughtsman; second, the workman should patiently and carefully study it, so that it is thoroughly understood.

In studying a drawing, the object it is intended to represent should be made as familiar as possible to the mind of the student, so that he may fill out in imagination the parts designedly left incomplete—as in a gear wheel where only two or three teeth are drawn in, that he may see, mentally, the whole.

The following is a description of reading drawings when dimensions are not figured. Here we have a piece of machinery represented by fig. 290, and the information we have is that it is to scale, three inches = one foot. Now, with scale and dividers, we can arrive at its actual dimensions.

Measurements should be first taken *with the dividers from the drawing*, and then the dividers applied to the scale to which the drawing is made; this scale is always marked on the working drawing; if the dividers are set to the length of the base of the example, fig. 290, they will measure, on an ordinary two-foot rule, three and three-fourths inches, *but if applied to the three-inch scale they will read* one foot three inches, the actual length of the part; the "reading" is from the scale; thus, in both figures the drawings are "three-inch scale."

Now, 3 inches is one-fourth of a foot, hence $3\frac{3}{4} \times 4 = 1$ ft. 3 in., the full size, and so on for all parts of the drawing.

Fig. 291 shows *a side view* of the "steady rest," illustrated in front elevation, fig. 290; from the scale as before we get the sizes; the two views combined give length, breadth and thickness of the parts.

In some figures it is necessary to show end views, also section views, to enable all measurements to be read from the drawing.

Patent Office Drawing Rules.

U. S. PATENT OFFICE RULES.

AS APPLIED TO PREPARATION OF DRAWINGS.

Each applicant for a patent is required by law to furnish a drawing of his invention whenever the nature of the case admits of it. The drawing must be signed by the inventor or the name of the inventor may be signed on the drawing by his attorney-in-fact, and in either case must be attested by two witnesses. The drawing must show every feature of the invention covered by the claims.

When the invention consists of an improvement on an old machine, the drawing must exhibit, in one or more views, the invention proper, disconnected from the old structure, and also, in another view, so much only of the old structure as will clearly show the connection of the invention with the old machine.

Several editions of the patent-drawings are printed, the smallest of which is about $3 \times 4\frac{3}{4}$ inches, so that the drawing must be so made that it will stand a reduction of about one-fourth. This work is done by the photo-lithographic process, and therefore the character of the original drawing must be brought as nearly as possible to a uniform standard of excellence suited to the requirements of the process.

NOTE.—These rules will be found most useful to many readers of this work—hence their introduction at this point. Nearly 50,000 patents are "applied for" in the United States every year.

The following rules are given by the Patent Office for guidance:

1. Drawings must be made upon pure white paper of a thickness corresponding to three-sheet Bristol board. The surface of the paper must be calendered and smooth. India ink alone must be used, so as to secure perfectly black and solid lines.

2. The size of a sheet on which a drawing is made must be exactly 10×15 inches. One inch from its edges a single marginal line is to be drawn, leaving the "sight" precisely 8×13 inches. Within this margin all work and

signatures must be included. One of the shorter sides of the sheet is regarded as its top, and measuring downwardly from the marginal line, a space of not less than $1\frac{1}{4}$ inches is to be left blank for the heading of title, name, number and date.

3. All drawings must be made with the pen only. Every line and letter, signature included, must be absolutely black. This direction applies to all lines, however fine, to shading, and to lines representing cut surfaces in sectional views. All lines must be clean, sharp, and solid, and they must not be too fine or crowded. Surface shading, when used, should be open. Sectional shading should be made by oblique parallel lines about $\frac{1}{20}$ of an inch apart. Solid black should not be used for sectional or surface shading.

4. Drawing must be made of the fewest lines possible, consistent with cleanness. The plane upon which a sectional view is taken should be indicated by a broken or dotted line. Heavy lines on the shade side of objects should be used, except where they tend to thicken the work and obscure letters of reference. The light is always supposed to come from the upper left hand corner at an angle of 45 degrees.

5. The scale to which a drawing is made should be large enough to show the mechanism without crowding. The number of sheets used must never be more than is absolutely necessary.

Fig.1
10
4
12
8
3
2
11
7
1
9
5
6
Fig.2
10
4
12
3
8
2
11
7
1
9
5
6
Witnesses.
Inventor.
Clarence M. Kemp.
By
Att'y

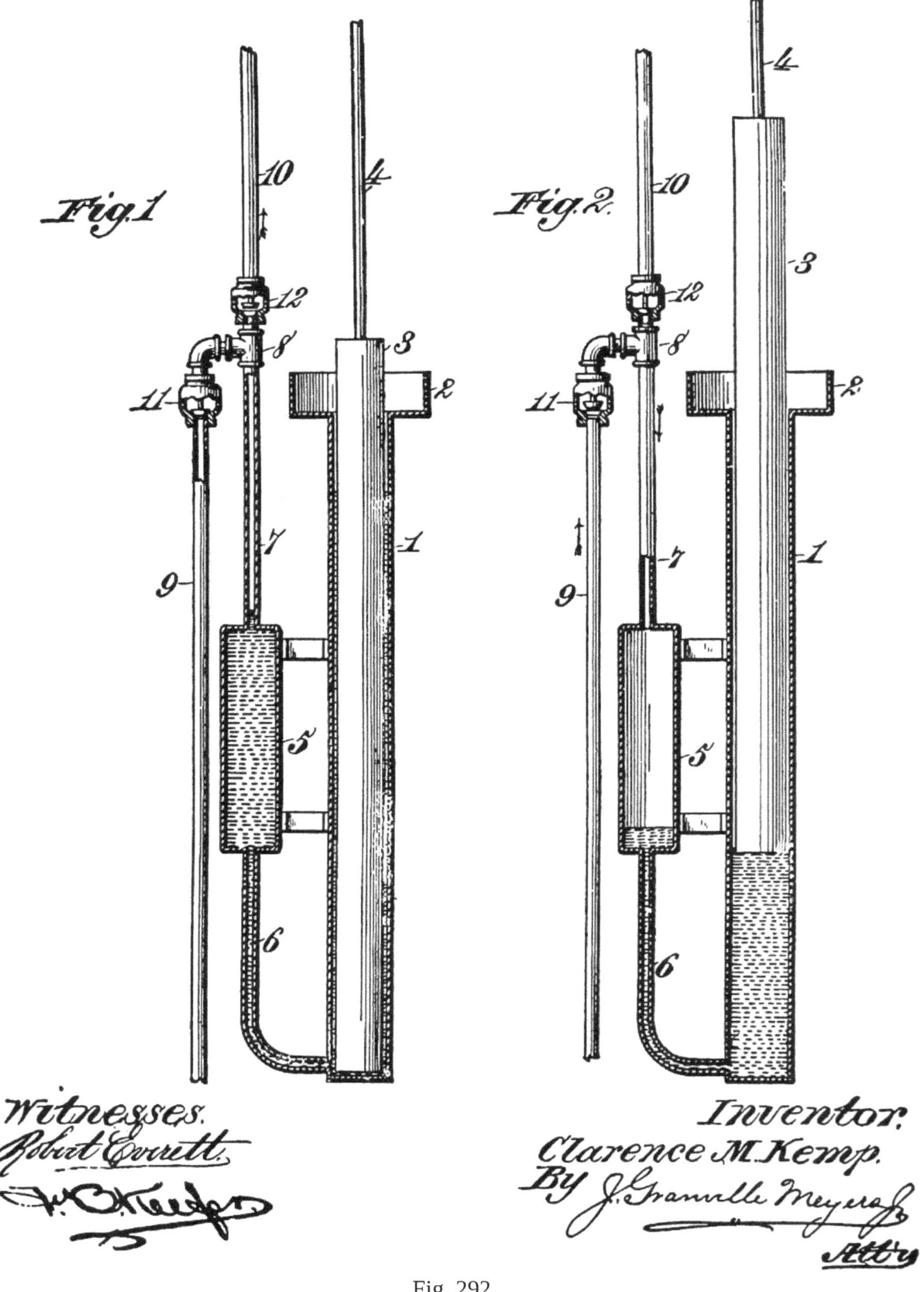

Fig. 292.

6. The different views should be consecutively numbered. Letters and figures of reference must be carefully formed. They should, if possible, measure at least one-eighth of an inch in height.

If the same part of an invention appears in more than one view of the drawing it must always be represented by the same character.

7. The signature of the inventor is to be placed in the lower right-hand corner of each sheet, and those of the witnesses at the lower left-hand corner.

The title should be written with pencil on the back of the sheet.

Drawings should be rolled for transmission, never folded.

On page 235, fig. 292 exhibits a reproduction of a patent office drawing, used in connection with specification papers in an application for a United States patent.

ENGLISH PRACTICE.

The rules for patent drawings in England are practically the same as in the United States; the paper sizes are, however, different. They must be on sheets of one of the two following sizes (the smaller being preferable), 13 inches at the sides by 8 inches at the top and bottom, or 13 inches at the sides by 16 inches at the top and bottom, including margin, which must be one-half an inch wide.

If there are more figures than can be shown on one of the smaller-sized sheets, two or more of these sheets should be used in preference to employing the large size. When an exceptionally large drawing is required, it should be *"continued"* on subsequent sheets. There is no limit to the number of sheets that may be sent in.

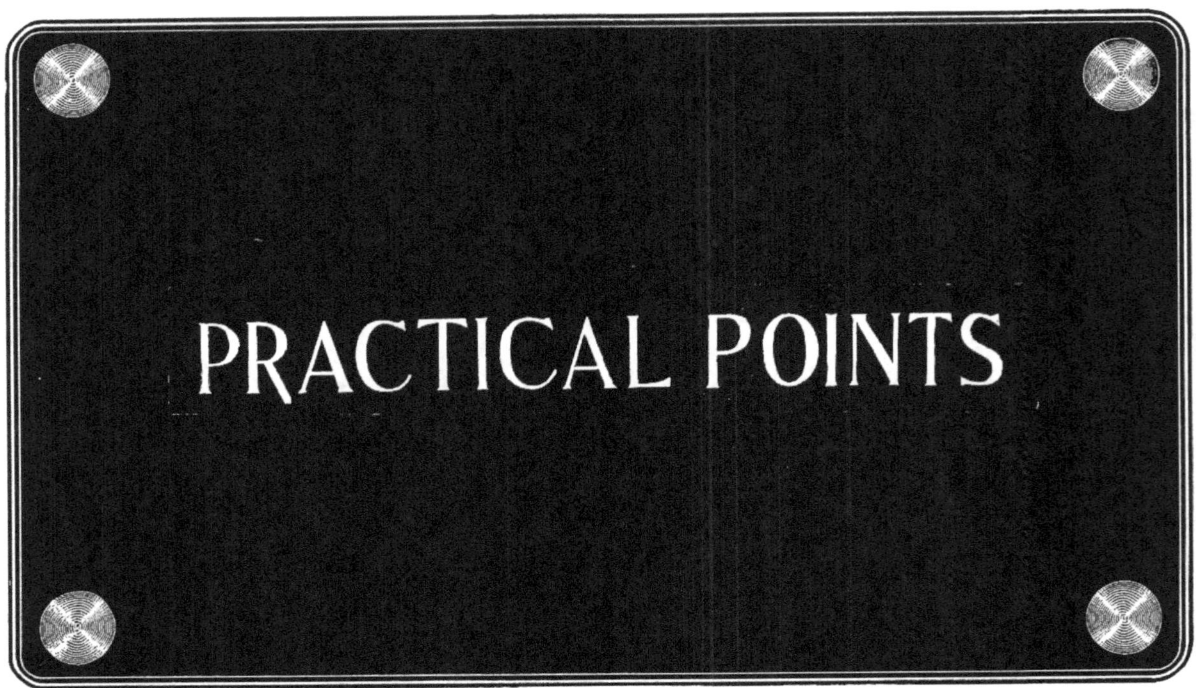

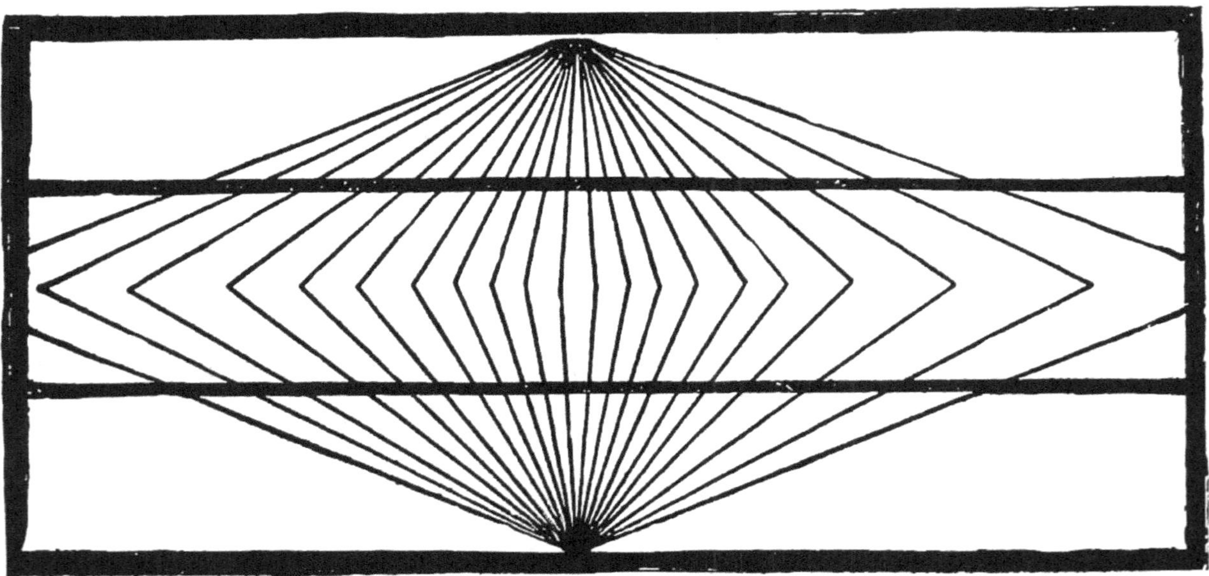

Fig. 293. See page 244.

Useful Hints and "Points."

Many of these "points" are repetitions, with but little variation from the way they have been previously stated; they are thus repeated to emphasize their practical worth.

A good draughtsman leaves his work in such a state that any competent person can without difficulty ink in what he has drawn.

The criterion of a good set of drawings is that with a properly prepared specification they are complete in themselves and require no explanation.

A "break" in a figure or object in a drawing is shown in rough irregular lines, as in fig. 134, on page 131; this is useful when the paper is not large enough to show the whole.

Never use a sloping line in writing fractions on a drawing. The objection arises from the fact that such a dimension as $1\frac{3}{16}$, if written with the inclined line, unless very distinctly executed, may be read as $\frac{13}{16}$.

In inking do not draw the lines further than you wish them to go, but in penciling it is well to extend the lines, free up.

Never use a scale for a ruler.

Do not overload the pen with ink.

Having filled the pen, nearly close the nibs and try the width of the line on a piece of paper or the margin of the drawing.

Never refill or lay the pen aside without first cleaning it.

The application of the science of geometry to the drawing-board is absolutely necessary to success, for the reason that the whole fabric of mechanical drawing rests on the principles of geometry, which is well termed the science of measurements.

Section lines should be the last inked and always without previous penciling.

Center lines are necessary in working drawings.

In choosing T-squares, care should be exercised to see that the head slides up and down the *left*-hand side of the board easily, and that when pressed against the board with the left hand there is no "slogging" of the blade up or down, or in other words, that the head is bearing firmly for its whole length against the board.

The best place for the title of a drawing is said to be the upper left-hand corner; this facilitates the filing of the sheet.

Never use a soft pencil except for finishing in shadow lines.

The rubber should always be kept clean.

Great care should be taken to keep drawing boards out of the way of heat or damp, as these cause the wood to warp.

Circles and curves are to be "inked in" before straight lines. First ink the smallest and afterwards the larger curves.

Do not press heavily on the pencil so as to cut the paper, but draw lightly, so that the mark can be erased and leave no trace, especially if the drawing is to be inked.

The draughtsman should commence his work at the top of the paper, keeping the lower part covered over until he needs to use it.

Shade lines should be avoided in all working drawings, as their use interferes with accurate measurements.

To make ink stick to the tracing cloth, with a woolen cloth rub some powdered chalk or pounce over the surface on which the ink lines are to be drawn, then wipe the surface clean and use a good quality of ink.

For striking small circles a small bow pen should be used.

To fix lead pencil marks on sketches so that they cannot be readily erased, sponge them with milk carefully skimmed, then lay blotting paper over them and iron with a hot flat-iron.

To have the ink preserve its fluidity and to keep out all dirt and dust, keep the cover on the ink slab; the mistake is often made of putting too liberal a supply of water in ink well, which causes a waste of both time and ink; no more should be prepared than to meet immediate requirements.

Always draw on the right side of the sheet, which can be found by holding the sheet up to the light and looking across its surface with the eye nearly in the same plane as the paper; note which side is the smoothest and has the least number of blemishes on it; this is the right side to draw on.

As to sharpening pencils, it is always best to cut a chisel point on the pencil used for drawing, and put a circular point on the pencils in the bow pencil and pencil leg. The chisel point makes a finer line and lasts much longer than a round point.

The varnish used in many large drawing-rooms is simply white shellac dissolved in alcohol; it requires a little experience to mix these to a proper consistency, but this is soon acquired.

Never sharpen your pencil over the drawing.

A center line of a drawing is the line upon which the figure is to be constructed; the center line is the first line to be drawn.

The T-square belongs to the left side of the drawing-board, and is operated by the left hand. The right hand should be kept free for the purpose of picking up pencil, pen and bows, adjusting and marking off. The left hand controls the T-square and the triangle that slides along the upper edge of the square; the right hand is for the instruments.

The advantage of a paper rule or scale is that the paper will expand and contract under varying degrees of atmospheric moisture the same as the drawing does.

Avoid rubbing out and constantly cleaning the drawing with India rubber; if wrong lines are made or it is desired to make alterations, the part to be changed should be rubbed out and completely re-drawn.

When using the bows see to it that the steel-pointed leg that is put down first on the paper, to secure a center for a curve or a circle, is a trifle longer than the pencil or pen leg.

To clearly indicate the position of a center which is to be used again, lightly pencil a small circle about it; never put the point of a pencil in the center hole to enlarge or blacken it; the prick point made by the dividers and needle points should be no more than can be just seen, hence the circle to be made as advised above.

Be particular in having the legs of the dividers exactly the same length, and sharp, so that in pricking off distances, and dimensions, and centers, the indent or hole made in the paper is as small as possible.

The term "plane" means a perfectly flat surface; that is, something which has length and breadth but no thickness.

The best way to indicate on the drawing the surfaces which are to be finished is to write on the lines which represent the finished surfaces "finished," tool-finish, or "faced," according to the degree of finish required. The single letter f is frequently used.

Avoid fingering the drawing sheet as much as possible; in pointing to any part of the drawing use a pencil and not the finger.

Remember that a drawing is made to be read.

The skill in inking does not depend on the fineness of the line, but on its clearness.

A soft pencil should never be used on a mechanical drawing unless in rare cases when it is used for pencil shading; the hardness or softness of pencils is denoted by letters.

Never ink any portion of a drawing until the penciling is entirely finished.

Stretching or pasting the paper to the board is very seldom resorted to, for the reason that the mechanical drawings are *to scale* and the paper is natural when pinned to the board and more correct than if under a strain. Mechanical drawings are always required in practice *right away*, and time would be wasted and lost in damping and pasting and drying again.

A working drawing, whether made to a scale or not, must have all the dimensions plainly written upon it, for a workman should never be compelled to measure a drawing.

In marking off distances, centers, etc., a fine needle point is useful; the hole should not be punctured through the paper, merely a prick point, so that it will leave an impression, which will not be obliterated by the use of rubber; drawing-pens are often equipped with such a needle point in the end of the handle, that is visible only when the pen is unscrewed from the handle; but in the absence of one of this kind the point of the divider leg will be of use.

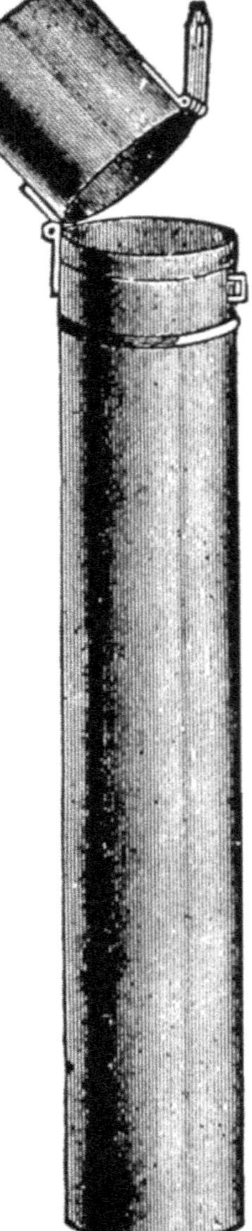

Fig. 294.

Mechanical construction drawings represent a large amount of mental and manual work, as well as a considerable cost in money; hence, they are of value quite as much as property which has been acquired by the expenditure of either labor or capital. It is wise to keep copies of original designs and sketches, as well as data and formulæ, for record and comparison.

The best system for keeping drawings is to make them of certain standard sizes, and to keep them flat, unrolled, in drawers, numbered, lettered and labeled.

In an office where space is limited and drawings have to be rolled it is well to use a number of pasteboard cases about three feet long and three inches in diameter. These are shown in fig. 294.

A puncture can be made near the top and, when a new drawing or blue-print is inserted in this cylindrical case, a cardboard tag can be looped through the puncture. This label will give the title and number of drawings in that case.

A manuscript book methodically and neatly kept should tell immediately the number of the drawing and the case.

Fig. 293 is good for practice in line drawing and also as an optical illusion. "You look and are deceived. At first glance you say, 'Of course, those two lines are curved.' You are mistaken. They are exactly parallel. In order to prove this hold them up edgewise to the eye. It is, of course, the subsidiary lines which lead the vision astray. It is a case of first impressions being quite wrong."

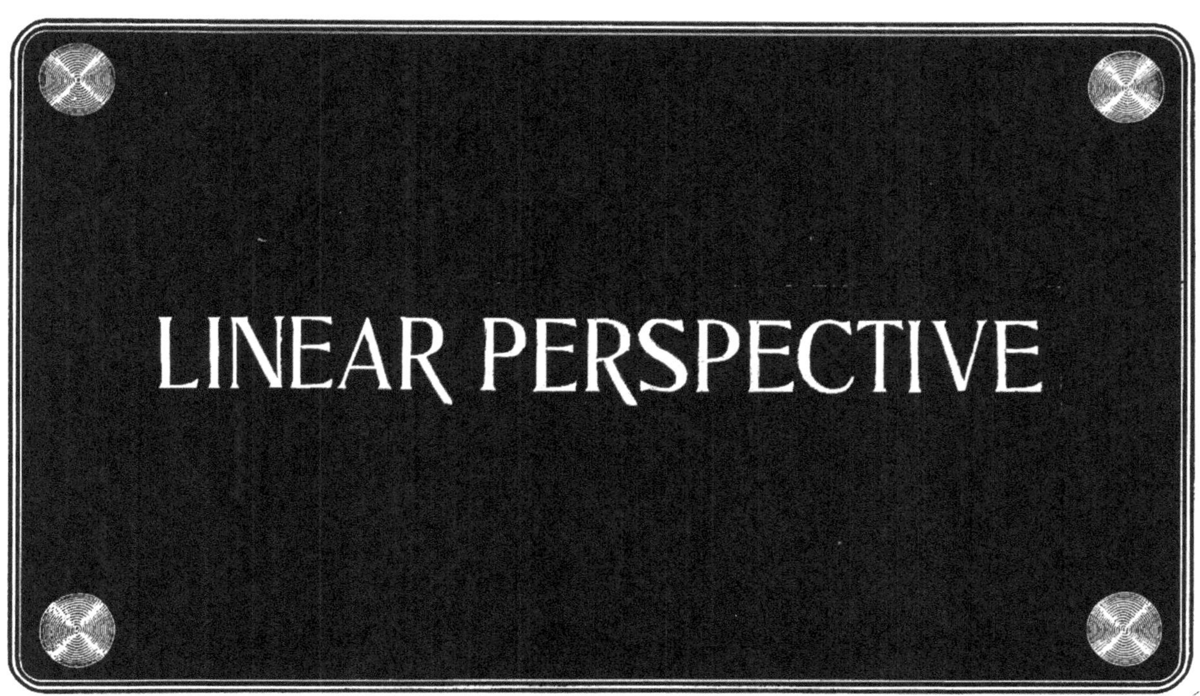

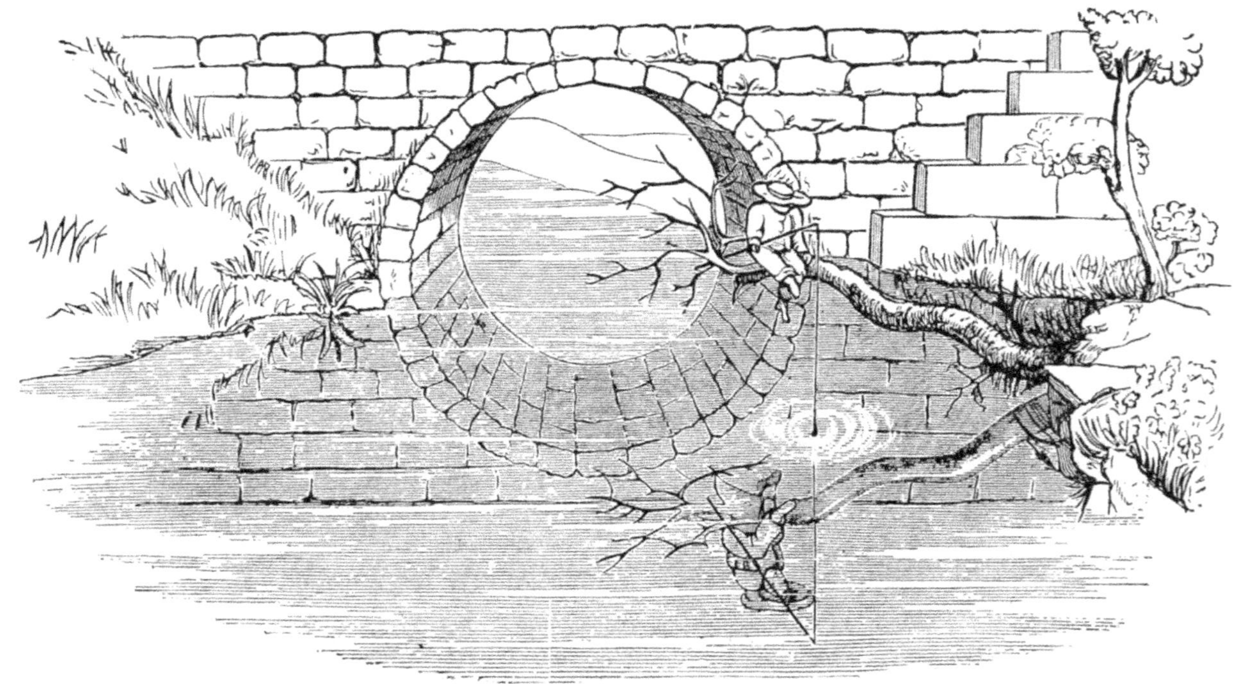

Fig. 295.

Linear Perspective.

It should be mentioned that this subject is outside the limits of mechanical drawing, which only deals with objects that can be measured, projected or dimensioned to an accurate scale.

But, in rounding out the more formal subjects it is well to look a little outside the rigid lines of mechanics into the methods of nature, for no system of teaching drawing is complete that does not include some explanations for sketching from nature—the objects being always around the student, the eye always clear to see and the hand only needing the training to make permanent the impressions received.

The word perspective means to *see through*; the word perspective being derived from the Latin word *perspicere*, to look through, hence, perspective is a science which teaches us to *see* correctly and enables us to represent the *appearance* of anything we may wish to draw; care should be taken in perspective drawing, to select objects interesting in themselves, and the best specimens of their class, so as to cultivate taste, while they at the same time afford useful and instructive drawing lessons.

The meaning of the term linear perspective is a line view; the previous examples have been composed of surfaces placed fronting the eye; perspective is the science which treats of the changes of form produced by viewing them in various oblique positions.

The slightest alteration of *position* will change the *appearance* of an object; this can be easily shown—for illustration take a coin, the actual shape of which is a perfect round; or, strictly speaking, a circle. If we take the coin between the thumb and the first finger, holding it in an upright position, and exactly facing the eyes, as in Fig. 296, it appears of its true form, viz., a circle. If we alter its position, balancing it upon the thumb, in a level position, with its edge directly opposite the eye, as in Fig. 297, its appearance is changed, and what we know to be really a circle, appears to us as a straight line.

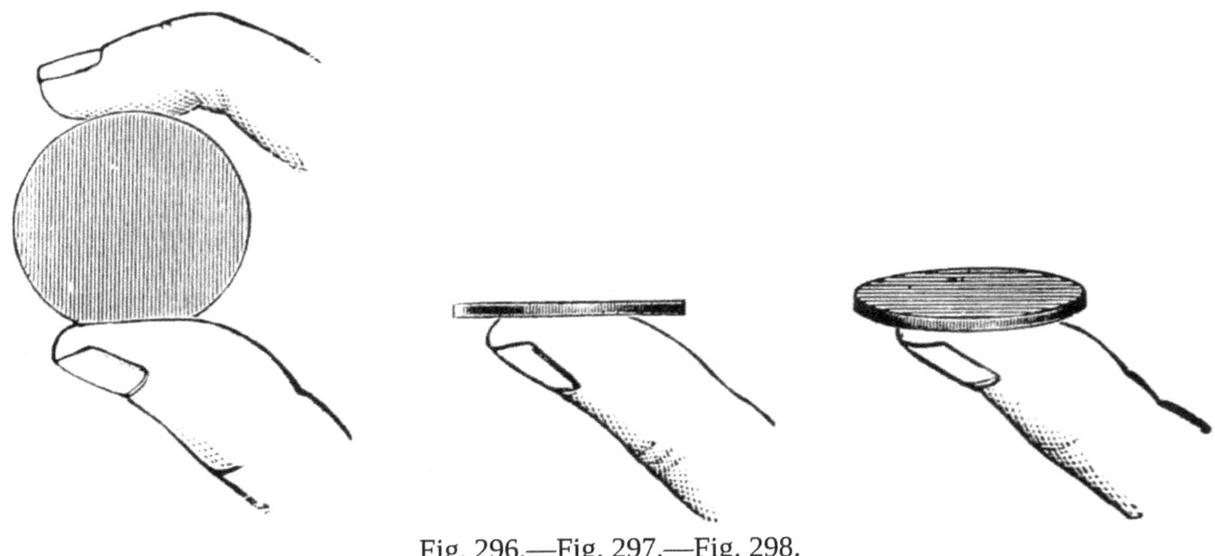

Fig. 296.—Fig. 297.—Fig. 298.

Now, still balancing the coin upon the thumb, but changing its position with regard to the eye, by holding it a little lower than in the last position, that is slightly beneath the level of the eye, as in fig. 298, we see both the edge and the surface, the coin now appearing neither a circle nor a straight line, but a curved figure of an elliptical form. Thus the same coin held in three different positions has assumed three different shapes.

Let us take two coins of the same size, holding (in the position shown at fig. 296) one in each hand. Now, closing one eye, (which will make the experiment more clear), hold one coin out at arm's length, and the other at about the distance of a foot from the eye. On comparing them, we find that the coin which is further from the eye appears less than the nearer one. We know that the coins are really equal in size, yet one appears smaller than the other.

We thus see that when we change the position of an object, we have as a consequence a change of appearance; also that the change of appearance may affect both the shape and the size of the object.

These diversities of appearance may be remarked in everything around us. We can observe them in the street by looking at a building from different points of view, or by comparing the apparent sizes of the street lamps; in the railway station, by watching the arriving or departing train; and at sea, by noticing the vessels as they approach, or as they retire, ultimately vanishing from our sight in that line where the sea and sky appear to meet.

All these interesting variations of appearance are in strict accordance with the laws of **GEOMETRY** and **OPTICS**. The former subject has been enlarged upon beginning with page 81 of this work, where a line, a point, an angle, etc., are defined; other terms are explained at page 41 and the following pages; to these we add a few definitions essential to the subject.

A PLANE is a surface which is perfectly even and flat; to use a familiar illustration, a plane is like the surface of a sheet of plate glass; recollect particularly, that a surface which is at all curved, is not a plane.

The **GROUND-PLANE** is the plane on which we stand; the *base-line* is an imaginary line passing through the middle of the feet as we stand square and erect; and the *vertical plane* is supposed to stand on the base-line and perpendicular to it.

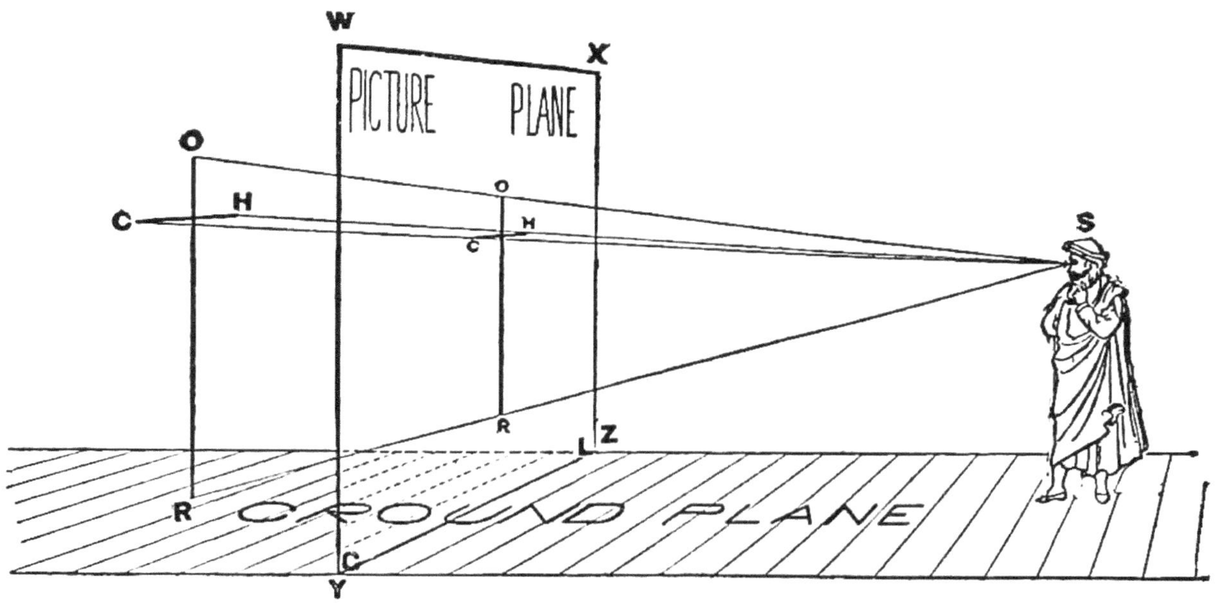

Fig. 299.—See page 255.

Planes are parallel to each other when they are throughout their entire surfaces the same distance apart.

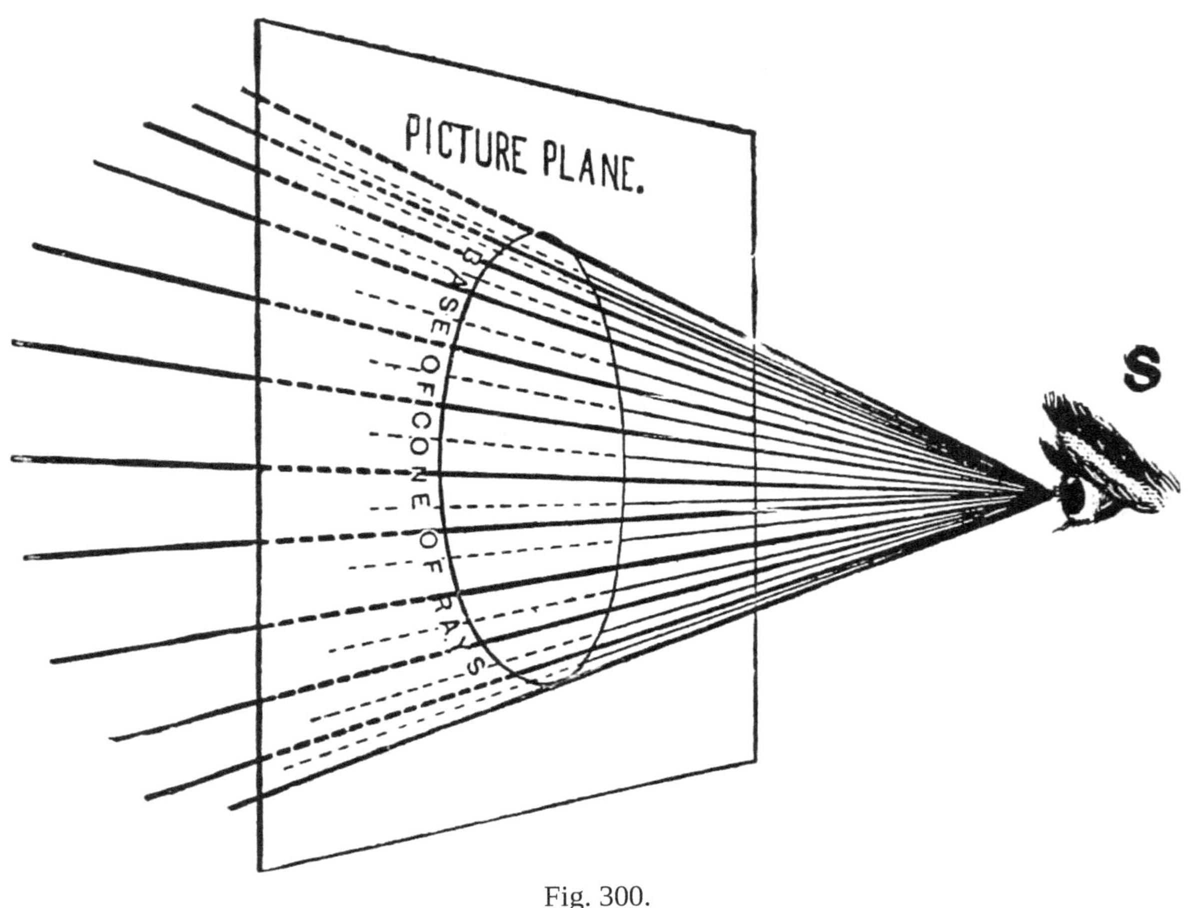

Fig. 300.

THE PERSPECTIVE PLANE is an upright square of glass, usually framed like a picture, with a base, so that it can stand up alone. This is placed between the eye of the spectator and the subject to be drawn, and as the drawing is sometimes made directly upon it, it is sometimes called the *Picture* or the *Plane of the Picture*.

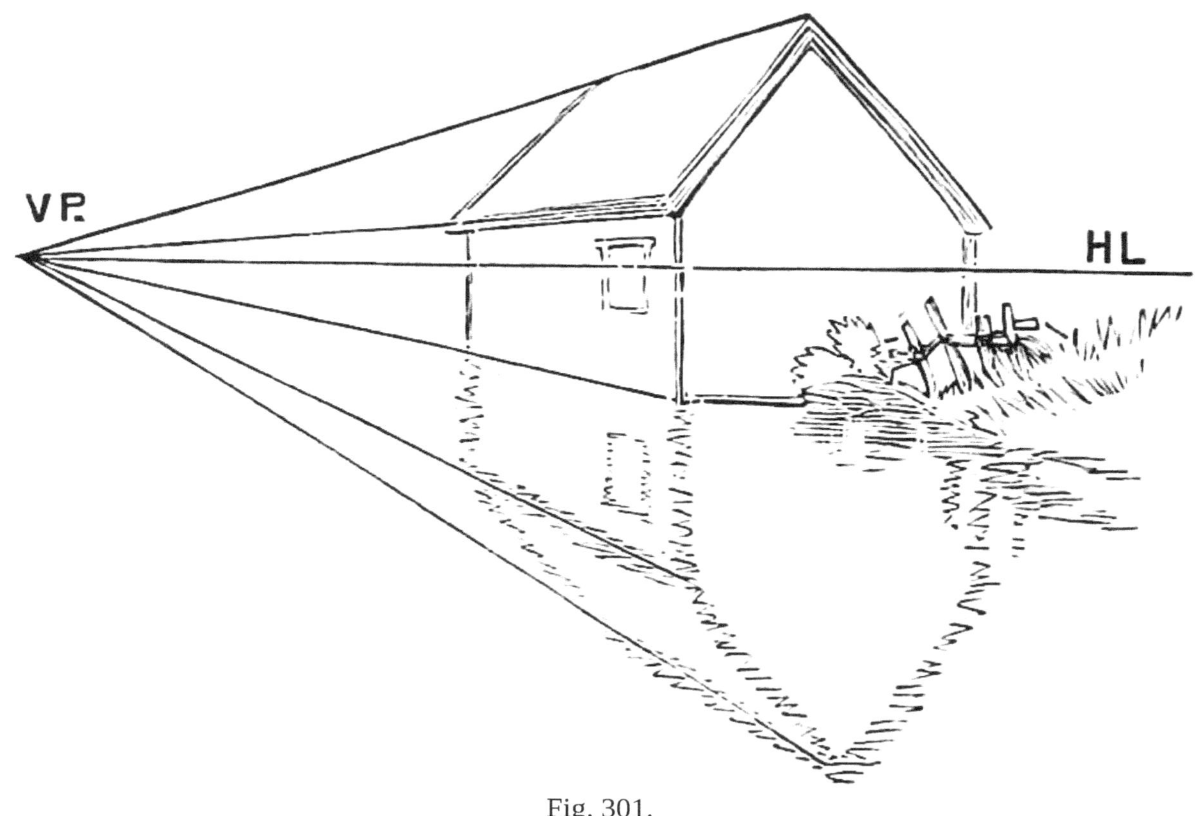

Fig. 301.

HORIZONTAL means perfectly level, like the surface of still water. We must be careful to understand perfectly the difference between the terms "level" and "even" or "flat." A surface may be even or flat, without being level. Thus the wall is even and flat, but it is upright, not level; level means a fixed, constant position.

In fig. 301 a house is shown in perspective in which the line $H L$ is the line of the horizon and $V P$ is the,—

VANISHING POINT.—The vanishing point is familiarly represented by the rails on a trolley track on a straight road, which seem to approach each other in the distance, as shown in fig. 302 at $V P$.

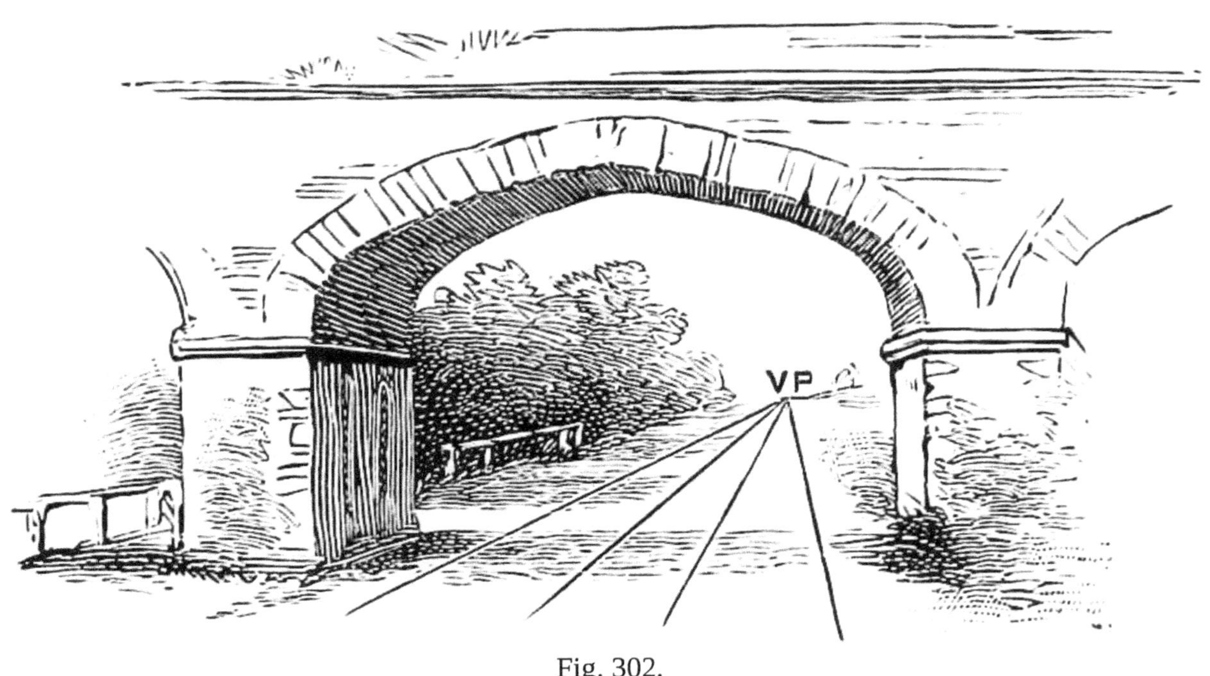

Fig. 302.

All parallel lines seen in perspective appear to meet in the same vanishing point.

The value of the vanishing point may be seen in the view of a wooden house, fig. 303, where it (*V P*) gives direction to the retiring lines of the roof, side planks and door.

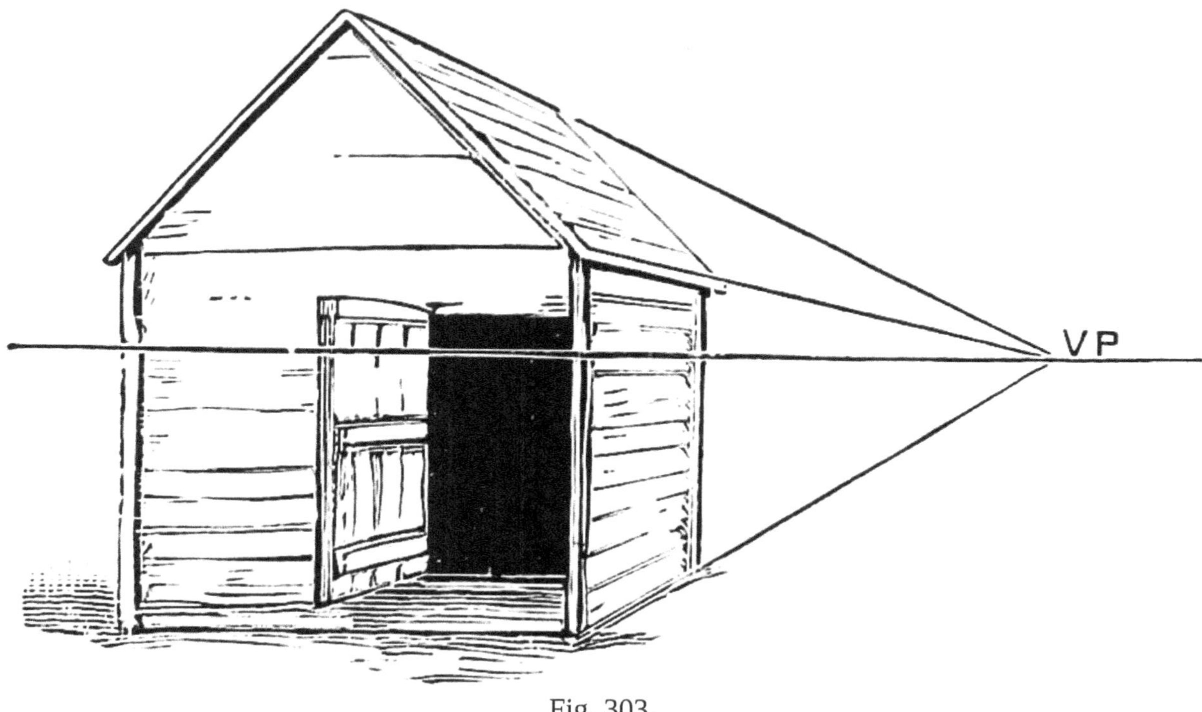

Fig. 303.

POINT OF SIGHT.—This is that point in the eye where the lines or rays from the object cross each other, as shown at *P* in fig. 305, also in fig. 299 at *S*.

VERTICAL means perfectly upright. If we attach a piece of thread to a weight, a small piece of lead for example, and hold the thread with the lead hanging downwards, the thread will fall in an upright or vertical position.

PARALLEL lines are said to be parallel to each other when they are throughout their whole lengths the same distance apart.

PERPENDICULAR. When one straight line, meeting another, makes the angles at the point of contact equal, each of the angles is called a right angle, and the lines are said to be perpendicular to each other. Remember especially that perpendicular and vertical have not the same meaning. Vertical means an unvarying upright position. Perpendicular means that one line or plane meets another line or plane at right angles.

The fig. 295 on page 246 is a study in perspective, showing a water reflection. As rays from every visible part of the object are reflected, all following the same law, the reflection will appear to the eye *inverted*, and of the *same size as the object*. The arch itself forms the upper half of a hollow cylinder, and the reflection forms the lower half. The reflection shows much more of the interior of the arch than can be seen directly. The leaning tree, the boy fishing, and the receding banks, all are seen in accordance with the laws of reflection and perspective.

THE HORIZONTAL LINE, THE POINT OF SIGHT AND THE VANISHING POINTS are the principal items. These should be studied in every room and during every walk, and the more pleasing accidents of form stored in the mind or committed to paper for future use.

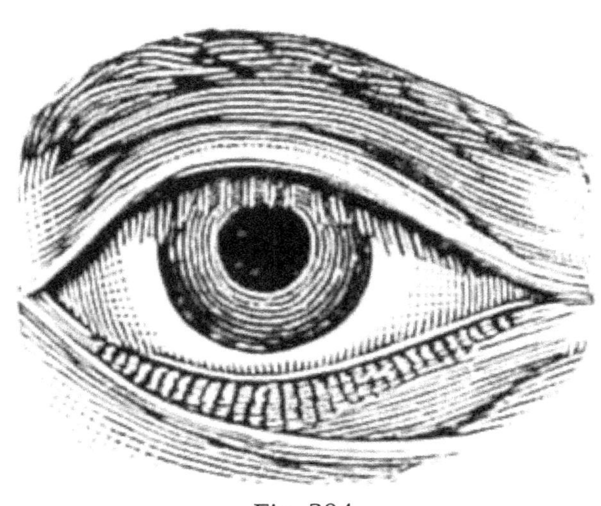

Fig. 304.

OPTICS, the science of sight, gives us the following laws:

1. That we see by the agency of light.

2. That light passes from objects to our eyes.

3. That light travels in straight lines, which are called Visual Rays.

The human eye may be briefly described as a chamber of a spherical or globular form, with a circular opening in front. This circular opening is called the pupil, and through it the visual rays pass to the interior of the eye. The visual rays, passing from space in all directions through the small pupil, are received upon what may be called the interior wall of the globular chamber forming the eye (see fig. 305). This interior wall is called the retina, and upon it the impressions of external objects are received, just as they are received upon a screen in a dark chamber. These impressions are conveyed by the optic nerve from the retina to the brain.

In front of the pupil is a segment of a small sphere, composed of the cornea and the aqueous humor, both of which are transparent, and from their shape and density have a convergent effect upon the rays passing through them.

Behind the pupil is the transparent crystalline lens, which, from its shape and its elasticity, is a powerful agent in aiding the convergence of the rays, and in bringing objects at various distances to a clear focus upon the retina.

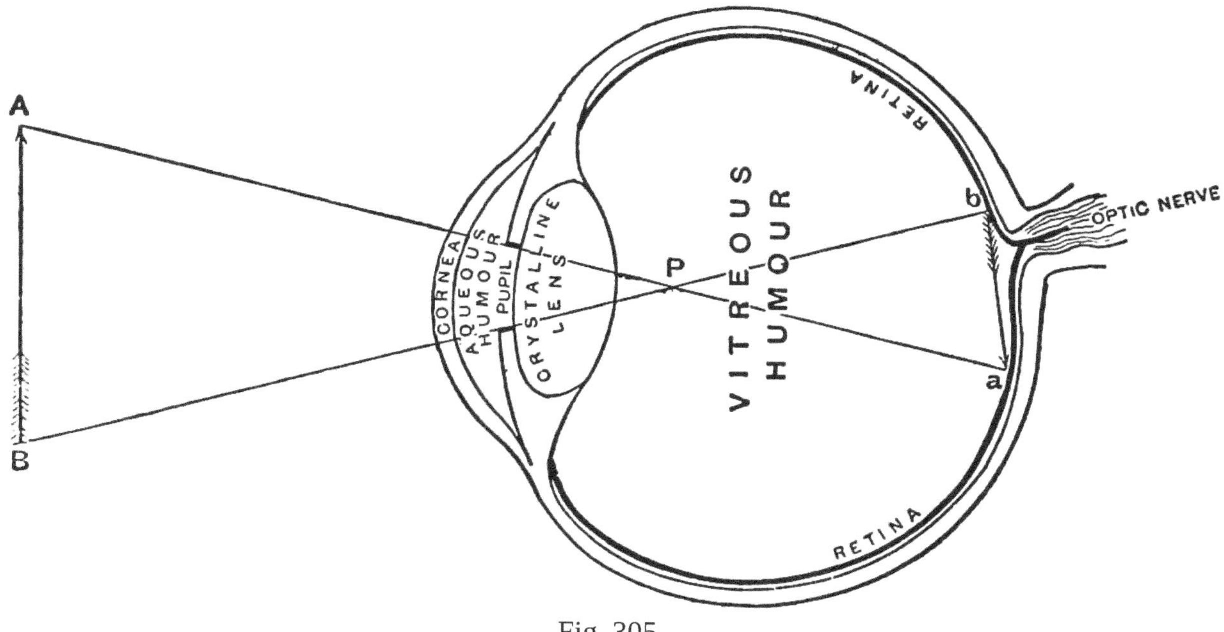

Fig. 305.

The pupil has the power of contraction and dilation, which is influenced by the quantity of light entering the eye, but when it is dilated to the utmost its size is very small in comparison with the great chamber forming the body of the eye.

In fig. 305 we have a rough sectional diagram of the eye and an object in front of it. This object, an arrow, is seen by means of the visual rays proceeding from it, the principal two of which are shown. The visual ray from *A* passes through the pupil and is received upon the retina at *a*. In the same way the visual ray from *B* passes through the pupil and is received upon the retina at *b*. It will thus be seen that the impressions or images received upon the retina are inverted; but, by long reason and experience, the mind has acquired the habit of determining the real positions of objects, and does not, though the image is so received, imagine them to be upside down.

It will also be observed, in the same way, that that portion of an object which is upon the right will be pictured upon the retina upon the left, and *vice versa*, but the mind, for the reasons before stated, never imagines the object to be reversed. This fact is another proof that, as mentioned at the commencement of our study, to see accurately is a matter of education and practice.

And first of Optics; it was asserted, page 252, that we see by the agency of light which passes from objects to our eyes in straight lines which are called Visual Rays.

We see by the agency of light, as all objects, except such as may be styled self-luminous, when placed in a dark chamber are not perceivable by us, except by touch, smell or hearing; we cannot *see* them; they are invisible. But when, by removing a shutter or igniting a flame, we introduce something to the chamber which was not present when the chamber was dark, we become at once conscious of the appearance of the object, we perceive it by the sense of sight.

This something which must always be present to enable us to see, is called Light; all objects are made visible to the sense of seeing by its agency.

Without light, natural or artificial, it would be impossible to distinguish one object from another.

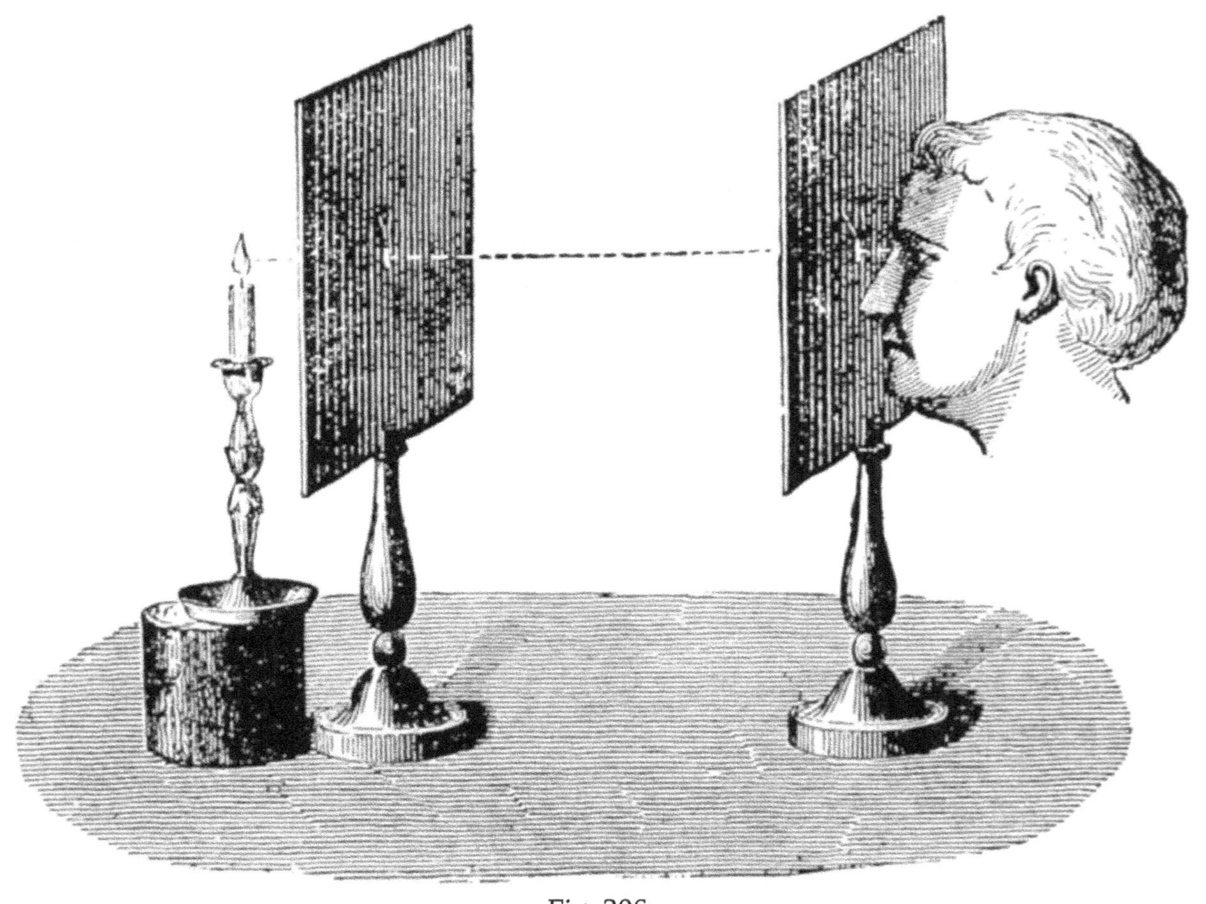

Fig. 306.

That the Visual Rays pass from objects in straight lines to the eye may be proved by the following experiment (see fig. 306):—Pierce two screens with a large pin, and place them so that the holes are in a straight line with a flame, as the light of a candle or lamp. On fixing the eye to one of these holes we are able to see the flame; but if we slightly move the flame, one of the screens, or the eye, the flame is no longer visible. To be visible, the flame, the holes in the screens, and the eye must all be in the same straight line. See fig. 306.

In fig. 299 the picture plane is represented by the rectangle $W\,X\,Y\,Z$. Although the picture plane is here shown as a rectangle, it may be of any shape or of any size.

The observer is at S, looking through the picture plane at the cross $R\,C\,O\,H$. The observer is standing upon a horizontal surface, which is called the ground plane. If we are in a room, the window may be called a picture plane and the floor a ground plane.

The picture plane rests, as it were, upon the ground plane, in a line which passes from Y to Z. The two planes meet or intersect in this line, which is called the ground line. The ground line is sometimes called the picture line, or the measuring line.

The visual rays, by means of which the observer sees the cross, will, in their course from it to the eye, pass through the picture plane. These visual rays will intersect the picture plane in a number of points, and if we mark the true positions of these points the result will be a perspective image of the cross.

The rays are shown passing from the cross to the eye of the observer, and meeting the picture plane in points r, c, o, h; r being joined to o, and c to h, we have the perspective image of the cross as it would appear to the observer at S. Of course an infinite number of rays proceed from the cross to the eye of the observer; but it is quite evident that we need only consider those proceeding from the extremities of the object.

Scale or Approximate Perspective.

Real, or true perspective, represents the object exactly as it is seen in nature, where the parts that are far away from the eye of the observer appear smaller than those nearby. Occasions arise, however, in practical life, with its numerous phases of industrial requirements, where the convenience of showing the complete form of the object in a single view might preferably be coupled with the convenience of scale dimensions.

This has led to a modified perspective, that sacrifices some of the accuracy in the appearance of the object to gain the advantage of scale dimensions; this form of perspective may be distinguished by the name—*approximate or scale perspective*—which does not represent the object exactly as seen in nature, but where those parts that are afar off are shown of the same size as those that are near by, and where the lines that run out into space are parallel to each other and do not converge into a vanishing point.

To represent an object in perspective, the horizon and the point of vision will have to appear in the drawing as the fundamental starting points.

Three dimensions are distinguished for the fixing of an object in space from a certain reference point. They are height, breadth and thickness, and are in their direction square to each other. The height is the fundamental direction, being derived from the direction of gravity, that invariably extends to the center of the earth.

All directions in the perspective determination of an object are parallel to these.

Vertical lines and planes point toward the center of the earth, while horizontal planes, including the directions of breadth and thickness, are square to the vertical direction. In this, the principal visual ray extends in the direction of thickness.

For a clear understanding of perspective, it must be firmly fixed in mind, that for each prominent point of the object behind the picture plane, a corresponding point lies in the picture plane, in that position where a straight line or ray of sight that is going from the eye to the point of the object, cuts through the picture plane.

Suppose we could replace these rays of sight by thin, visible threads of wire that would go through little holes in the picture plane, we could then walk around this bundle of rays, and by looking at it from three different directions, we would get three different views of it. We may look upon it from the top, from the side or from the end, where the bundle of rays all concentrate in the eye of the observer.

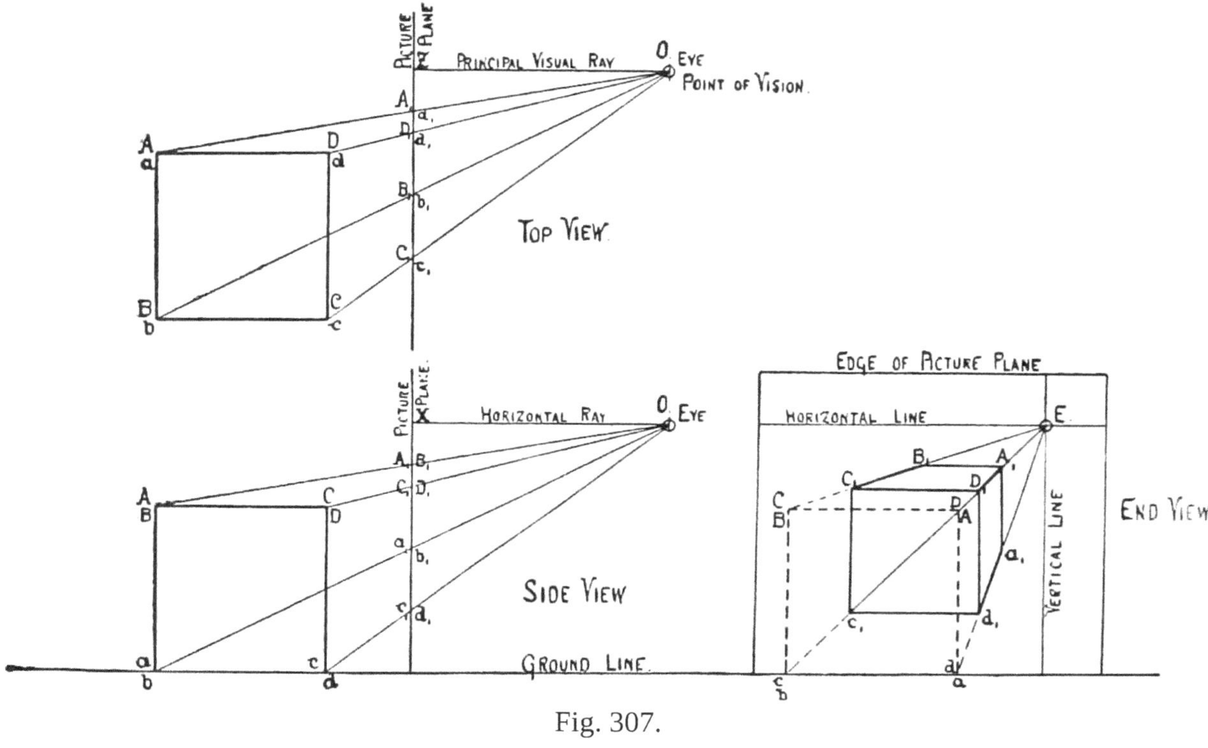

Fig. 307.

Figs. 307 and 308 show, in two cases, how these three views would appear. The end views are those where the perspective picture appears on the plane, while the top and side views only show where the rays intersect the picture plane. The top view shows how far, for example, point *A* is distant from a vertical line *O Z*, while the side view shows how far point *A* is below horizontal line *O X*, which is at the same height above the ground as the eye of the observer, *O*. Thus, all points of the cube can be located on the picture plane, and the outlines of the cube reproduced in perspective.

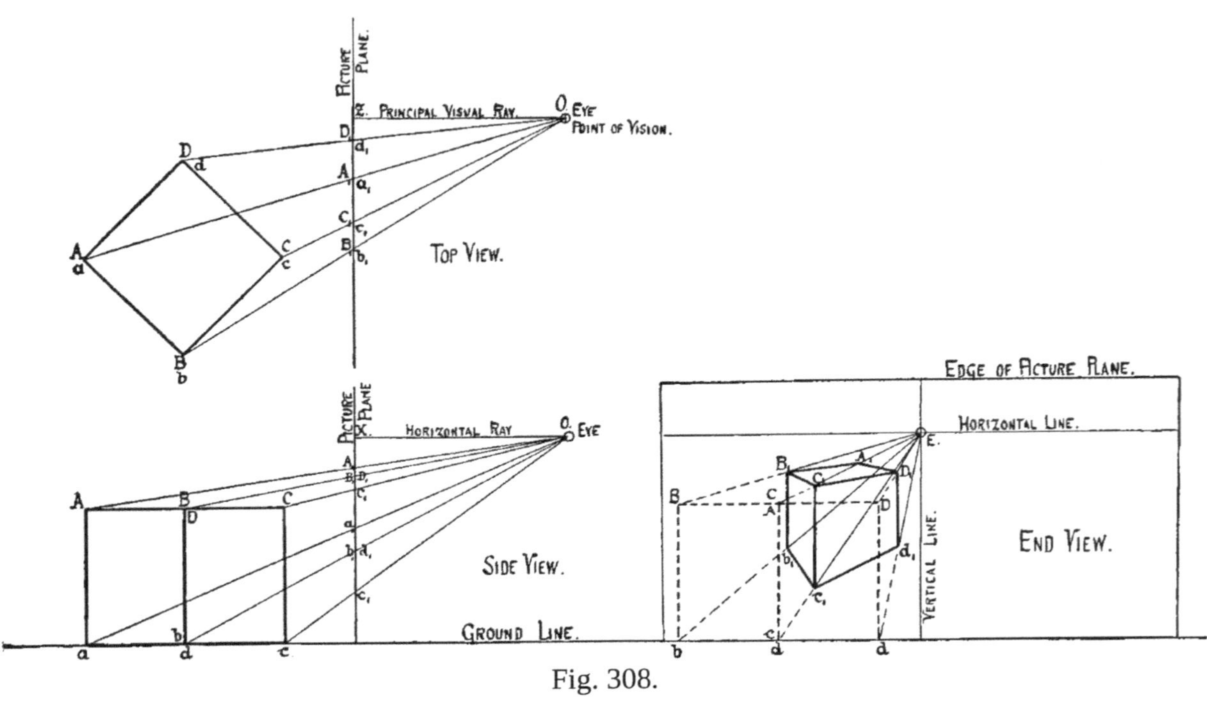

Fig. 308.

Modified arrangements are shown in figs. 309 and 310 for parallel and angular perspective.

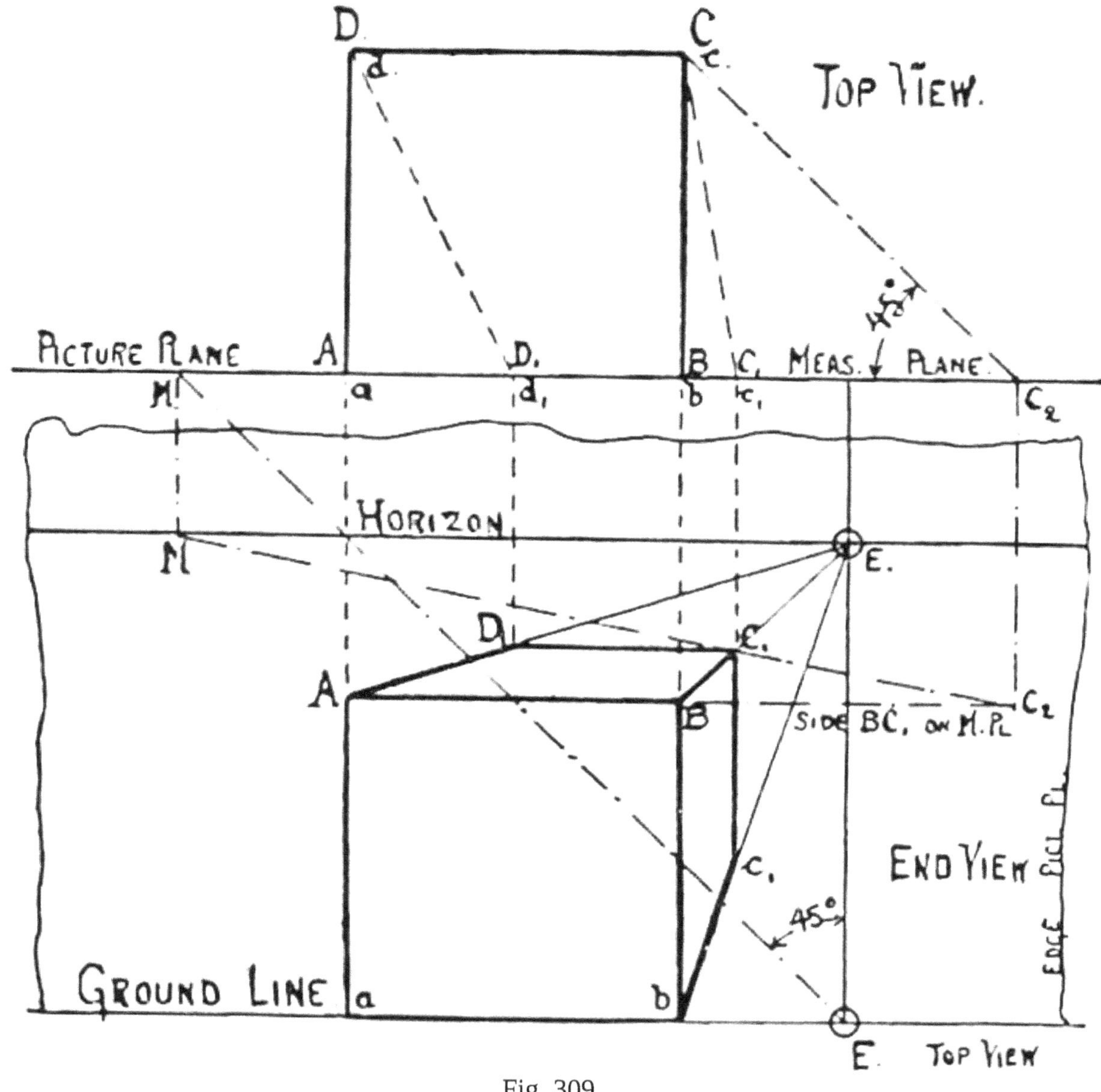

Fig. 309.

The views are so arranged in relation to each other that the picture plane in the top view is parallel to the horizon and the ground-line, which latter is the intersection of the picture plane with the level ground of the end or perspective view. At the same time the eye of the observer is in one and the same vertical line for both views, two vanishing points may be found in the horizon outside of the principal visual ray. To find the position of these two vanishing points in the picture plane, the modified top view, fig. 310, is used.

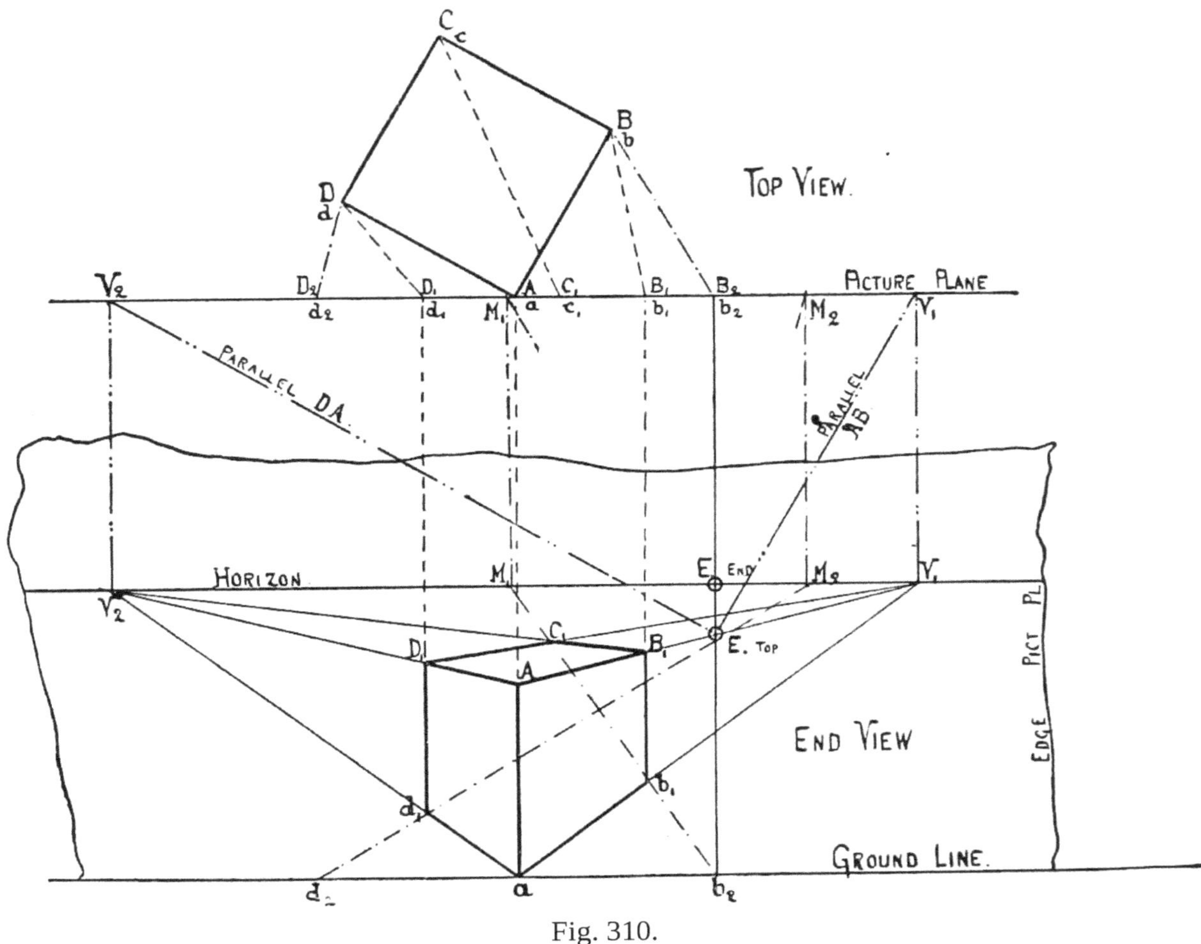

Fig. 310.

As all lines that end in a vanishing point must be parallel in reality, this parallelism may be seen in the top view and lines through the eye of the observer, parallel to the directions of the main lines of the object, will cut the picture plane at the vanishing points.

Through these two vanishing points the directions of two sets of lines are found, the starting points of which are determined from the plane of measurement. The third set of lines, being vertical, also appears vertical and parallel in the picture.

The position of each vertical line is found in the top view, where the light rays from the observing eye to the ends of the vertical lines intersect with the picture plane. Projecting these points down upon the rays to the vanishing points produces the vertical lines in the picture.

For example, in fig. 311, the purpose of perspective is entirely defeated by placing the eye of the observer directly in front of the object and arriving at the view taken in mechanical drawing which needs supplementary views for complete comprehension of the form of the object.

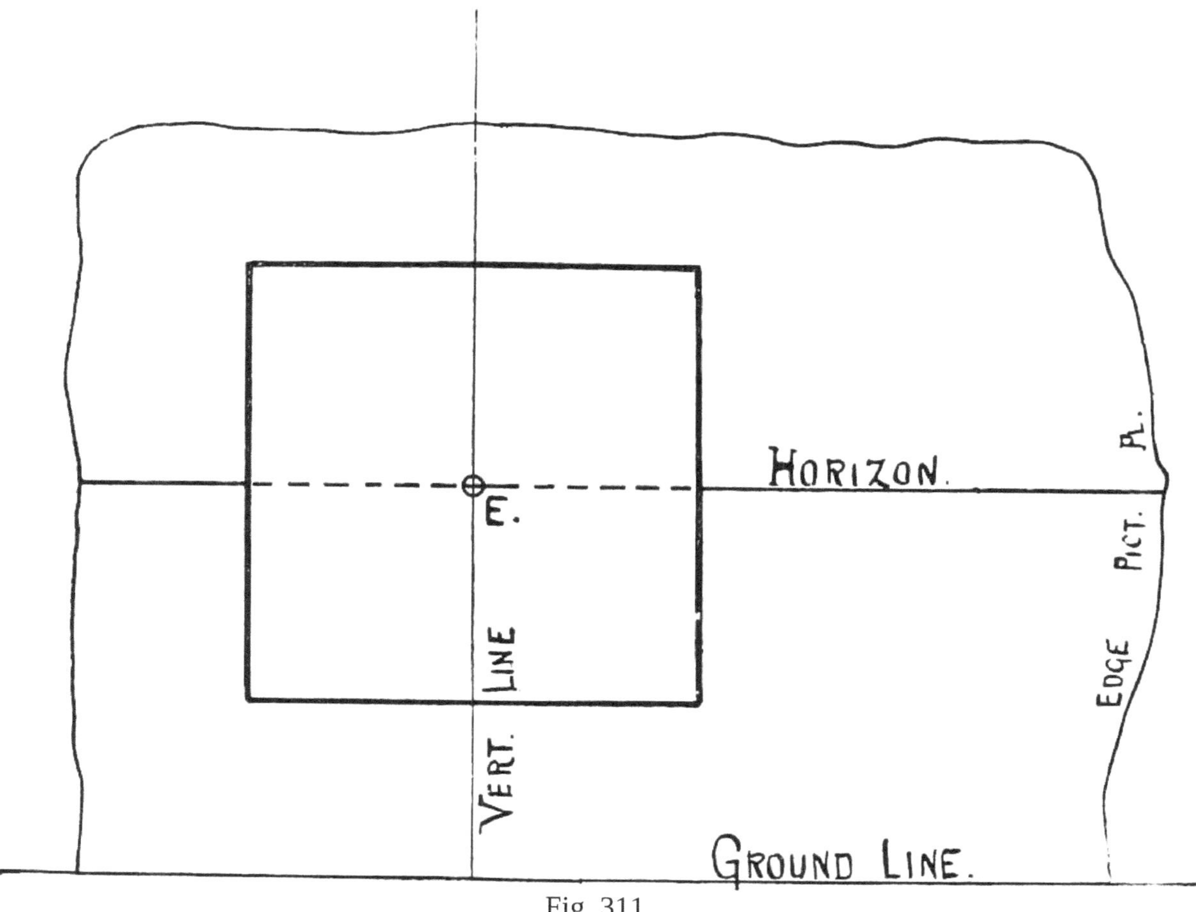

Fig. 311.

In fig. 312 the eye of the observer is first placed directly opposite the object, then it sees the object to the left but a short distance away, while in the third figure the observer is farther away from the object. In each case the picture plane and plane of measurement is at the front face of the cube.

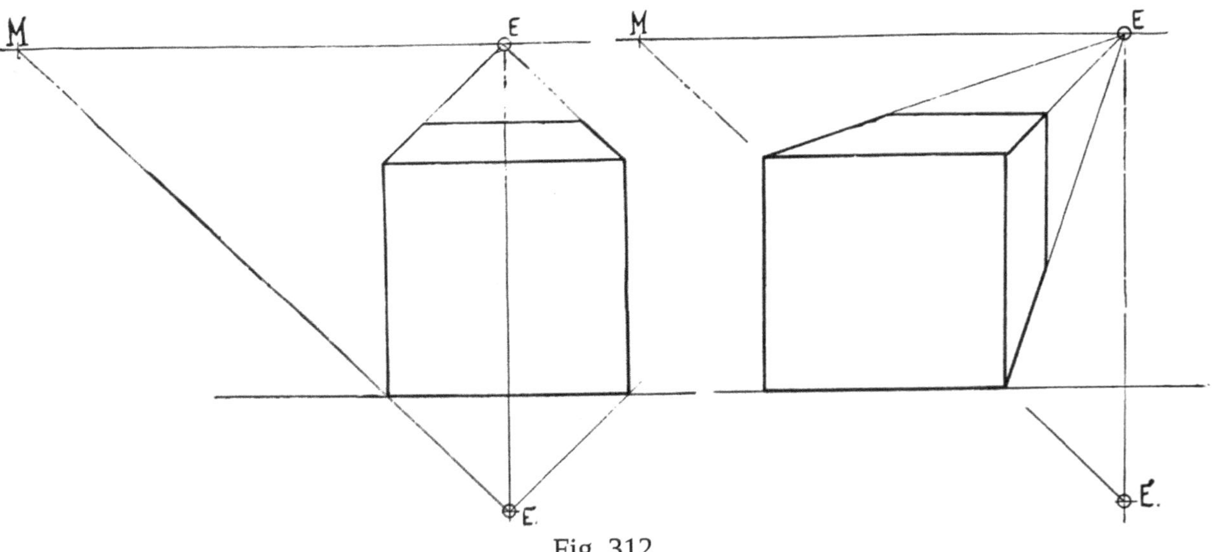

Fig. 312.

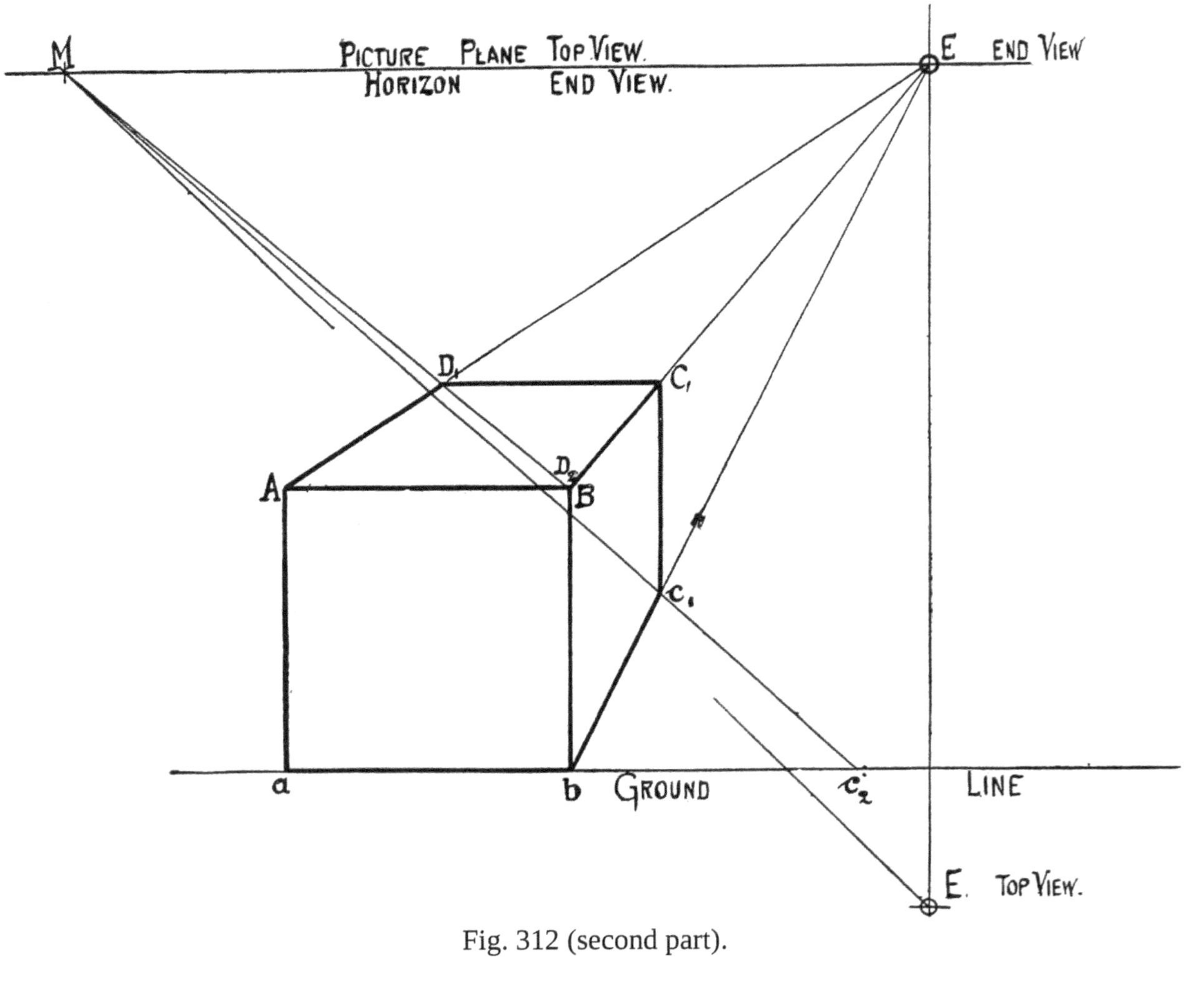

Fig. 312 (second part).

For such simple objects, it is not necessary to draw the top view at all. The only reminder of the top view is the eye or point of vision, the picture plane that falls together for the sake of convenience with the horizon of the end view and the ray that determines the measurement point M, which is, in this suppressed reproduction, absolutely necessary, in order to find the apparent position of the real corners behind the picture plane.

So far, only square or sharp-cornered objects have been represented in perspective.

It is evident, however, that round objects can also be shown in linear perspective, placing reference lines on the object and representing these as if they were real lines. A cylinder is thus shown in fig. 313 of which the end planes will appear very distinctly in sharp outlines.

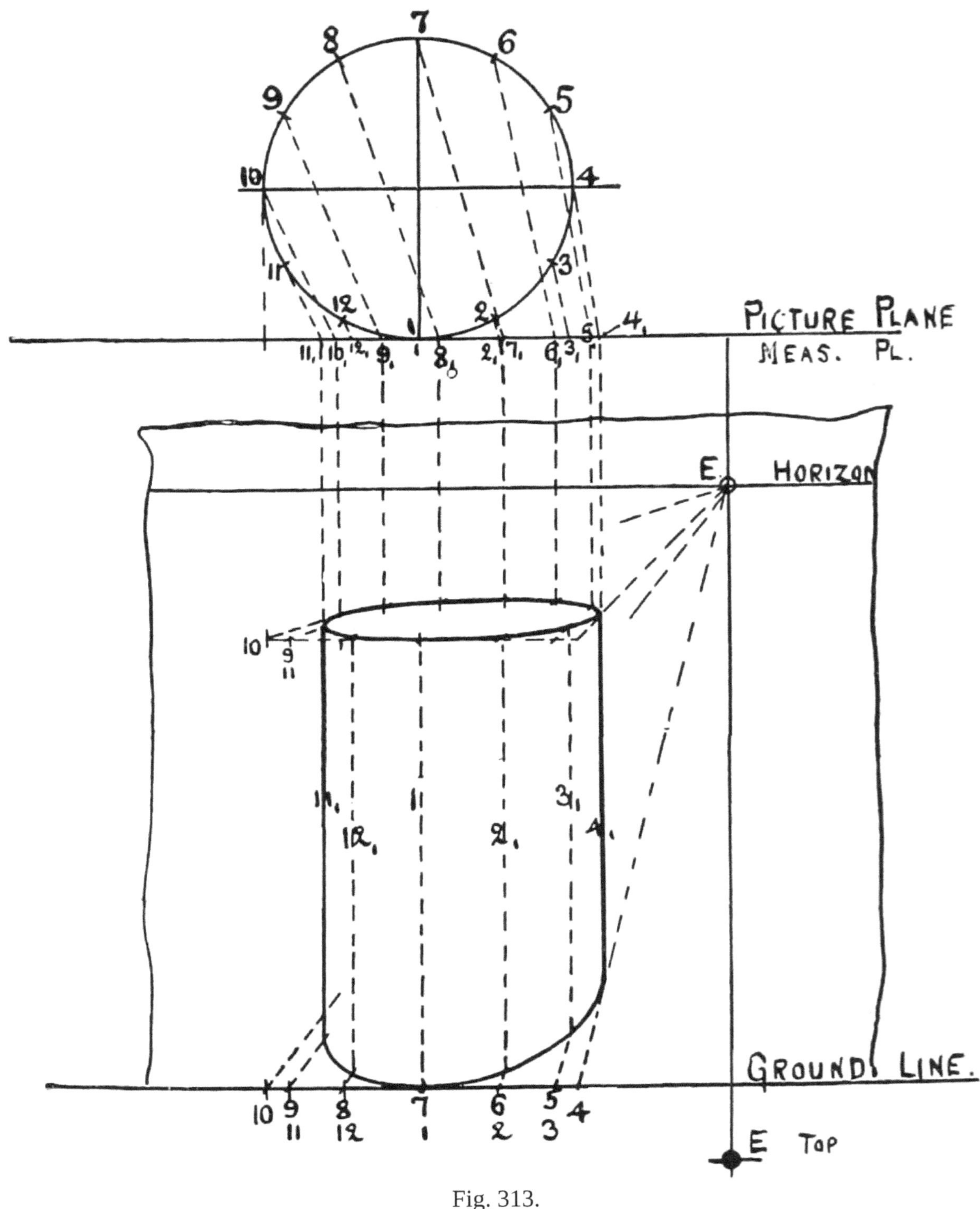

Fig. 313.

Vertically, only the outlines of the cylinder, as contrasted against space, will appear as distinct outlines, while the reference lines will not appear and are therefore shown only as dotted lines.

Fig. 314 shows the approximate or scale perspective with all the axes drawn and the corresponding angles and scales marked. The outlines of the object running in these directions appear all parallel to the axes.

The approximate or scale perspective completely avoids all the difficulties of choosing a point of sight, of having several views, vanishing points and measurement points, and thus offers a representative view, with a great saving of time and labor. Particularly for mechanical purposes, where an artistic impression is not called for, it presents a distinct advantage over the true or real perspective.

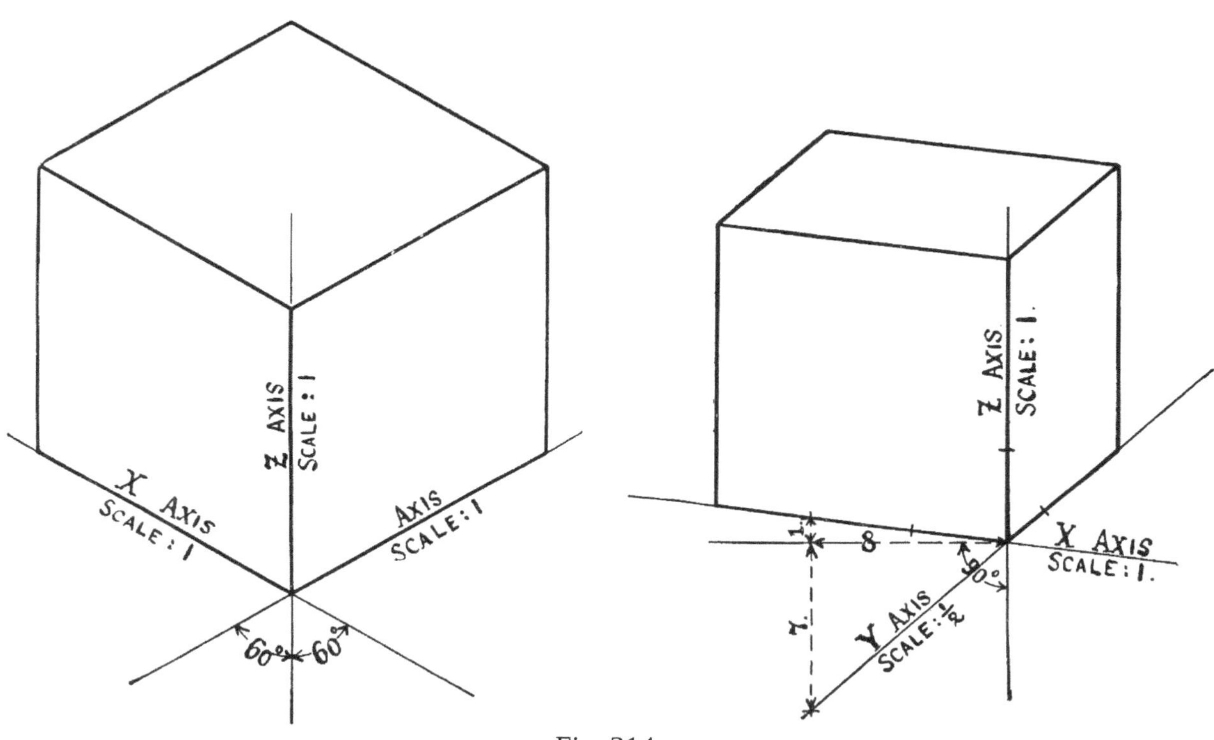

Fig. 314.

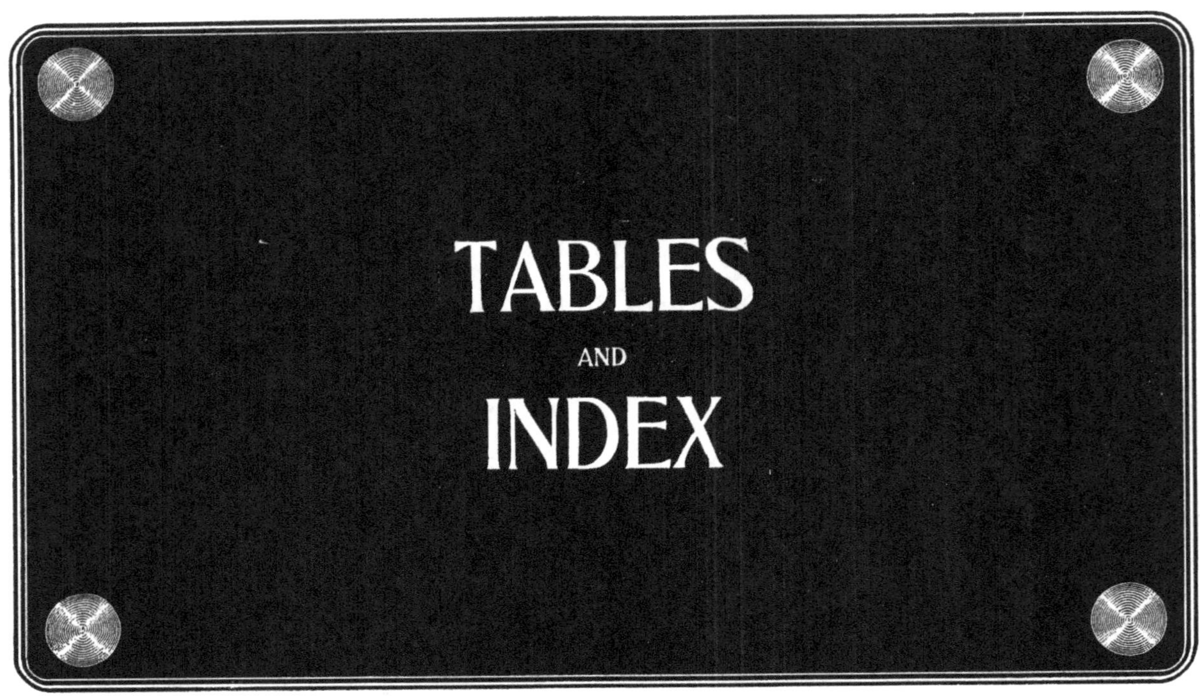

TABLES

AND

INDEX

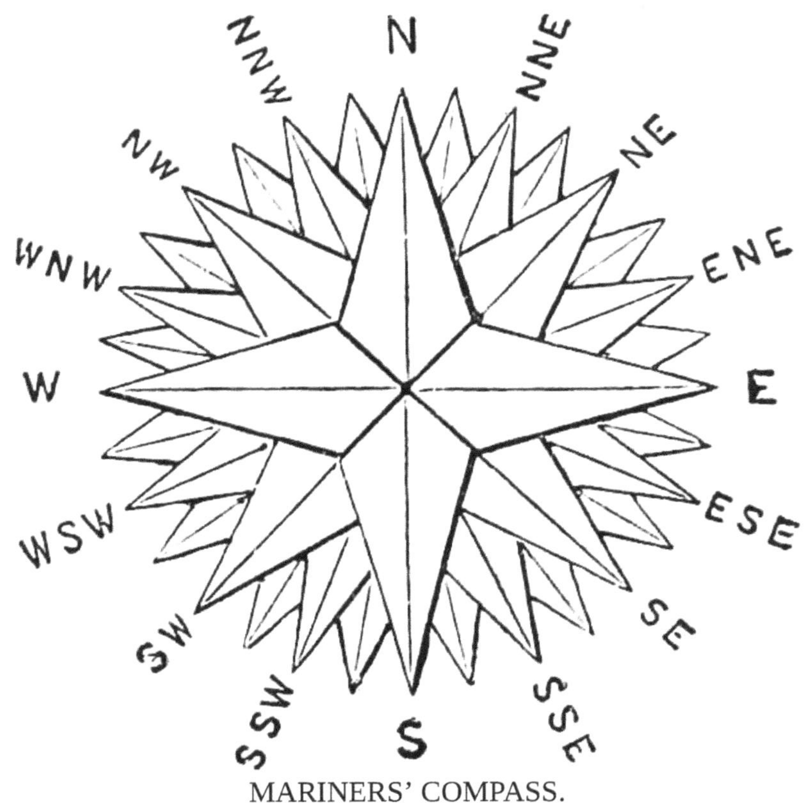

MARINERS' COMPASS.

Useful Tables for Draughtsmen.

TABLE OF DECIMAL EQUIVALENTS.
8ths, 16ths, 32ds and 64ths of an Inch.

8ths.

$\frac{1}{8} = .125$
$\frac{1}{4} = .250$
$\frac{3}{8} = .375$
$\frac{1}{2} = .500$
$\frac{5}{8} = .625$
$\frac{3}{4} = .750$
$\frac{7}{8} = .875$

16ths.

$\frac{1}{16} = .0625$
$\frac{3}{16} = .1875$
$\frac{5}{16} = .3125$
$\frac{7}{16} = .4375$
$\frac{9}{16} = .5625$
$\frac{11}{16} = .6875$
$\frac{13}{16} = .8125$
$\frac{15}{16} = .9375$

32nds.

$\frac{1}{32} = .03125$
$\frac{3}{32} = .09375$
$\frac{5}{32} = .15625$
$\frac{7}{32} = .21875$

$\frac{9}{32} = .28125$

$\frac{11}{32} = .34375$

$\frac{13}{32} = .40625$

$\frac{15}{32} = .46875$

$\frac{17}{32} = .53125$

$\frac{19}{32} = .59375$

$\frac{21}{32} = .65625$

$\frac{23}{32} = .71875$

$\frac{25}{32} = .78125$

$\frac{27}{32} = .84375$

$\frac{29}{32} = .90625$

$\frac{31}{32} = .96875$

64ths.

$\frac{1}{64} = .015625$

$\frac{3}{64} = .046875$

$\frac{5}{64} = .078125$

$\frac{7}{64} = .109375$

$\frac{9}{64} = .140625$

$\frac{11}{64} = .171875$

$\frac{13}{64} = .203125$

$\frac{15}{64} = .234375$

$\frac{17}{64} = .265625$

$\frac{19}{64} = .296875$

$\frac{21}{64} = .328125$

$\frac{23}{64} = .359375$

$\frac{25}{64} = .390625$

$\frac{27}{64} = .421875$

$\frac{29}{64} = .453125$

$\frac{31}{64} = .484375$

$\frac{33}{64} = .515625$

$\frac{35}{64} = .546875$

$\frac{37}{64} = .578125$

$\frac{39}{64} = .609375$

$^{41}/_{64} = .640625$

$^{43}/_{64} = .671875$

$^{45}/_{64} = .703125$

$^{47}/_{64} = .734375$

$^{49}/_{64} = .765625$

$^{51}/_{64} = .796875$

$^{53}/_{64} = .828125$

$^{55}/_{64} = .859375$

$^{57}/_{64} = .890625$

$^{59}/_{64} = .921875$

$^{61}/_{64} = .953125$

$^{63}/_{64} = .984375$

TABLE OF DECIMAL EQUIVALENTS
Of Millimeters and Fractions of Millimeters.

mm.   *Inches.*

$^{1}/_{50} = .00079$

$^{2}/_{50} = .00157$

$^{3}/_{50} = .00236$

$^{4}/_{50} = .00315$

$^{5}/_{50} = .00394$

$^{6}/_{50} = .00472$

$^{7}/_{50} = .00551$

$^{8}/_{50} = .00630$

$^{9}/_{50} = .00709$

$^{10}/_{50} = .00787$

$^{11}/_{50} = .00866$

$^{12}/_{50} = .00945$

$^{13}/_{50} = .01024$

$^{14}/_{50} = .01102$

$^{15}/_{50} = .01181$

$^{16}/_{50} = .01260$

$^{17}/_{50} = .01339$

$^{18}/_{50} = .01417$

$^{19}/_{50} = .01496$

$^{20}/_{50} = .01575$

$^{21}/_{50} = .01654$

$^{22}/_{50} = .01732$

$^{23}/_{50} = .01811$

$^{24}/_{50} = .01890$

$^{25}/_{50} = .01969$

$^{26}/_{50} = .02047$

$^{27}/_{50} = .02126$

$^{28}/_{50} = .02205$

$^{29}/_{50} = .02283$

$^{30}/_{50} = .02362$

$^{31}/_{50} = .02441$

$^{32}/_{50} = .02520$

$^{33}/_{50} = .02598$

$^{34}/_{50} = .02677$

$^{35}/_{50} = .02756$

$^{36}/_{50} = .02835$

$^{37}/_{50} = .02913$

$^{38}/_{50} = .02992$

$^{39}/_{50} = .03071$

$^{40}/_{50} = .03150$

$^{41}/_{50} = .03228$

$^{42}/_{50} = .03307$

$^{43}/_{50} = .03386$

$^{44}/_{50} = .03465$

$^{45}/_{50} = .03543$

$^{46}/_{50} = .03622$

$^{47}/_{50} = .03701$

$^{48}/_{50} = .03780$

$^{49}/_{50} = .03858$

$1 = .03937$

$2 = .07874$

$$3 = .11811$$
$$4 = .15748$$
$$5 = .19685$$
$$6 = .23622$$
$$7 = .27559$$
$$8 = .31496$$
$$9 = .35433$$
$$10 = .39370$$
$$11 = .43307$$
$$12 = .47244$$
$$13 = .51181$$
$$14 = .55118$$
$$15 = .59055$$
$$16 = .62992$$
$$17 = .66929$$
$$18 = .70866$$
$$19 = .74803$$
$$20 = .78740$$
$$21 = .82677$$
$$22 = .86614$$
$$23 = .90551$$
$$24 = .94488$$
$$25 = .98425$$
$$26 = 1.02362$$

10 mm.	= 1 Centimeter	= 0.3937	inches.
10 cm.	= 1 Decimeter	= 3.937	„
10 dm.	= 1 Meter	= 39.37	„
25.4 mm.	= 1 English Inch.		

RULES RELATIVE TO THE CIRCLE.

The circle contains a greater area than any other plane figure bounded by an

equal perimeter or outline.

TO FIND CIRCUMFERENCE—

Multiply diameter by 3.1416.
Or divide diameter by 0.3183.

TO FIND DIAMETER—

Multiply circumference by 0.3183.
Or divide circumference by 3.1416.

TO FIND RADIUS—

Multiply circumference by 0.15915.
Or divide circumference by 6.28318.

TO FIND SIDE OF AN INSCRIBED SQUARE—

Multiply diameter by   0.7071.
Or multiply circumference by 0.2251.
Or divide circumference by   4.4428.

TO FIND SIDE OF AN EQUAL SQUARE—

Multiply diameter by   0.8862.
Or divide diameter by   1.1284.
Or multiply circumference by 0.2821.
Or divide circumference by   3.545.

SQUARE—

A side multiplied   1.4142 equals diameter of its circumscribing circle.

by
A side multiplied   4.443 equals circumference of its circumscribing
by   circle.
A side multiplied
by   1.128 equals diameter   } of an
A side multiplied   equal
by   3.545 equals circumference   circle.
A side multiplied
by   1.273 equals circle inches

Multiply circumference by one-quarter of the diameter.
Or multiply the square of diameter by   0.7854.
Or multiply the square of circumference by   .07958.
Or multiply the square of ½ diameter by   3.1416.

Contents of cylinder = area of end × length. Contents of wedge = area of base × ½ altitude. Surface of cylinder = area of both ends × length × circumference. Surface of sphere = diameter squared × 3.1416, or = diameter × circumference. Contents of sphere = diameter cubed × .5236. Contents of pyramid or cone, right or oblique, regular or irregular = area of base × ⅓ altitude. Area of triangle = base × ½ altitude. Area of parallelogram = base × altitude. Area of trapezoid = altitude × ½ the sum of parallel sides.

ROMAN TABLE.

I. denotes One.
II.   „   Two.
III.   „   Three.
IV.   „   Four.
V.   „   Five.
VI.   „   Six.
VII.   „   Seven.
VIII.   „   Eight.

IX.	„	Nine.
X.	„	Ten.
XI.	„	Eleven.
XII.	„	Twelve.
XIII.	„	Thirteen.
XIV.	„	Fourteen.
XV.	„	Fifteen.
XVI.	„	Sixteen.
XVII.	„	Seventeen.
XVIII.	„	Eighteen.
XIX.	„	Nineteen.
XX.	„	Twenty.
XXX.	„	Thirty.
XL.	„	Forty.
L.	„	Fifty.
LX.	„	Sixty.
LXX.	„	Seventy.
LXXX.	„	Eighty.
XC.	„	Ninety.
C.	„	One hundred.
D.	„	Five hundred.
M.	„	One thousand.
$\overline{\text{X}}$.	„	Ten thousand.
$\overline{\text{M}}$.	„	One million.

SOLID MEASURE, OR CUBIC MEASURE.

This is used in measuring bodies, or things having length, breadth and height or depth.

TABLE.

1728 cubic inches (cu. in.) make	1 cubic foot (cu. ft.).
27 cubic feet,	„ 1 cubic yard (cu. yd.).
128 cubic feet,	„ 1 cord (C.).

CIRCULAR MEASURE.

60 seconds (") make 1 minute (').
60 minutes „ 1 degree (°).
360 degrees „ 1 circum. (C.).

The circumference of every circle whatever, is supposed to be divided into 360 equal parts, called *degrees*.

A degree is $\frac{1}{360}$ of the circumference of any circle, small or large.

A quadrant is a fourth of a circumference, or an arc of 90 degrees.

A degree is divided into 60 parts called minutes, expressed by the sign ('), and each minute is divided into 60 seconds, expressed by ("); so that the circumference of any circle contains 21,600 minutes, or 1,296,000 seconds.

LONG MEASURE—MEASURES OF LENGTH.

12 inches = 1 foot.
3 feet = 1 yard.
5½ yards = 1 rod.
40 rods = 1 furlong.
8 furlongs = 1 common mile.
3 miles = 1 league.

The mile (5,280 feet) of the above table is the legal mile of the United States and England, and is called the statute mile.

Tables of Diameters, Circumferences and Areas of Circles.

Diam.	Area.	Circum.
0.0		
.1	.007854	.31416
.2	.031416	.62832
.3	.070686	.94248
.4	.12566	1.2566
.5	.19735	1.5708
.6	.28274	1.8850
.7	.38485	2.1991
.8	.50266	2.5133
.9	.63617	2.8274
1.0	.7854	3.1416
.1	.9503	3.4558
.2	1.1310	3.7699
.3	1.3273	4.0841
.4	1.5394	4.3982
.5	1.7671	4.7124
.6	2.0106	5.0265
.7	2.2698	5.3407
.8	2.5447	5.6549
.9	2.8353	5.9690
2.0	3.1416	6.2832
.1	3.4636	6.5973
.2	3.8013	6.9115
.3	4.1548	7.2257
.4	4.5239	7.5398
.5	4.9087	7.8540
.6	5.3093	8.1681
.7	5.7256	8.4823
.8	6.1575	8.7965
.9	6.6052	9.1106
3.0	7.0686	9.4248
.1	7.5477	9.7389
.2	8.0425	10.0531
.3	8.5530	10.3673
.4	9.0792	10.6814
.5	9.6211	10.9956
.6	10.1788	11.3097
.7	10.7521	11.6239
.8	11.3411	11.9381
.9	11.9456	12.2522
4.0	12.5664	12.5664
.1	13.2025	12.8805
.2	13.8544	13.1947

.3	14.5220	13.5088
.4	15.2053	13.8230
.5	15.9043	14.1372
.6	16.6190	14.4513
.7	17.3494	14.7655
.8	18.0956	15.0796
.9	18.8574	15.3938
5.0	19.6350	15.7080
.1	20.4282	16.0221
.2	21.2372	16.3363
.3	22.0618	16.6504
.4	22.9022	16.9646
.5	23.7583	17.2788
.6	24.6301	17.5929
.7	25.5176	17.9071
.8	26.4208	18.2212
.9	27.3397	18.5354
6.0	28.2743	18.8496
.1	29.2247	19.1637
.2	30.1907	19.4779
.3	31.1725	19.7920
.4	32.1699	20.1062
.5	33.1831	20.4204
.6	34.2119	20.7345
.7	35.2565	21.0487
.8	36.3168	21.3628
.9	37.3928	21.6770
7.0	38.4845	21.9911
.1	39.5919	22.3053
.2	40.7150	22.6195
.3	41.8539	22.9336
.4	43.0084	23.2478
.5	44.1786	23.5619
.6	45.3646	23.8761
.7	46.5663	24.1903
.8	47.7836	24.5044
.9	49.0167	24.8186
8.0	50.2655	25.1327
.1	51.5300	25.4469
.2	52.8102	25.7611
.3	54.1061	26.0752
.4	55.4177	26.3894
.5	56.7450	26.7035
.6	58.0880	27.0177
.7	59.4468	27.3319

.8	60.8212	27.6460
.9	62.2114	27.9602
9.0	63.6173	28.2743
.1	65.0388	28.5885
.2	66.4761	28.9027
.3	67.9291	29.2168
.4	69.3978	29.5310
.5	70.8822	29.8451
.6	72.3823	30.1593
.7	73.8981	30.4734
.8	75.4296	30.7876
.9	76.9769	31.1018
10.0	78.5398	31.4159
.1	80.1185	31.7301
.2	81.7128	32.0442
.3	83.3229	32.3584
.4	84.9487	32.6726
.5	86.5901	32.9887
.6	88.2473	33.3009
.7	89.9202	33.6150
.8	91.6088	33.9292
.9	93.3132	34.2434
11.0	95.0332	34.5575
.1	96.7689	34.8717
.2	98.5203	35.1858
.3	100.2875	35.5000
.4	102.0703	35.8142
.5	103.8689	36.1283
.6	105.6832	36.4425
.7	107.5132	36.7566
.8	109.3588	37.0708
.9	111.2202	37.3850
12.0	113.0973	37.6991
.1	114.9901	38.0133
.2	116.8987	38.3274
.3	118.8229	38.6416
.4	120.7628	38.9557
.5	122.7185	39.2099
.6	124.6898	39.6841
.7	126.6769	39.8982
.8	128.6796	40.2121
.9	130.6981	40.5265
13.0	132.7323	40.8407
.1	134.7822	41.1549
.2	136.8478	41.4690

.3	138.9291	41.7832
.4	141.0261	42.0973
.5	143.1388	42.4116
.6	145.2672	42.7257
.7	147.4114	43.0398
.8	149.5712	43.3540
.9	151.7468	43.6681
14.0	153.9380	43.9823
.1	156.1450	44.2965
.2	158.3677	44.6106
.3	160.6061	44.9248
.4	162.8602	45.2389
.5	165.1300	45.5531
.6	167.4155	45.8673
.7	169.7167	46.1814
.8	172.0336	46.4956
.9	174.3662	46.8097
15.0	176.7146	47.1239
.1	179.0786	47.4380
.2	181.4584	47.7522
.3	183.8539	48.0664
.4	186.2650	48.3805
.5	188.6919	48.6947
.6	191.1345	49.0088
.7	193.5928	49.3230
.8	196.0668	49.6372
.9	198.5565	49.9513
16.0	201.0619	50.2655
.1	203.5831	50.5796
.2	206.1199	50.8938
.3	208.6724	51.2080
.4	211.2407	51.5221
.5	213.8246	51.8363
.6	216.4243	52.1504
.7	219.0397	52.4646
.8	221.6708	52.7788
.9	224.3176	53.0929
17.0	226.9801	53.4071
.1	229.6583	53.7212
.2	232.3522	54.0354
.3	235.0618	54.3496
.4	237.7871	54.6637
.5	240.5282	54.9779
.6	243.2849	55.2920
.7	246.0574	55.6062

.8	248.8456	55.9203
.9	251.6494	56.2345
18.0	254.4690	56.5486
.1	257.3043	56.8628
.2	260.1553	57.1770
.3	263.0220	57.4911
.4	265.9044	57.8053
.5	268.8025	58.1195
.6	271.7164	58.4336
.7	274.6459	58.7478
.8	277.5911	59.0619
.9	280.5521	59.3761
19.0	283.5287	59.6903
.1	286.5211	60.0044
.2	289.5292	60.3186
.3	292.5530	60.6327
.4	295.5925	60.9469
.5	298.6477	61.2611
.6	301.7186	61.5752
.7	304.8052	61.8894
.8	307.9075	62.2035
.9	311.0255	62.5177
20.0	314.1593	62.8319
.1	317.3087	63.1460
.2	320.4739	63.4602
.3	323.6547	63.7743
.4	326.8513	64.0885
.5	330.0636	64.4026
.6	333.2916	64.7168
.7	336.5353	65.0310
.8	339.7947	65.3451
.9	343.0698	65.6593
21.0	346.3606	65.9734
.1	349.6671	66.2876
.2	352.9894	66.6018
.3	356.3273	66.9159
.4	359.6809	67.2301
.5	363.0503	67.5442
.6	266.4354	67.8584
.7	369.8361	68.1726
.8	373.2526	68.4867
.9	376.6848	68.8009
22.0	380.1327	69.1150
.1	383.5963	69.4292
.2	387.0756	69.7434

.3	390.5707	70.0575
.4	394.0814	70.3717
.5	397.6078	70.6858
.6	401.1500	71.0000
.7	404.7078	71.3142
.8	408.2814	71.6283
.9	411.8707	71.9425
23.0	415.4756	72.2566
.1	419.0993	72.5708
.2	422.7327	72.8849
.3	426.3848	73.1991
.4	430.0526	73.5133
.5	433.7361	73.8274
.6	437.4354	74.1416
.7	441.1503	74.4557
.8	444.8809	74.7699
.9	448.6273	75.0841
24.0	452.3893	75.3982
.1	456.1671	75.7424
.2	459.9606	76.0265
.3	463.7693	76.3407
.4	467.5947	76.6549
.5	471.4352	76.9690
.6	475.2916	77.2832
.7	479.1636	77.5973
.8	483.0513	77.9115
.9	486.9547	78.2257
25.0	490.8739	78.5398
.1	494.8087	78.8540
.2	498.7592	79.1681
.3	502.7255	79.4823
.4	506.7075	79.7965
.5	510.7052	80.1106
.6	514.7185	80.4248
.7	518.7476	80.7389
.8	522.7924	81.0531
.9	526.8529	81.3672
26.0	530.9292	81.6814
.1	535.0211	81.9956
.2	539.1287	82.3097
.3	543.2521	82.6239
.4	547.3911	82.9380
.5	551.5459	83.2522
.6	555.7163	83.5664
.7	559.9025	83.8805

.8	564.1044	84.1947
.9	568.3220	84.5088
27.0	572.5553	84.8230
.1	576.8043	85.1372
.2	581.0690	85.4513
.3	585.3494	85.7655
.4	589.6455	86.0796
.5	593.9574	86.3938
.6	598.2849	86.7080
.7	602.6282	87.0221
.8	606.9871	87.3363
.9	611.3618	87.6504
28.0	615.7522	87.9646
.1	620.1582	88.2788
.2	624.5800	88.5929
.3	629.0175	88.9071
.4	633.4707	89.2212
.5	637.9397	89.5354
.6	642.4243	89.8495
.7	646.9246	90.1637
.8	651.4407	90.4779
.9	655.9724	90.7920
29.0	660.5199	91.1063
.1	665.0830	91.4203
.2	669.6619	91.7345
.3	674.2565	92.0487
.4	678.8668	92.3628
.5	683.4928	92.6770
.6	688.1345	92.9911
.7	692.7919	93.3053
.8	697.4650	93.6195
.9	702.1538	93.9336
30.0	706.8583	94.2478
.1	711.5786	94.5610
.2	716.3145	94.8761
.3	721.0662	95.1903
.4	725.8336	95.5044
.5	730.6167	95.8186
.6	735.4154	96.1327
.7	740.2299	96.4469
.8	745.0601	96.7611
.9	749.9060	97.0752
31.0	754.7676	97.3894
.1	759.6450	97.7035
.2	761.5380	98.0177

.3	769.4467	98.3319
.4	774.3712	98.6460
.5	779.3113	98.9602
.6	784.2672	99.2743
.7	789.2388	99.5885
.8	794.2260	99.9026
.9	799.2290	100.2168
32.0	804.2477	100.5310
.1	809.2821	100.8451
.2	814.3322	101.1593
.3	819.3980	101.4734
.4	824.4796	101.7876
.5	829.5768	102.1018
.6	834.6898	102.4159
.7	839.8185	102.7301
.8	844.9628	103.0442
.9	850.1229	103.3584
33.0	855.2986	103.6726
.1	860.4902	103.9867
.2	865.6973	104.3009
.3	870.9202	104.6150
.4	876.1588	104.9292
.5	881.4131	105.2434
.6	886.6831	105.5575
.7	891.9688	105.8717
.8	897.2703	106.1858
.9	902.5874	106.5000
34.0	907.9203	106.8142
.1	913.2688	107.1283
.2	918.6331	107.4425
.3	924.0131	107.7566
.4	929.4088	108.0708
.5	934.8202	108.3849
.6	940.2473	108.6991
.7	945.6901	109.0133
.8	951.1486	109.3274
.9	956.6228	109.6416
35.0	962.1128	109.9557
.1	967.6184	110.2699
.2	973.1397	110.5841
.3	978.6768	110.8982
.4	984.2296	111.2124
.5	989.7980	111.5265
.6	995.3822	111.8407
.7	1000.9821	112.1549

.8	1006.5977	112.4690
.9	1012.2290	112.7832
36.0	1017.8760	113.0973
.1	1023.5387	113.4115
.2	1029.2172	113.7257
.3	1034.9113	114.0398
.4	1040.6212	114.3540
.5	1046.3467	114.6681
.6	1052.0880	114.9823
.7	1057.8449	115.2965
.8	1063.6176	115.6106
.9	1069.4060	115.9248
37.0	1075.2101	116.2389
.1	1081.0299	116.5531
.2	1086.8654	116.8672
.3	1093.7166	117.1814
.4	1098.5835	117.4956
.5	1104.4662	117.8097
.6	1110.3645	118.1239
.7	1116.2786	118.4380
.8	1122.2083	118.7522
.9	1128.1538	119.0664
38.0	1134.1149	119.3805
.1	1140.0918	119.6947
.2	1146.0844	120.0088
.3	1152.0927	120.3230
.4	1158.1167	120.6372
.5	1164.1564	120.9513
.6	1170.2118	121.2655
.7	1176.2830	121.5796
.8	1182.3698	121.8938
.9	1188.4724	122.2080
39.0	1194.5906	122.5221
.1	1200.7246	122.8363
.2	1206.8742	123.1504
.3	1213.0396	123.4646
.4	1219.2207	123.7788
.5	1225.4175	124.0929
.6	1231.6300	124.4071
.7	1237.8582	124.7212
.8	1244.1021	125.0354
.9	1250.3617	125.3495
40.0	1256.6371	125.6637
.1	1262.9281	125.9779
.2	1269.2348	126.2920

.3	1275.5573	126.6062
.4	1281.8955	126.9203
.5	1288.2493	127.2345
.6	1294.3189	127.5487
.7	1301.0042	127.8628
.8	1307.4052	128.1770
.9	1313.8219	128.4911
41.0	1320.2543	128.8053
.1	1326.7024	129.1195
.2	1333.1663	129.4336
.3	1339.6458	129.7478
.4	1346.1410	130.0619
.5	1352.6520	130.3761
.6	1359.1786	130.6903
.7	1365.7210	131.0044
.8	1372.2791	131.3186
.9	1378.8529	131.6227
42.0	1385.4424	131.9469
.1	1392.0476	132.2611
.2	1398.6685	132.5752
.3	1405.3051	132.8894
.4	1411.9574	133.2035
.5	1418.6254	133.5177
.6	1425.3092	133.8318
.7	1432.0086	134.1460
.8	1438.7238	134.4602
.9	1445.4546	134.7743
43.0	1452.2012	135.0885
.1	1458.9635	135.4026
.2	1465.7415	135.7168
.3	1472.5352	136.0310
.4	1479.3446	136.3451
.5	1486.1697	136.6593
.6	1493.0105	136.9734
.7	1499.8670	137.2876
.8	1506.7393	137.6018
.9	1513.6272	137.9159
44.0	1520.5308	138.2301
.1	1527.4502	138.5442
.2	1534.3853	138.8584
.3	1541.3360	139.1726
.4	1548.3025	139.4867
.5	1555.2847	139.8009
.6	1562.2826	140.1153
.7	1569.2063	140.4292

.8	1576.3255	140.7434
.9	1583.3706	141.0575
45.0	1590.4313	141.3717
.1	1597.5077	141.6858
.2	1604.5999	142.0000
.3	1611.7077	142.3142
.4	1618.8313	142.6283
.5	1625.9705	142.9425
.6	1633.1255	143.2566
.7	1640.2962	143.5708
.8	1647.4826	143.8849
.9	1654.6847	144.1991
46.0	1661.9025	144.5133
.1	1669.1360	144.8274
.2	1676.3853	145.1416
.3	1683.6502	145.4557
.4	1690.9308	145.7699
.5	1698.2272	146.0841
.6	1705.5392	146.3982
.7	1712.8670	146.7124
.8	1720.2105	147.0265
.9	1727.5697	147.3407
47.0	1734.9445	147.6550
.1	1742.3351	147.9690
.2	1749.7414	148.2832
.3	1757.1635	148.5973
.4	1764.6012	148.9115
.5	1772.0546	149.2257
.6	1779.5237	149.5398
.7	1787.0086	149.8540
.8	1794.5091	150.1681
.9	1802.0254	150.4823
48.0	1809.5574	150.7964
.1	1817.1050	151.1105
.2	1824.6684	151.4248
.3	1832.2475	151.7389
.4	1839.8423	152.0531
.5	1847.4528	152.3672
.6	1855.0790	152.6814
.7	1862.7210	152.9956
.8	1870.3786	153.3097
.9	1878.0519	153.6239
49.0	1885.7409	153.9380
.1	1893.4457	154.2522
.2	1901.1662	154.5664

.3	1908.9024	154.8805
.4	1916.6543	155.1947
.5	1924.4218	155.5088
.6	1932.2051	155.8230
.7	1940.0042	156.1372
.8	1947.8189	156.4513
.9	1955.6493	156.7655
50.0	1963.4954	157.0796
.1	1971.3572	157.3938
.2	1979.2348	157.7080
.3	1987.1280	158.0221
.4	1995.0370	158.3363
.5	2002.9617	158.6504
.6	2010.9020	158.9646
.7	2018.8581	159.2787
.8	2026.8299	159.5929
.9	2034.8174	159.9071
51.0	2042.6206	160.2212
.1	2050.8895	160.5354
.2	2058.8742	160.8495
.3	2066.9245	161.1637
.4	2074.9905	161.4779
.5	2083.0723	161.7920
.6	2091.1697	162.1062
.7	2099.2829	162.4203
.8	2107.4118	162.7345
.9	2115.5563	163.0487
52.0	2123.7166	163.3628
.1	2131.8926	163.6770
.2	2140.0843	163.9911
.3	2148.2917	164.3053
.4	2156.5149	164.6195
.5	2164.7537	164.9336
.6	2173.0082	165.2479
.7	2181.2785	165.5619
.8	2189.5644	165.8761
.9	2197.8661	166.1903
53.0	2206.1834	166.5044
.1	2214.5165	166.8186
.2	2222.8653	167.1327
.3	2231.2298	167.4469
.4	2239.6100	167.7610
.5	2248.0059	168.0752
.6	2256.4175	168.3894
.7	2264.8448	168.7035

.8	2273.2879	169.0177
.9	2281.7466	169.3318
54.0	2290.2210	169.6460
.1	2298.7112	169.9602
.2	2307.2171	170.2743
.3	2315.7386	170.5885
.4	2324.2759	170.9026
.5	2332.8289	171.2168
.6	2341.3976	171.5310
.7	2349.9820	171.8451
.8	2358.5821	172.1593
.9	2367.1979	172.4735
55.0	2375.8294	172.7876
.1	2384.4767	173.1017
.2	2393.1396	173.4159
.3	2401.8183	173.7301
.4	2410.5126	174.0442
.5	2419.2227	174.3584
.6	2427.9485	174.6726
.7	2436.6899	174.9867
.8	2145.4471	175.3009
.9	2454.2200	175.6150

UNITED STATES STANDARD SIZES OF WROUGHT IRON WELDED PIPE.

Inside diam-eter nom.	Actual outside Diam-eter.	Thick-ness.	Actual Inside Diam-eter.	External circum-ference.	Internal circum-ference.	Length of pipe per square foot of outside surface.	Length of pipe per square foot of inside surface.	External area.	Actual internal area.	Length of pipe con-taining one cubic foot.	Weight per foot of length.	No. of threads per Inch of screw.	Length perfect screw.
⅛	.405	.068	0.269	1.272	0.848	9.440	14.15	.129	.0572	2500.	.243	27	0.19
¼	.54	.088	0.364	1.696	1.144	7.075	10.50	.229	.1041	1385.	.422	18	0.29
⅜	.675	.091	0.493	2.121	1.552	5.657	7.67	.358	.1916	751.5	.561	18	0.30
½	.840	.109	0.622	2.652	1.957	4.502	6.13	.554	.3048	472.4	.845	14	0.39
¾	1.050	.113	0.824	3.299	2.589	3.637	4.635	.866	.5333	270.0	1.126	14	0.40
1	1.315	.134	1.047	4.134	3.292	2.903	3.679	1.357	.8627	166.9	1.670	11½	0.51
1¼	1.660	.140	1.38	5.215	4.335	2.301	2.768	2.164	1.496	96.25	2.258	11½	0.54
1½	1.90	.145	1.61	5.969	5.061	2.010	2.371	2.835	2.038	70.65	2.694	11½	0.55
2	2.375	.154	2.067	7.461	6.494	1.611	1.848	4.430	3.355	42.36	3.667	11½	0.58
2½	2.875	.204	2.467	9.032	7.754	1.328	1.547	6.491	4.783	30.11	5.773	8	0.89
3	3.50	.217	3.066	10.996	9.636	1.091	1.245	9.621	7.388	19.40	7.547	8	0.95
3½	4.0	.226	3.548	12.566	11.146	.955	1.077	12.566	9.837	14.56	9.055	8	1.00
4	4.50	.237	4.026	14.137	12.648	.849	0.949	15.901	12.730	11.31	10.728	8	1.05
4½	5.0	.247	4.506	15.708	14.153	.765	0.848	19.635	15.939	9.03	12.492	8	1.10
5	5.563	.259	5.045	17.475	15.849	.629	0.757	24.299	19.990	7.20	14.564	8	1.16
6	6.625	.280	5.065	20.813	19.054	.577	0.630	34.471	28.889	4.98	18.767	8	1.26
7	7.625	.301	7.023	23.954	22.063	.505	0.544	45.663	38.737	3.72	23.410	8	1.36
8	8.625	.322	7.981	27.096	25.076	.444	0.478	58.426	50.039	2.88	28.348	8	1.46
9	9.688	.344	9.00	30.433	28.277	.394	0.425	73.715	63.633	2.26	34.677	8	1.57
10	10.750	.366	10.018	33.772	31.475	.355	0.381	90.762	78.838	1.80	40.641	8	1.68

Thread taper three-fourths inch to one foot.

All pipe below 1½ inches is butt-welded, and proved to 300 pounds per square inch; 1½ inch and above is lap-welded and proved to 500 pounds per square inch.

STANDARDS FOR WIRE GAUGES IN USE IN THE UNITED STATES.
Dimensions of Sizes in Decimal Parts of an Inch.

Number of Wire Gauge.	American or Brown & Sharpe.	Birming-ham, or Stubs' Wire.	Washburn & Moen Mfg. Co., Worces-ter, Ms.	Impe-rial Wire Gauge.	Stubs' Steel Wire.	U. S. Stand. for Plate.	Number of Wire Gauge.
000000	....	....	....	.464	....	.46875	000000
00000	....	....	....	.432	....	.4375	00000

0000	.46	.454	.3938	.400	....	.40625	0000
000	.40964	.425	.3625	.372	....	.375	000
00	.3648	.38	.3310	.348	....	.34375	00
0	.32486	.34	.3065	.324	....	.3125	0
1	.2893	.3	.2830	.300	.227	.28125	1
2	.25763	.284	.2625	.276	.219	.265625	2
3	.22942	.259	.2437	.252	.212	.25	3
4	.20431	.238	.2253	.232	.207	.234375	4
5	.18194	.22	.2070	.212	.204	.21875	5
6	.16202	.203	.1920	.192	.201	.203125	6
7	.14428	.18	.1770	.176	.199	.1875	7
8	.12849	.165	.1620	.160	.197	.171875	8
9	.11443	.148	.1483	.144	.194	.15625	9
10	.10189	.134	.1350	.128	.191	.140625	10
11	.090742	.12	.1205	.116	.188	.125	11
12	.080808	.109	.1055	.104	.185	.109375	12
13	.071961	.095	.0915	.092	.182	.09375	13
14	.064084	.083	.0800	.080	.180	.078125	14
15	.057068	.072	.0720	.072	.178	.0703125	15
16	.05082	.065	.0625	.064	.175	.0625	16
17	.045257	.058	.0540	.056	.172	.05625	17
18	.040303	.049	.0475	.048	.168	.05	18
19	.03589	.042	.0410	.040	.164	.04375	19
20	.031961	.035	.0348	.036	.161	.0375	20
21	.028462	.032	.03175	.032	.157	.034375	21
22	.025347	.028	.0286	.028	.155	.03125	22
23	.022571	.025	.0258	.024	.153	.028125	23
24	.0201	.022	.0230	.022	.151	.025	24
25	.0179	.02	.0204	.020	.148	.021875	25
26	.01594	.018	.0181	.018	.146	.01875	26
27	.014195	.016	.0173	.0164	.143	.0171875	27
28	.012641	.014	.0162	.0149	.139	.015625	28
29	.011257	.013	.0150	.0136	.134	.0140625	29
30	.010025	.012	.0140	.0124	.127	.0125	30
31	.008928	.01	.0132	.0116	.120	.0109375	31
32	.00795	.009	.0128	.0108	.115	.01015625	32
33	.00708	.008	.0118	.0100	.112	.009375	33
34	.006304	.007	.0104	.0092	.110	.00859375	34
35	.005614	.005	.0095	.0084	.108	.0078125	35

36	.005	.004	.0090	.0076	.106	.00703125	36
37	.004453	....	....	.0068	.103	.006640625	37
38	.003965	....	....	.0060	.101	.00625	38
39	.003531	....	....	.0052	.099	....	39
40	.003144	....	....	.0048	.097	....	40

UNITED STATES STANDARD SIZES OF BOLTS.

DIAM-ETER.	DISTANCE ACROSS FLATS, SQUARE AND HEX.	DISTANCE ACROSS CORNERS, HEX.	THICKNESS OF HEAD.
$\frac{1}{4}''$	$\frac{1}{2}''$	$\frac{9}{16}''$	$\frac{1}{4}''$
$\frac{3}{8}$	$\frac{11}{16}$	$\frac{25}{32}$	$\frac{11}{32}$
$\frac{1}{2}$	$\frac{7}{8}$	1	$\frac{7}{16}$
$\frac{5}{8}$	$1\frac{1}{16}$	$1\frac{7}{32}$	$\frac{17}{32}$
$\frac{3}{4}$	$1\frac{1}{4}$	$1\frac{7}{16}$	$\frac{5}{8}$
$\frac{7}{8}$	$1\frac{7}{16}$	$1\frac{21}{32}$	$\frac{21}{32}$
1	$1\frac{5}{8}$	$1\frac{7}{8}$	$\frac{13}{16}$
$1\frac{1}{8}$	$1\frac{13}{16}$	$2\frac{3}{32}$	$\frac{29}{32}$
$1\frac{1}{4}$	2	$2\frac{5}{16}$	1
$1\frac{3}{8}$	$2\frac{3}{16}$	$2\frac{1}{2}$	$1\frac{3}{32}$
$1\frac{1}{2}$	$2\frac{3}{8}$	$2\frac{3}{4}$	$1\frac{3}{16}$
$1\frac{5}{8}$	$2\frac{9}{16}$	$2\frac{15}{16}$	$1\frac{9}{32}$
$1\frac{3}{4}$	$2\frac{3}{4}$	$3\frac{3}{16}$	$1\frac{3}{8}$
$1\frac{7}{8}$	$2\frac{15}{16}$	$3\frac{13}{32}$	$1\frac{15}{32}$
2	$3\frac{1}{8}$	$3\frac{5}{8}$	$1\frac{9}{16}$
$2\frac{1}{4}$	$3\frac{1}{2}$	$4\frac{1}{16}$	$1\frac{3}{4}$
$2\frac{1}{2}$	$3\frac{7}{8}$	$4\frac{1}{2}$	$1\frac{15}{16}$
$2\frac{3}{4}$	$4\frac{1}{4}$	$4\frac{7}{8}$	$2\frac{1}{8}$
3	$4\frac{5}{8}$	$5\frac{11}{32}$	$2\frac{5}{16}$

UNITED STATES STANDARD SCREW THREAD GAUGE.

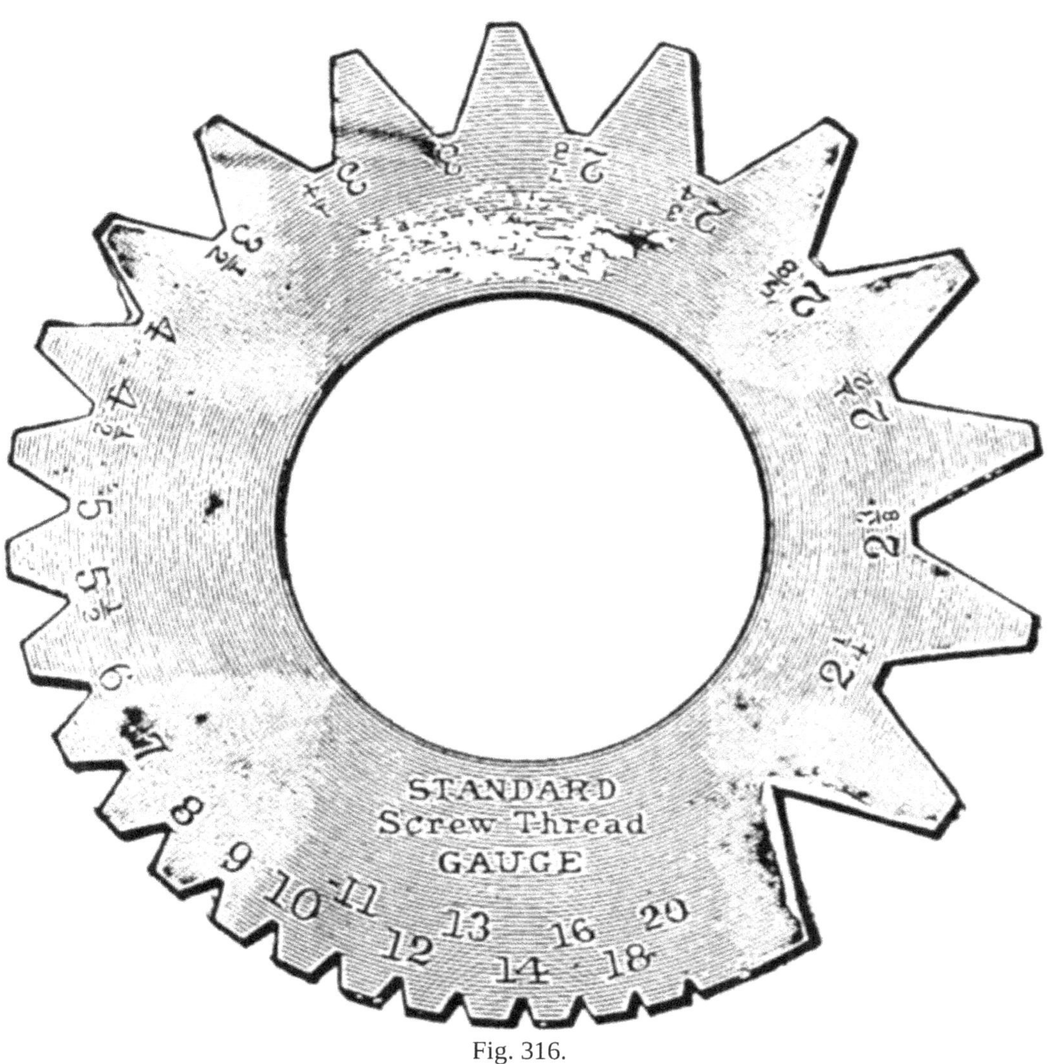

Fig. 316.

www.ingramcontent.com/pod-product-compliance
Lightning Source LLC
Chambersburg PA
CBHW080442030726
47592CB00011B/2930